sock
knitting
MASTER CLASS

Innovative Techniques + Patterns
from Top Designers

Ann Budd

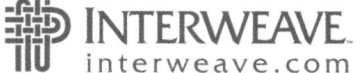

INTERWEAVE.
interweave.com

TECHNICAL EDITOR	Lori Gayle
ART DIRECTOR	Liz Quan
PHOTOGRAPHER	Joe Hancock
PHOTO STYLIST	Carol Beaver
COVER & INTERIOR DESIGN	Julia Boyles
ILLUSTRATION	Gayle Ford
	Ann Swanson
PRODUCTION	Katherine Jackson

Interweave Press LLC
201 East Fourth Street
Loveland, CO 80537-5655 USA
Interweave.com

Printed in China by Asia Pacific Offset, Ltd.

Library of Congress Cataloging-in-Publication Data

Budd, Ann, 1956–
 Sock knitting master class : innovative techniques +
patterns from top designers / Ann Budd.
     p. cm.
 Includes bibliographical references and index.
 ISBN 978-1-59668-312-9
 1. Knitting--Patterns. 2. Socks.   I. Title.
 TT825.B824 2011
 746.43'2--dc22
 2010049008

10 9 8 7 6 5 4 3 2

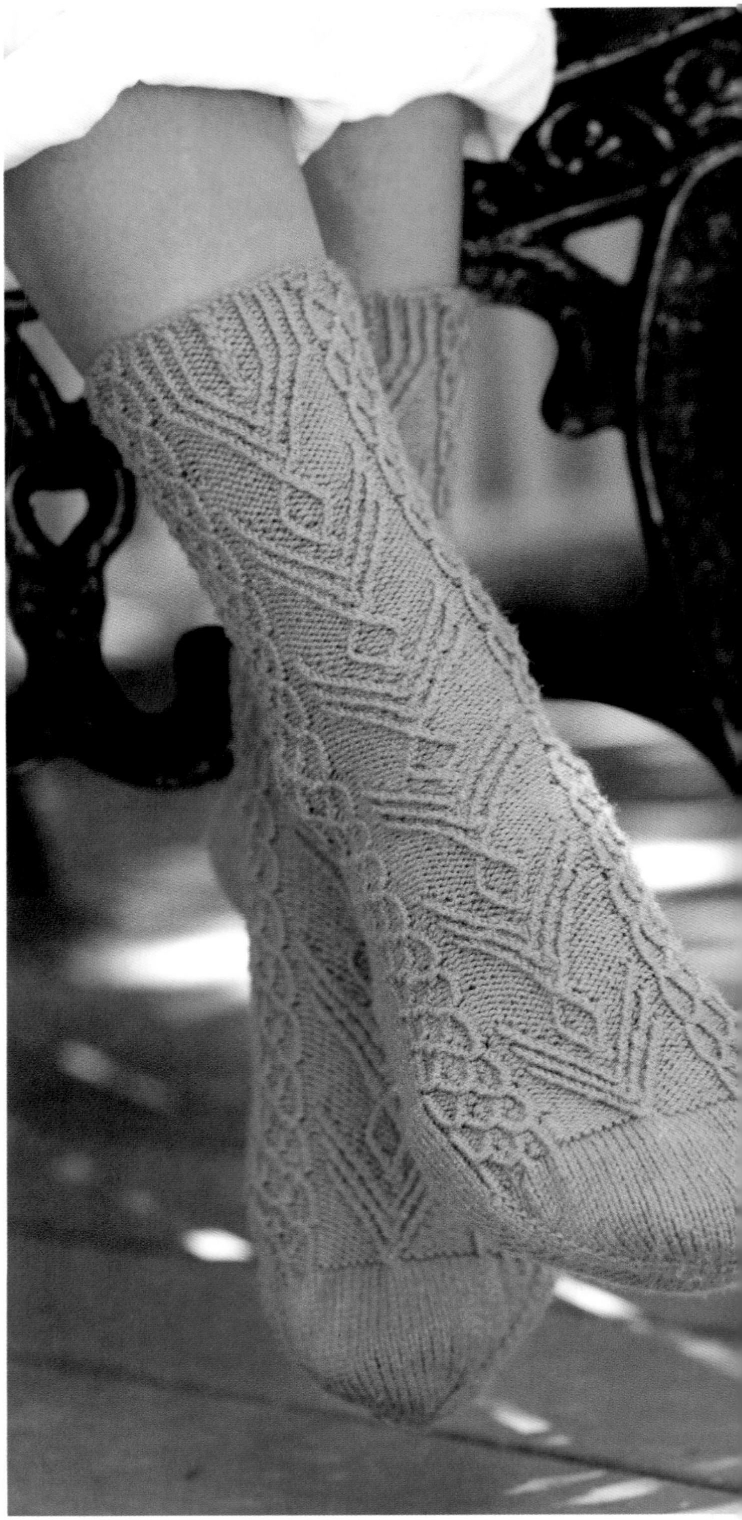

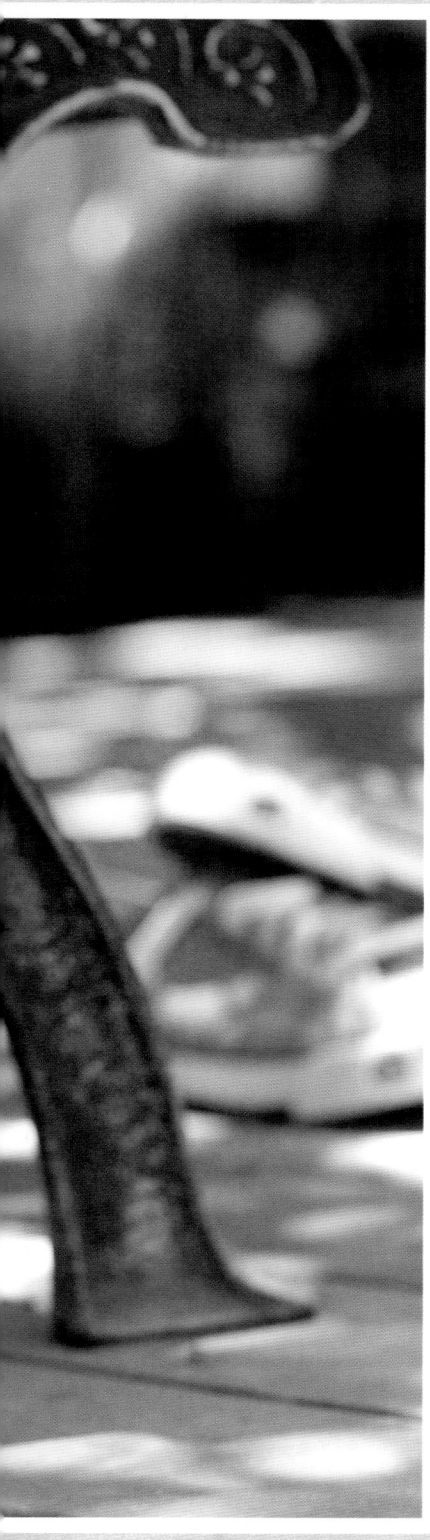

" *For sock knitters everywhere who continue to think up good designs and techniques.*

The masters of this book are the designers who so generously shared their sock-knitting expertise: Cookie A, Kathryn Alexander, Véronik Avery, Cat Bordhi, Nancy Bush, Evelyn A. Clark, Chrissy Gardiner, Priscilla Gibson-Roberts, Anne Hanson, Eunny Jang, Melissa Morgan-Oakes, Deborah Newton, Clara Parkes, Meg Swansen, and Anna Zilboorg. Thank you for providing so many ways to make feet warm and comfortable.

Equally important are the makers of the yarn. Yarns for the socks in this book were contributed by Brown Sheep Company, Cascade Yarns, Classic Elite Yarns, Elemental Affects, Fleece Artist, Kathryn Alexander Kits, Knitting Fever Inc., Lorna's Laces, Pagewood Farm, Quince & Company, Satakieli, Schaefer Yarn, Shalimar Yarns, Simply Socks Yarn Company, and String Theory. Without your yarns, there would be so much less to enjoy in handknitted footwear.

For making this book a visual treat, thanks go to Joe Hancock for his mastery of light and composition, Carol Beaver for her keen style sense, models Sheila Baldwin, Boo Edwards, Lindsay Hudson, and Kirsten Warner for their patience and good humor, illustrators Gayle Ford and Ann Swanson for clear drawings, Julia Boyles for an excellent layout and design, and Liz Quan for ensuring high standards every step of the way.

Thanks also to Interweave for believing in this book, to Anne Merrow for expert advice and guidance, to Lori Gayle for ensuring the instructions are clear and correct, and to Katherine Jackson for perfecting all the files and getting everything to the printer on time.

Special thanks go to Jane Patrick and Barry Schacht for opening their home and garden for the photo shoot.

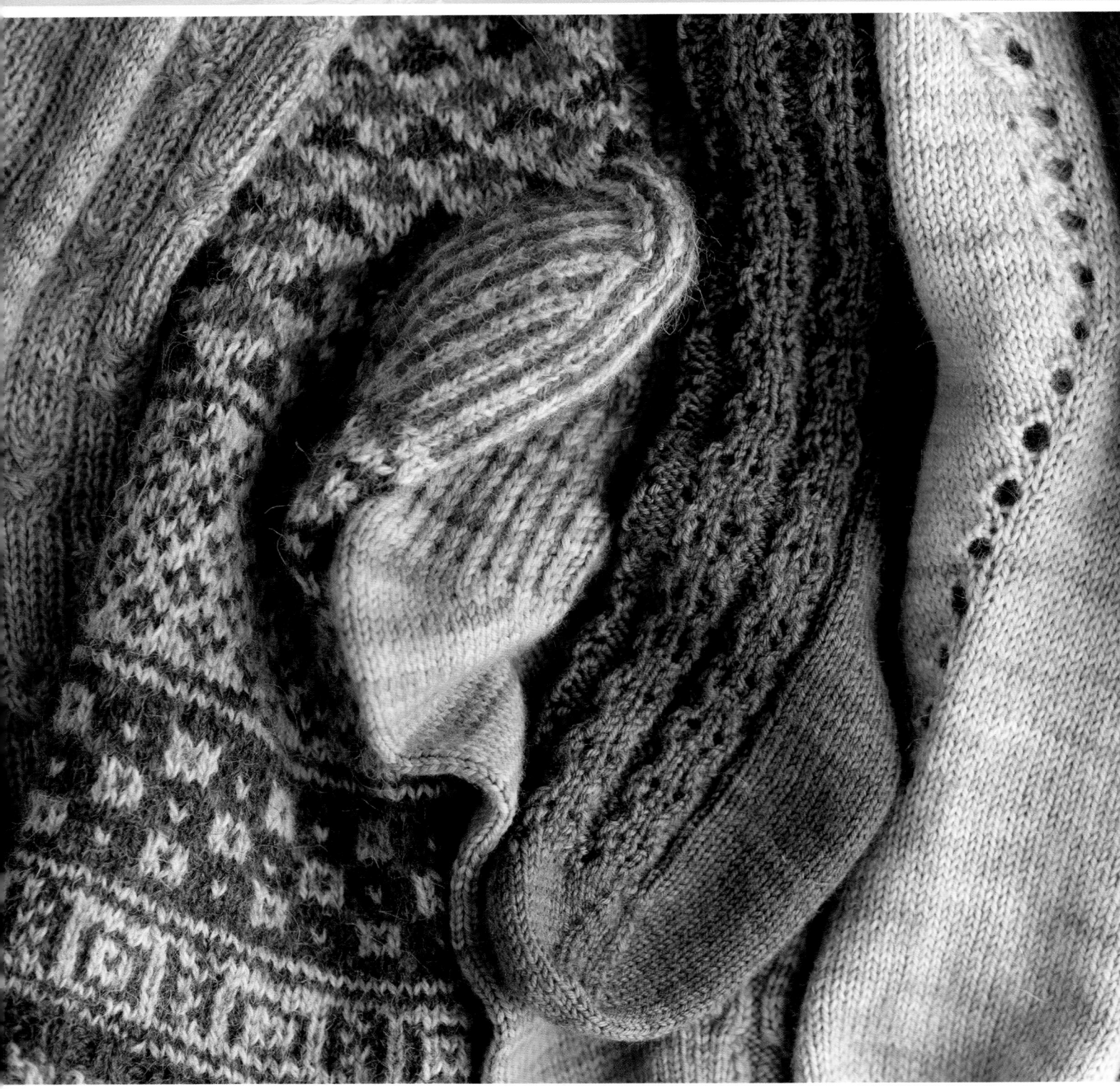

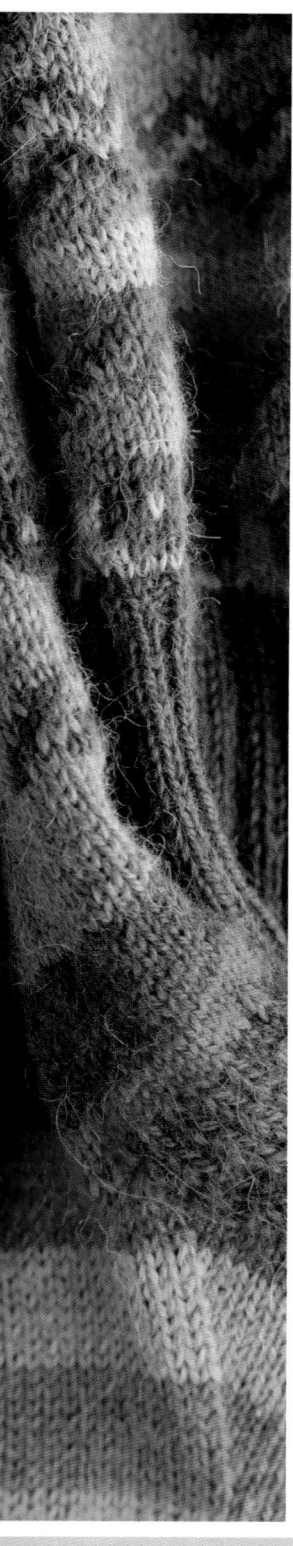

CONTENTS

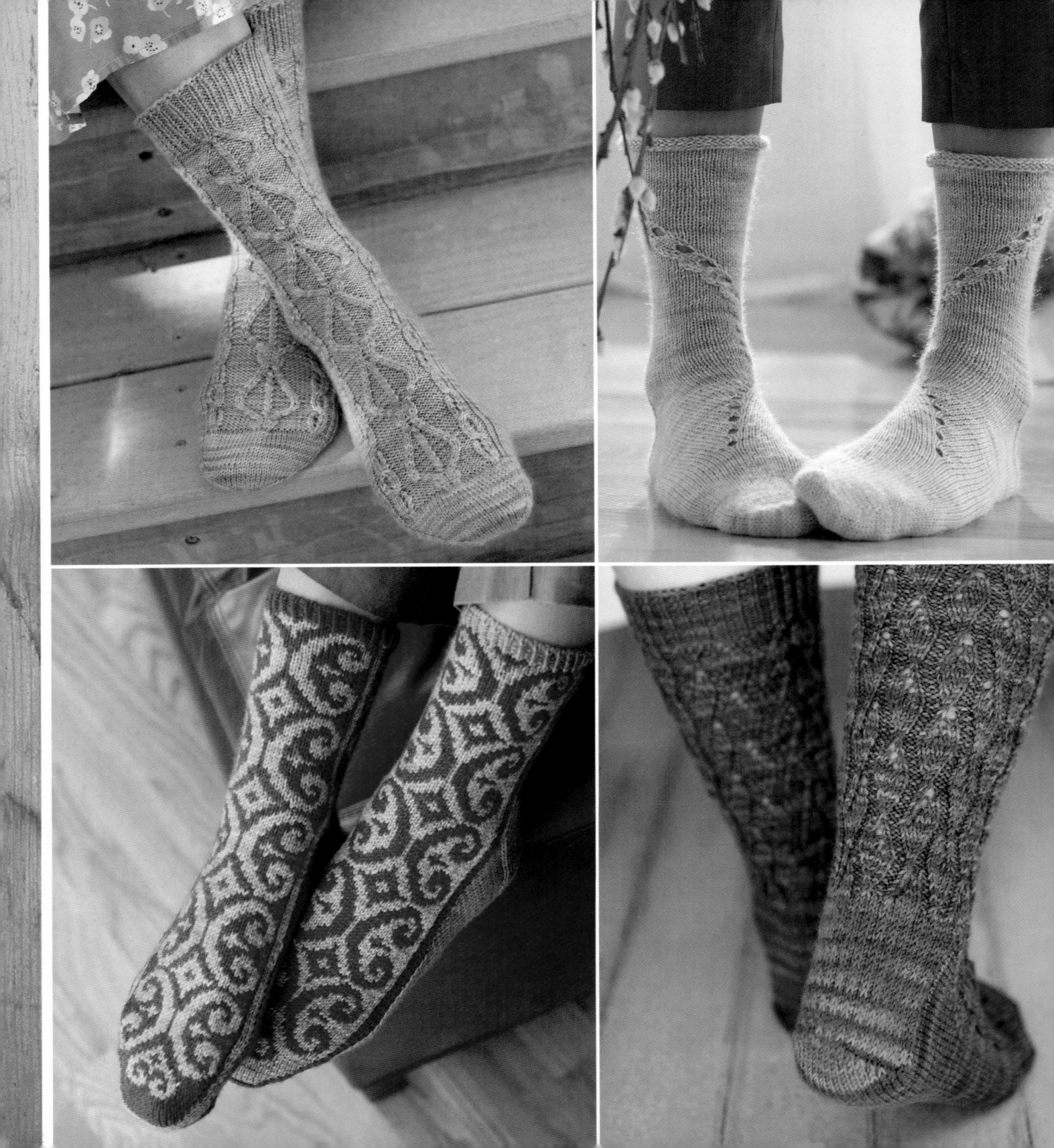

Mastering
Good Sock Design

For years, my favorite knitting project has been socks. Besides enjoying the portability and relatively quick gratification, I continue to marvel at the magical way the heel turns into something that fits so beautifully.

For years now, I've worn only handknitted socks because they look and feel so good. Although I often fall back on a basic pattern when knitting socks for myself, the number of innovative and exciting designs continues to astonish and inspire me, which is how this book came to be.

For *Sock Knitting Master Class*, I asked fifteen renowned sock knitters and experts to contribute their designs and sock-knitting knowledge. In addition to the spectacular patterns, you'll learn a variety of design approaches and techniques that will provide the foundation for creating beautiful socks of your own. While some designers begin by choosing a skein of yarn for its color, fiber content, or structure, then design a sock that makes the most of those properties, others begin with an idea for a particular stitch or color pattern. Still others sketch and doodle until something speaks to them, then they find the appropriate yarn and work out "filler" stitches as necessary to translate their ideas into wearable socks.

However they begin, the most successful sock designs follow the Bauhaus principle that form follows function. In socks, this means that each part—cuff, leg, heel, instep, sole, and toe—has a pleasing design that accomplishes the necessary function. The true art in designing comes from the integration of the different parts into an overall plan that is greater than the sum of its individual parts. For many designers, this integration is the result of trial and error—excellent design usually requires some amount of ripping out and making adjustments.

The patterns in this book are organized by direction of construction—top down followed by toe up. Within each construction type you'll find an assortment of color and texture techniques—stripes, slip stitches, color stranding, intarsia, entrelac, lace, cables, and traveling stitches—and an assortment of heel and toe shapings. Within each pattern you'll find sidebar boxes that highlight design principles, special techniques, and (my favorite) a description by the esteemed Clara Parkes of the type of yarn best suited to each design. Even if you don't plan to knit every pair of socks in this book, I encourage you to take a few minutes to read all the sidebar boxes. They give valuable tips for design and execution, no matter how a sock is knitted.

Fit

Like all practical things, good design takes into account both form (or shape) and function. Socks need to fit the human foot comfortably and withstand friction caused by walking and rubbing inside shoes. A well-designed sock accomplishes all of this and is interesting to look at as well.

The best way to determine what size to make your sock is to wrap a tape measure around the widest part of your foot, pulling the tape snug, but not tight (figure 1). To measure your foot length, place a ruler on the floor and lightly step on it, aligning the back of your heel with the "0" and measuring the length to your longest toe (figure 2). To measure your leg length, hold a ruler against a wall with the "0" on the floor, then place the back of your leg against the ruler and measure how high up your leg you want the sock to extend (figure 3). If you are knitting socks as a gift, use the table below to get a general idea of foot size based on shoe size. Keep in mind that a sock should have a bit of negative ease so that the stitches stretch somewhat around the foot.

But there's more to good sock design than just getting the right fit.

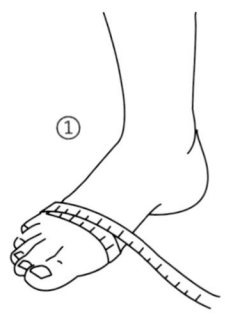
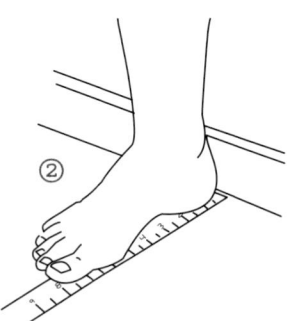
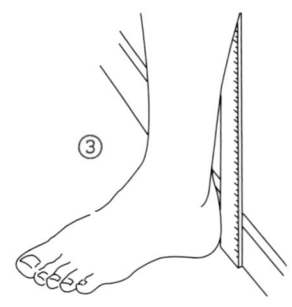

Sock Size as a Function of Shoe Size

U.S. (EUROPEAN) SHOE SIZE	FOOT CIRCUMFERENCE	TOTAL FOOT LENGTH
Children's 9–12 (26–30)	6½" (16.5 cm)	7" (18 cm)
Children's 1–4 (31–34)	7½" (19 cm)	8¼" (21 cm)
Women's 5–7 / Men's 4–6 (35–38)	8" (20.5 cm)	9½" (24 cm)
Women's 8–10 / Men's 7–9 (38.5–43)	9" (23 cm)	10¼" (26 cm)
Women's 11–14 / Men's 10–13 (44–48)	9¾" (25 cm)	11" (28 cm)

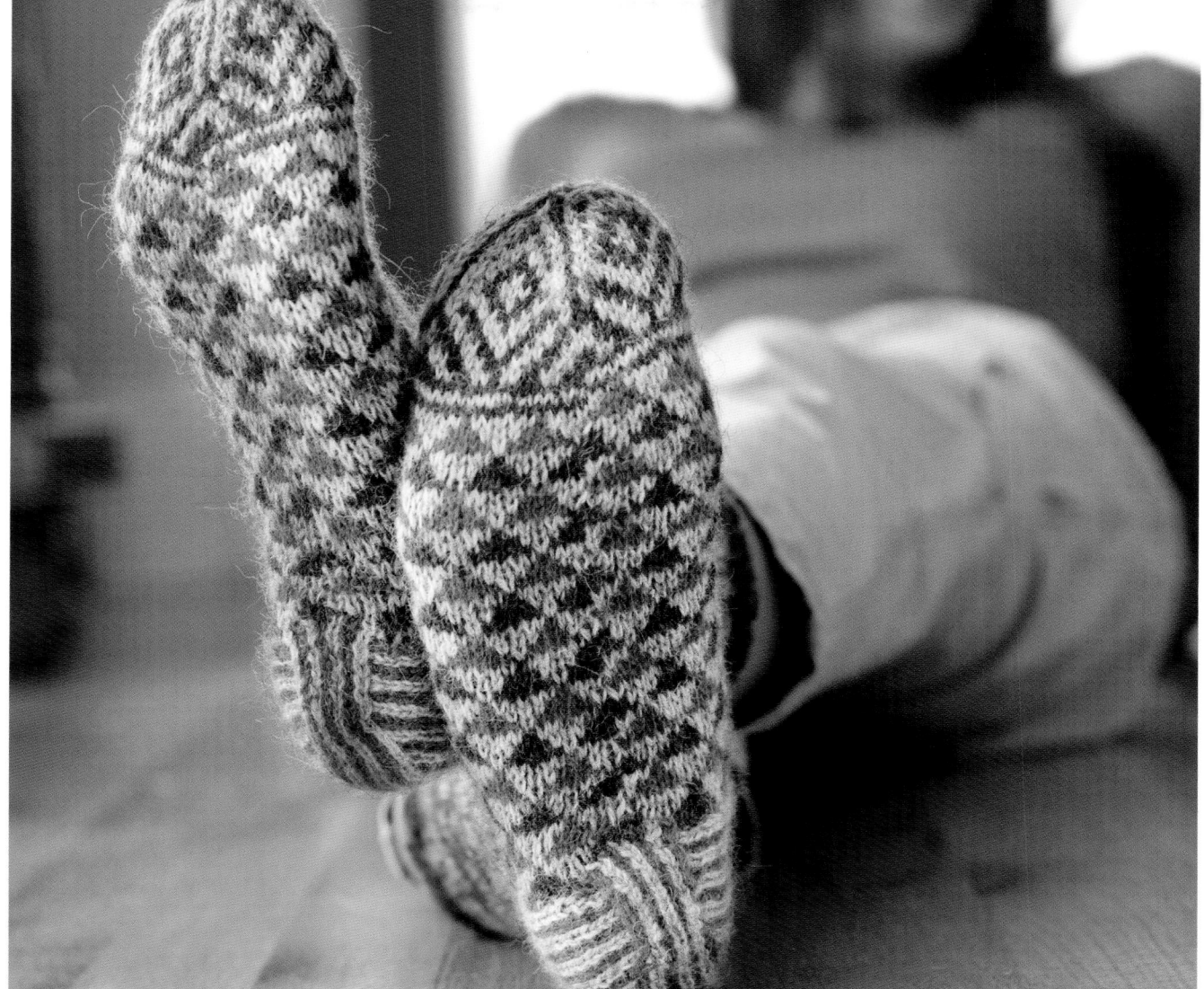

FRENCH MARKET SOCKS, PAGE 56

Comfort

Socks are most comfortable if they have enough stretch to hug (but not bind) the leg and instep. To ensure maximum elasticity, many designers include some sort of ribbed component on the leg and instep. You also want to take into account how a sock will fit in a shoe. While highly textured cable patterns can look lovely around the leg, they will add bulk at the back of the heel and along the instep that can be potentially uncomfortable inside a shoe. Therefore, plan to end bulky patterns at the ankle. The bottom of the foot is another place where comfort is key. The sole of a sock should be smooth and soft. Because uneven stitches or texture patterns can be annoying to sensitive feet, the bottoms of most socks are worked in plain stockinette stitch. The toe should be wide enough to accommodate the toes without bagging or binding. This is an area that can be tight in a shoe so you want to be cautious about adding texture in this area as well—like the sole, most designers work the toes in stockinette stitch.

Yarn and Gauge

Many dedicated wool or cotton sock yarns contain some percentage of man-made fiber (such as nylon) to add longevity to the yarn. While these fibers don't prevent the wool or cotton from wearing thin, they are much slower to wear themselves and provide a thin foundation of stitches when the other fibers wear away. If your yarn doesn't contain one of these additions, consider working a strand of reinforcing nylon thread or yarn (available at most knitting stores that carry sock yarn) along with the heel and toe, or be prepared to mend the inevitable holes.

The knitted fabric of a sock should be sturdy enough to withstand the friction that results from walking and rubbing inside a shoe. A perfectly fitting sock will not wear well if the stitches are so loose that they slide along the path of friction at the toes, bottom of foot, or back of heel. For me, the sturdiest socks are knitted at a gauge that is one or two stitches per inch tighter than recommended on the ball band. Denser stitches wear better because only the outer fibers are subject to abrasion. Just be careful not to knit the sock so densely that elasticity is lost.

How Much Yarn Do You Need?

The amount of yarn you'll need for a pair of socks depends on the gauge and sock size. In general, the finer the yarn and the bigger the sock, the more yarn you'll need. If you plan to add a heavily textured pattern such as cables, you'll also need more yarn. Use the table here as a guideline for yarn amounts based on gauge and foot circumference.

	FOOT CIRCUMFERENCE			
	8¼" (21 cm)	9½" (24 cm)	10¼" (26 cm)	11" (28 cm)
6 stitches/inch	266 yd (243 m)	317 yd (290 m)	394 yd (361 m)	466 yd (426 m)
7 stitches/inch	293 yd (268 m)	349 yd (319 m)	434 yd (397 m)	513 yd (469 m)
8 stitches/inch	322 yd (294 m)	384 yd (351 m)	477 yd (437 m)	564 yd (516 m)
9 stitches/inch	357 yd (326 m)	423 yd (387 m)	524 yd (479 m)	620 yd (567 m)

GAUGE

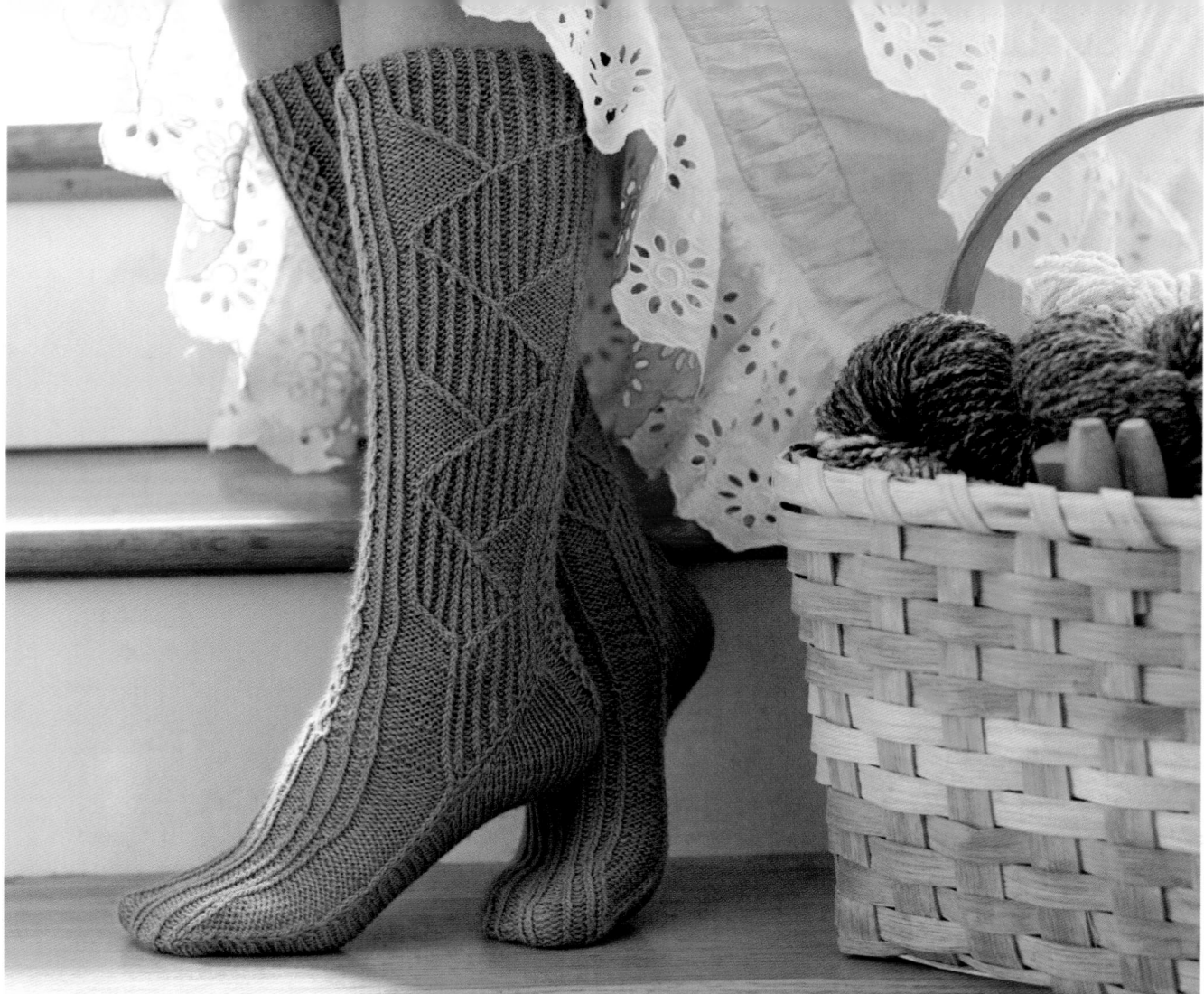

TWISTED-STITCH STOCKINGS, PAGE 86

Be sure to measure your gauge on a swatch that has been knitted in the round with the yarn, needles, and stitch pattern you plan to use for the sock. Many knitters knit more tightly than they purl, or vice versa, so that the gauge they get working in rounds (when the right side is always facing forward) is different from the gauge they get knitting back and forth in rows (in which the stockinette stitches are alternately knitted and purled). Stitch patterns such as lace, cables, stranded colorwork, and slip stitches can cause the stitches to become wider or narrower, which can produce a significantly different gauge from the stockinette gauge worked with the same yarn and needles. Work a swatch large enough that you can measure at least 2" (5 cm) both horizontally (stitch gauge) and vertically (row gauge) well away from the edges of the swatch. To ensure an accurate reading, take measurements in two or three places. Also be sure to include any partial stitches in your gauge measurements. While a half stitch may not seem significant over a 2" (5 cm) width, it can add up to an inch or more around the entire sock circumference.

Needle Choice

Historically, most socks were knitted with double-pointed needles in which the stitches are held on three or four needles, and a fourth or fifth needle is used to knit. More recently, many knitters find that circular needles are easier to manage and reduce the number of transitions between needles within each round of knitting. All of these methods are demonstrated in the accompanying DVD.

"The projects in this book specify the technique used by the designer, but as long as you keep track of the instep (or front-of-leg) stitches, the sole (or back-of-leg) stitches, and any other key sections of the pattern, you can use the type of needles you prefer."

Four Double-Pointed Needles

Most Americans learn to knit socks with four double-pointed needles—the stitches are distributed between three needles and the fourth is used for knitting. When working from the top down, the stitches are typically arranged so that half of the back-of-leg or heel stitches are on the first needle (Needle 1), all of the front-of-leg or instep stitches are on the second needle (Needle 2), and the remaining half of the back-of-leg or heel stitches are on the third needle (Needle 3). The round typically begins at the back of the leg and along the bottom of the sole. Note that the stitches are rearranged at the start of the heel flap so that the heel stitches are worked on one needle while the instep stitches are distributed equally on the other two.

This method was used for Asymmetrical Cables (page 48), Almondine (page 62), Knot Socks (page 96), Slip-n-Slide (page 108), Stealth Argyles (page 138), and Toe-Up Travelers (page 166).

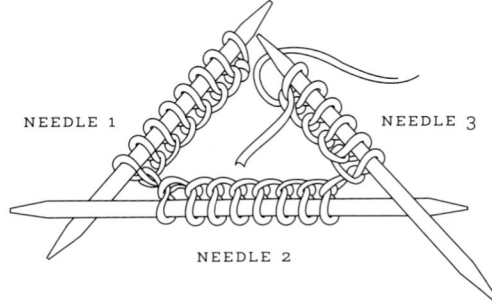

Five Double-Pointed Needles

Europeans typically learn to knit socks with five double-pointed needles—the stitches are distributed between four needles and the fifth is used for knitting. The stitches are arranged so that the back-of-leg, heel, and sole stitches are equally divided between two needles (half on Needle 1 and half on Needle 4), and the front-of-the-leg and instep stitches are equally divided between the other two (half on Needle 2 and half on Needle 3). The round typically begins at the back of the leg and along the bottom of the sole.

This method was used for French Market Socks (page 56), Happy-Go-Lucky Boot Socks (page 68), Thigh-High Stripes (page 74), Rose Ribs (page 80), Up-Down Entrelac (page 122), Bulgarian Blooms (page 130), Half-Stranded Socks (page 152), and Toe-Up Travelers (page 166).

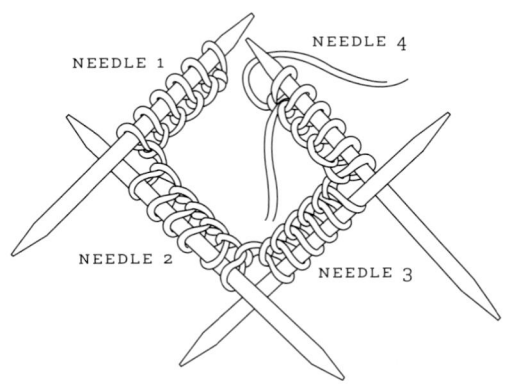

One Very Short Circular Needle

Recently, 9" and 12" (23 and 30.5 cm) circular needles have been manufactured specifically to accommodate the relatively small number of stitches around a sock. The rigid needle sections at the tips of these needles are quite short and take some getting used to, but the advantage is that all of the stitches are on a single needle, and you can knit around and around without interruption. It's a good idea to use markers to separate the front-of-leg (instep) stitches from the back-of-leg (sole) stitches to ensure that the heel and toe stitches are perfectly aligned. The round typically begins at the back of the leg and along the bottom of the sole.

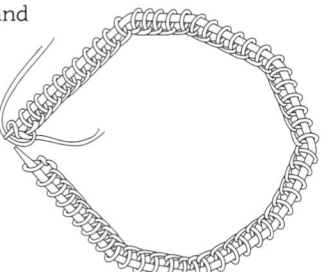

This method is not specified for any of the socks in this book but could be substituted for any other needle type.

Two Circular Needles

Some knitters prefer to knit socks on two circular needles. The back-of-leg, heel, and sole stitches are worked on one needle, and the front-of-leg and instep stitches are worked on the second. For this method, the round begins at the side of the leg (between the instep and sole). The key is to keep the stitches and the needles separate—each needle is used only for the stitches it holds. Most followers of this method use 24" (60 cm) circulars, which have longer rigid needle sections that are easy to handle. The advantages are that there are only two breaks between the needles, no needle is ever completely empty so it's difficult to lose one, and the stitches can stretch over the cables, allowing the sock to be tried on as it is in progress. Some knitters find that the needle not in use flops about in an annoying way.

This method was used for Twisted-Stitch Stockings (page 86) and Pussy Willow Stockings (page 160).

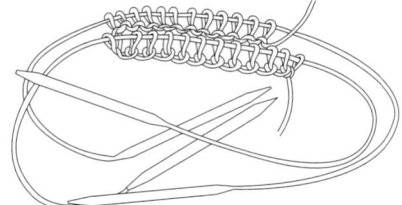

One Long Circular Needle (Magic Loop)

In a method called the "magic loop," Sarah Hauschuka simplified the method of working socks circularly by using a single 40" (100 cm) circular needle. To use this method, cast on the stitches as usual, then slide them to the center of the cable, fold the cable and stitches exactly at the midpoint, pull out a loop of cable in the center of the cast-on to make two sets of stitches, then slide each group toward a needle point. Half of the stitches will be on one needle tip and the other half will be on the other tip (figure 1). Hold the needle tips parallel so that the working yarn comes out of the right-hand edge of the back needle tip. *Pull the back needle tip out to expose about 6" (15 cm) of cable and use that needle to knit the stitches off the front needle tip (figure 2). At the end of those stitches, pull the cable so that the two sets of stitches are at the ends of their respective needle tips again, turn the work around, and repeat from *. When working the socks, the back-of-leg, heel, and sole stitches are in one group, and the front-of-leg and instep stitches are in the other group. The round begins at one side of the leg, between the two sections. The advantage to this method is that all of the stitches are on a single needle so there's no chance of loosing the needle. Some knitters are distracted by the "wings" of cable loops between the groups of stitches.

This method was used for Mock Cables and Lace (page 102) and Terpander (page 144).

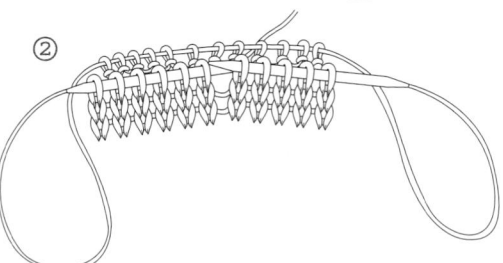

Heels

Round Heel Worked from the Top Down

The round heel is one of the most common top-down heel shapings used in the Western world. It is worked in three parts—a heel flap followed by a short-row heel turn, which in turn is followed by stitches picked up along the sides of the heel flap and decreased to form the gussets. The round heel is used in Asymmetrical Cables (page 48), Almondine (page 62), Happy-Go-Lucky Boot Socks (page 68), Thigh-High Stripes (page 74), Rose Ribs (page 80), Mock Cables and Lace (page 102), and Slip-n-Slide (page 108).

Heel Flap

The heel flap extends along the back of the heel from the ankle to the base of the heel. It is typically worked over about half of the leg stitches and is usually positioned so that the former beginning of the round is in the center of the heel stitches. It often begins with a wrong-side row and is worked for the same number of rows as there are heel stitches. For example, if there are 64 leg stitches, the heel flap might be worked on 32 stitches for 32 rows. Because the heel flap is an area of increased friction in shoes, it is typically worked in a reinforcing stitch pattern that alternates slipped stitches with knit or purl stitches. The slip-stitch pattern is typically set up so that the first stitch of every row is slipped, which produces one chain edge stitch along the selvedges for every two rows of knitting. In our example, there would be 16 slipped chain edge stitches for the 32-row heel flap.

Heel Turn

The heel turn is worked in short-rows, beginning with a center section of about 5 stitches. Then 1 more stitch is worked farther out toward the end of the needle in each row while decreases are worked to form the familiar cup shape. Once the number of center stitches has been established, the heel turn can follow the same formula, no matter what size sock you're knitting.

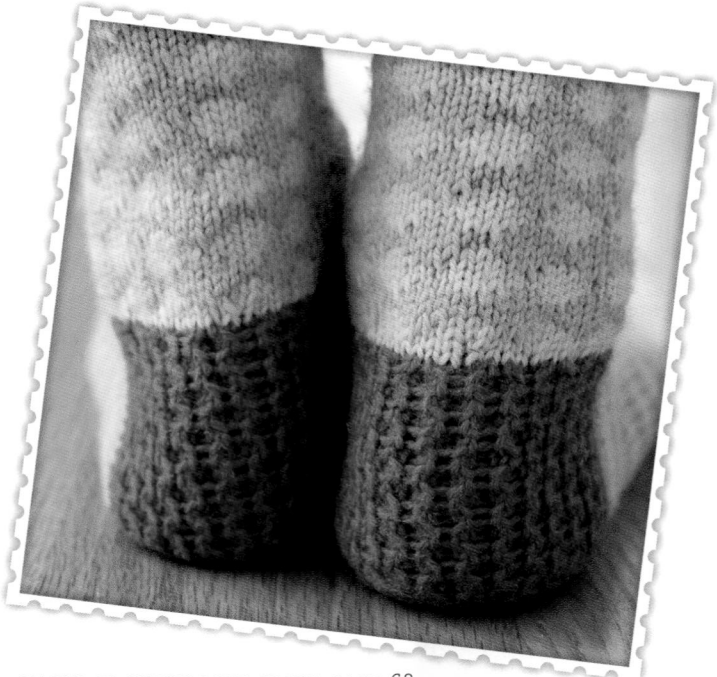

HAPPY-GO-LUCKY BOOT SOCKS, PAGE 68

Gussets

The gussets connect the heel with the instep so that the foot can be worked in rounds to the tip of the toe. To form the gussets, new stitches are picked up at a rate of about one stitch for every two heel flap rows along each side of the heel flap (ways to do this are demonstrated on the accompanying DVD) to connect the live stitches of the turned heel with the live instep stitches. Many designers like to pick up an extra stitch at the base of the heel flap (in the corner between the flap and the adjacent instep stitch) to help close up any hole that might form between the two. In our example with a 32-row heel, we'd pick up and knit a total of 17 stitches along each side of the heel flap—1 stitch every other round 16 times, then 1 extra stitch in the corner.

Once the gusset stitches are picked up, 1 stitch is decreased on each side of the instep stitches every other row until the original number of leg stitches or the desired number of foot stitches remains. The gusset decreases form pronounced diagonal lines between the beginning of the heel flap and the foot. You can work the gusset decreases on the stitches at the edge, right next to the instep, or several stitches in from the edge if you prefer. This allows you to align the gusset decreases with a particular stitch in the leg pattern.

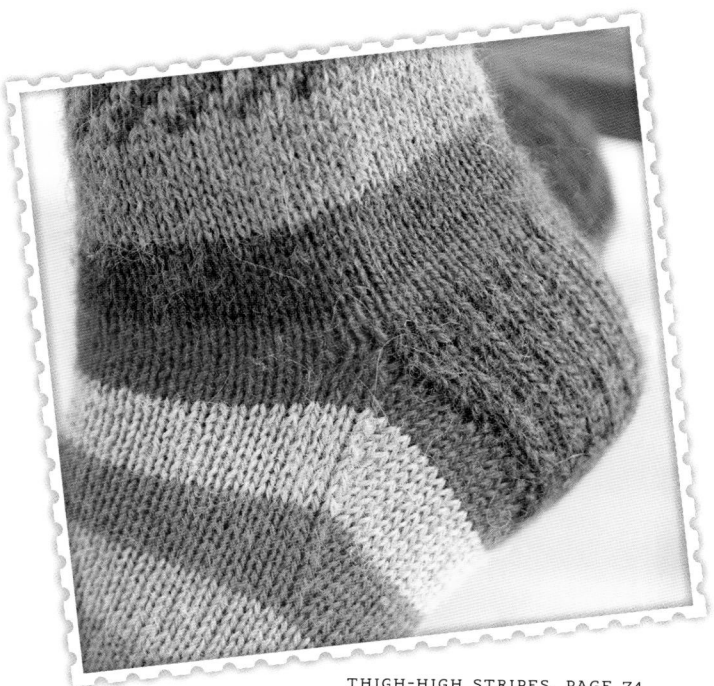

THIGH-HIGH STRIPES, PAGE 74

Common Heel Flap Stitch Patterns

Standard Slip 1, Knit 1 Pattern

This pattern is worked over an even number of stitches. On right-side rows, it alternates a slipped stitch with a knitted stitch; on wrong-side rows, only the first stitch is slipped, then the rest are purled.

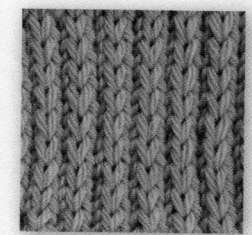

Row 1: (WS) Sl 1 purlwise with yarn in back, purl to end.

Row 2: (RS) *Sl 1 purlwise with yarn in back, k1; rep from *.

Repeat Rows 1 and 2 for pattern.

Reversed Slip 1, Knit 1 Pattern

This is similar to the standard pattern, but the yarn is held on the right side of the knitting when the stitches are slipped.

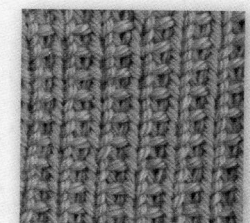

Row 1: (WS) Sl 1 purlwise with yarn in back, purl to end.

Row 2: (RS) *Sl 1 purlwise with yarn in front, k1; repeat from *.

Repeat Rows 1 and 2 for pattern.

Alternating Slip 1, Knit 1 Pattern

The stitches that are slipped alternate from row to row, brick fashion. This is commonly called "eye of the partridge."

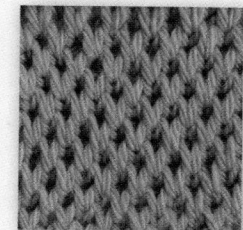

Rows 1 and 3: (WS) Sl 1 purlwise with yarn in front, purl to end.

Row 2: (RS) *Sl 1 purlwise with yarn in back, k1; rep from *.

Row 4: Sl 1 purlwise with yarn in back, k2, *sl 1 purlwise with yarn in back, k1; rep from * to last st, k1.

Repeat Rows 1–4 for pattern.

Round Heel Worked from the Toe Up

You can get the look of a round heel (page 14) on a toe-up sock by reversing the order in which the three elements are worked and modifying the way the gusset and heel flap are worked to accommodate the change in direction. When a round heel is worked from the toe up, the gussets are worked first, followed by the heel turn, and ending with the heel flap. This type of heel is used for Terpander (page 144), Half-Stranded Socks (page 152), and Pussy Willow Stockings (page 160).

Gussets

The gussets begin when the foot is between 3½" and 4¾" (9 and 12 cm) less than that desired total length. The exact starting point depends on your foot length, gauge, and type of shaping; the pattern instructions will specify when to start the gusset. To make it easier to distinguish the heel stitches from the gusset stitches, place a marker on each side of the original heel stitches. To form the gussets, 1 stitch is increased each side of the instep stitches every other round until there is about twice the number of original sole stitches. For example, if there are 64 foot stitches, the heel is generally worked on the 32 sole stitches, which are increased to 64 stitches by increasing 16 gusset stitches on each side of the marked center 32 stitches. Cat Bordhi broke with tradition and discovered that the increases, which serve the same purpose as designated gusset increases, can be worked anywhere on the foot, and not just at the sides of the instep.

Heel Turn

The heel is turned in a series of short-rows in which 1 less stitch is worked each row and a stitch is wrapped at each turning point until about 1" (2.5 cm) of stitches remain between wrapped stitches.

Heel Flap

The wraps are worked together with the wrapped stitches to close holes, then the heel flap is worked in short-rows while the gusset stitches are decreased. Just like heel flaps worked from the top down, a reinforcing slip-stitch pattern (page 14) can be used to reinforce the flap. The last heel flap stitch is worked together with the first gusset stitch at the end of every row until all of the gusset stitches have been eliminated.

TERPANDER, PAGE 144

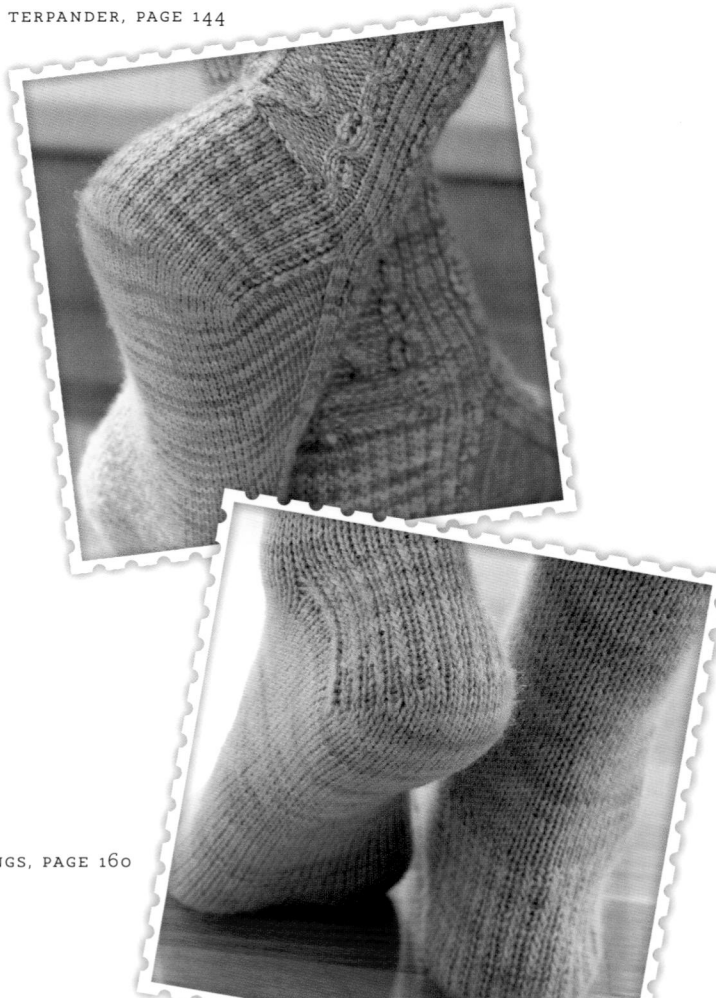

PUSSY WILLOW STOCKINGS, PAGE 160

Band Heel

The band heel is a variation of the three-part round heel (page 15) in which a band of stitches extends along the center of the base of the heel. Although the band can vary in width, it is generally worked over the center one-third of the heel stitches. The heel flap stitch pattern can be continued through the heel turn to produce a bit of reinforcement (and padding) along the base of the heel. This type of heel, which is distinctive in its lack of diagonal gusset decreases, is used for French Market Socks (page 56).

Heel Flap

The heel flap is typically worked in a slip-stitch pattern over half of the leg stitches. It is worked for the same number of rows as there are stitches in the heel flap, minus 8. For example, if we had 32 heel stitches, we'd work the heel flap for 24 rows.

Heel Turn

As for the round heel, the band heel is turned with a combination of short-rows and decreases. The difference is that the decreases are worked each side of a set number of center stitches (usually 6 to 8) to end up with 2 more than the number of center stitches (the center stitches plus 1 decrease stitch at each side).

Gussets

Gusset stitches are picked up along the sides of the heel flap to connect the turned-heel stitches with the waiting instep stitches. There are no gusset decreases to work.

FRENCH MARKET SOCKS, PAGE 56

Dutch Heel

The Dutch heel, also called the square heel, is a variation of the band heel (page 17) that shares three elements with the round heel—heel flap, heel turn, and gussets. This type of heel is used for Knot Socks (page 96).

Heel Flap

The heel flap is typically worked in a slip-stitch pattern the same as the heel flap for a round heel.

Heel Turn

To turn the heel, the heel stitches are divided into thirds. If the original number of stitches is not divisible by three, make sure that there is the same number of stitches on each side of the center section. For example, if we have 32 heel stitches, we'd place a marker after the first 11 stitches, then another marker 10 stitches beyond that for a 10-stitch center section with 11 stitches on each side. The stitches are worked in short-rows with decreases at each side of the marked center stitches. For our example, 12 heel stitches would remain (the center 10 stitches plus the last decrease at each side).

Gussets

The gussets are worked in the same manner as the gussets for a round heel.

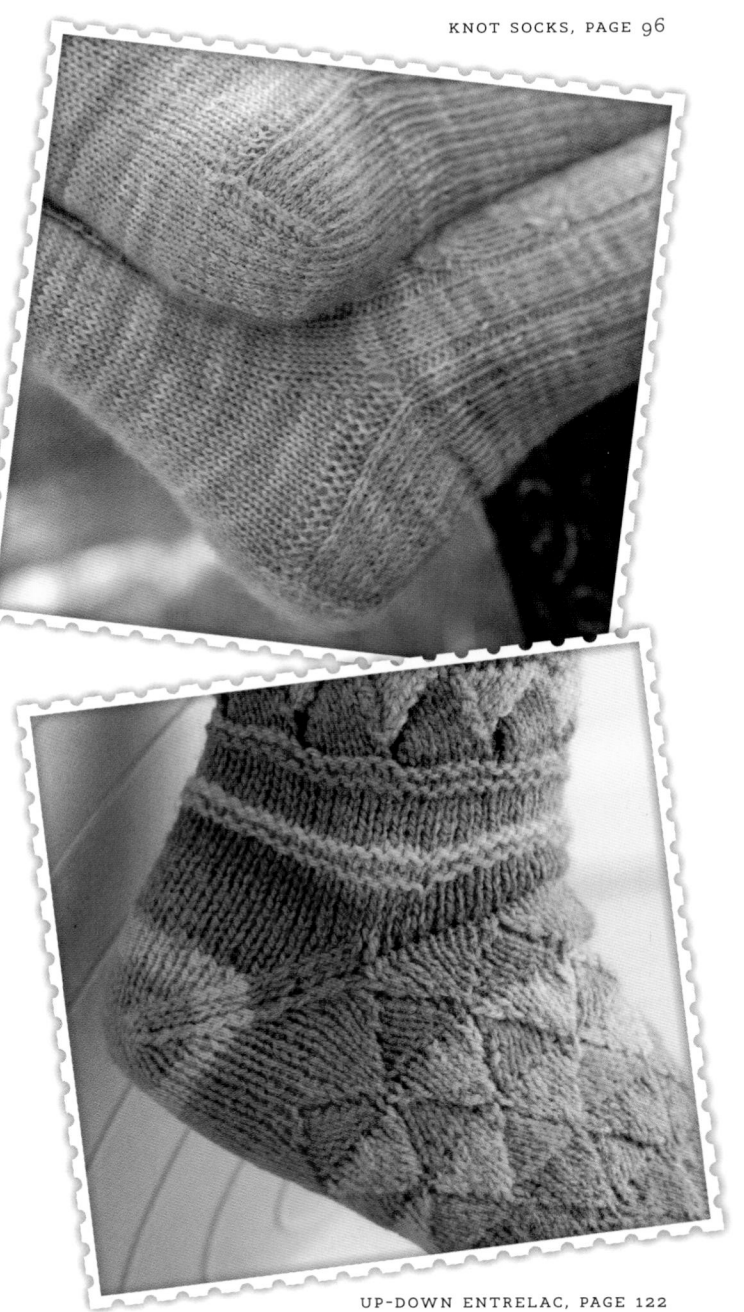

KNOT SOCKS, PAGE 96

UP-DOWN ENTRELAC, PAGE 122

Peasant Heel

The peasant heel, also called an afterthought heel, is worked as the last step of a sock. This type of heel has no heel flap or gusset and is worked the same whether the sock is knitted from the top down or from the toe up. It is relatively easy to replace if it develops a hole or wears thin.

To set up for a peasant heel, the stitches for the heel are typically worked on a length of waste yarn to mark the heel placement and make it easier to expose the heel stitches later. The same stitches are then knitted again with the working yarn, and the sock is completed in the round to the toe if knitting from the top down or to the top of cuff if knitting from the toe up. After the main body of the sock is completed, the waste yarn is carefully removed, and the live stitches are placed on needles for working in the round. The heel is shaped with decreases at each side, much the same as a wedge toe is worked (page 21) to reduce the stitches to a rounded point. The remaining stitches are then grafted together, the same as for closing the tip of a toe.

STEP 1: At the desired heel location, drop the working yarn and knit the desired heel stitches with contrasting waste yarn (a smooth cotton yarn is preferable). Typically, this is about half the stitches, so if there are 64 leg stitches, knit 32 stitches with waste yarn. For ease of working, you may want to isolate these stitches on one or two needles.

STEP 2: Pick up the working yarn and use it to knit across the stitches just worked with waste yarn. There will be one extra row of knitting across these stitches, but it's the waste-yarn row that will be removed later. Continue to work in rounds as established to the toe if knitting from the top down or to the cuff if knitting from the toe up.

STEP 3: Carefully remove the waste yarn that marks the heel stitches and place the exposed stitches on double-pointed needles for working in the round. Because of the nature of the loops that form stitches, there will be one less exposed stitch on one half of the heel. In our example, there will be 32 stitches on one half and 31 stitches on the other. Divide the loops so that there are 16 stitches each on two needles for one half of the heel; divide the remaining half so that there are 16 stitches on a third needle and 15 stitches on a fourth.

STEP 4: Join the working yarn at the boundary between the two halves so that you'll work the half with the same number of stitches on both needles first. Pick up and knit 1 stitch at the boundary between the two halves, then knit the 16 stitches on the first needle. Knit the 16 stitches on the second needle. Pick up and knit 1 stitch at the boundary between the two halves, then knit the 16 stitches on the third needle. Knit the 15 stitches on the fourth needle, then pick up and knit another stitch in the boundary between the two halves—there will be 66 stitches total; 17 stitches on the first needle, 16 stitches on the second needle, 17 stitches on the third needle, and 16 stitches on the fourth needle.

STEP 5: To shape the heel, decrease 1 stitch at each side of each half every other round until about 1" (2.5 cm) of stitches remains on each half, or about ½" (1.3 cm) of stitches on each needle. For example, if your gauge is 8 stitches per inch, you'll decrease until 8 stitches remain in each half, or 4 stitches on each needle.

STEP 6: Use the Kitchener stitch (see page 44) to graft the remaining stitches together.

Kathryn Alexander used a variation of this method to shape the heel of her Up-Down Entrelac socks (page 122). Instead of marking the heel stitches with waste yarn, Kathryn worked the heel on the live stitches that remained after she grafted the instep stitches from the toe-up foot to the leg stitches from top-down portion of the sock.

Short-Row Heel

A short-row heel is similar to a peasant heel (page 19) in its lack of heel flap and gusset shaping and, like the peasant heel, a short-row heel is worked the same whether the sock is knitted from the top down or from the toe up. This type of heel is also relatively easy to replace if it develops a hole or wears thin.

For this type of heel, just a portion of the stitches are worked back and forth in short-rows to create a pouch of knitting that accommodates the shape of the heel. Like most types of heel shaping, the short-row heel is typically worked over half of the leg stitches. You can imagine the heel as an hourglass shape of knitting that begins by working 1 less stitch at the end of every row until about 20% of the heel stitches remain in the center between the turning points (the "waist" of the hourglass). Then 1 more stitch is worked at the end of every row until all of the heel stitches are worked. To bring the height of the short-row heel even with the ankle bone, about an inch is worked plain along the back half of the leg (work the instep stitches in the established pattern) before beginning the heel when working from the top down or after the heel when working from the toe up.

The key to a successful short-row heel is to close the gaps that form at the short-row turning points. There are a variety of ways to accomplish this, the most common of which involve working a yarnover or wrapping the stitch at the turning point, then working the yarnover or wrap with the adjacent stitch on a following row to close the hole. The differences are subtle, but the principles are the same.

This type of heel works equally well for socks knitted from the top down as those knitted from the toe up. It is used in Bulgarian Blooms (page 130), Stealth Argyles (page 138), and Toe-Up Travelers (page 166).

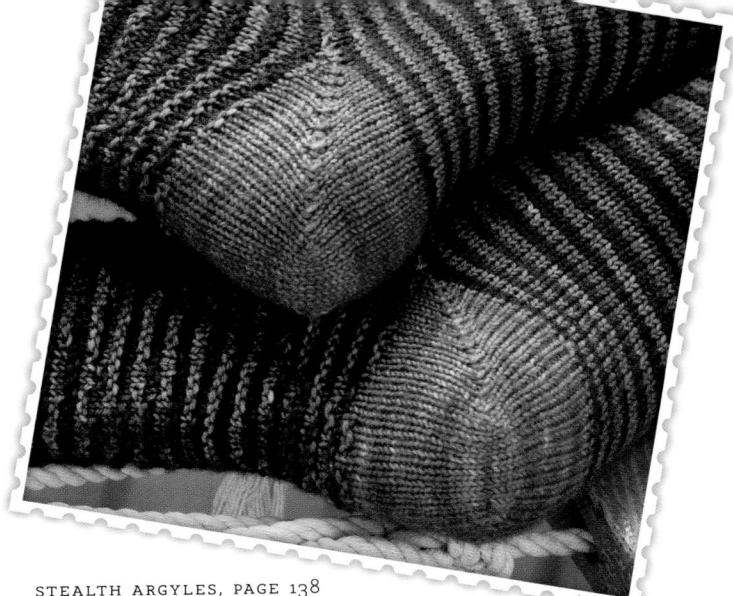

STEALTH ARGYLES, PAGE 138

STEP 1: Place the heel stitches on one needle for ease of working back and forth in rows. For example, if there are 64 leg stitches, place the 32 heel stitches on one needle.

STEP 2: For the first half of the heel, work 1 less stitch every row until about 20% of the heel stitches remain worked in the middle. To close the gaps at the turning points, work a yarnover before the first stitch of every row, working backward yarnovers on wrong-side rows. This will create a paired stitch (the regular stitch plus its accompanying yarnover) at every turning point.

STEP 3: The second half of the heel continues on the same right-side row that ended the first half of the heel. For the second half of the heel, work 1 more stitch every row until all of the heel stitches have been worked. Because this half of the heel is also worked in short-rows, continue to work a yarnover at the beginning of every row and at the same time close the gaps at the turning points by working the yarnovers together with the first "real" stitch of the following pair.

STEP 4: With the right side facing, rejoin for working in rounds and close the gaps between the heel and instep stitches by working the yarnovers at each end of the heel needle together with the stitches at the ends of the instep. If desired, the heel stitches can then be divided onto two needles again for working the sole.

Toes

Wedge Toe

The wedge toe is arguably the most common way to shape a toe. And with good reason—it has a comfortable fit and is easy to execute. In general, 2 stitches are decreased at each side of the foot (at the boundaries between the instep and sole stitches) every other round until half of the original number of stitches remain. Then the decreases are worked every round until about 1" (2.5 cm) of stitches remain each for the instep and sole. The Kitchener stitch (see page 44) is used to graft these stitches together for the tip of the toe.

This type of shaping is used for Asymmetrical Cables (page 48), Almondine (page 62), Happy-Go-Lucky Boot Socks (page 68), Thigh-High Stripes (page 74), Rose Ribs (page 80), and Slip-n-Slide (page 108).

STEP 1: To set up for this type of toe shaping, arrange the stitches so that the instep stitches are easily distinguished from the sole stitches. For example, place the instep stitches on one needle and divide the sole stitches equally between two needles so that the round begins at the center of the sole stitches. If working with 64 foot stitches, for example, there will be 16 heel stitches on the first needle, 32 instep stitches on the second needle, and the remaining 16 heel stitches on the third needle.

STEP 2: Decrease 1 stitch each side of the instep stitches and each side of the sole stitches (4 stitches decreased total) every other round until half the original number of stitches remain. The decreases can be worked on the edge stitches or up to a few stitches in from the edge. In our example, we'd decrease 4 stitches every other round until 32 stitches remain; 16 stitches each for the instep and sole.

STEP 3: Decrease 1 stitch each side of the instep stitches at each side of the sole stitches every round until about 1" (2.5 cm) of stitches remain each for the instep and sole. This gives a rounded shape to the tip of the toe. In our example, we'll decrease 4 stitches every round until 6 or 8 stitches remain each for the instep and sole—12 or 16 stitches total.

STEP 4: Use the Kitchener stitch (see page 44) to graft the remaining stitches together.

ROSE RIBS, PAGE 80

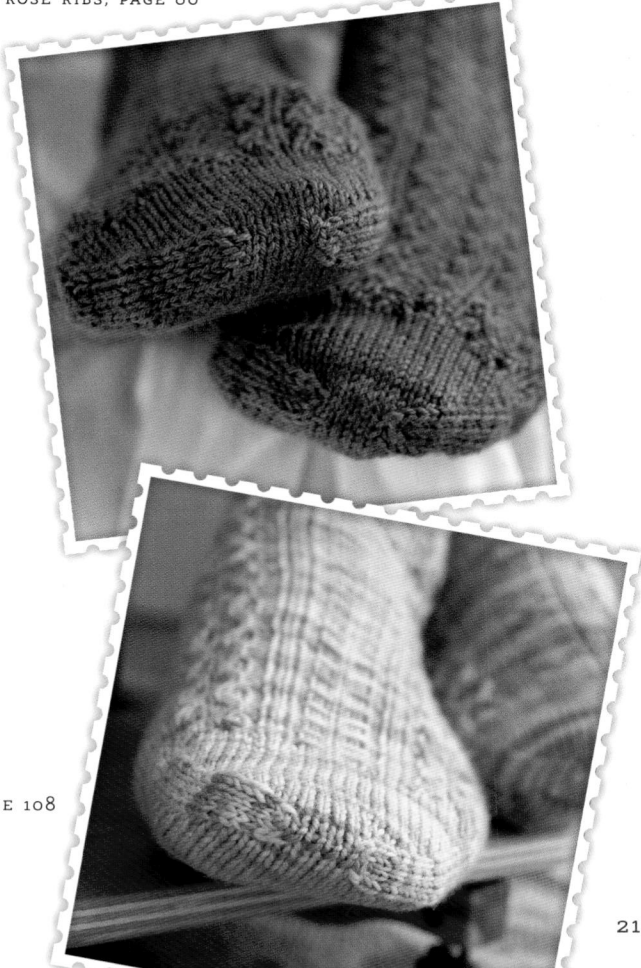

SLIP-N-SLIDE, PAGE 108

Three-Point Toe

This type of toe forms a three-pointed star when viewed straight at the tip of the toe. It requires a number of stitches that is evenly divisible by 3, such as 60 stitches. This type of shaping is used for Knot Socks (page 96).

STEP 1: Arrange the stitches on three double-pointed needles so that there is the same number of stitches on each needle. If there isn't a multiple of 3 stitches for the foot, decrease 1 or 2 stitches in the first round to achieve the necessary number. For example, if we have 62 stitches in the foot, we'll decrease 2 stitches in the first toe round to achieve a multiple of 3 stitches (60 stitches), then place 20 stitches each on three needles.

STEP 2: Decrease 2 stitches on each needle (6 stitches total) every other round until half of the original number of stitches remains, ending with the same number of stitches on each needle. In our example, we'll decrease 6 stitches every other round until 30 stitches remain—10 stitches on each needle.

STEP 3: Decrease 2 stitches on each needle every round until about an inch's worth of stitches remains. For example, if our gauge is 8 stitches per inch, we'd decrease until 6 stitches remain—2 stitches on each needle.

STEP 4: Use the gathered tip method (page 47) to close the tip of the toe.

Four-Point Toe

For this variation of the three-point toe, the toe stitches are divided into four equal sections and 2 stitches are decreased in each section (8 stitches decreased total) every other round until half of the original number of stitches remains. Then 2 stitches are decreased in each section every round until about an inch of stitches remains. This type of shaping is used for French Market Socks (page 56).

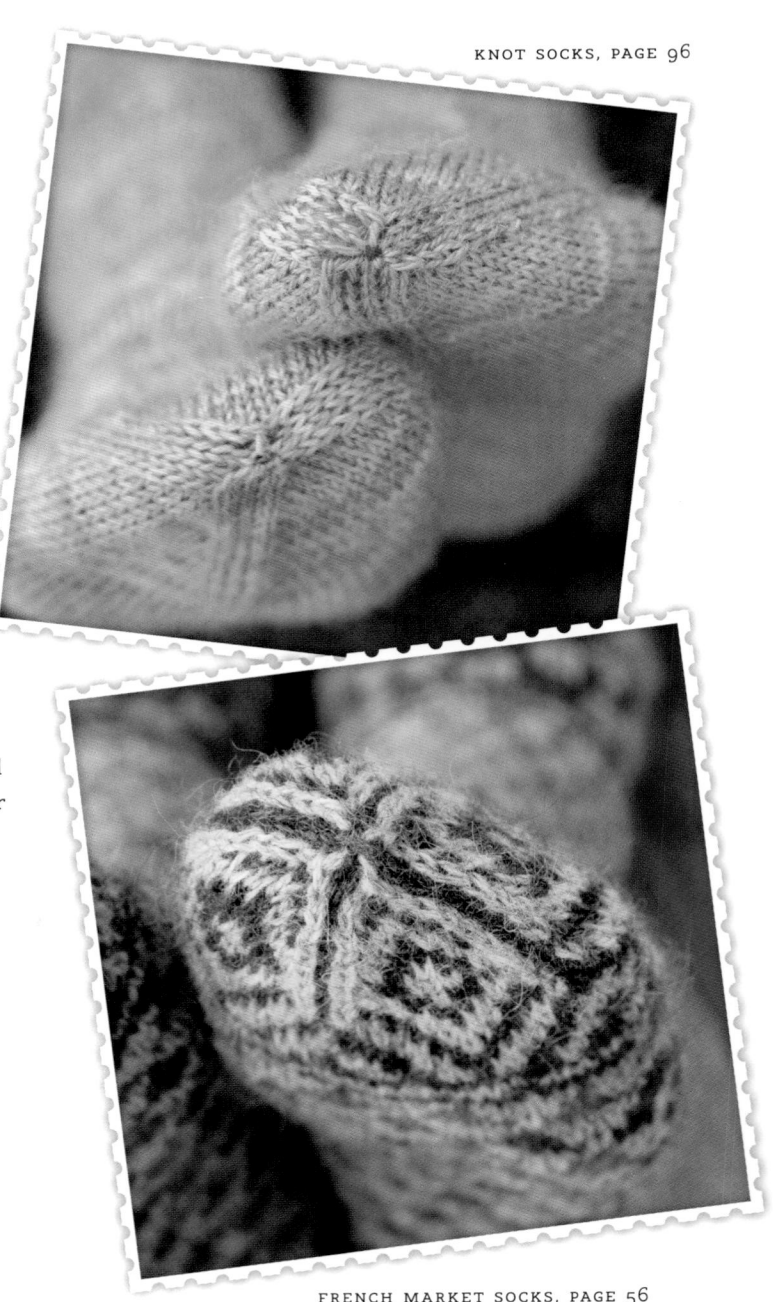

KNOT SOCKS, PAGE 96

FRENCH MARKET SOCKS, PAGE 56

Horizontal Band Toe

This method, developed by Anna Zilboorg so that the sole and instep could be worked separately in her Half-Stranded Socks (page 152), involves knitting a narrow strip that extends from the side of the little toe, around the tips of all the toes, and down the side of the big toe. Anna worked the band on just a few stitches, but it could probably be as much as 1" (2.5 cm) in width. About 1¼" to 1½" (3.2 to 3.8 cm) of stitches are then picked up at the center of the band for the center of the instep (or sole), and these stitches are worked back and forth in rows, picking up 1 more stitch from the band at each end of every right-side row until there is the desired number of instep (or sole) stitches.

STEP 1: Figure out how many stitches you want around the ball of the foot based on your size and gauge.

STEP 2: Subtract the band stitches that will remain visible at each side of the finished sock (usually the number of cast-on stitches minus 2 because 1 stitch at each side of the band is consumed by joining). The result is the total number of stitches for the foot (combined instep and sole stitches). For example, if there are 64 stitches around the foot and 2 stitches of the band visible at each side, subtract 4 band stitches from 64 total stitches to get 60.

STEP 3: Slipping the first stitch of every row, knit the toe band in stockinette stitch for the same number of rows as there are foot stitches. In our example, we'll work the toe band for 60 rows; there will be 30 slipped selvedge stitches at each edge.

STEP 4: Pick up and knit 1 stitch in each slipped selvedge stitch for the instep. In our example, we'll pick up 30 stitches from one selvedge for the instep stitches and another 30 stitches from the other selvedge for the sole stitches. There will be 30 stitches each for the instep and sole and 2 band stitches at each side for a total of 64 stitches for the foot.

HALF-STRANDED SOCKS, PAGE 152

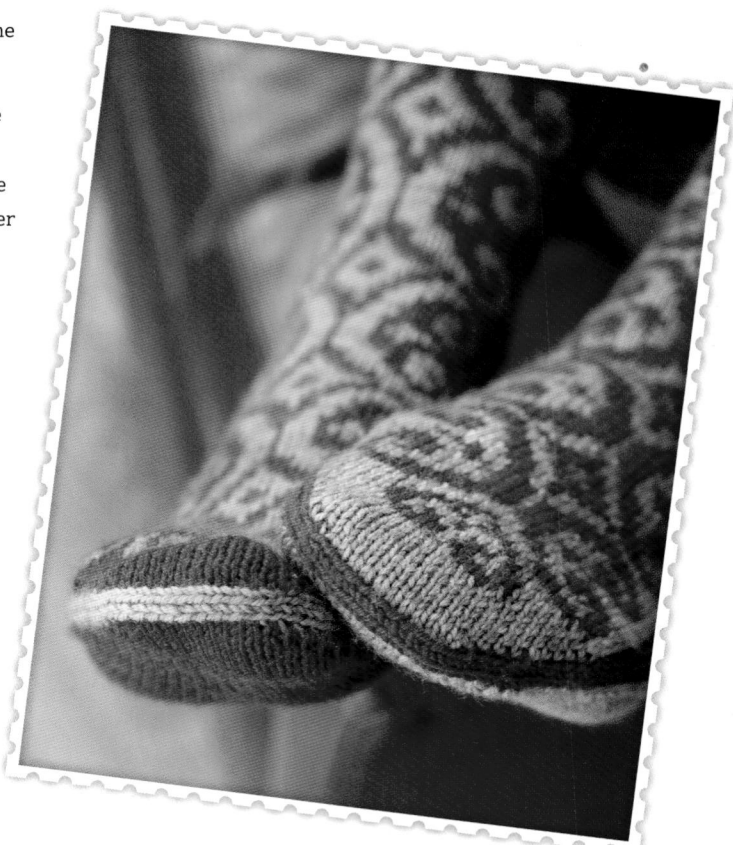

Cat's Moccasin Toe

Cat Bordhi used this variation of the wedge toe (page 21) for her Pussy Willow Stockings (page 160). For this type of shaping, the increases are worked each side of a center panel of sole stitches and each side of a similar center panel of instep stitches (instead of at the boundaries between the sole and instep). It begins with about 1½" (3.8 cm) of stitches cast on each for the sole and instep. The center 1" (2.5 cm) of stitches is marked and the increases are worked each side of these marked stitches.

STEP 1: Cast on about 1½" (3.8 cm) of stitches each for the sole and instep. For example, if our gauge is 8 stitches to the inch, we'd cast on 12 stitches each for the sole and instep (24 stitches total).

STEP 2: Mark the center 1" (2.5 cm) of stitches each on the sole and instep. In our example, we'd mark the center 8 or 10 sole and instep stitches.

STEP 3: Increase 1 stitch each side of each set of marked stitches every other round until the desired number of foot stitches is reached. In our example, we'd increase 1 stitch every other round until there were 64 stitches—32 stitches each for the sole and instep. Then the start of the round is moved ¼ of the way around the sock to the middle of the center panel at the side of the foot. When the sock is worn, the center panel wraps around the tips of the toes from side to side.

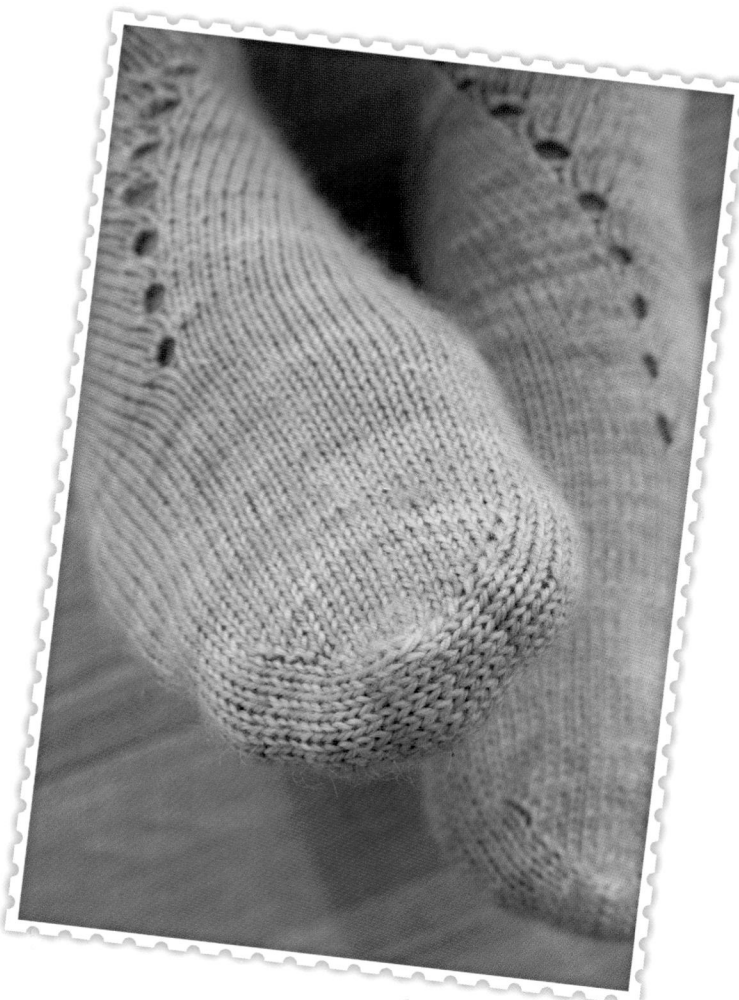

PUSSY WILLOW STOCKINGS, PAGE 160

Short-Row Toe

When worked from the top-down, a short-row toe is worked exactly like short-row heel (page 20). The sole half of the stitches are worked in short-rows in an hourglass shape, with 1 fewer stitch worked every short-row until about a third or an inch's worth of stitches remains between the center between the turning points. Then 1 more stitch is worked every short-row until all of the sole stitches have been worked. This type of toe is used for Bulgarian Blooms (page 130) and Mock Cables and Lace (page 102).

When knitting from the toe up, as for Bulgarian Blooms, simply use a provisional cast-on (page 43) to cast on half the desired number of foot stitches, work these stitches the same as the short-row heel. Finally, remove the waste yarn from the provisional cast-on, place the exposed stitches on the needles, and work the foot in the round on all the stitches.

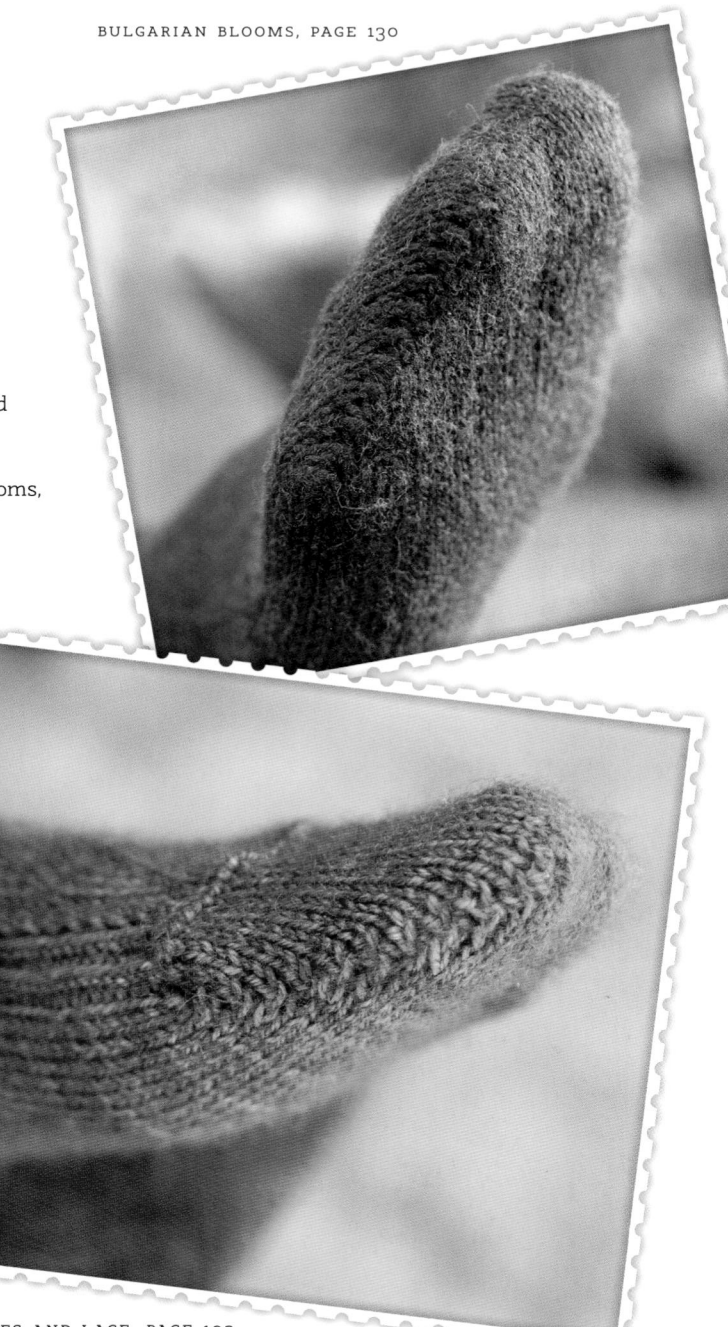

BULGARIAN BLOOMS, PAGE 130

MOCK CABLES AND LACE, PAGE 102

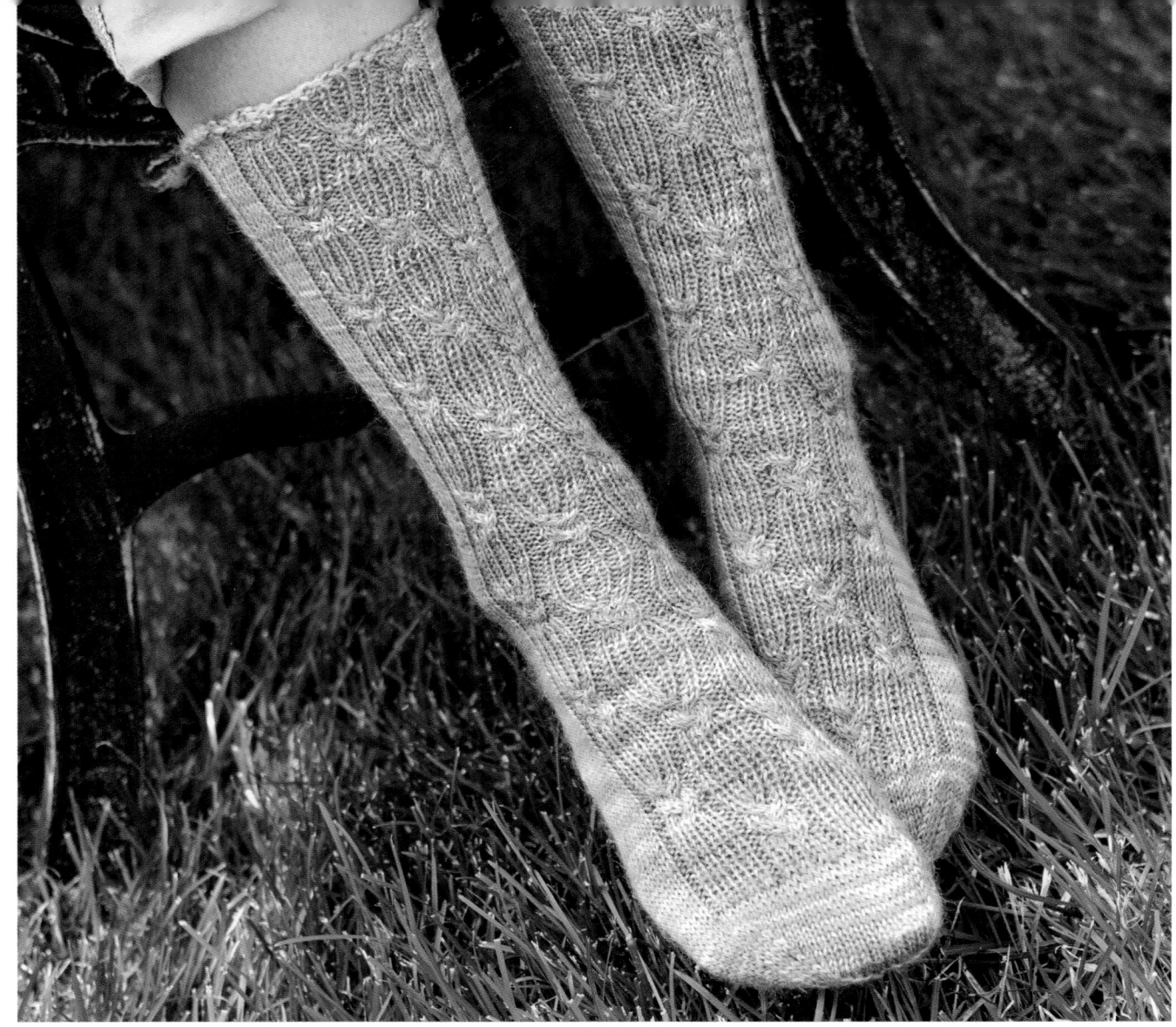

KNOT SOCKS, PAGE 96

Aesthetics

Beyond fit and comfort, the most important aspect of sock design is aesthetics. Whether you choose color or texture patterns or a combination of the two, a sock is most successful if the parts relate to one another and involve logical transitions from the cast-on (at the top of the leg or the tip of the toe) to the bind-off (at the tip of the toe or the top of the leg). Once you understand the basic construction of a well-fitting sock, you can channel your creative ideas into a great design that enhances the unity between form and function. As you'll see from the designs in this book, there is no end to how color and texture can be added in pleasing ways. Read the tips and sidebars accompanied with each project to learn how a variety of designers have accomplished this task beautifully.

Designing with Cables

Cables are worked by twisting two groups of stitches so that they exchange the order in which they are worked. In general, one set of stitches is placed on a cable needle, the next set of stitches is worked, then the stitches on the cable needle are worked. Depending on whether the first set of stitches is held in back or in front of the second set, the cable will lean to the right or left. Cables are typically worked as knit stitches against a background composed of purl stitches (reverse stockinette) or a combination of knit and purl stitches (garter stitch or seed stitch, for example). Because cables involve overlapped stitches, they use up more yarn and draw in the knitting to narrow the width. The overlapped stitches produce bulk, which can be uncomfortable along the instep in a shoe. The advantage is that the thicker cable fabric traps more air and produces warm socks. And because cables are based on rib patterns, they can be planned to evolve organically into or out of ribbing at the sock cuff.

The trick to designing socks with cables is to account for the draw-in caused by each cable. Typically, an individual cable is as wide as the average of its two halves. For example, a 4-stitch cable—one that crosses 2 stitches over 2 stitches—will average out to about 2 stitches wide at the crossing point. In between the crossing points, the stitches will try to spread out to their full 4-stitch width. In general, the closer the spacing of the cable-crossing rounds, the less the cable stitches can expand between crossings, and the tighter the fabric will be. Therefore, stitches are often added to cable patterns to counteract their tendency to draw in and prevent the sock from becoming too narrow.

Many cables, especially those involving 4 or fewer stitches, can be maneuvered without a cable needle at all. This shortcut works best with "sticky" yarns that contain a significant percentage of wool; there is a greater chance of dropped stitches with slippery yarns such as alpaca or cotton. The directions here are for working a cable that involves just 2 stitches in which 1 stitch crosses the other. The same principles apply to cables worked over more stitches.

Twisting Cables Without a Cable Needle

Step 1: Slip the first stitch off of the left-hand needle and let it drop in the front of the work for a left-leaning cable (figure 1) or in the back of the work for a right-leaning cable.

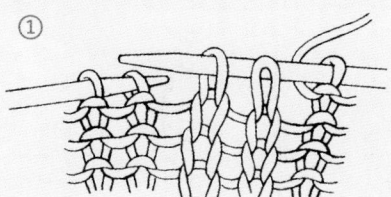

Step 2: Slip the next stitch onto the right-hand needle to temporarily hold it, keeping the dropped stitch in front or back.

Step 3: Return the dropped stitch onto the left-hand needle, then return the held stitch from the right-hand needle onto the left-hand needle (figure 2).

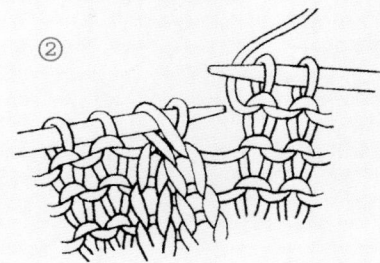

Step 4: Knit these 2 stitches in their new order (figure 3) to complete the cable.

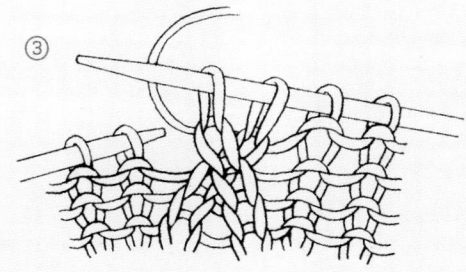

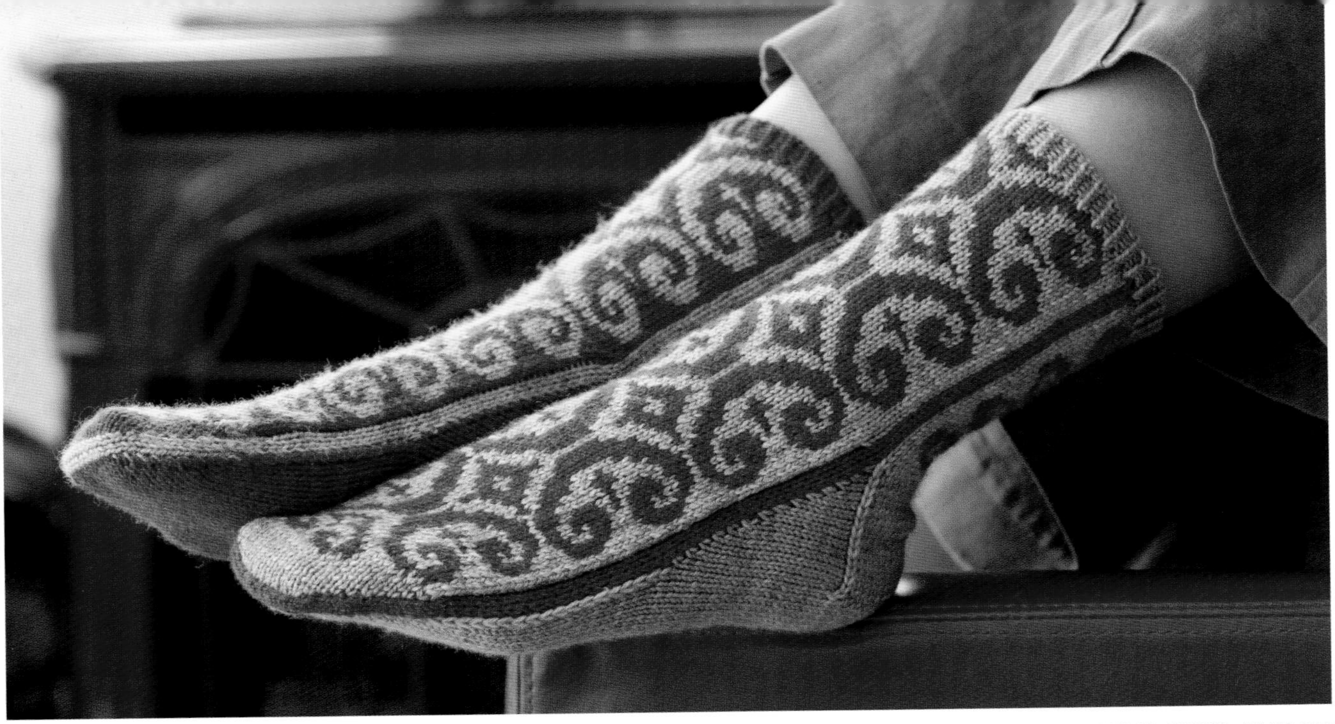

HALF-STRANDED SOCKS, PAGE 152

Designing with Stranded Colorwork

Stranded colorwork is a method of working with two (or more) colors in a single row of knitting. The colors are alternated according to a charted pattern so that while one color is being used, the other is carried across the wrong side of the fabric. The carried strands add a second layer to the knitted stitches that makes the fabric strong and insulating.

The key to successful stranded colorwork is maintaining even tension between the two (or more) yarns, both in the stitches and in the stranded lengths (also called floats). For many people, this is easier to do when working the round because the right side of the work is always facing forward, and there are no purl rows, which is good news for sock knitters. The bad news is that the floats do not have the same amount of stretch as the knitted stitches, which can affect how easily the sock stretches to slide over the heel. To ensure that the floats are long enough to allow the fabric to stretch fully, stretch the stitches as far apart as possible on the right needle at each color change. Another way is Joyce Williams's method of knitting "on the far side." Simply turn the sock inside out so that the wrong side faces outward and the right side (the public side) is on the inside of the sock tube. This forces the floats to travel a greater distance along the outside circumference of the knitted tube.

Even if you're diligent about keeping the floats loose, stranded colorwork is almost always tighter than stockinette stitch worked with the same yarn and needles. Therefore, be sure to measure your gauge in the colorwork pattern. If you plan to combine bands of stranded colorwork with bands of plain stockinette stitch (as in the Thigh-High Stripes on page 74), you may want to work the stranded sections using a needle one size larger to ensure that these sections do not draw in the circumference.

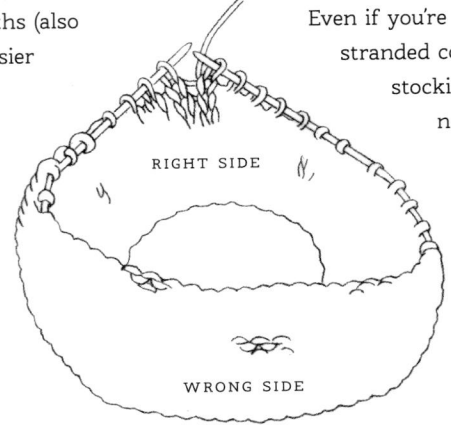

RIGHT SIDE

WRONG SIDE

Knitting on the far side.

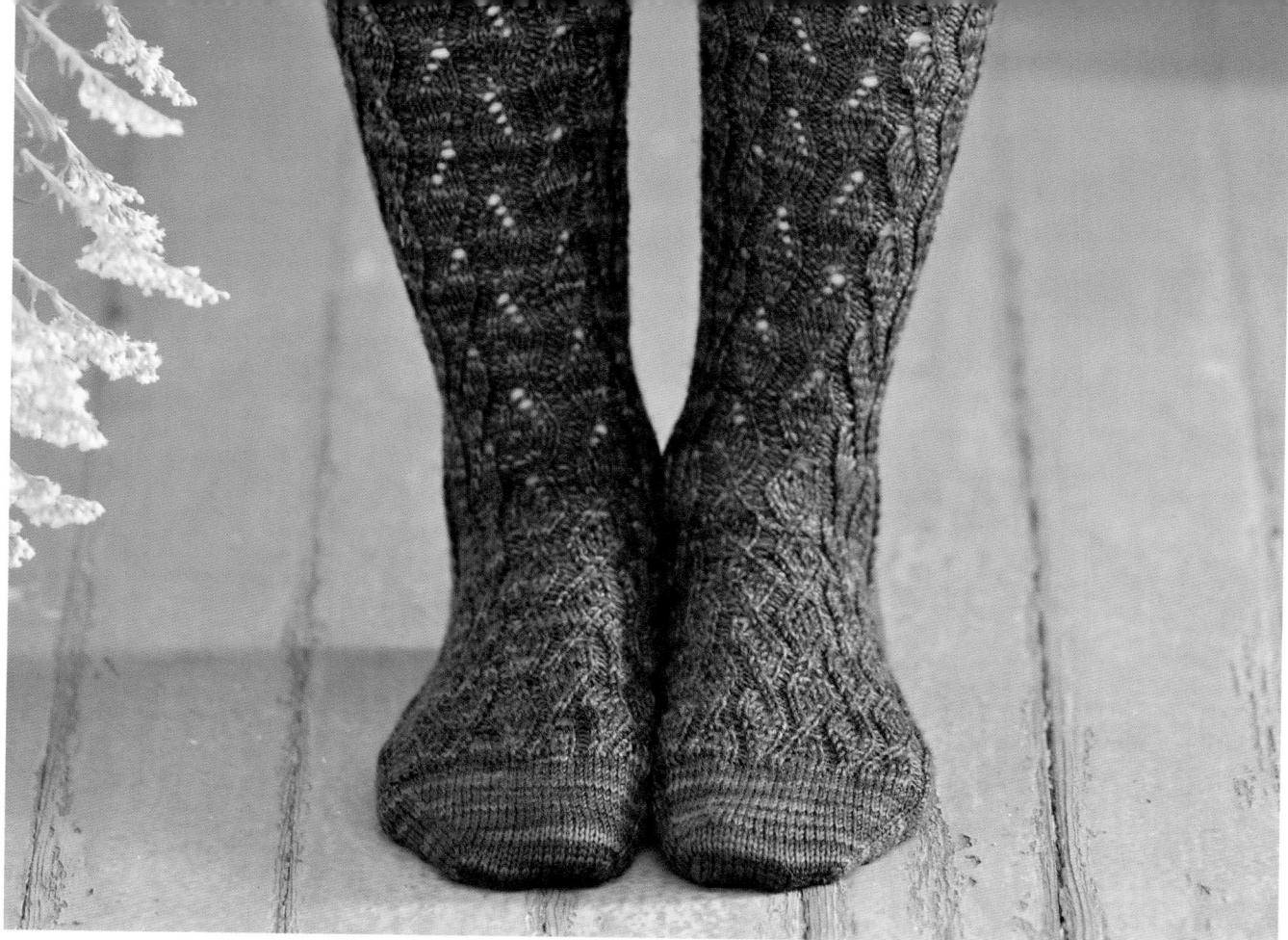

ALMONDINE, PAGE 62

Designing with Lace

Lace is produced by pairing yarnover increases with decreases to produce openwork holes in the knitting—generally without changing the overall stitch count. The pattern shows up best when the knitting is stretched, so lace socks are typically worked with negative ease so that they stretch to reveal the pattern when worn. Keep in mind that lace patterns can be stretched to various amounts during blocking; be sure to knit a generous sample and block it to achieve the desired appearance before measuring the gauge.

Lace patterns that have been stretched fully by vigorous blocking are no longer very elastic, so it's a good idea to combine lace panels with some type of vertical arrangement of knit and purl stitches to give the sock a ribbed effect. If the lace panels are relatively narrow, a single purl stitch between individual stockinette-based lace panels is often sufficient. If the lace panels are wider, you may want to separate them with wider ribbed panels that will draw in the fabric and counteract the tendency of openwork pattern to expand.

In general, lace socks are worked on fewer stitches than stockinette-stitch socks worked with the same yarn and needles.

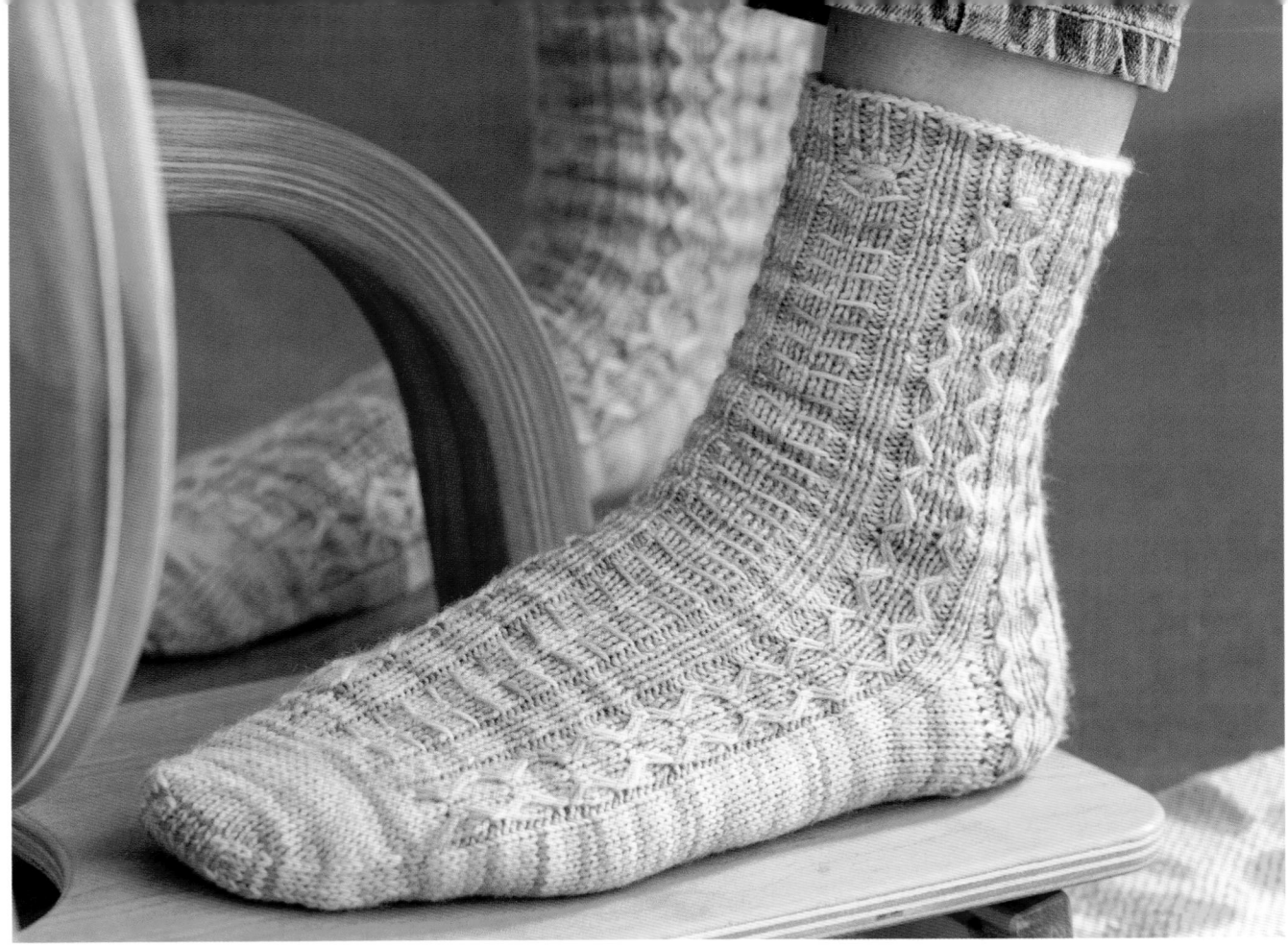

SLIP-N-SLIDE, PAGE 108

Designing with Slip Stitches

You can add texture by simply slipping instead of knitting designated stitches in a round of knitting. Stitches can be slipped for up to a couple of rounds before they are knitted, at which point they appear a bit longer than the adjacent knitted (or purled) stitches. Many slip-stitch patterns are worked in conjunction with color changes to create the look of color-stranded patterns, as in the Happy-Go-Lucky Boot Socks (page 68). When worked in a single color, slip-stitch patterns can create lively textural patterns, especially when the slipped stitches travel over the background stitches similar to small cables or traveling stitches, such as for the Slip-n-Slide socks on page 108.

When designing with slip stitches, keep in mind that that the slipped stitches tend to spread horizontally after blocking. Therefore, it's important to measure your gauge on a swatch that's been blocked. Otherwise, you may find that the leg and foot will become wide and short after the sock is washed. In general, slip-stitch socks are worked with fewer stitches than stockinette-stitch socks worked with the same yarn and needles.

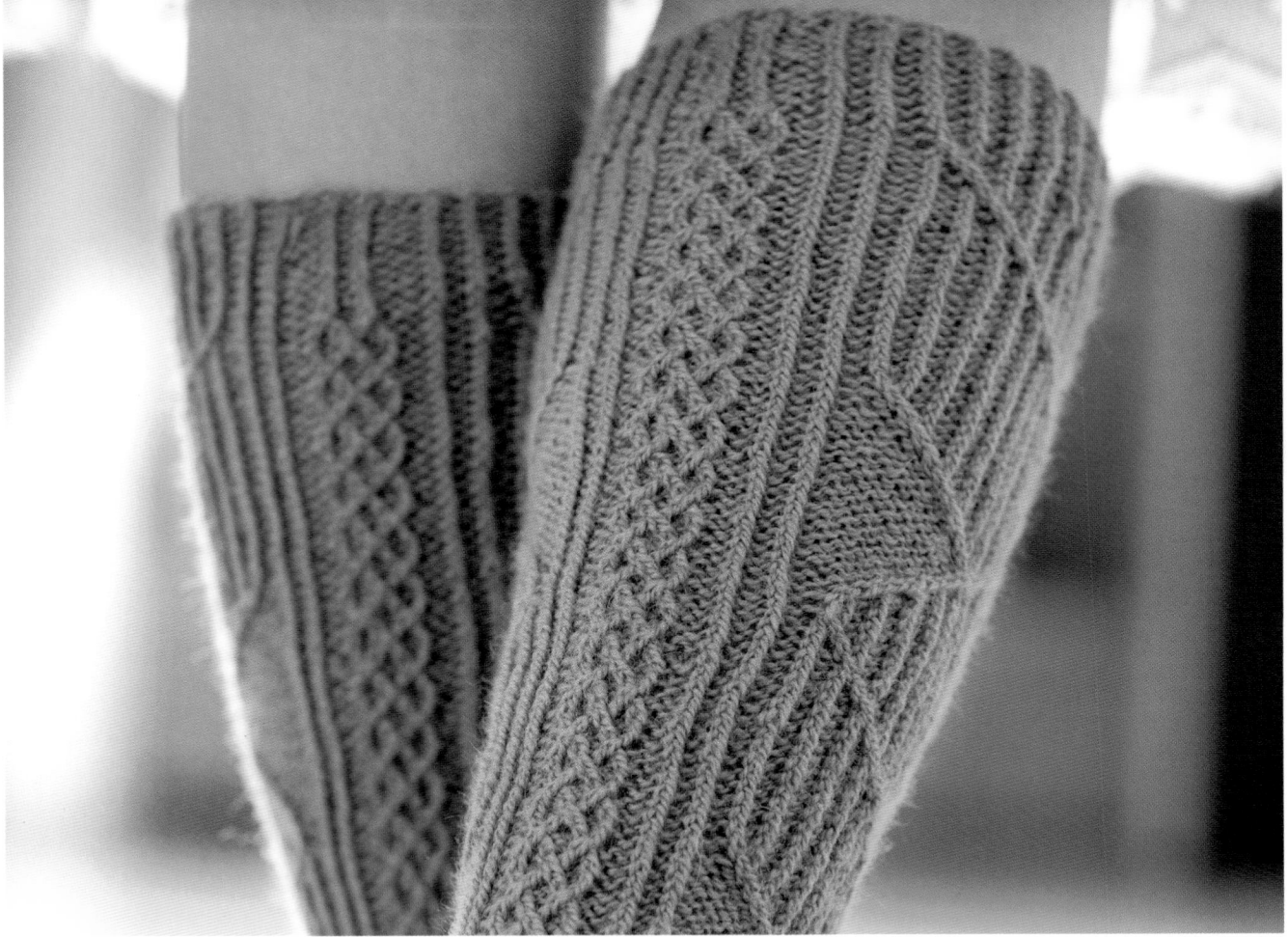

TWISTED-STITCH STOCKINGS, PAGE 86

Designing with Twisted Traveling Stitches

Twisted traveling stitches are similar to cables (page 27) in that stitches are worked out of order across a row. Typical twisted traveling-stitch patterns involve a single knit stitch that crosses over another single knit or purl stitch. The knit stitches are always worked through the back loop to twist them. The twisted knit stitches stand out in relief against a background that is typically purled to create beautiful embossed designs.

Because traveling stitches involve just one stitch crossing over another stitch to produce diagonal patterns, the crossed stitches cause less draw-in and less bulk than other cable patterns, but they still require a bit more yarn than stockinette-stitch patterns worked over the same number of stitches. In general, socks that feature traveling stitches are worked with slightly more stitches than stockinette-stitch socks worked with the same yarn and needles and twisted knit stitches have slightly less elasticity than regular knit stitches. When combined with some type of ribbed pattern to provide additional stretch, traveling-stitch patterns can produce socks with substantial durability.

31

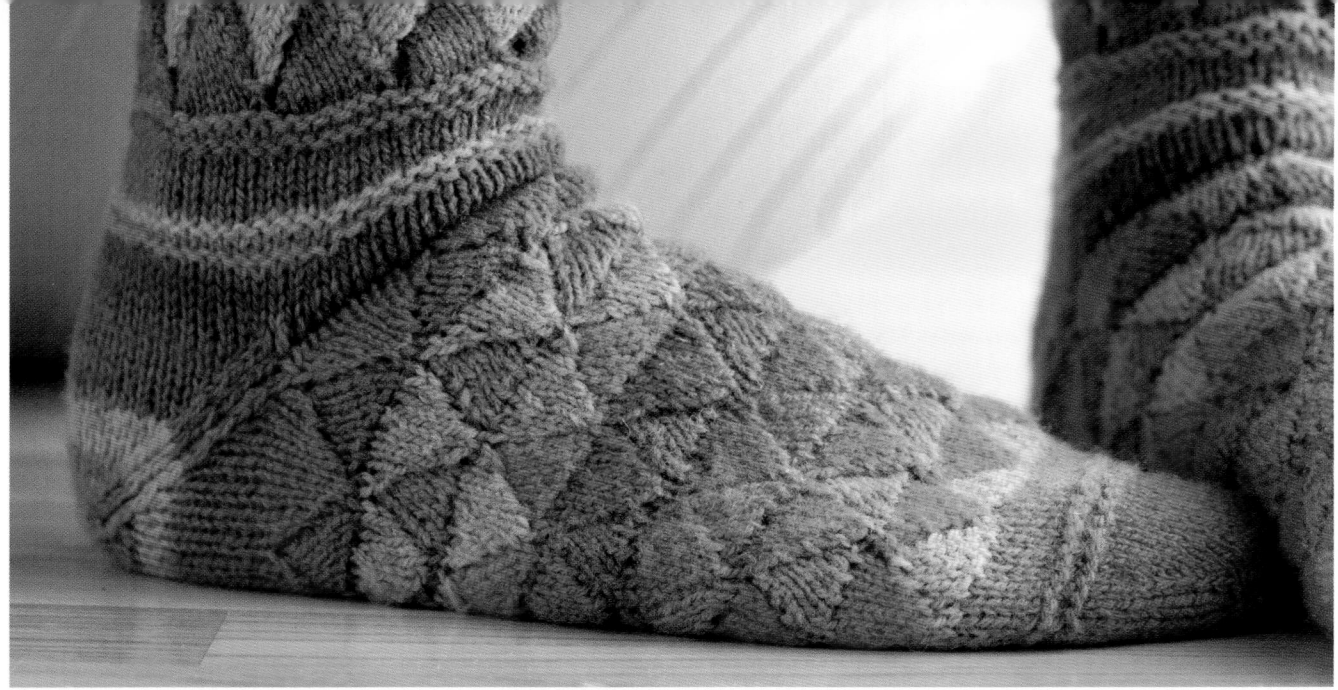

UP-DOWN ENTRELAC, PAGE 122

Designing with Entrelac

Entrelac is an ingenious way to combine small sections of knitting to form a larger piece. It involves knitting a few stitches at a time in horizontal bands, or tiers, of tilted blocks that build one upon another. Within a tier, the blocks are worked individually over a small number of stitches before proceeding to the next block, which is worked on the following group of stitches. After establishing the first tier, each block in the following tiers begins by picking up stitches along the edge of a block from the tier below and is joined to the live stitches of another block in the tier below as it is worked. When entrelac is worked flat, the tiers alternate between being worked from left to right and from right to left, so all the blocks of one tier slant to the left, and all the blocks of the following tier slant to the right. A block can be worked over as many stitches as desired (the more stitches, the larger the block) and is typically worked for twice as many rows as there are stitches. Although entrelac can be worked in a single color, a characteristic basketweave effect can be produced using two colors and alternating them for each tier. Other effects using more colors or self-patterning yarns are also possible.

Entrelac tends to have the same elasticity as plain stockinette stitch. There is no opportunity to add intervening purl stitches to provide a ribbed effect. When designing socks with entrelac, the fabric must be tight enough to hug the leg so that they don't fall down. Because the blocks are tilted in each tier, the block's diagonal measurement from corner to corner determines how much width each block contributes to the circumference. Plan the total number of stitches to be a multiple of the stitches needed for one full block; there can be an even or odd number of blocks.

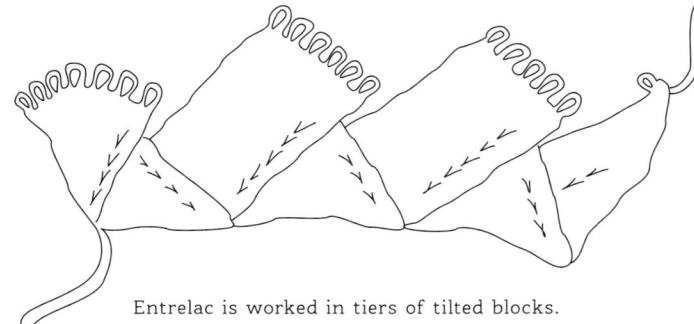

Entrelac is worked in tiers of tilted blocks.

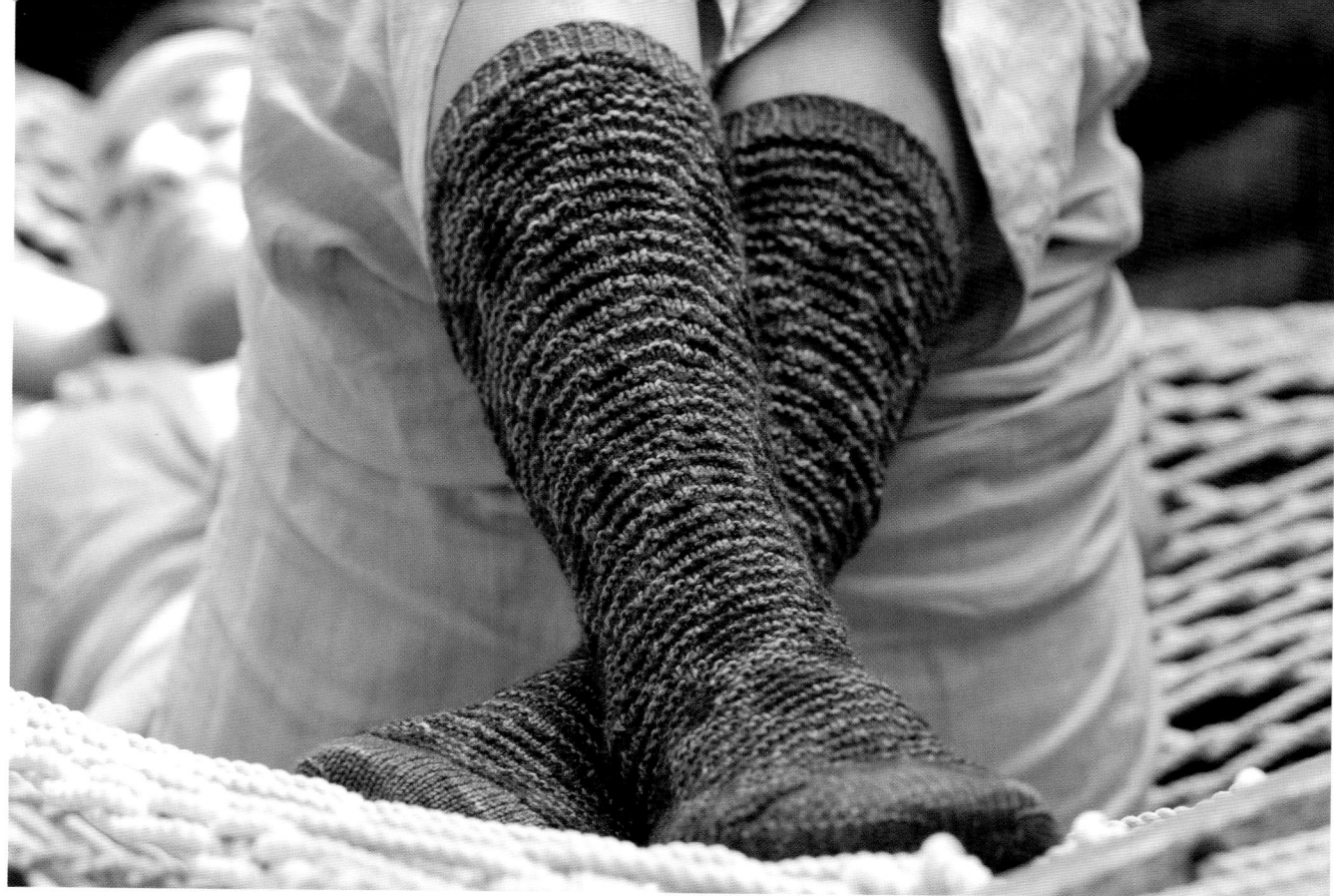

STEALTH ARGYLES, PAGE 138

Designing with Shadow Knitting

Shadow knitting, so named by Vivian Høxbro, is an ingenious technique of combining two-row stripes of knit and purl stitches in such a way that purl ridges form a pattern on the right side of the work. The pattern changes from nearly imperceptible to bold and distinct depending on the direction from which it is viewed: straight-on, the pattern appears as simple stripes; at an angle, the charted pattern comes to life. How fun is that?

The challenge with designing socks with shadow knitting is that it takes a few inches of patterning for the design to show up. This can be a challenge on the relatively short length and circumference of a sock. Another limitation is that shadow knitting is worked in a combination of stockinette and garter stitch, which doesn't have the same widthwise elasticity of ribbed patterns. Therefore, you want to be sure to knit the sock tight enough that when the fabric is slightly stretched, it will hold the sock up and hug the foot. Keep in mind that the pattern shows up best with a round, tightly spun yarn knitted at a tight gauge—consider working at one to two stitches per inch tighter than recommended by the ball band. The garter ridges of the shadow pattern tend to contract lengthwise, so take careful measurements to ensure that the leg and foot are long enough.

Because the colors change every two rounds, you can carry the unused color up the inside of the sock at the boundary between rounds; there's no need to cut and rejoin yarns at each color change.

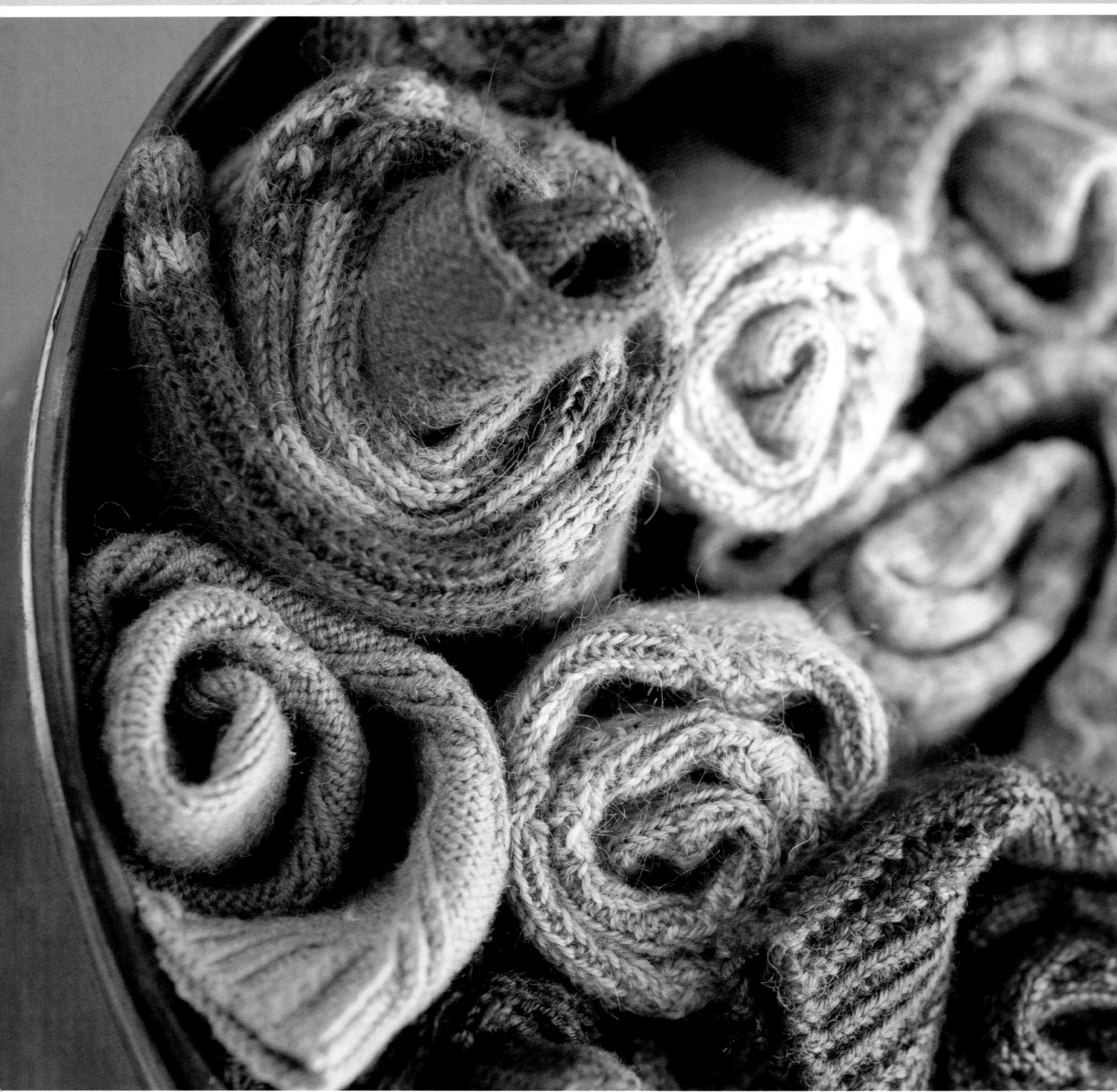

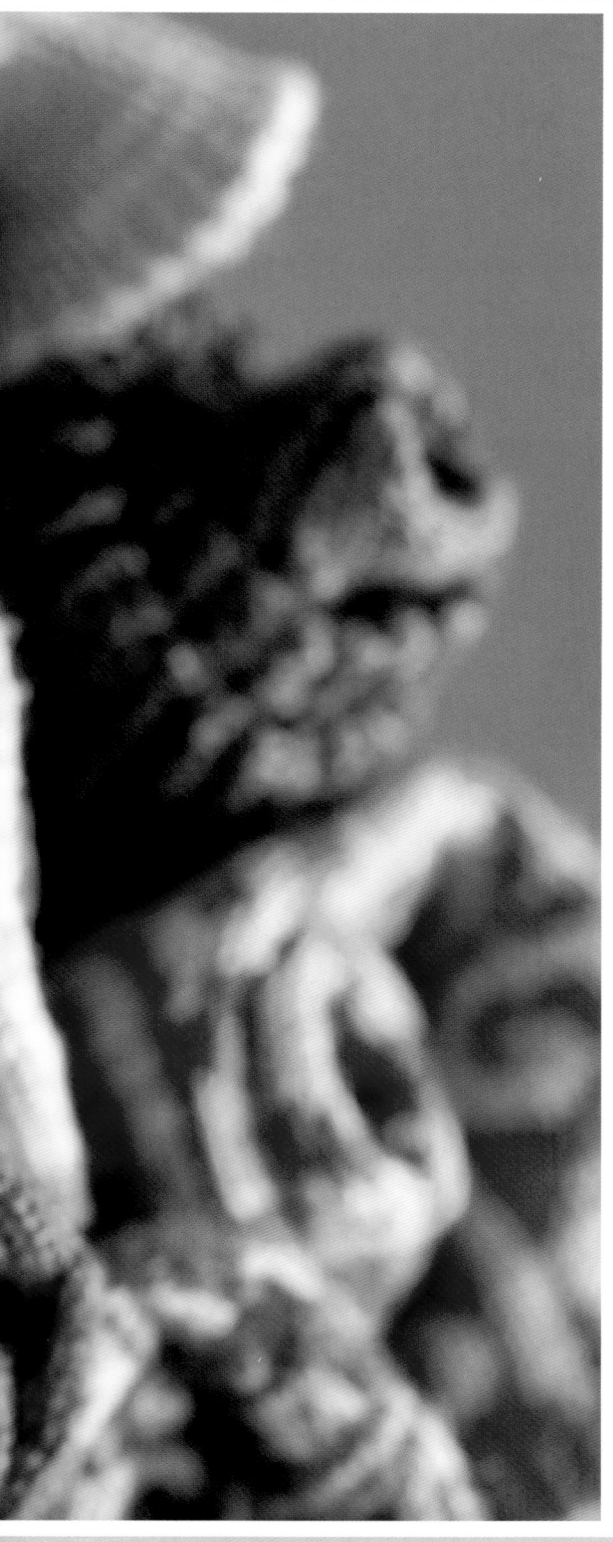

PROJECTS

"The projects that follow demonstrate the varied approaches and techniques that can be used to create a cohesive sock design. Whether you like to knit from the top (cuff) down or bottom (toe) up, you'll find lots of ideas and inspiration from these sock-knitting masters."

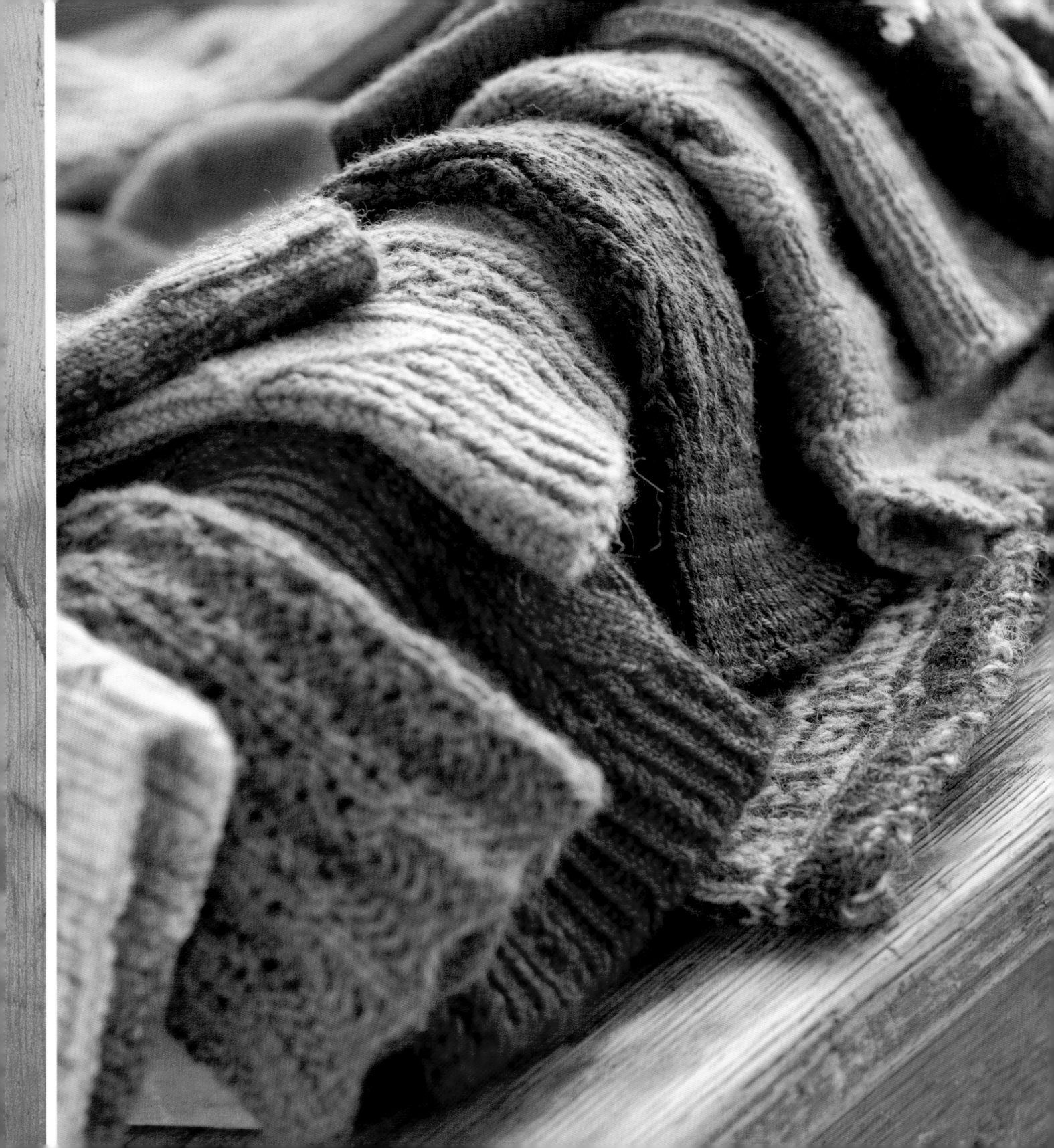

Top-Down Construction

Traditionally, most sock patterns written for American knitters are worked from the top down. To begin, stitches are cast on for the cuff, then the leg is worked down to the heel, at which point the stitches are divided with half of the stitches worked back in forth in rows to shape the heel while the other half are put on a holder to work later for the instep.

If a round heel is worked (page 14), gusset stitches are picked up along the selvedges of the heel flap, then the heel and instep stitches are rejoined for working in rounds to the toe, with the gusset stitches decreased along the way. The gusset is eliminated if a short-row heel (page 20) is worked. The foot is worked in rounds to the toe, then the toe is shaped with decreases and most commonly finished off by grafting with Kitchener stitch (page 44) at the tip.

The advantage to working from the top down is that once the pattern is figured out for the leg, everything else falls into place. The heel can be placed anywhere around the circumference of the tube that forms the leg. This makes it easy to continue the most suitable part of the design along the top of the instep and even to extend all or some portion of the design into the heel flap.

A disadvantage to this direction of construction is that the foot cannot be tried on and checked for fit until the entire sock is finished. Working from the top down can also pose a serious problem if you run out of yarn before the foot is completed. Unless you're willing to buy another ball of yarn or use a contrasting yarn to finish the sock, there's no choice but to rip out everything to the top of the heel, shorten the leg, then reknit the heel and the foot. Many knitters shy away from top-down construction because they dislike picking up stitches for the gussets and abhor working the Kitchener stitch to finish the toe. However, both of these issues can be eliminated by working a short-row heel and gathered tip (page 47) at the toe.

The ten patterns in this section are all worked from the top down. In terms of construction, they demonstrate a variety of cast-ons, several heel and toe shapings, and two ways to finish the toe that don't involve the Kitchener stitch. In terms of design, they offer exciting studies in texture, color, and design integration.

Top-Down Cast-Ons

The key to a comfortable fit at the top of the leg of a top-down sock is to choose an elastic cast-on. There are dozens of ways to cast on, but the ones shown here will ensure a sturdy, stretchy edge that will fit over the heel and will not bind at the top of the leg.

Long-Tail (Continental) Cast-On

This cast-on is worked with two ends of yarn to make a strong, stable edge. Some designers suggest using a larger needle for the cast-on to ensure a looser, more elastic edge. I find that this simply makes the cast-on row loose and sloppy. Instead, I like to leave a small gap—about 1/16" to 1/8" (1.5 to 3 mm)—between the stitches as they are formed on the needle. This particular method is not specified for any of the socks in this book, but it is appropriate anytime an elastic edge is desired. This technique is demonstrated on the accompanying DVD.

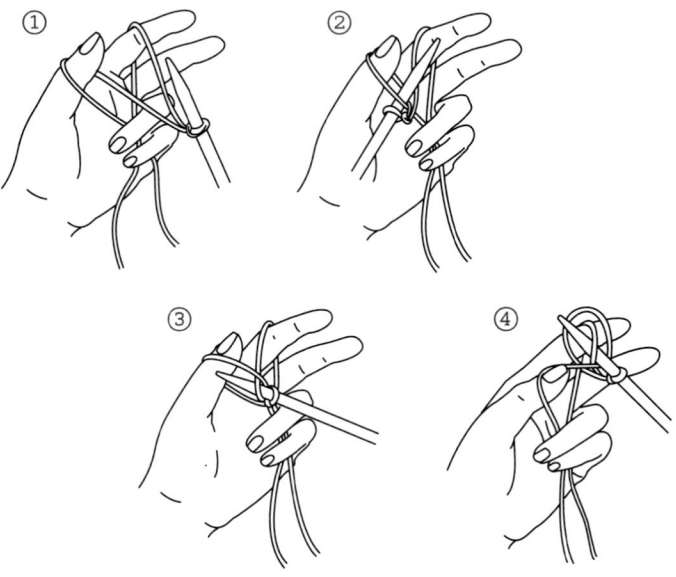

Leaving a long tail (see How Long is "Long"? at right), make a slipknot and place it on the right needle.

Place the thumb and index finger of your left hand between the yarn ends so that the working yarn is around your index finger and the tail end is around your thumb. Secure both yarn ends with your other fingers. Hold your palm upward, making a V of yarn (figure 1).

*Bring the needle up through the loop on your thumb (figure 2), catch the first strand around your index finger, and bring the needle back down through the loop on your thumb (figure 3).

Drop the loop off your thumb and place your thumb back in the V configuration while tightening the resulting stitch on the needle (figure 4).

Repeat from * for the desired number of stitches.

How Long is "Long"?

The length of tail needed for the long-tail cast-on depends on the size of the needles and the number of stitches to cast on. A good estimate is to measure the length of yarn needed to wrap around the needle the number of times as stitches to be cast on, then add about 6" (15 cm) for safety. For speed and simplicity, I usually allow about 1" (2.5 cm) of tail for each stitch to be cast on. This ensures that the tail won't run out before I've cast on the proper number of stitches, but it does tend to leave a considerable length of unused tail when finished.

Old Norwegian Cast-On

This modification of the long-tail method ensures a strong elastic edge because the two yarns are wrapped around each other an additional time along the cast-on edge. It gives a somewhat bumpy appearance that is similar on both the right and wrong sides of the knitting. Although it is not specified for any of the socks in this book, this method is excellent for socks knitted from the top-down. This technique is demonstrated on the accompanying DVD.

Leaving a long tail (see How Long is "Long"? at left), make a slipknot and place it on the right needle.

Place the thumb and index finger of your left hand between the yarn ends so that the working yarn is around your index finger and the tail end is around your thumb. Secure both yarn ends with your other fingers. Hold your palm upward, making a V of yarn (figure 1).

*Bring needle in front of your thumb, under both yarns around your thumb, then down into the center of the thumb loop, forward in front of your thumb, and then over the top of the yarn around your index finger (figure 2).

Catching the yarn on your index finger, bring the needle back down through the thumb loop (figure 3) and to the front, turning your thumb slightly to make room for the needle to pass through.

Drop the loop off your thumb (figure 4) and place your thumb back in the V configuration while tightening the resulting stitch on the needle (figure 5).

Repeat from * for desired number of stitches.

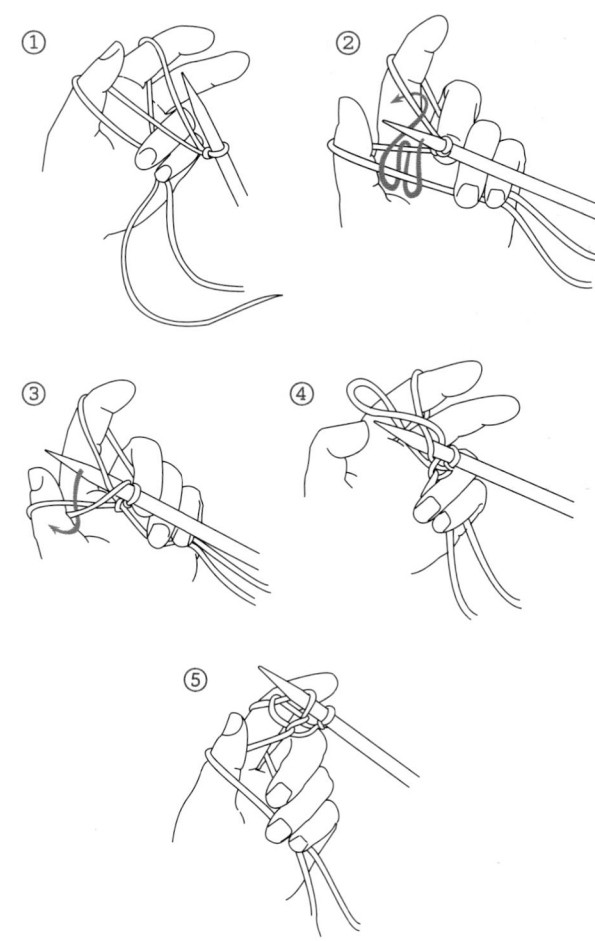

39

Cable Cast-On

This method creates a sturdy elastic edge with a somewhat ropy appearance. Although it is not specified for any of the socks in this book, it is appropriate for any sock worked from the top down. This technique is demonstrated on the accompanying DVD.

Make a slipknot of working yarn and place it on the left needle.

Insert the right needle tip into the slipknot knitwise, wrap the yarn around the needle as if to knit, pull the loop through (figure 1), and place it on the left needle in front of the slipknot (figure 2).

*Insert right needle between the first 2 stitches on left needle (figure 3), wrap yarn around needle as if to knit, draw yarn through (figure 4), and place new loop on left needle (figure 5) to form a new stitch.

Repeat from * for the desired number of stitches, always working between the first 2 stitches on the left needle.

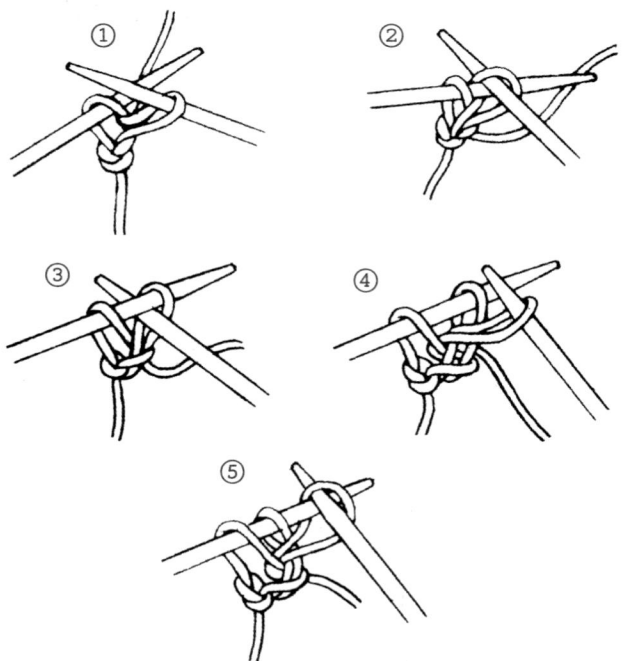

Joining for Working in Rounds

To begin working in rounds, you'll need to join the first cast-on stitch with the last cast-on stitch to form a ring. There are different ways to do this, many of which Nancy Bush describes in *Folk Knitting in Estonia,* and three of which are described here and are demonstrated on the accompanying DVD.

Simple Join

As the name implies, this method is simple. Beginning with the first cast-on stitch, just start knitting. There will be a small gap at the join, but this can be effectively tidied up later when the cast-on tail is woven in.

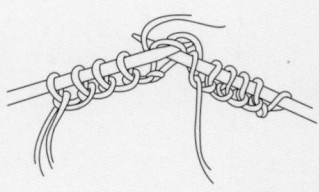

Crossover Join

Step 1: Slip the first cast-on stitch (it will be on the left needle tip) onto the right needle (figure 1).

Step 2: Use the left needle tip to pick up the last cast-on stitch (now the second-to-last stitch on the right needle), bring this stitch up and over the top of the previously slipped stitch (figure 2), and place it on the left needle tip (figure 3). The first and last stitches have exchanged places and the last stitch cast on surrounds the first.

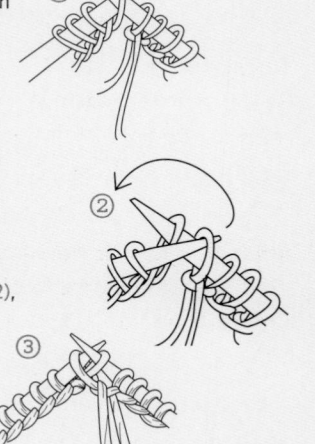

Two-End Join

Work the first 2 or 3 stitches of the round while holding both ends to yarn (the one attached to the ball and the tail end) that were used for the cast-on. Then, drop the tail end and continue on with the yarn attached to the ball. On the next round, be sure to work the two strands together as if they were a single stitch.

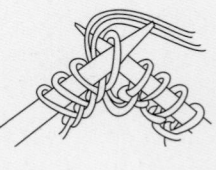

K1, P1 Cable Cast-On

This variation of the cable method can create any sequence of knit and purl stitches on the needle. But be aware that the working yarn will be at the right end of the cast-on stitches so that you either have to turn the work around to begin knitting in the round (in which case, what was cast-on as a knit stitch will appear as a purl stitch and vice versa), or you have to work an initial straight row before joining the stitches into a round. The one-row gap at the top of the sock is easily closed when weaving in the cast-on tail. This method is used for Mock Cables and Lace on page 102 and is demonstrated on the accompanying DVD.

Make a slipknot of working yarn and place it on the left needle.

Insert the right needle tip into the slipknot knitwise, wrap the yarn around the needle as if to knit, pull the loop through (figure 1), and place it on the left needle in front of the slipknot (figure 2). This forms the knit stitch as viewed from the right side.

Bring the working yarn around the tip of the left needle to the front of the work, then insert the right needle tip from back to front between the first 2 stitches on the left needle (figure 3), wrap yarn around needle as if to purl, draw yarn through (figure 4), and place the new loop on the left needle (figure 5) to form a new stitch. This forms a purl stitch when viewed from the right side.

Bring the working yarn around the tip of the left needle to the back of the work, then insert the right needle tip from front to back between the first 2 stitches on the left needle to form the next knit stitch when viewed from the right side.

Continue to alternate knit and purl stitches until there is the desired number of stitches, counting the slipknot for an odd number of stitches and not counting the slipknot for an even number of stitches.

Work 1 row in rib as established, working the slipknot tog with the first stitch cast on if you want an even number of stitches, then join for working in rounds and continue in rib as desired.

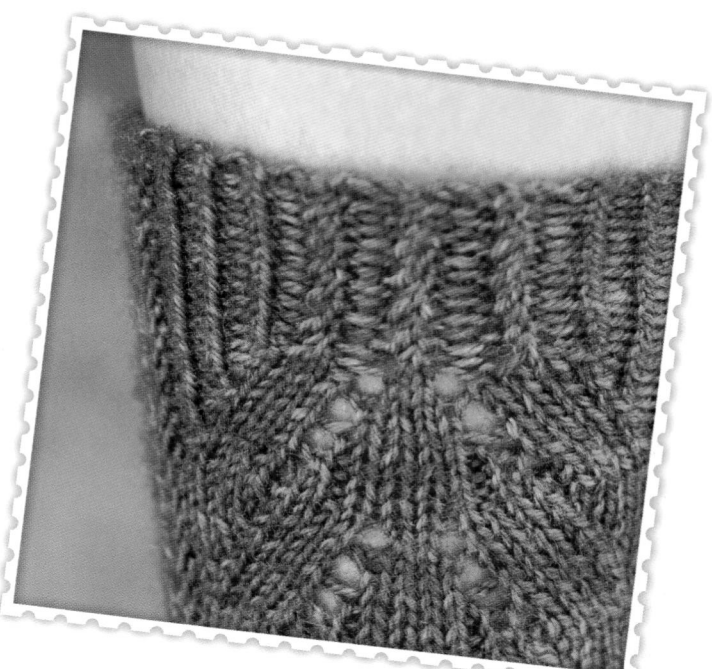

MOCK CABLES AND LACE, PAGE 102

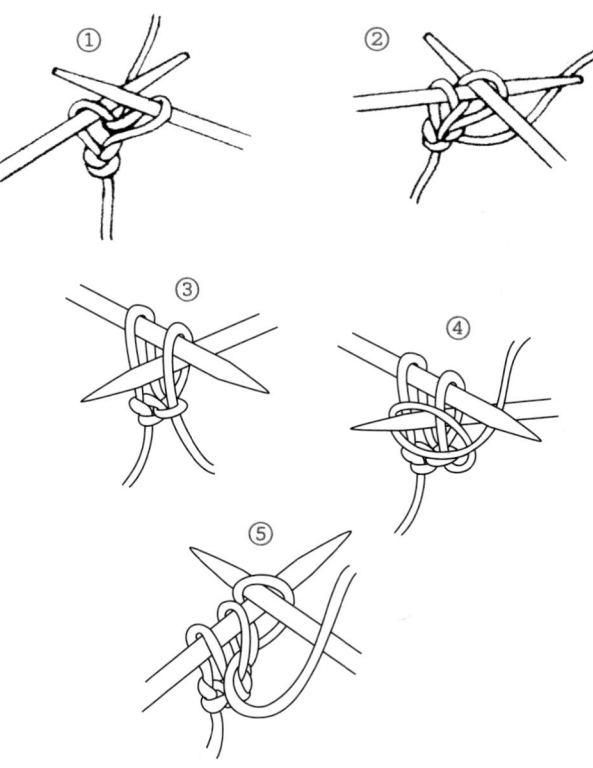

41

Double-Start Cast-On

This decorative cast-on, based on the long-tail method, was introduced in Folk Knitting of Estonia *by Nancy Bush. Worked in two parts, this cast-on results in a double strand of yarn in front of every 2 stitches. Nancy used this method in her Knot Socks on page 96. For a more prominent edge, you can work this method with two or three strands of yarn around your thumb.*

Leaving a long tail, set up as for the long-tail cast-on (page 38). The slipknot will count as the first stitch (A).

To make stitch B, remove your thumb from the loop and reinsert it so that the yarn wraps in the opposite direction (figure 1).

Bring the needle under the yarn on the inside of your thumb (the yarn between your index finger and thumb), then go over the yarn around your index finger, and back through the thumb loop (figure 2).

Drop the loop off your thumb and, placing your thumb back in the original V formation, tighten up the resulting stitch on the needle—there will be 2 stitches on the needle: the slipknot (A) and the next stitch (B).

Cast on the next stitch (A) following the long-tail method.

Continue to alternate stitches B and A for the desired number of stitches. The stitches will be grouped in pairs on the needle (figure 3).

NOTE: To cast on with a double or triple yarn, measure yarn for the number of stitches required, then fold the yarn, measure one or two more length(s), and hold the lengths parallel. Make a slipknot using all the strands about 5" (12.5 cm) from the end with the cut tail and place it on the needle (does not count as a cast-on stitch). When you begin the cast-on, place the doubled or tripled yarn around your thumb and the single strand around your index finger (figure 4). Drop the slipknot from the needle before joining in the round.

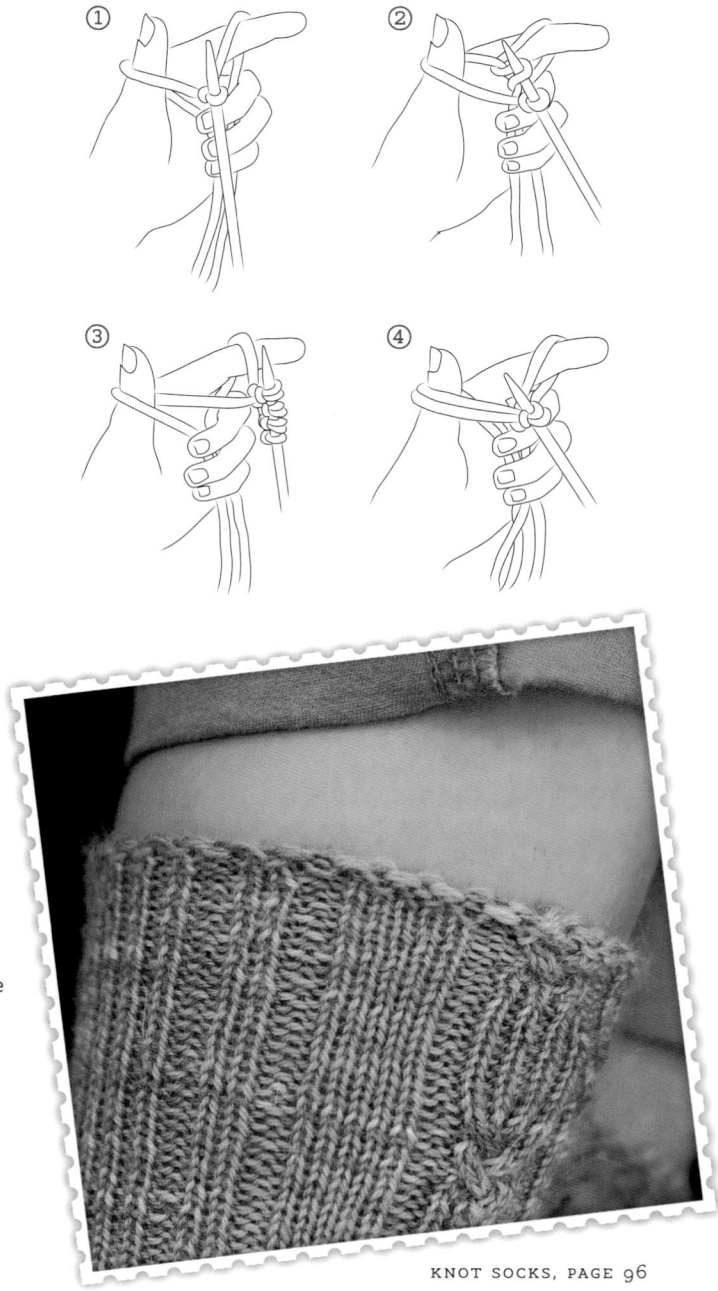

KNOT SOCKS, PAGE 96

Invisible Provisional Cast-On

A provisional cast-on is used when an edging will be added to the cast-on edge later, as was done for Up-Down Entrelac on page 122. For these socks, Kathryn Alexander worked a strip of small triangles beginning with a provisional cast-on, then joined the live stitches at the end of the strip to the cast-on stitches to form a tube.

This method, dubbed the "twisty-wrap" method by Meg Swansen (and demonstrated on the accompanying DVD), catches a strand of waste yarn at the base of each stitch on the needle. The waste yarn is later pulled out to reveal loops at the base of the cast-on row.

Make a loose slipknot of working yarn and place it on the right needle.

Hold a length of contrasting waste yarn (shaded dark) next to the slipknot and around your left thumb; hold the working yarn over your left index finger.

*Bring the right needle forward under the waste yarn, over the working yarn, grab a loop of working yarn (figure 1), then bring the needle back behind the working yarn and grab a second loop (figure 2).

Repeat from * for the desired number of stitches, always adding stitches in pairs.

When you're ready to work in the opposite direction, place the exposed loops on a knitting needle as you pull out the waste yarn.

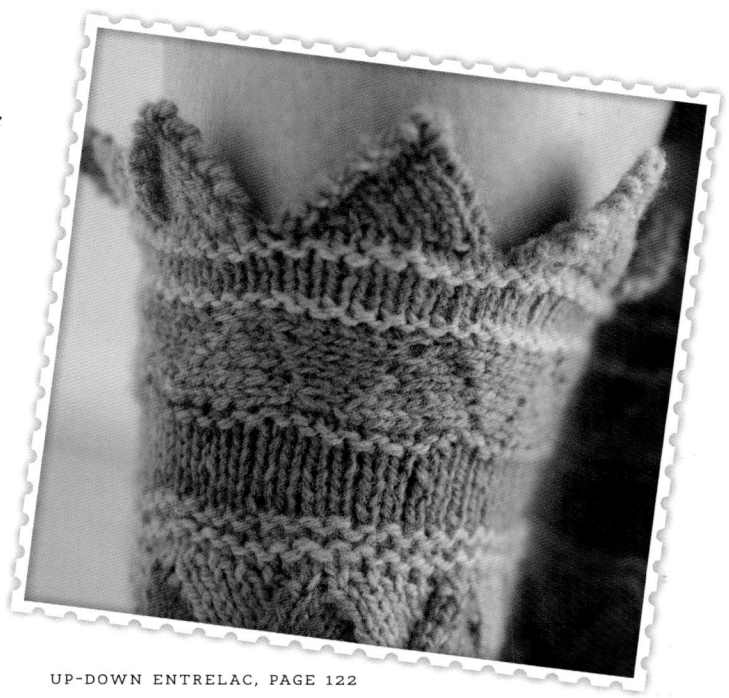

UP-DOWN ENTRELAC, PAGE 122

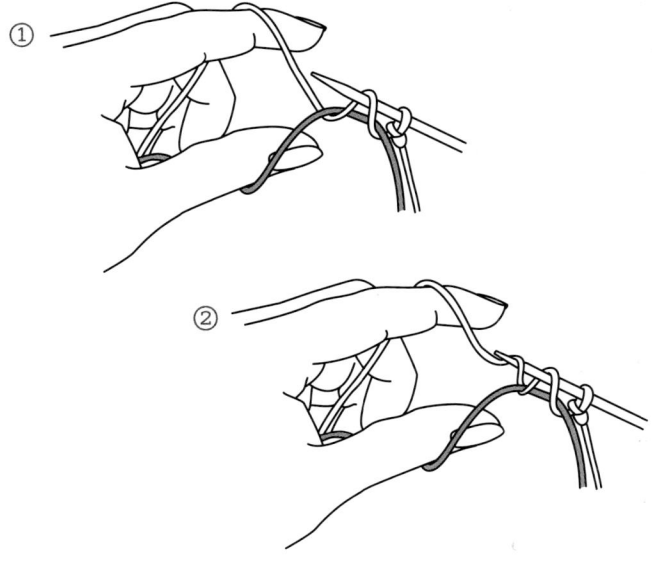

Top-Down Bind-Offs

Most socks that are knitted from the top down end with a few stitches remaining at the tip of the toe. These stitches can be secured in a number of ways, depending on the look you want.

Kitchener Stitch

The Kitchener stitch is the most common way to end the toe of socks knitted from the top down. It is an ingenious way to mimic a row of knitting that connects the stitches at the top of the toe with the stitches on the bottom of the toe. The instructions may look intimidating on first reading, but if you watch the demonstration on the accompanying DVD and follow the shortcut notation in the box at right, you'll find that it's really quite simple. This technique was used for Asymmetrical Cables (page 48), Almondine (page 62), Happy-Go-Lucky Boot Socks (page 68), Thigh-High Stripes (page 74), Rose Ribs (page 80), and Slip-n-Slide (page 108). It is also used in Meg Swansen's Twisted-Stitch Stockings (page 86), but in that case it joins stitches along the entire length of the sole, not just at the tip of the toe.

STEP 1: Bring tapestry needle through the first stitch on the front needle as if to purl and leave the stitch on the needle (figure 1).

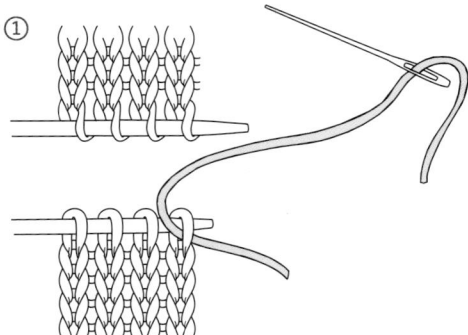

STEP 2: Bring tapestry needle through the first stitch on the back needle as if to knit and leave that stitch on the needle (figure 2).

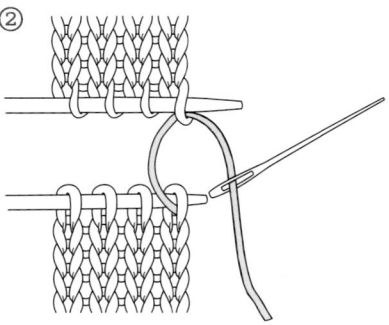

STEP 3: Bring tapestry needle through the first front stitch as if to knit and slip this stitch off the needle, then bring the tapestry needle through the next front stitch as if to purl and leave this stitch on the needle (figure 3).

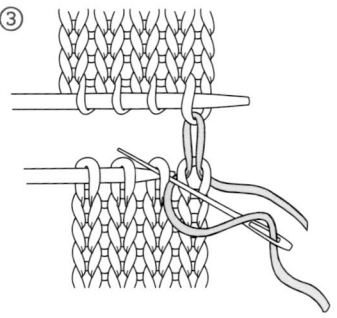

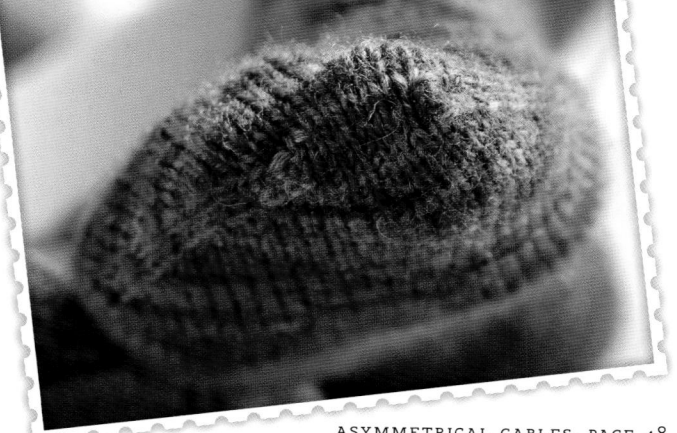

ASYMMETRICAL CABLES, PAGE 48

STEP 4: Bring tapestry needle through the first back stitch as if to purl and slip this stitch off the needle, then bring the tapestry needle through the next back stitch as if to knit and leave this stitch on the needle (figure 4).

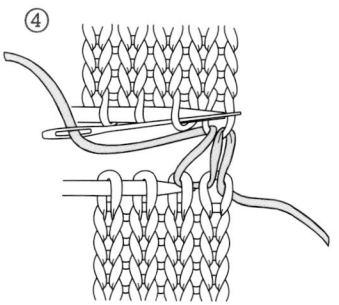

Repeat Steps 3 and 4 until 1 stitch remains on each needle, adjusting the tension to match the rest of the knitting as you go. To finish, bring the tapestry needle through the front stitch as if to knit and slip this stitch off the needle, then bring the tapestry needle through the back stitch as if to purl and slip this stitch off the needle.

Insert the tapestry needle into the center of the last stitch worked, pull the yarn to the wrong side, and weave the tail into the purl bumps on the wrong side of the toe.

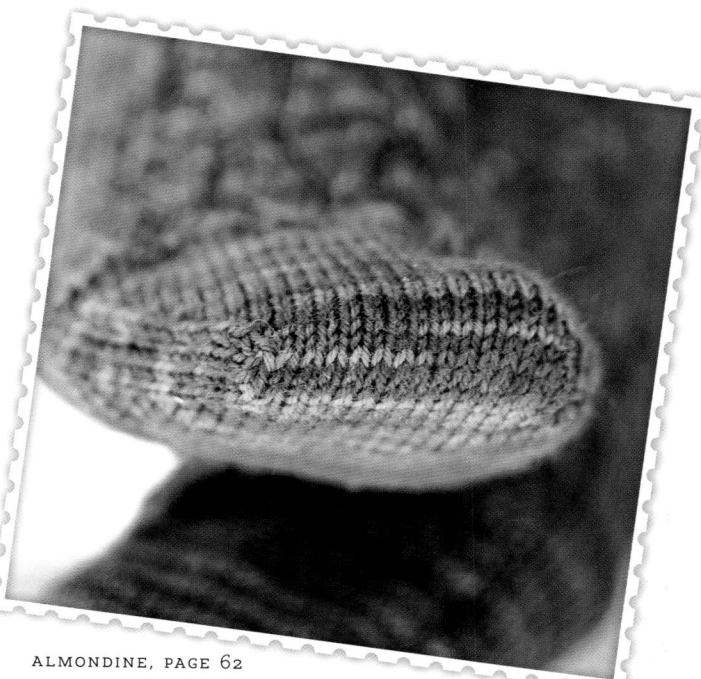

ALMONDINE, PAGE 62

Kitchener Stitch Simplified

Once you get going, the Kitchener stitch is worked in a series of steps that alternates between inserting the tapestry needle knitwise or purlwise through the stitch on the front and back needles and alternates between leaving a stitch on the needle and dropping one off. I recite the following chant with perfect results every time.

Set-up Step 1: Purlwise on front needle, leave on.

Set-up Step 2: Knitwise on back needle, leave on.

Step 1: Knitwise on front needle, drop off;
 Purlwise on front needle, leave on.

Step 2: Purlwise on back needle, drop off;
 Knitwise on back needle, leave on.

Repeat Step 1 and 2 until all of the stitches have been joined.

Zigzag Bind-Off

This variation of the three-needle bind-off comes from historic Greek knitting. It produces a small decorative ridge that is not noticeable when worn in a shoe. This method is used to join the top of a short-row toe to the instep in Mock Cables and Lace on page 102 and is demonstrated on the accompanying DVD.

Place the toe and instep stitches to be joined on two separate needles and hold the needles parallel so that the right sides of the knitting are facing out.

With a third needle, purl 1 from the back needle, then knit 1 from the front needle, then pass the first stitch over the second and off the third needle—1 stitch remains on the third needle.

*Purl 1 from the back needle (figure 1), then pass the previous stitch over it and off the needle—1 stitch remains on the third needle.

Knit 1 from the front needle (figure 2), then pass the remaining stitch over it and off the needle (figure 3)—1 stitch remains on the third needle.

Repeat from * until no stitches remain on the first two needles (working the last stitch together with its yarnover if working Priscilla Gibson-Roberts' method of a short-row toe).

Cut the yarn and pull the tail through the last stitch to secure. Alternately, cut the yarn and pull the last stitch until the tail comes free; both methods will secure the last stitch.

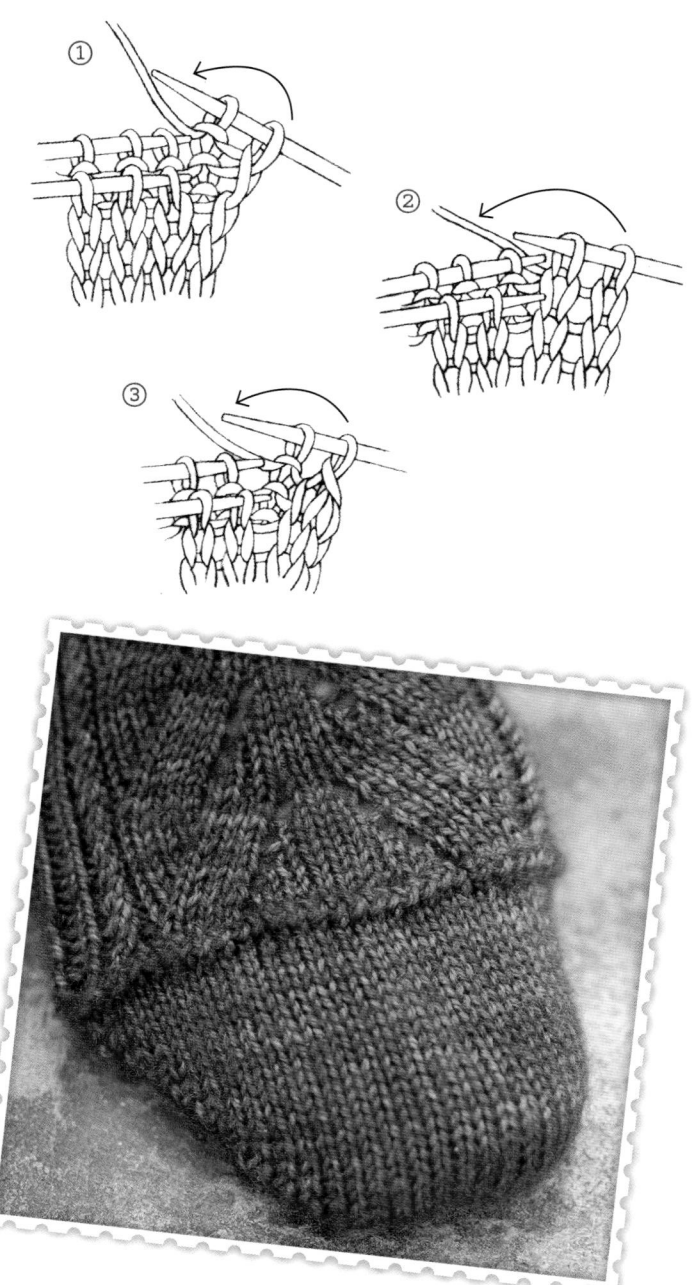

MOCK CABLES AND LACE, PAGE 102

Gathered Tip

This simple method is ideal when the toe has been decreased to about 8 stitches; more than that results in a bulky toe, fewer results in a pointy tip. Nancy Bush used this method to finish the toes of both French Market Socks on page 56 and Knot Socks on page 96, and it is demonstrated on the accompanying DVD.

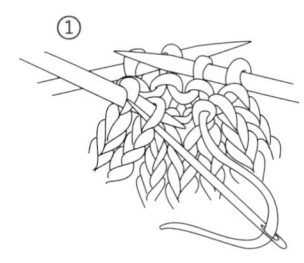

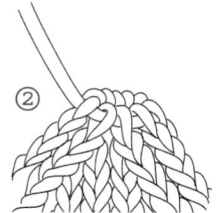

Cut the yarn leaving a 10" (25.5 cm) tail. Thread the tail on a tapestry needle, then draw the needle through all of the remaining stitches (figure 1) once (or twice for a sturdier join) and pull the yarn tight to close the hole (figure 2). Insert the tapestry needle through the center of the hole and weave in the loose end on the wrong side.

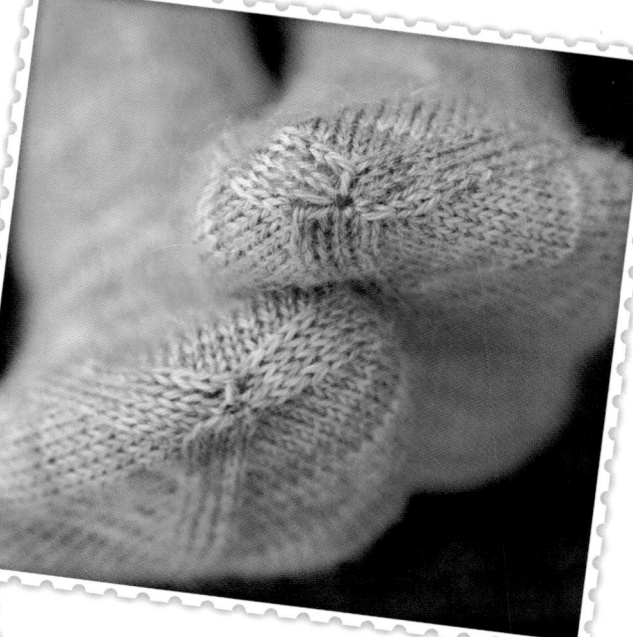

KNOT SOCKS, PAGE 96

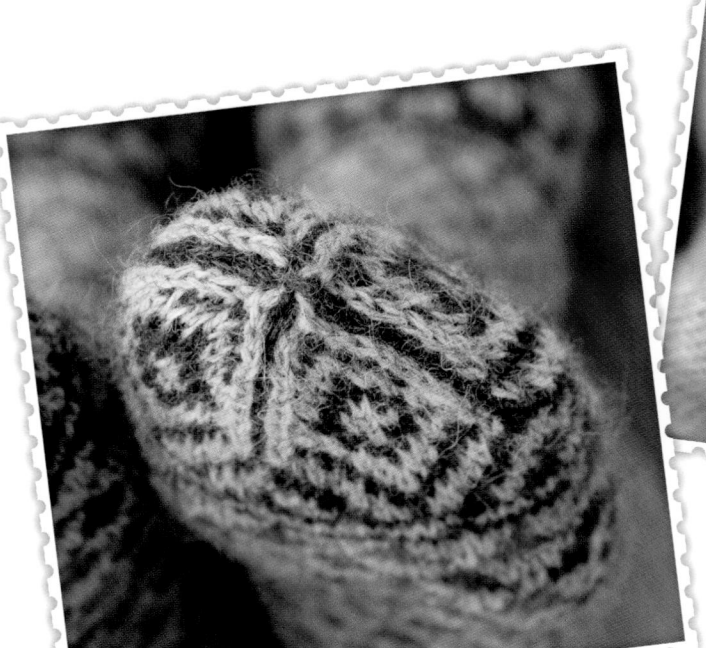

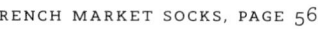

FRENCH MARKET SOCKS, PAGE 56

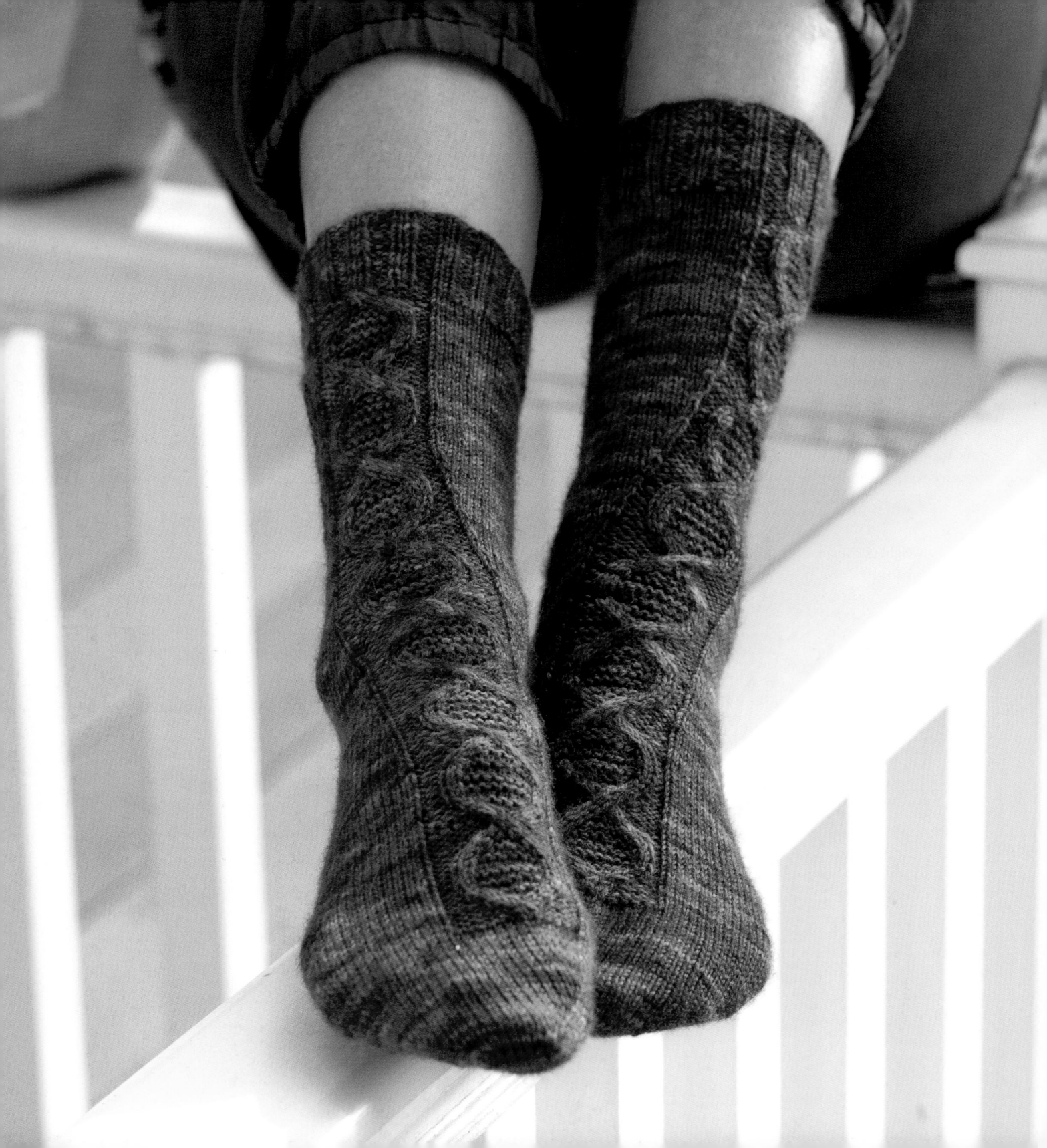

Asymmetrical Cables

DESIGNED BY *Cookie A*

finished size

About 7 (8, 9)" (18 [20.5, 23] cm) foot circumference, 8¾ (9¼, 9¾)" (22 [23.5, 25] cm) foot length from back of heel to tip of toe (with option for adjusting foot length), and 9¼ (9½, 9¾)" (23.5 [24, 25] cm) leg length from top of cuff to base of heel. Socks shown measure 8" (20.5 cm) in circumference.

yarn

Fingering weight (#1 Super Fine).

Shown here: Pagewood Farm St. Elias (80% Bluefaced Leicester wool, 20% nylon; 450 yd [411 m]/4 oz [113.4 g]): #S2 purple, 1 skein.

needles

Size U.S 1.5 (2.5 mm): set of 4 double-pointed (dpn).

Adjust needle size if necessary to obtain the correct gauge.

notions

Markers (m); cable needle (cn); tapestry needle.

gauge

16 sts and 23 rnds = 2" (5 cm) in St st worked in rnds.

16 sts of Left and Right Cable Panels each measure 1¾" (4.5 cm) wide.

The semi-solid color and texture of the Pagewood Farm St. Elias yarn I chose for these socks called for a bold pattern. I therefore decided to knit hefty yet simple cable panels with garter-stitch interiors. Each sock has a stockinette background that showcases the movement of the cable panels. The panels start out in parallel on each side of the end-of-round marker at the side of the leg, then they diverge as one panel swoops across the front of the leg and the top of the foot to create a strong but elegant visual line. The concept of symmetry is employed throughout: the diverging cable panels are mirror images of each other and the panels travel in mirror image directions as well.

> *Although this description may make the socks sound challenging, they are actually quite easy and enjoyable to knit."*

These socks are worked from the top down, beginning with k2, p2 ribbing that aligns with the cable pattern. The heel flap and gusset construction easily accommodate changes to customize the fit. Although this description may make the socks sound challenging, they are actually quite easy and enjoyable to knit.

⊕ **DESIGN TIP:** *When using double-pointed needles, position the beginning of the round at the boundary between two needles. To keep the end-of-round marker on the needle, place it between the last and second-to-last stitches of the round. When you come to the marker, you'll know to begin the next round with the first stitch of the next needle.*

⊕ **DESIGN TIP:** *Work asymmetrical patterns as mirror images on the two socks.*

Stitch Guide

2/2LC (WORKED OVER 4 STS)
Sl 2 sts onto cn and hold in front of work, k2, k2 from cn.

2/2RC (WORKED OVER 4 STS)
Sl 2 sts onto cn and hold in back of work, k2, k2 from cn.

2/2LC DEC (4 STS DECREASED TO 2 STS)
Sl 2 sts onto cn and hold in front of work, *insert right needle tip into first st on both cn and left needle and k2tog (1 st from each needle); rep from * once more—4 sts dec'd to 2 sts.

2/2RC DEC (4 STS DEC'D TO 2 STS)
Sl 2 sts onto cn and hold in back of work, *insert right needle tip into first st on both left needle and cn and k2tog (1 st from each needle); rep from * once more—4 sts dec'd to 2 sts.

2/2LCP (WORKED OVER 4 STS)
Sl 2 sts onto cn and hold in front of work, p2, k2 from cn.

2/2RCP (WORKED OVER 4 STS)
Sl 2 sts onto cn and hold in back of work, k2, p2 from cn.

LEFT CABLE PANEL (WORKED OVER 16 STS)
Rnd 1: P6, 2/2LC, p6.

Rnd 2: P6, k4, p6.

Rnd 3: P4, 2/2RC, 2/2LC, p4.

Rnd 4: [P4, k2] 2 times, p4.

Rnd 5: P2, 2/2RC, k4, 2/2LC, p2.

Rnds 6, 8, 10, and 12: P2, k2, p8, k2, p2.

Rnds 7, 9, and 11: P2, k12, p2.

Rnd 13: P2, 2/2LCP, k4, 2/2RCP, p2.

Rnd 14: Rep Rnd 4.

Rnd 15: P4, 2/2LCP, 2/2RCP, p4.

Rnd 16: Rep Rnd 2.

Rep Rnds 1–16 for patt.

RIGHT CABLE PANEL (WORKED OVER 16 STS)
Rnd 1: P6, 2/2RC, p6.

Rnd 2: P6, k4, p6.

Rnd 3: P4, 2/2RC, 2/2LC, p4.

Rnd 4: [P4, k2] 2 times, p4.

Rnd 5: P2, 2/2RC, k4, 2/2LC, p2.

Rnds 6, 8, 10, and 12: P2, k2, p8, k2, p2.

Rnds 7, 9, and 11: P2, k12, p2.

Rnd 13: P2, 2/2LCP, k4, 2/2RCP, p2.

Rnd 14: Rep Rnd 4.

Rnd 15: P4, 2/2LCP, 2/2RCP, p4.

Rnd 16: Rep Rnd 2.

Rep Rnds 1–16 for patt.

Leg

CO 56 (64, 72) sts. Arrange sts as evenly as possible on 3 dpn, place marker (pm), and join for working in rnds, being careful not to twist sts.

CUFF

NEXT RND: K1, *p2, k2; rep from * to last 3 sts, p2, k1.

Rep the last rnd until piece measures 1½" (3.8 cm) from CO.

INC RND: K1, p6, k1, [knit into the front, back, and front of next st] to inc 1 st to 3 sts, p6, k26 (34, 42), p6, [knit into the front, back, and front of next st] to inc 1 st to 3 sts, k1, p6, k1—60 (68, 76) sts; rnd begins at side of leg.

LEG PANEL

NEXT RND: K1, pm, work Rnd 1 of left cable panel (see Stitch Guide) over 16 sts, k26 (34, 42), pm, work Rnd 1 of right cable panel (see Stitch Guide) over 16 sts, k1.

Working sts outside cable panels in St st, cont in established patts until Rnds 1–16 of cable panels have been worked 2 times—32 cable panel rnds total; piece measures 4¼" (11 cm) from CO.

TRAVELING LEG SECTION

Cont cable panels as established, work the right and left sock separately as foll.

Right Sock

NEXT RND: (Rnd 1 of cable panels) M1 (see Glossary), k1, slip marker (sl m), work 16 sts of left cable panel, ssk, knit to next m, sl m, work 16 sts of right cable panel, k1—2 St sts before cable panel at beg of rnd, 25 (33, 41) St sts between cable panels.

Working inc'd st in St st, work 3 rnds even, ending with Rnd 4 of cable panels.

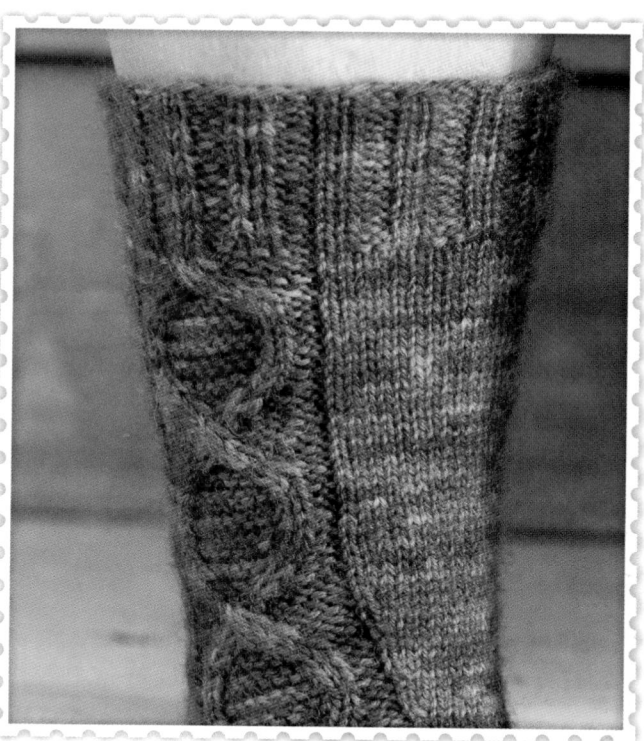

TRAVEL RND: Knit to 1 st before m, M1, k1, sl m, work 16 sts of left cable panel, ssk, knit to next m, work 16 of sts right cable panel, k1—1 St st inc'd before cable panel at beg of rnd, 1 St st dec'd between cable panels.

Cont in patt as established, work travel rnd every 4th rnd 6 more times, then work 3 rnds even to end with Rnd 16 of cable panels—piece measures 7" (18 cm) from CO.

NEXT RND: Knit to 1 st before m, M1, k1, work Rnd 1 of left cable panel over 16 sts, ssk, knit to next m, p6, 2/2RC Dec (see Stitch Guide), p6, k1—58 (66, 74) sts rem; 2 sts dec'd in right cable panel at end of rnd.

NEXT RND: (Rnd 2 of left cable panel) Work 30 (34, 38) sts in patt, place sts just worked on 2 needles to work later for instep (keeping travel rnd marker before left cable panel in position), knit rem 28 (32, 36) sts onto a single needle for heel flap—piece measures 7¼" (18.5 cm) from CO.

Left Sock

NEXT RND: (Rnd 1 of cable panels) K1, sl m, work 16 sts of left cable panel, knit to 2 sts before next m, k2tog, sl m, work 16 sts of right cable panel, k1, M1—2 St sts after cable panel at end of rnd, 25 (33, 41) St sts between cable panels.

Working inc'd st in St st, work 3 rnds even, ending with Rnd 4 of cable panels.

TRAVEL RND: K1, sl m, work 16 sts of left cable panel, knit to 2 sts before next m, k2tog, sl m, work 16 sts of right cable panel, k1, M1, knit to end—1 St st inc'd after cable panel at end of rnd, 1 St st dec'd between cable panels.

Cont in patt as established, work travel rnd every 4th rnd 6 more times, then work 3 rnds even to end with Rnd 16 of cable panels—piece measures 7" (18 cm) from CO.

NEXT RND: K1, p6, 2/2LC Dec, p6, knit to 2 sts before next m, k2tog, sl m, work Rnd 1 of right cable panel over 16 sts, k1, M1, knit to end—58 (66, 74) sts rem; 2 sts dec'd in left cable panel at beg of rnd.

NEXT RND: (Rnd 2 of right cable panel) Knit the first 28 (32, 36) sts onto a single needle for heel flap, work next 30 (34, 38) sts in patt and place sts just worked on 2 needles to work later for instep (keeping traveling rnd marker before right cable panel in position)—piece measures 7¼" (18.5 cm) from CO. Knit 1 row across the 28 (32, 36) heel flap sts.

Heel

For both socks, work heel back and forth in rows on 28 (32, 36) sts as foll:

HEEL FLAP

ROW 1: (WS) *Sl 1 pwise with yarn in front (wyf), p1; rep from *.

ROW 2: (RS) Sl 1 pwise with yarn in back (wyb), knit to end.

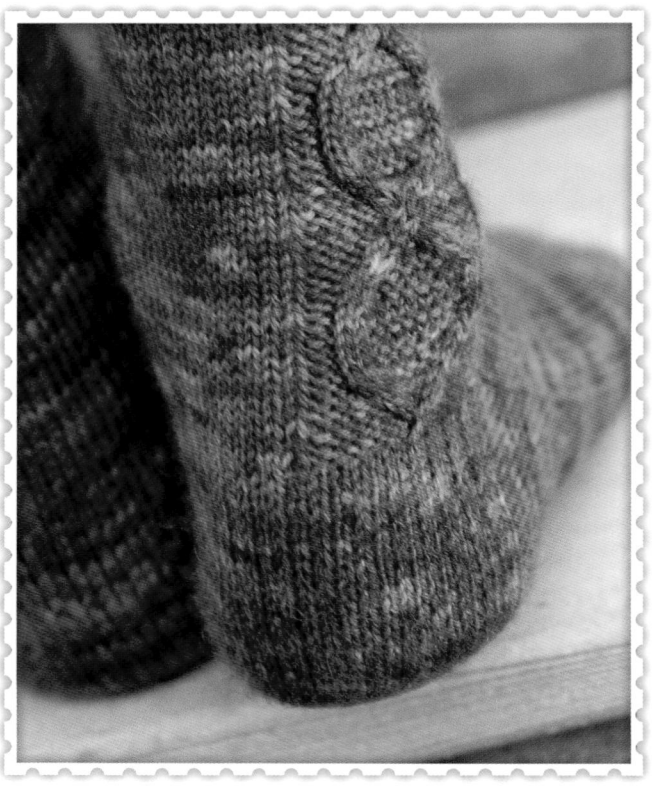

Rep Rows 1 and 2 for flap 15 (16, 17) more times, then work Row 1 once more, ending with a WS row—heel flap measures about 2 (2¼, 2½)" (5, 5.5, 6.5 cm).

TURN HEEL

Work short-rows as foll:

ROW 1: (RS) Sl 1 pwise wyb, k15 (17, 19), ssk, k1, turn work.

ROW 2: (WS) Sl 1 pwise wyf, p5, p2tog, p1, turn.

ROW 3: Sl 1 pwise wyb, knit to 1 st before gap formed on previous row, ssk (1 st each side of gap), k1, turn.

ROW 4: Sl 1 pwise wyf, purl to 1 st before gap formed on previous row, p2tog (1 st each side of gap), p1, turn.

Rep Rows 3 and 4 until all heel sts have been worked, ending with a WS Row 4 and omitting the k1 or p1 after the decrease on the last repeat—16 (18, 20) heel sts rem.

SHAPE GUSSETS

Pick up sts along gussets (see Glossary) and resume working in rnds for right and left socks as foll.

Right Sock

PICK-UP RND: With Needle 1, sl 1 pwise wyb, k15 (17, 19), pick up and knit 17 (18, 19) sts along selvedge of heel flap (about 1 st for each chain edge st), then pick up and knit 1 st in corner at base of heel flap; with Needle 2, knit to travel m, sl m, work Rnd 3 of left cable panel over 16 sts, knit to end of instep sts; with Needle 3, pick up and knit 1 st in corner at base of heel flap, then pick up and knit 17 (18, 19) sts along selvedge of heel flap, then knit across first 8 (9, 10) heel sts again—82 (90, 98) sts; 26 (28, 30) sts each on Needles 1 and 3, and 30 (34, 38) instep sts on Needle 2.

Left Sock

PICK-UP RND: With Needle 1, sl 1 pwise wyb, k15 (17, 19), pick up and knit 17 (18, 19) sts along selvedge of heel flap (about 1 st for each chain edge st), then pick up and knit 1 st in corner at base of heel flap; with Needle 2, knit to travel m, sl m, work Rnd 3 of right cable panel over 16 sts, knit to end of instep sts; with Needle 3, pick up and knit 1 st in corner

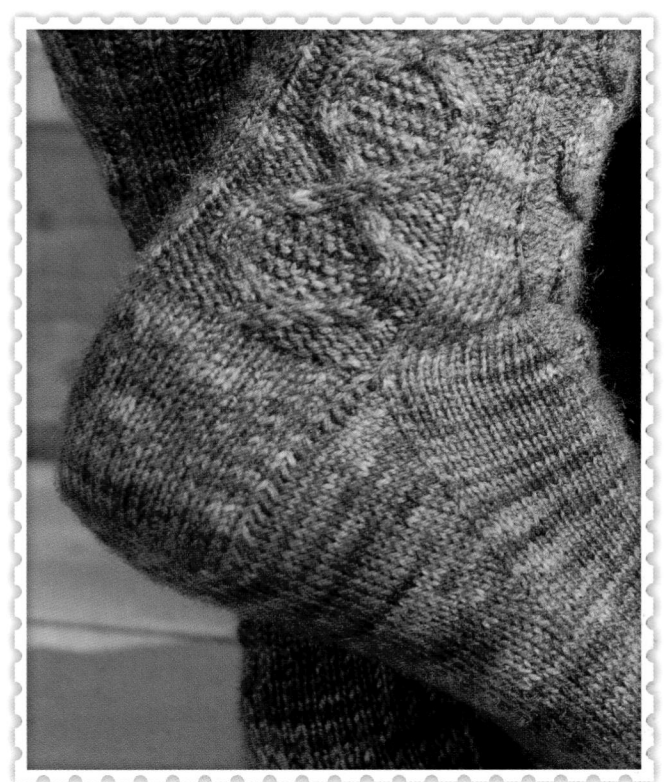

Yarn Note

Some socks clearly require a specific kind of yarn, but these would work well with several different yarn personalities. You could knit them in a smooth, slick, well-rounded yarn, or you could knit them with a softer, earthier yarn. The first would produce near sculptural precision in the cable panels and broad swaths of stockinette. The second would give a gentler, more blurred, lower-relief effect while still doing justice to the exquisite beauty of Cookie's cable motif. Whichever effect you desire, consider yarns with three or more plies to render the raised cable pattern in clean, well-defined lines. Should you choose a yarn with two plies, especially a springy one whose plies are spun at a near-perpendicular angle, be aware that the cable motif will lose some of its three-dimensional quality. In terms of color, you'll definitely want to stick with a solid or flickering semisolid because more strongly contrasting colors will create jarring horizontal lines that detract from the graceful downward flow of the cables.

—Clara Parkes

at base of heel flap, then pick up and knit 17 (18, 19) sts along selvedge of heel flap, then knit across first 8 (9, 10) heel sts again—82 (90, 98) sts; 26 (28, 30) sts each on Needles 1 and 3, and 30 (34, 38) instep sts on Needle 2.

Both Socks

NOTE: For each instep cable panel, cont to work travel rnds every 4th rnd as established on Rnds 1, 5, 9, and 13 of patt until only 1 knit st rem between the p6 at the edge of the cable panel and the end of the instep needle. After that, discontinue the travel rnds and work the cable panels without traveling to the end of the foot.

RND 1: On Needle 1, knit to last 2 sts, k2tog; on Needle 2, cont instep patt as established; on Needle 3, ssk, knit to end—2 sts dec'd.

RND 2: On Needle 1, knit; on Needle 2, cont instep patt as established; on Needle 3, knit.

Rep Rnds 1 and 2 for gusset 11 more times for all sizes—58 (66, 74) sts rem; 14 (16, 18) sts each on Needles 1 and 3 and 30 (34, 38) instep sts on Needle 2.

Foot

Cont even as established until Rnds 1–16 of cable panel on instep have been worked a total of 8 times from beg, ending with Rnd 16—foot measures about 6¾ (7, 7¼)" (17 [18, 18.5] cm) from back of heel.

NEXT RND: On Needle 1, knit; on Needle 2, knit to cable panel, p6, work 2/2LC Dec for right sock or 2/2RC Dec for left sock over next 4 sts (dec'd to 2 sts), p6, knit to end of needle; on Needle 3, knit—56 (64, 72) sts rem; no change to Needles 1 and 3; 28 (32, 36) instep sts on Needle 2.

NEXT RND: Knit all sts—piece measures about 7 (7¼, 7½)" (18 [18.5, 19] cm) from back of heel.

If adjusting foot length, work even in St st until piece measures 1¾ (2, 2¼)" (4.5 [5, 5.5] cm) less than desired total length from back of heel.

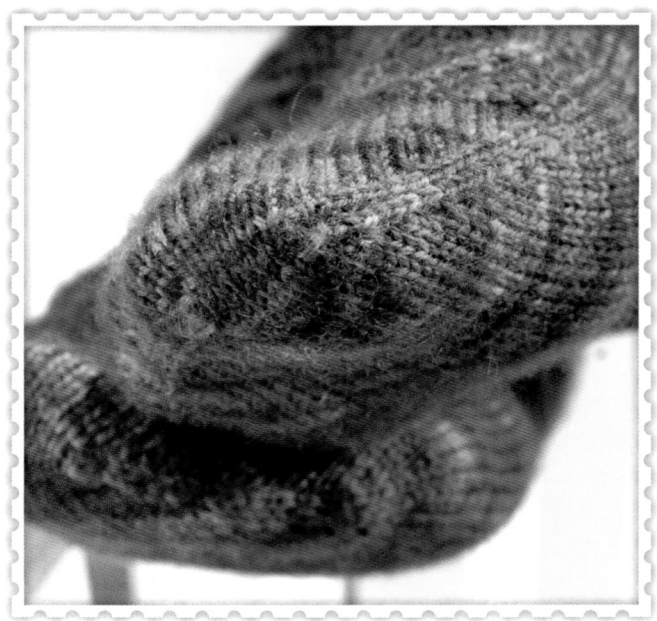

Toe

Dec each side of toe as foll:

RND 1: On Needle 1, knit to last 2 sts, k2tog; on Needle 2, ssk, knit to last 2 sts, k2tog; on Needle 3, ssk, knit to end—4 sts dec'd.

RND 2: Knit.

Rep Rnds 1 and 2 for toe 10 (11, 12) more times—12 (16, 20) sts rem; 3 (4, 5) sts each on Needles 1 and 3, and 6 (8, 10) sts on Needle 2.

Finishing

Knit sts from Needle 1 onto the end of Needle 3—6 (8, 10) sts each on 2 needles. Cut yarn, leaving a 12" (30.5 cm) tail. Thread tail on a tapestry needle and use the Kitchener st (see page 44) to graft sts tog.

Weave in loose ends. Block lightly.

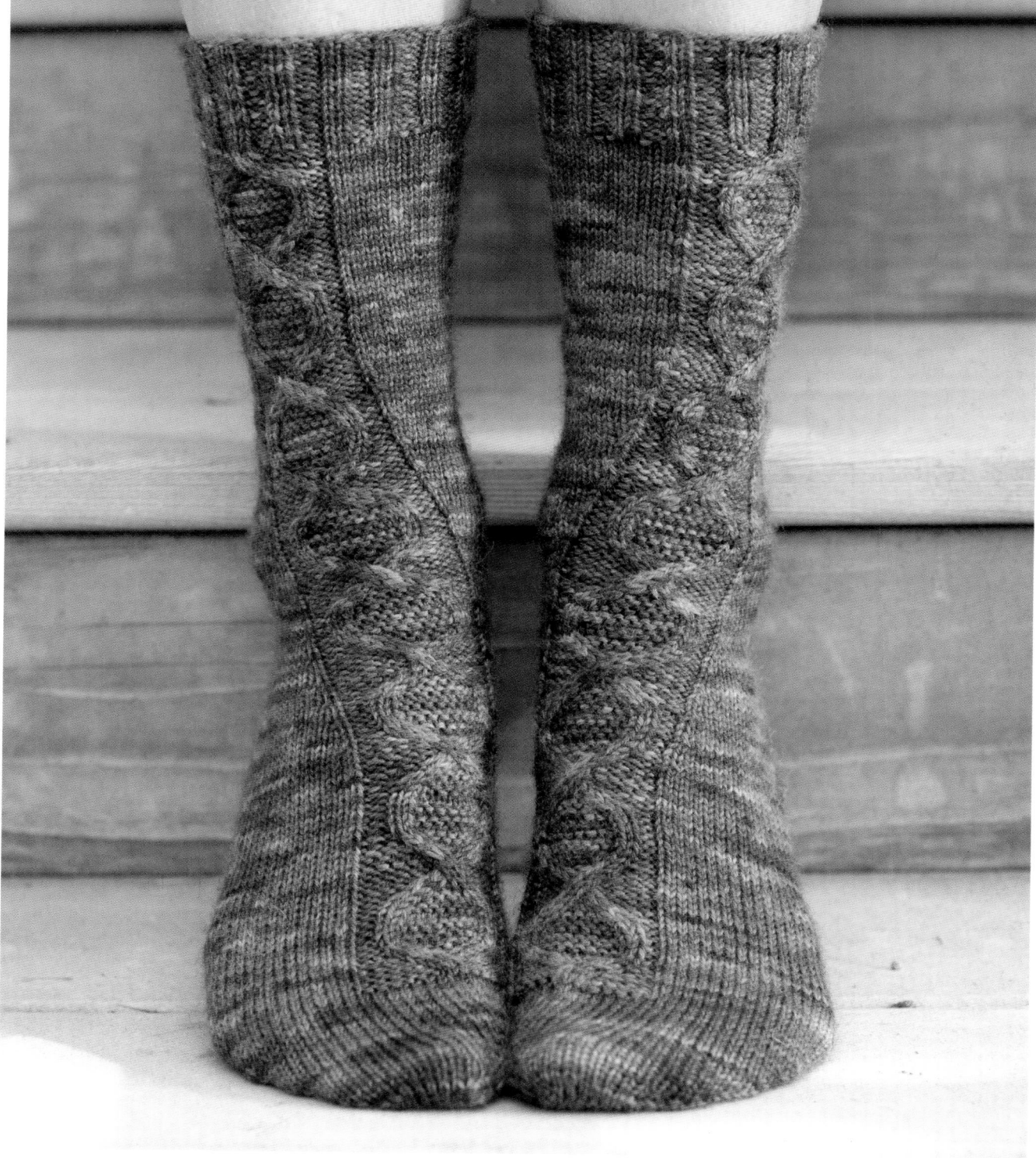

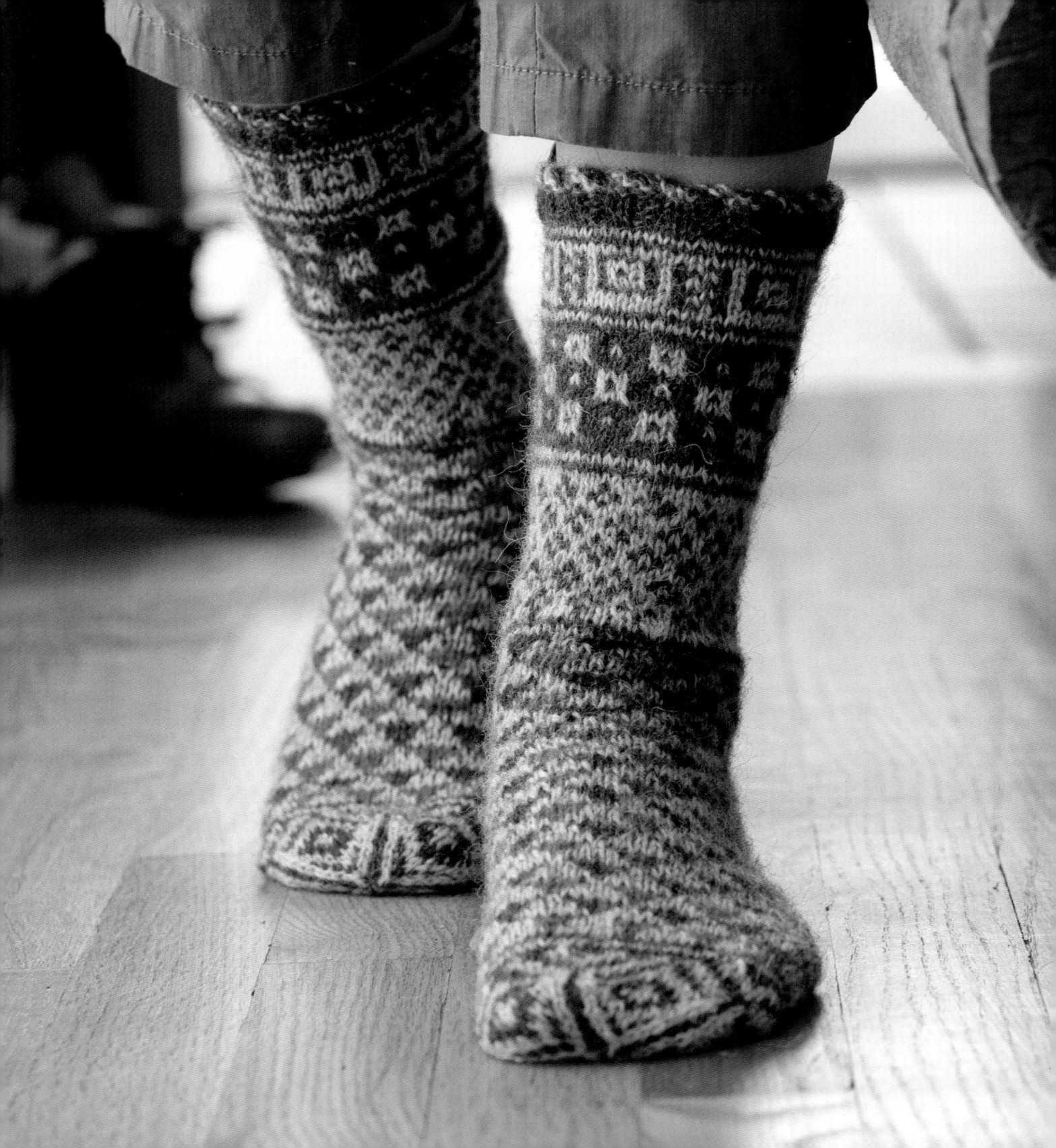

French Market Socks

DESIGNED BY *Nancy Bush*

finished size

About 8" (20.5 cm) foot circumference, 9¾" (25 cm) foot length from back of heel to tip of toe (with option for adjusting foot length), and 11" (28 cm) leg length from top of cuff to base of heel.

yarn

Fingering weight (#1 Super Fine).

Shown here: Elemental Affects Shetland Fingering Yarn (100% Shetland wool; 115 yd [105 m]/1 oz [28.4 g]): Mediterranean night (dark green; A) and ciel (light gray-green; B), 2 skeins each; agave (medium teal; C), 1 skein.

needles

Size U.S. 2 (2.75 mm): set of 5 double-pointed (dpn).

Adjust needle size if necessary to obtain the correct gauge.

notions

Marker (m); tapestry needle.

gauge

15 sts and 16 rnds = 2" (5 cm) in stranded St st color pattern, worked in rnds.

These socks were originally designed for a workshop I taught a couple of years ago in Provence, France. My goal was to teach a class in color theory, as it relates to knitting. I designed the first pair in a three-color palette of natural shades. I used cool blues for the socks shown here. When working with multiple colors, I like to make color decisions as I go to ensure that each color blends with or plays off its neighbors. The challenge is to choose colors that do this in interesting ways.

> "I like to make color decisions as I go to ensure that each color blends with or plays off its neighbors."

I began the socks with a decorative Latvian twist cast-on (which I learned from Lucy Neatby) that makes use of all three colors. The band heel allows the color pattern to continue throughout the entire foot. Because the heel flap had an odd number of stitches, I was able to work it in single-stitch vertical stripes, which added a visual delight of color and reinforced the heel. To continue the color patterning to the tip of the toe, I shaped the toe in four segments, working the shaping into the stitch pattern for a kaleidoscopic effect.

notes

+ The leg and foot of both socks are worked the same, but the heel flap is worked on the first 31 stitches of the round for the right sock and on the last 31 stitches for the left sock in order to place the beginning of the round on the inside of the leg where any interruptions in the pattern will be less obvious.

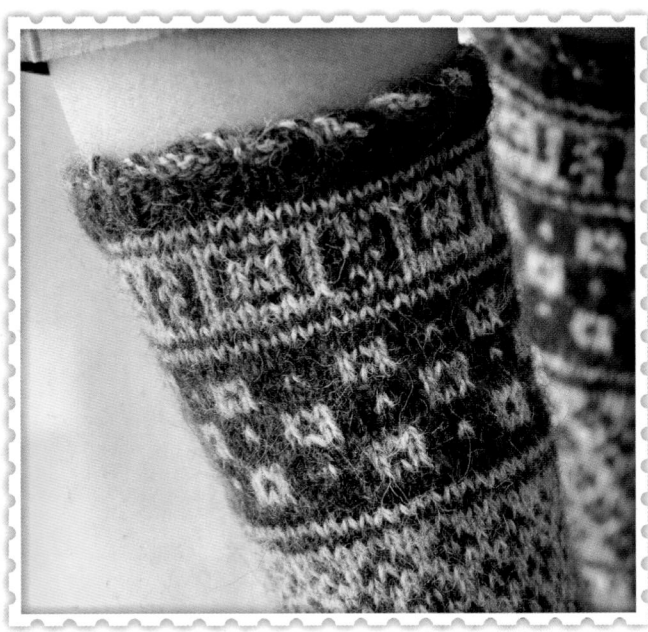

Leg

With A, use an elastic method (page 38) to CO 68 sts onto 1 dpn. Join B and knit 2 rows. Join C and knit 2 rows.

TWIST ROW: (RS) With A, *k4, twist the left-hand needle counterclockwise one full turn to insert a full twist in the fabric between the needles; rep from * to end of row.

Distribute sts onto 4 needles so that there are 17 sts on each needle. Join for working in rnds, using the crossover method (see page 40). Place marker (pm) to indicate beg of rnd.

With A, work in k2, p2 ribbing for 3 rnds—piece measures about ¾" (2 cm).

RND 1: With A, knit.

RND 2: With B, knit.

RND 3: With A, knit, working k2tog at the beg of Needle 1 and Needle 3—66 sts rem; 16 sts each on Needle 1 and Needle 3; 17 sts each on Needle 2 and Needle 4.

RNDS 4–11: Work Rnds 1–8 of Chart 1.

RND 12: With A, knit, working k2tog at beg of Needle 1 and Needle 3—64 sts rem; 15 sts each on Needle 1 and Needle 3; 17 sts each on Needle 2 and Needle 4.

RND 13: With B, knit.

RNDS 14–28: Work Rnds 1–15 of Chart 2.

RND 29: With B, knit.

RND 30: With A, knit.

RNDS 31–47: Work Rnds 1–17 of Chart 3.

RND 48: With A, knit, working k2tog at beg of all 4 needles—60 sts rem; 14 sts each on Needle 1 and Needle 3; 16 sts each on Needle 2 and Needle 4.

RND 49: With B, knit.

RNDS 50–61: Work Rnds 1–6 of Chart 4 two times—piece measures about 8½" (21.5 cm) from CO.

DESIGN TIP: *Whether working from the top down or toe up, the cuff should provide a non-curling band at the top of the leg.*

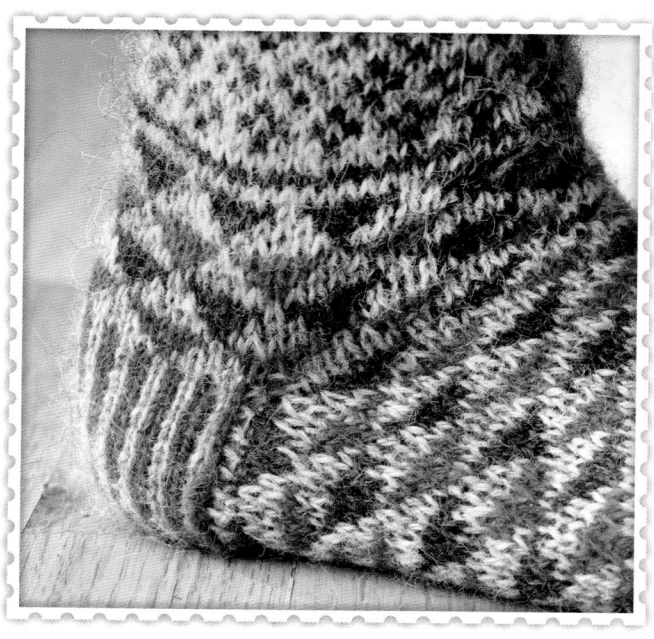

Heel

The heel is worked on different sts for the right and left sock (see Notes). Both heels are worked in two colors that alternate in vertical stripes.

HEEL FLAP
Right Sock

SET-UP ROW: Work first 31 sts onto a single needle for heel as [k1 with B, k1 with C] 15 times, k1 with B, then place rem 29 sts on 2 needles to work later for instep—31 heel sts.

Working each st in its matching color as established, work heel sts back and forth in rows as foll:

ROW 1: (WS) Sl 1 pwise with yarn in front (wyf), purl to end.

ROW 2: Sl 1 pwise with yarn in back (wyb), knit to end.

Rep these 2 rows 6 more times, then work WS Row 1 once more—16 rows total, including set-up row.

	A		+	C		/	k2tog with B			no stitch
	B		\	sl 1, k1, psso with B			pattern repeat			

Chart 1

Chart 2

Chart 3

Chart 4

Toe

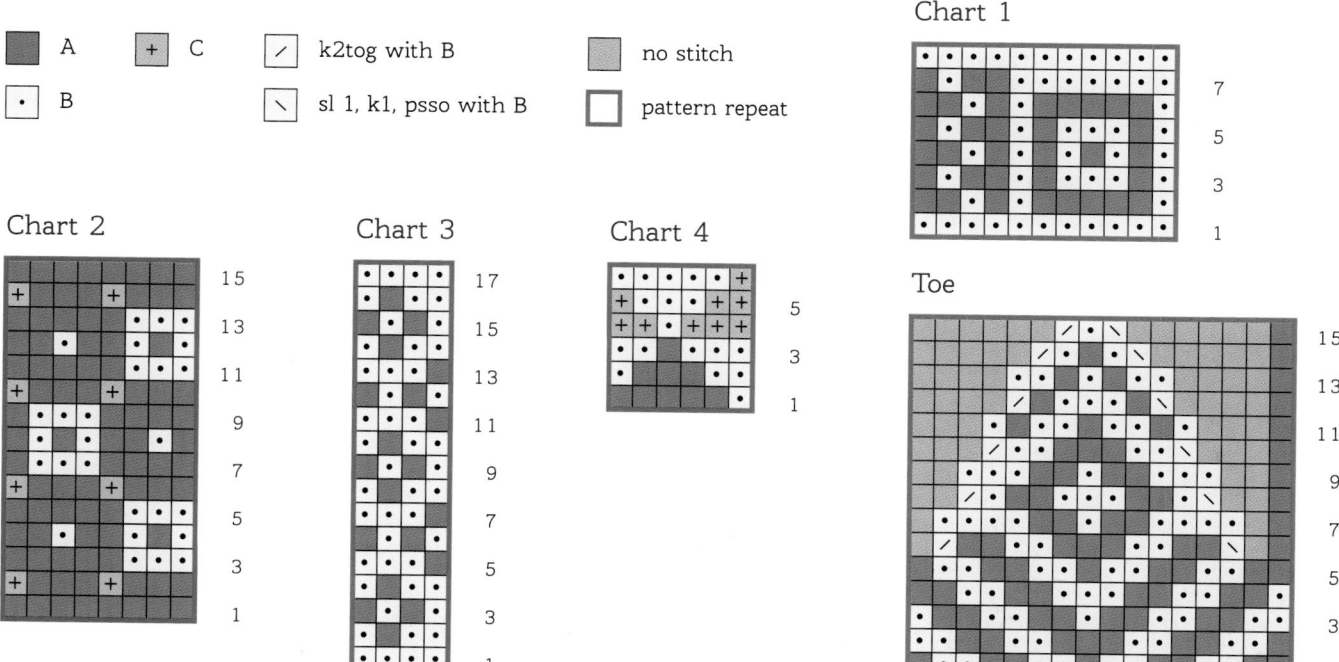

Left Sock

Sl the last 31 sts onto a single needle for heel without working them, then place rem 29 sts on 2 needles to work later for instep—31 heel sts. Rejoin B and C to beg of heel sts with RS facing.

SET-UP ROW: [K1 with B, k1 with C] 15 times, k1 with B.

Working each st in its matching color as established, work heel sts back and forth in rows as foll:

ROW 1: (WS) Sl 1 pwise wyf, purl to end.

ROW 2: Sl 1 pwise wyb, knit to end.

Rep these 2 rows 6 more times, then work WS Row 1 once more—16 rows total, including set-up row.

TURN HEEL, FIRST PART

Working both socks the same and working sts in their matching colors unless otherwise noted, work short-rows as foll:

ROW 1: (RS) Sl 1 pwise wyb, k10, k2tog with B, k5, ssk with B, k11, turn work—29 sts rem.

ROWS 2, 4, AND 6: Sl 1 pwise wyf, purl to end.

ROW 3: Sl 1 pwise wyb, k9, k2tog with B, k5, ssk with B, k10, turn—27 sts rem.

ROW 5: Sl 1 pwise wyb, k8, k2tog with B, k5, ssk with B, k9, turn—25 sts rem.

ROW 7: Sl 1 pwise wyb, k7, k2tog with B, k5, ssk with B, k8, turn—23 sts rem.

ROW 8: Sl 1 pwise wyf, purl to end.

TURN HEEL, SECOND PART

Working both socks the same and working sts in their matching colors unless otherwise noted, work short-rows as foll:

ROW 1: (RS) K14, ssk with B, turn work—22 sts rem.

ROW 2: Sl 1 pwise wyf, p5, p2tog with B, turn—21 sts rem.

ROW 3: Sl 1 pwise wyb, k5, ssk with B, turn—20 sts rem.

ROW 4: Sl 1 pwise wyf, p5, p2tog with B, turn—19 sts rem.

Rep Rows 4 and 5 six more times, ending with a WS row—7 sts rem.

Yarn Note

A yarn's durability comes from the length of its fibers and the amount of twist used to hold the fibers together. Too much twist and the yarn becomes rope; too little twist and it falls apart. With this in mind, you may think that a gently twisted two-ply Shetland yarn with its relatively short fibers would not be the wisest choice for a sock yarn, and yet in this pattern it is perfectly suited because the pattern calls for stranded colorwork, creating a double layer of fabric throughout. If you like what you see here, do stick with a more fuzzy woolen-spun yarn. The fuzz and bloom are what give the socks their muted, mossy look, and also help conceal the colors being stranded along the back of the fabric. Worked in a smooth worsted-spun yarn, this sock would take on the much louder, brighter shine and clarity of, say, a tile mosaic—and your tension would need to be spot-on. The leg has no ribbing for elasticity, so if this is a concern, seek a woolen-spun yarn that uses springier fibers with greater elasticity, such as Cormo or Targhee.

—*Clara Parkes*

Foot

Right Sock

With RS facing, sl 1 pwise wyb, k2 with A—4 heel sts rem unworked.

JOINING RND: With Needle 1, work last 4 heel sts as k3 with A, k1 with B, then pick up and knit 12 sts along side of heel flap as [k5 with B, k1 with A] 2 times; with Needle 2, work Rnd 1 of Chart 4 as established over first 15 instep sts; with Needle 3, cont Rnd 1 of chart patt over last 14 instep sts; with Needle 4, pick up and knit 12 sts along other side of heel flap as [k1 with B, k5 with A] 2 times, then work first 3 heel sts as k1 with B, k2 with A—60 sts total; 16 sts on Needle 1; 15 sts on Needle 2; 14 sts on Needle 3; 15 sts on Needle 4.

Left Sock

With RS facing, sl 1 pwise wyb, k2 with A—4 heel sts rem unworked.

JOINING RND: With Needle 1, work last 4 heel sts as k4 with A, then pick up and knit (see Glossary) 12 sts along side of heel flap as [k1 with B, k5 with A] 2 times; with Needle 2, work Rnd 1 of Chart 4 as established over first 15 instep sts; with Needle 3, cont Rnd 1 of chart patt over last 14 instep sts; with Needle 4, pick up and knit 12 sts along other side of heel flap as k1 with A, k1 with B, k5 with A, k1 with B, k4 with A, then work first 3 heel sts as k1 with A, k1 with B, k1 with A—60 sts total; 16 sts on Needle 1; 15 sts on Needle 2; 14 sts on Needle 3; 15 sts on Needle 4.

Both Socks

Cont in even in patt from Chart 4 until Rnds 1–6 have been worked a total of 7 times from joining rnd—foot measures 5¼" (13.5 cm) from edge of heel flap and about 7½" (19 cm) from back of heel. For a longer or shorter foot, work more or fewer rnds here until foot measures 2¼" (5.5 cm) less than desired length, ending with Rnd 3 or Rnd 6 of chart patt; every 3 rnds added or removed will lengthen or shorten the foot by about ⅜" (1 cm).

Toe

Knit 1 rnd with A, then knit 1 rnd with B.

NEXT RND: Knit with A, inc 1 st on each needle—64 sts; 17 sts on Needle 1; 16 sts on Needle 2; 15 sts on Needle 3; 16 sts on Needle 4.

Rearrange sts so there are 16 sts on each needle. Work Rnds 1–15 of Toe chart—16 sts rem.

NEXT RND: *K1 A, sl 2 kwise wyb, k1 B, p2sso; rep from *— 8 sts rem.

Cut yarn, leaving an 8" (20.5 cm) tail.

Finishing

Thread tail on a tapestry needle, draw through rem sts, pull tight to close hole, and fasten off on WS.

Weave in loose ends. Block on sock blockers or under a damp towel.

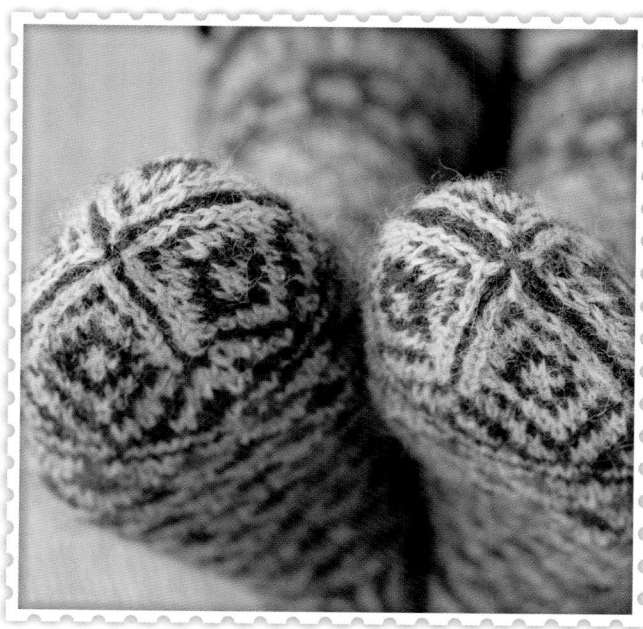

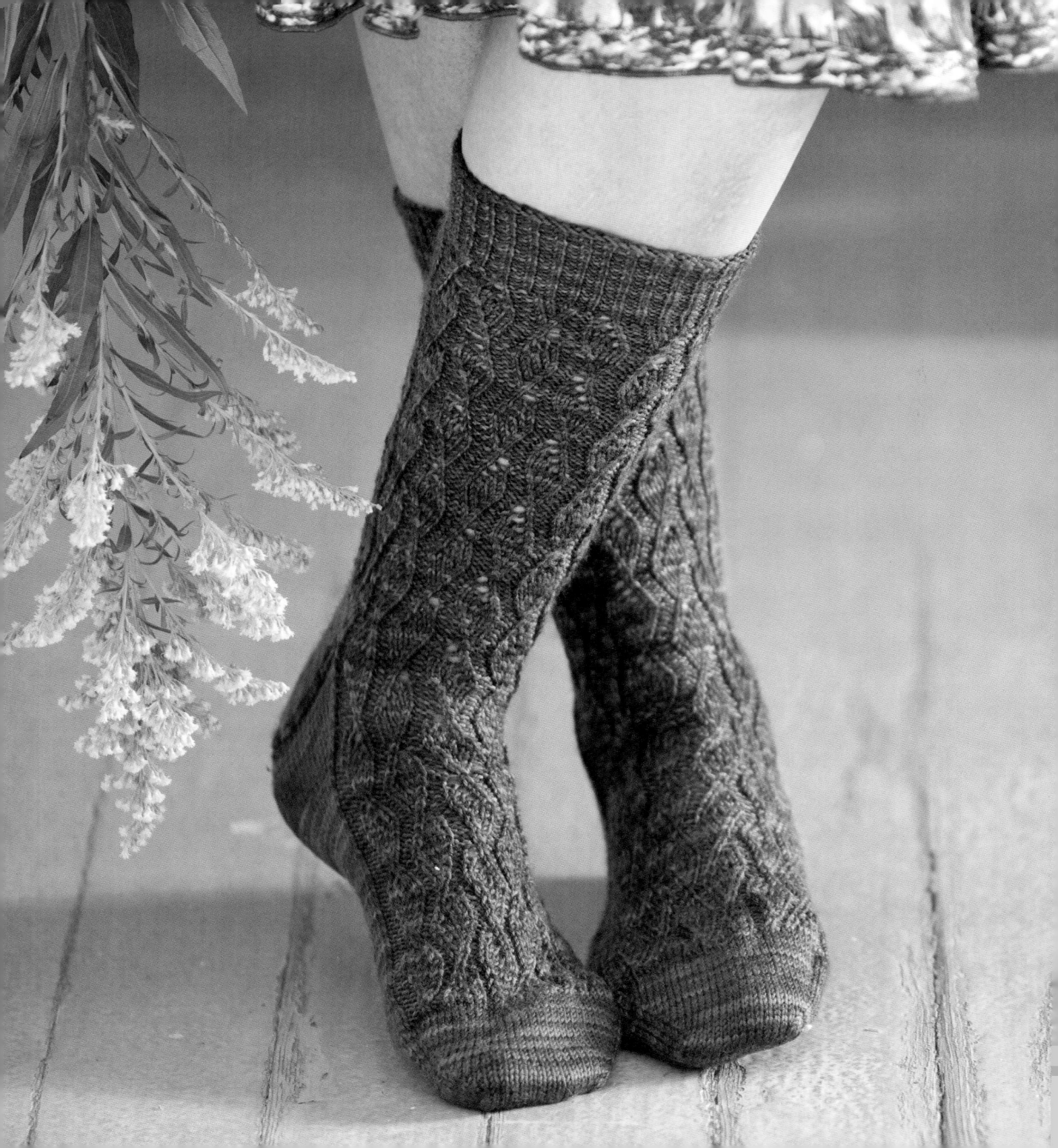

Almondine

DESIGNED BY *Anne Hanson*

finished size

About 6½ (7½, 9, 10)"
(16.5 [19, 23, 25.5] cm) foot
circumference, 10¼" (26 cm)
foot length from back of heel
to tip of toe (with option for
adjusting foot length), and 7 (9,
11, 12¾)" (18 [23, 28, 32.5] cm)
leg length from top of cuff to
base of heel. To fit feet up to 7½
(8½, 10, 11)" (19 [21.5, 25.5,
28] cm) foot circumference.
Socks shown measure 9"
(23 cm) in circumference.

yarn

Fingering weight (#1 Super Fine).

Shown here: Cascade Heritage
Paints (75% merino, 25% nylon;
437 yd [400 m]/100 g): #9824
forest, 1 (1, 1, 2) skein(s).

needles

Size U.S. 1 (2.25 mm): set of 4
double-pointed (dpn).

*Adjust needle size if necessary
to obtain the correct gauge.*

notions

Marker (m); tapestry needle.

gauge

16 sts and 24 rnds = 2" (5 cm)
in stockinette stitch, worked in
rounds.

14½ sts and 23 rnds = 2"
(5 cm) in Almondine pattern
from chart, worked in rounds.

My love for openwork patterns is often apparent in the
socks I knit. I find such patterns an appealing alternative
to the more solid foot coverings. Especially during periods
of transitional weather, a little openwork can go a long
way in making sock fabric breathable and comfortable.
And although convention dictates that lace is feminine,
I find that many of the less
fussy openwork patterns are as
suitable for men as women.

> **Because this simple
> pattern is easily
> memorized, it is an
> ideal take-along project."**

For these unisex socks, I chose
a simple pattern that involves a
small percentage of openwork.
The result is an elegant "vintage" feel, rather than a "lacy"
or "floral" effect. I arranged the narrow openwork motifs
in vertical panels separated by purl stitches. In addition
to giving vertical definition to the motifs, the purl stitches
add a springy ribbed effect that makes the socks hug the
foot nicely. To give the illusion of an allover lace pattern,
I staggered the lace panels so that the wide parts of
one panel nestled into the narrow parts of the adjacent
panels. Because this simple pattern is easily memorized,
it is an ideal take-along project. Knitted in a smooth,
springy yarn, these socks can be worn from season to
season.

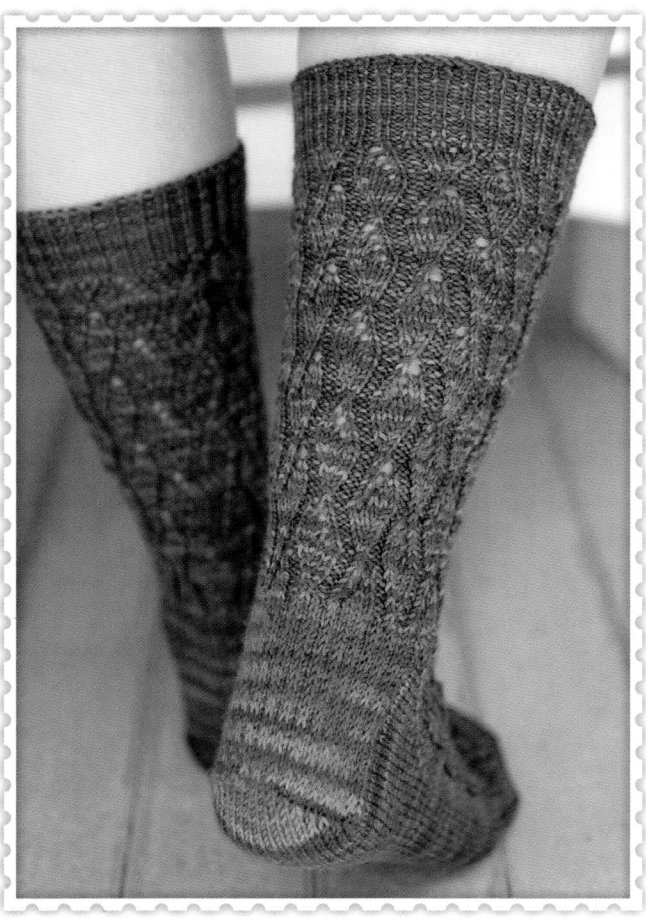

Leg

Using an elastic method (page 38), CO 50 (60, 70, 80) sts. Arrange sts on 3 dpn so that there is a multiple of 10 sts on each needle. Place marker (pm) and join for working in rnds, being careful not to twist sts. Rnd begins at back of leg. Work k1, p1 rib for cuff until piece measures 1½ (1½, 1¾, 1¾)" (3.8 [3.8, 4.5, 4.5] cm) from CO. Change to patt from Almondine chart and rep Rnds 1–16 of chart 3 (4, 5, 6) times, ending with Rnd 16—piece measures about 5¾ (7, 8¾, 10¼)" (14.5 [18, 22, 26] cm) from CO.

Heel

Knit the first 3 (0, 3, 0) sts from Needle 1 onto the end of Needle 3. Place the next 24 (30, 34, 40) sts on a single dpn for heel, then divide the rem 26 (30, 36, 40) sts evenly on 2 dpn to work later for instep.

HEEL FLAP

Work the 24 (30, 34, 40) back-of-leg sts back and forth in rows for the heel as foll:

ROW 1: (RS) Sl 1 pwise with yarn in back (wyb), knit to end.

ROW 2: (WS) *Sl 1 pwise with yarn in front (wyf), p1; rep from *.

Rep these 2 rows 12 (14, 16, 19) more times, then rep Row 1 once again—13 (15, 17, 20) chain sts along each selvedge edge.

TURN HEEL

Work short-rows as foll:

ROW 1: (WS) Sl 1 pwise wyf, p13 (16, 18, 21), p2tog, p1, turn work.

ROW 2: (RS) Sl 1 pwise wyb, k5, ssk, k1, turn.

ROW 3: Sl 1 pwise wyf, purl to 1 st before gap formed on previous row, p2tog (1 st each side of gap), p1, turn.

Almondine

- ⬜ knit
- · purl
- O yo
- ╱ k2tog
- ╲ ssk
- ⬜ pattern repeat

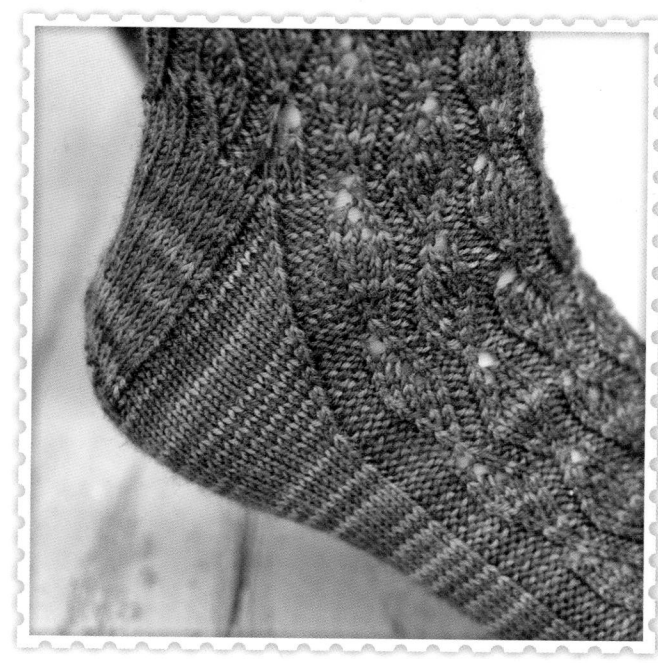

ROW 4: Sl 1 pwise wyb, knit to 1 st before gap formed on previous row, ssk (1 st each side of gap), k1, turn.

Rep Rows 3 and 4 until all heel sts have been worked, ending with RS Row 4 and ending the last rep as p2tog or ssk if there are not enough sts to work the final p1 or k1 after the dec—14 (18, 20, 22) heel sts rem.

GUSSETS

Pick up sts along selvedges of heel flap (see Glossary) and rejoin for working in rnds as foll:

RND 1: With Needle 1, pick up and knit 14 (16, 18, 21) sts (1 st in each chain st) along selvedge of heel flap; with Needle 2, p3 (0, 3, 0), then work Rnd 1 of Almondine chart over 20 (30, 30, 40) sts, p3 (0, 3, 0); with Needle 3, pick up and knit 14 (16, 18, 21) sts (1 st in each chain st) along other selvedge of heel flap, then knit the first 7 (9, 10, 11) heel sts from Needle 1 again—68 (80, 92, 104) sts total; 21 (25, 28, 32) sts each on Needles 1 and 3, 26 (30, 36, 40) instep sts on Needle 2. Rnd begins at back of heel.

RND 2: On Needle 1, knit to last 2 sts, k2tog; on Needle 2, cont instep sts in patt with 3 (0, 3, 0) purl sts at each end of needle; on Needle 3, ssk, knit to end—2 sts dec'd.

RND 3: On Needle 1, knit; on Needle 2, cont instep in patt with 3 (0, 3, 0) purl sts at each end of needle; on Needle 3, knit.

Rep Rnds 2 and 3 for gusset 7 (9, 9, 11) more times—52 (60, 72, 80) sts rem; 13 (15, 18, 20) sts each on Needles 1 and 3, 26 (30, 36, 40) sts on Needle 2.

Foot

Working sts on Needles 1 and 3 in St st, cont sts on instep needle as established until piece measures 7¾" (19.5 cm) from back of heel, or about 2½" (6.5 cm) less than desired total foot length, ending with Rnd 8 or 16 of chart. If ending on the correct chart rnd produces a foot that is shorter than the target length, after the final patt rnd work all sts even in St st until piece reaches desired length to start of toe.

TOE

Cont in St st, dec at each side of foot as foll:

RND 1: On Needle 1, knit to last 3 sts, k2tog, k1; on Needle 2, k1, ssk, knit to last 3 sts, k2tog, k1; on Needle 3, k1, ssk, knit to end—4 sts dec'd.

RND 2: Knit.

Rep Rnds 1 and 2 for toe 6 (7, 9, 10) more times—24 (28, 32, 36) sts rem. Knit the 6 (7, 8, 9) sts from Needle 1 onto the end of Needle 3—12 (14, 16, 18) sts each on 2 needles. Cut yarn, leaving a 10" (25.5 cm) tail.

Finishing

Thread tail on a tapestry needle and use the Kitchener st (see page 44) to graft live sts tog. Weave in loose ends. With yarn threaded on a tapestry needle, tighten up any holes at gussets, if necessary. Block lightly.

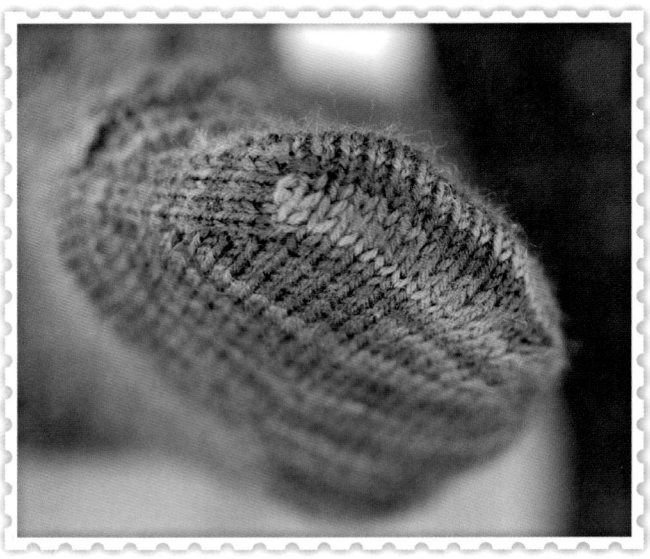

Yarn Note

Depending on the colorway and yarn, these socks can go quite easily from crisp high-relief to a much more muted low-relief effect. The well-rounded multiple-ply yarn used here renders the raised lace motifs in a particularly clear sculptural manner. If you want to soften the stitch pattern at all, simply choose a variegated or semisolid yarn—steering clear of higher-contrast color changes that would overpower the pretty little diamonds in the motif. Another option for toning down the definition of the stitch pattern is to try a two-ply yarn, which would give the diamond pattern a slightly more textured nuance. Extra nylon (25%) and a thicker slipped-stitch heel lend great abrasion resistance to this project, which is especially welcome because of the vulnerable openings formed by the yarnovers along the leg and top of the foot. Because there are purl ridges between each diamond motif and extra ribbing at the top, you can also consider using yarns with less-elastic fibers including silk or cotton.

—*Clara Parkes*

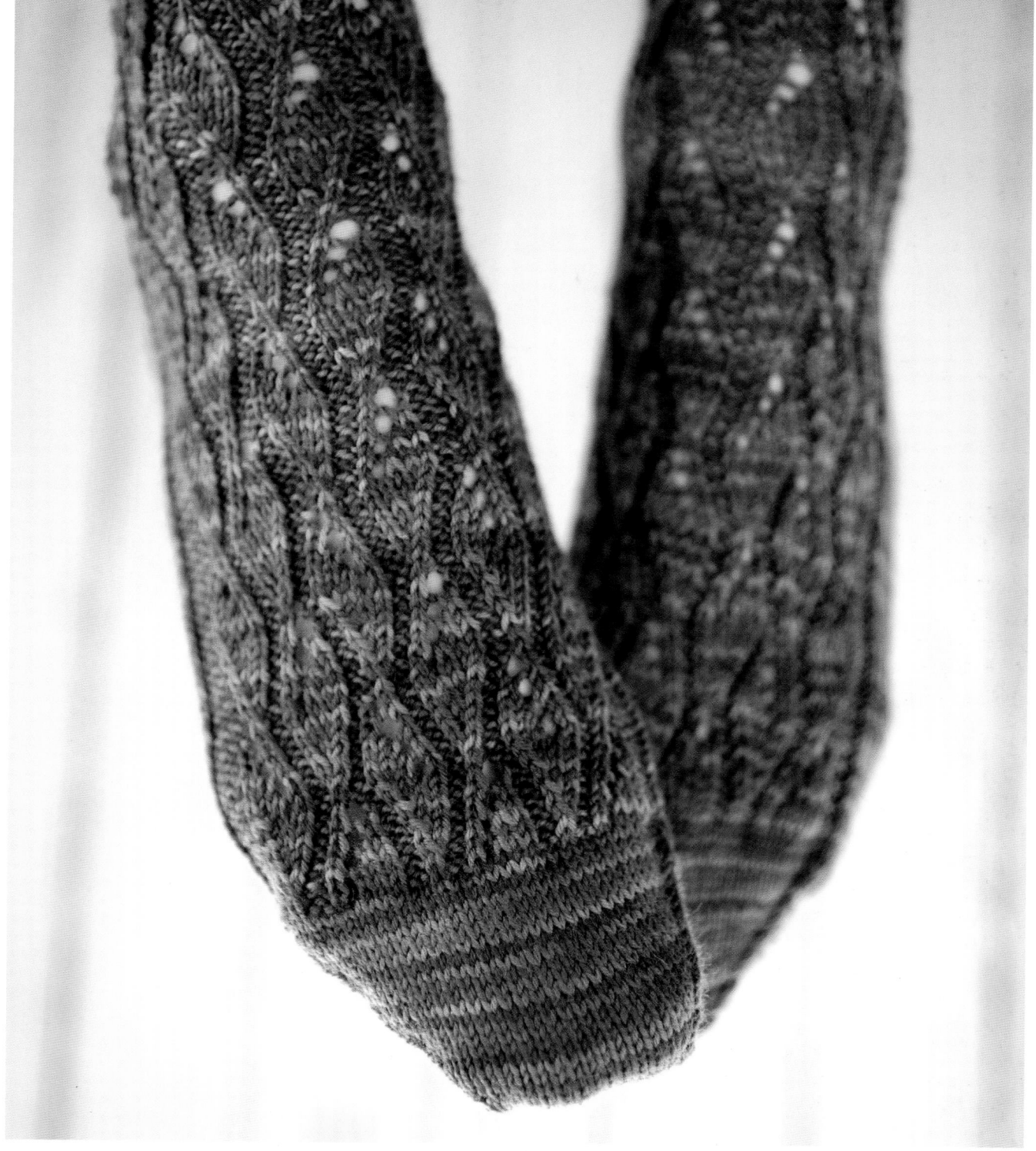

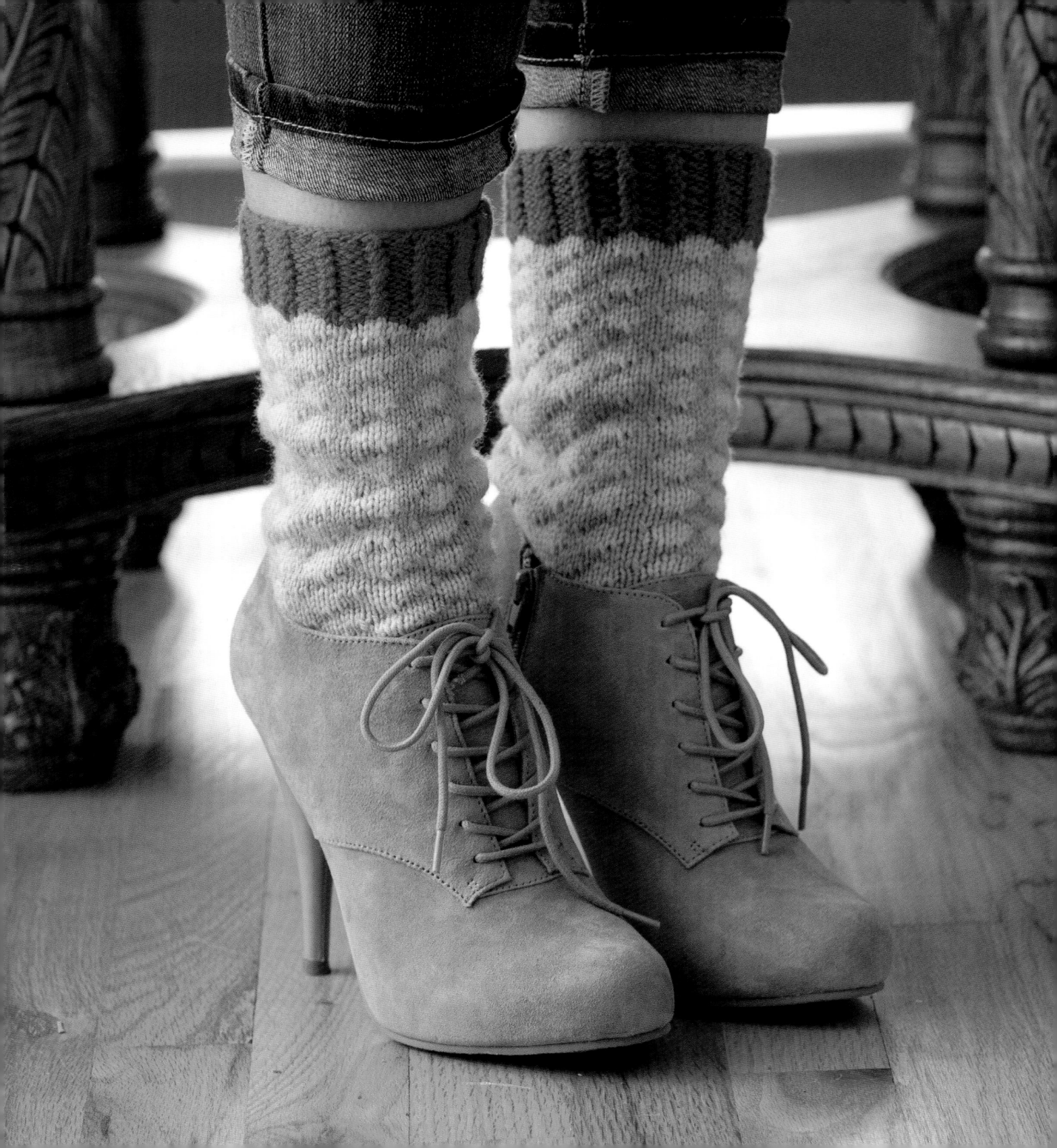

Happy-Go-Lucky Boot Socks

DESIGNED BY *Véronik Avery*

finished size

About 8½" (21.5 cm) foot circumference, 9¾" (25 cm) foot length from back of heel to tip of toe (with option for adjusting foot length), and 9¼" (23.5 cm) leg length from top of cuff to base of heel.

yarn

Sportweight (#2 Fine).

Shown here: St-Denis Nordique (100% wool; 150 yd [137 m]/50 g): #5831 peacock (A), #5804 chalk blue (light blue; B), and #5805 aurora (lavender-gray; C), 1 ball each.

needles

Size U.S. 2 (2.75 mm): set of 5 double-pointed (dpn).

Adjust needle size if necessary to obtain the correct gauge.

notions

Marker (m); waste yarn or stitch holder; tapestry needle.

gauge

15 stitches and 27 rounds = 2" (5 cm) in slip-stitch pattern, worked in rounds.

13 stitches and 21 rounds = 2" (5 cm) in stockinette stitch, worked in rounds.

> *I set out to knit socks she could pair with her distressed high-heel boots."*

These socks were inspired by Poppy, a fictional character interpreted by Sally Hawkins in Mike Leigh's *Happy-Go-Lucky*. In the opening scene, Poppy cycles through London wearing a characteristically colorful outfit comprised of a crocheted cardigan (in shades of blues and purples) with a turquoise tee and stonewashed jeans. While the combination sounds jarring and unfashionable, the overall effect was one of a *jolie laide* or unconventional beauty.

With Poppy as my imaginary recipient, I set out to knit socks she could pair with her distressed high-heel boots. I imagined they'd peek slightly over the top edge, so one could glimpse a generous cuff followed by a slouchy leg. I chose colors that would suit Poppy—bright turquoise paired with soft lavender and pale blue.

I used a simple slip-stitch pattern that let me use multiple colors without compromising the stretchy nature of the fabric. This allowed me to use just one color per round with the slipped stitches adding a pleasing texture, which is enhanced when the legs slouch. The bright turquoise accentuates the cuffs, heels, and toes, and gives a playful touch reminiscent of sock monkeys. Bright footwear is not just for females—next time you watch a "hoofer" movie featuring perhaps Fred Astaire or Gene Kelley, take a look at their feet.

notes

+ Carry the unused color up the inside of the sock at the boundary between rounds, instead of joining a new strand at each color change.

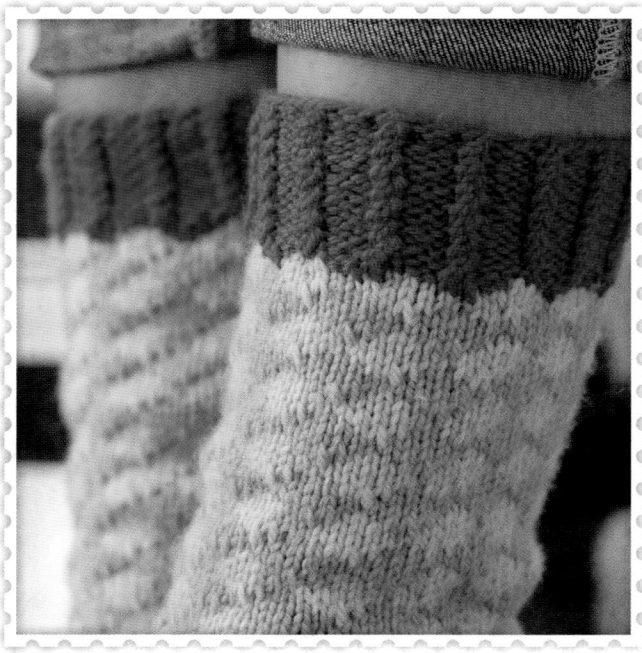

Stitch Guide

RIGHT CROSS (RC; WORKED OVER 2 STS)

K2tog but leave both sts on left-hand needle, knit the first st again, then slip both sts off left-hand needle.

LEFT CROSS (LC; WORKED OVER 2 STS)

Bring right needle tip behind first st on left-hand needle, knit the second st through the back loop but leave this st on the left-hand needle, then knit the first st and slip both sts off left-hand needle.

BABY CABLE RIB (MULTIPLE OF 4 STS)

Rnd 1: *K2, p2; rep from *.

Rnd 2: *RC (see above), p2; rep from *.

Rep Rnds 1 and 2 for patt.

SLIP-STITCH PATTERN (MULTIPLE OF 6 STS)

Rnd 1: With B, *k1, sl 4 with yarn in back (wyb), k1; rep from *.

Rnd 2: With B, *k2, sl 2 wyb, k2; rep from *.

Rnds 3 and 4: With B, knit.

Rnd 5: With C, *Sl 2 wyb, k2, sl 2 wyb; rep from *.

Rnd 6: With C, *sl 1 wyb, k4, sl 1 wyb; rep from *.

Rnds 7 and 8: With C, knit.

Rep Rnds 1–8 for patt.

⊕ **DESIGN TIP:** *Invariably, small holes form at the boundary between the top of the heel flap and the instep stitches. To help alleviate the problem, pick up an extra stitch at the boundary between the heel flap and each side of the instep, then decrease the extra stitches on the next round. Alternatively, simply use a bit of yarn threaded on a tapestry needle to sew the hole closed after the sock is finished.*

Leg

With A, CO 64 sts. Arrange sts evenly on 4 dpn, place marker (pm), and join for working in rnds, being careful not to twist sts—16 sts on each needle. Rep Rnds 1 and 2 of baby cable rib (see Stitch Guide) 8 times—16 rnds total; piece measures about 1½" (3.8 cm) from CO.

INC RND: With A, k2, M1 (see Glossary), k32, M1, k30—66 sts.

Work Rnds 1–8 of slip-st patt (see Stitch Guide) 9 times, then work Rnds 1–3 once more—piece measures about 7" (18 cm) from CO.

DEC RND: (counts as Rnd 4 of patt) With B, [k4, k2tog] 6 times, k30—60 sts rem.

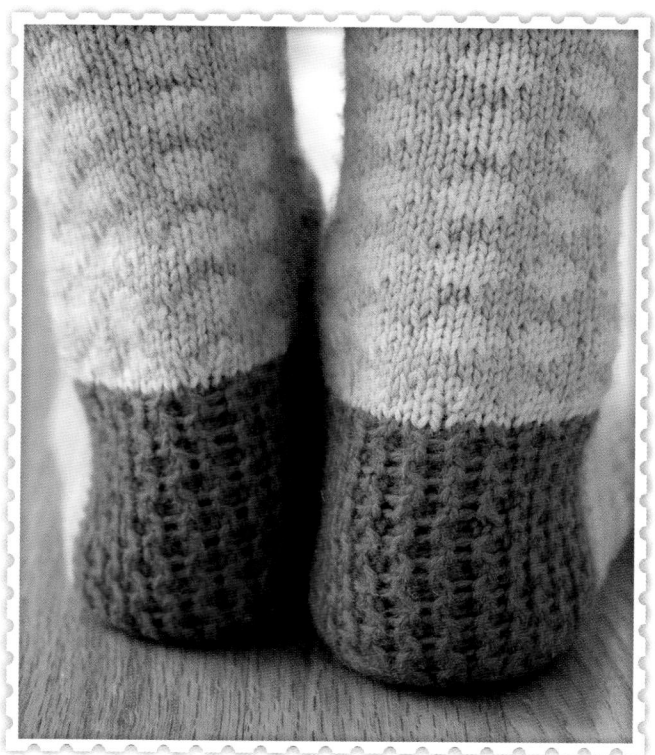

Heel

Change to A and work heel flap back and forth in rows as foll.

HEEL FLAP

ROW 1: (RS) Sl 1 pwise with wyb, k29—30 heel sts; place these 30 heel sts on a single dpn, then place rem 30 sts on waste yarn or holder to work later for instep.

ROWS 2 AND 4: (WS) Sl 1 with yarn in front (wyf), purl to end.

ROW 3: Sl 1 with yarn in back (wyb), *LC (see Stitch Guide), RC (see Stitch Guide); rep from * to last st, end k1.

ROW 5: Sl 1 wyb, *RC, LC; rep from * to last st, end k1.

ROW 6: Rep Row 2.

Rep Rows 3–6 five more times, then work Rows 3 and 4 once more, ending with a WS row—28 rows total; heel flap measures about 2¼" (5.5 cm).

TURN HEEL

Work short-rows as foll:

ROW 1: (RS) Sl 1 wyb, k16, ssk, k1, turn work.

ROW 2: (WS) Sl 1 wyf, p5, p2tog, p1, turn work.

ROW 3: Sl 1 wyb, knit to gap formed on previous row, ssk (1 st each side of gap), k1, turn work.

ROW 4: Sl 1 wyf, purl to gap formed on previous row, p2tog (1 st each side of gap), p1, turn work.

Rep Rows 3 and 4 four more times, ending with a WS row—18 heel sts rem. Cut off A.

GUSSET

With RS of heel flap facing, join C in corner at base of right-hand side of heel flap. Pick up and knit sts along selvedges of heel flap (see Glossary) and rejoin for working in rnds as foll:

JOINING RND: With Needle 1, pick up and knit 1 st in corner at base of heel flap, 14 sts along selvedge of flap, then knit the first 9 heel sts; with Needle 2, knit rem 9 heel sts, pick up and knit 14 sts along other selvedge of flap, then 1 st in corner at base of heel flap; with Needle 3, work Rnd 5 of patt across 30 held instep sts—78 sts total; 24 sts each on Needle 1 and Needle 2; 30 instep sts on Needle 3. Rnd begins at start of sole sts.

NOTE: The gusset decs slant in the opposite direction from the angle of the shaping.

RND 1: On Needle 1, k2tog, knit to end; on Needle 2, knit to last 2 sts, ssk; on Needle 3, cont in established patt—2 sts dec'd.

RND 2: On Needle 1 and Needle 2, knit; on Needle 3, cont in established patt.

Rep Rnds 1 and 2 eight more times—60 sts rem; 15 sts each on Needle 1 and Needle 2, 30 instep sts on Needle 3.

Foot

Cont even in patt until piece measures 7¾" (19.5 cm) from back of heel, or 2" (5 cm) less than desired total foot length, ending with Rnd 4 or 8 of slip-stitch patt.

Toe

Change to A and knit 4 rnds.

RND 1: On Needle 1, k1, ssk, knit to end; on Needle 2, knit to last 3 sts, k2tog, k1; on Needle 3, k1, ssk, knit to last 3 sts, k2tog, k1—4 sts dec'd.

RND 2: Knit.

Rep Rnds 1 and 2 five more times—36 sts rem. Rep Rnd 1 (dec every rnd) 6 times—12 sts rem; 3 sts each on Needle 1 and Needle 2, 6 sts on Needle 3.

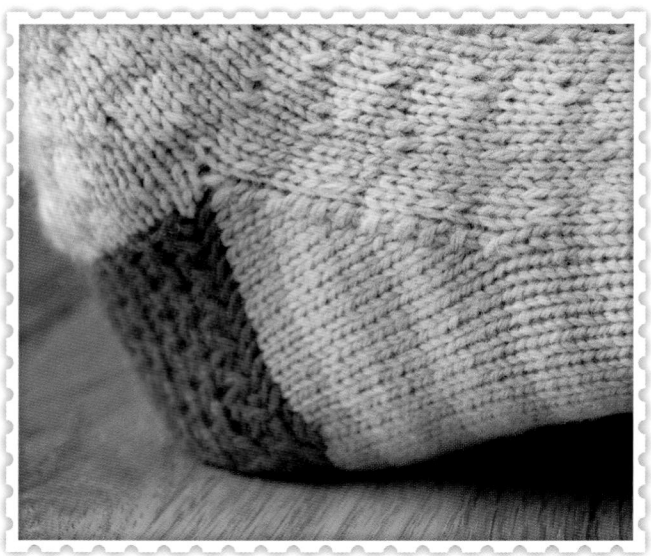

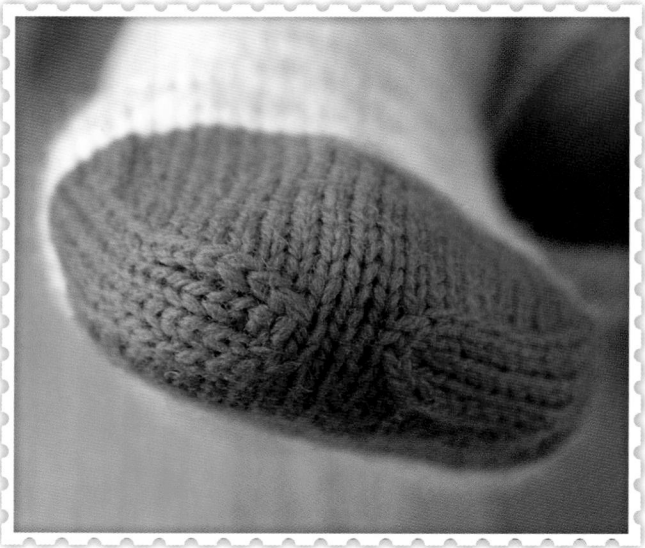

Finishing

Place sts of Needle 1 and Needle 2 on single needle for bottom of toe—6 sts each on 2 needles. Cut yarn, leaving a 12" (30.5 cm) tail. With tail threaded on a tapestry needle, use the Kitchener st (see page 44) to graft sts tog. Weave in loose ends. Block lightly.

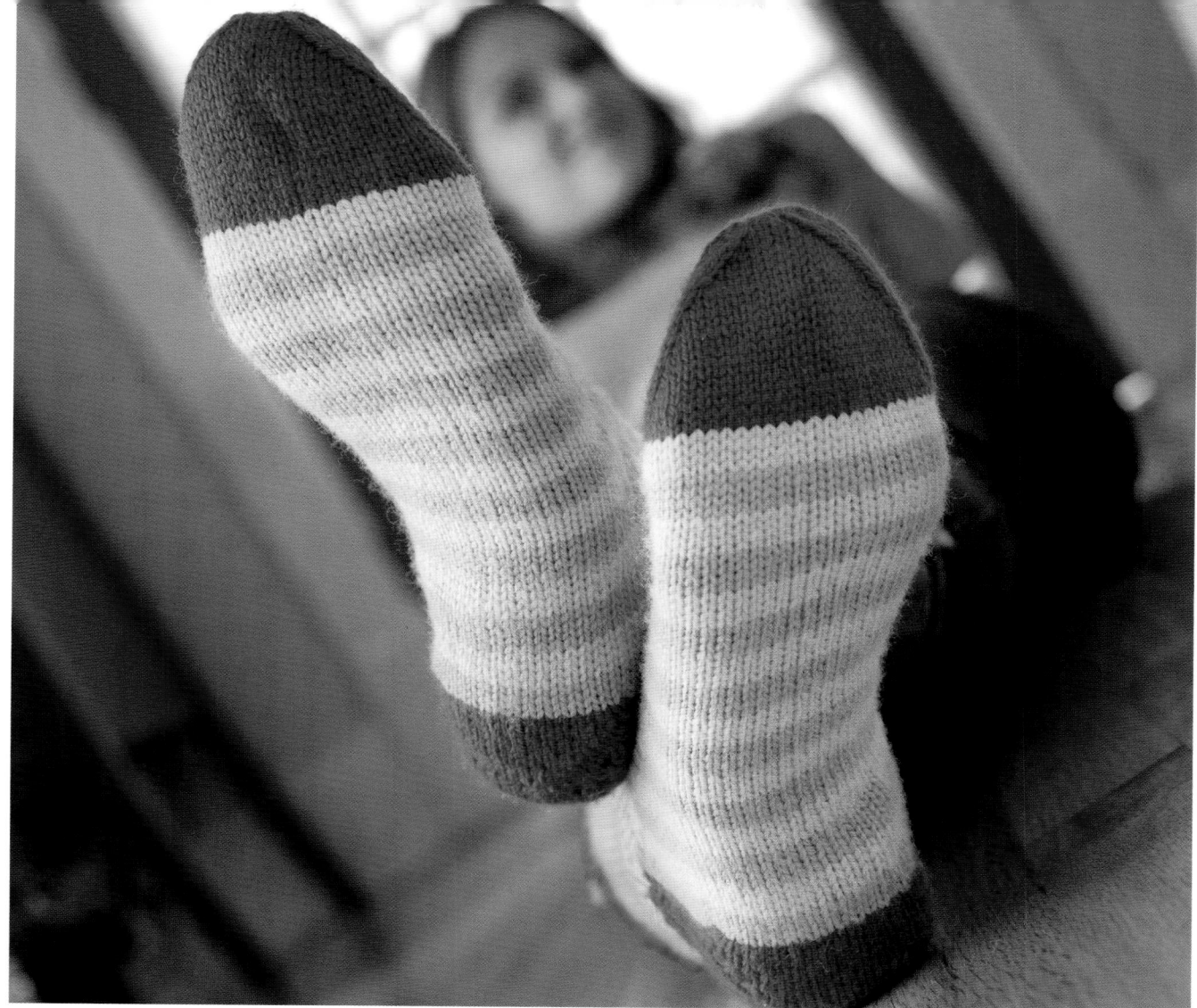

Yarn Note

Conceived as a heavier sock to be worn under boots, this pattern gives you permission to seek out more plump, earthy wool yarns that knit up at a heavier gauge than traditional sock yarns. But those woolier yarns tend to have a lower twist (hence lower abrasion resistance) and tend not to have any nylon for reinforcement. That's where the textured slipped-stitch heel pattern comes in handy by giving needed padding and strength. This particular yarn has a welcoming halo, especially after blocking, that can help conceal any puckers or contrasting color stranded along the background. Be aware that the smoother the yarn, the less halo and the more precise your colorwork will need to be. Because these socks have only a minimal amount of decorative ribbing at the top of the cuff, you'll want to stick with a wool or wool blend for maximum elasticity.

—*Clara Parkes*

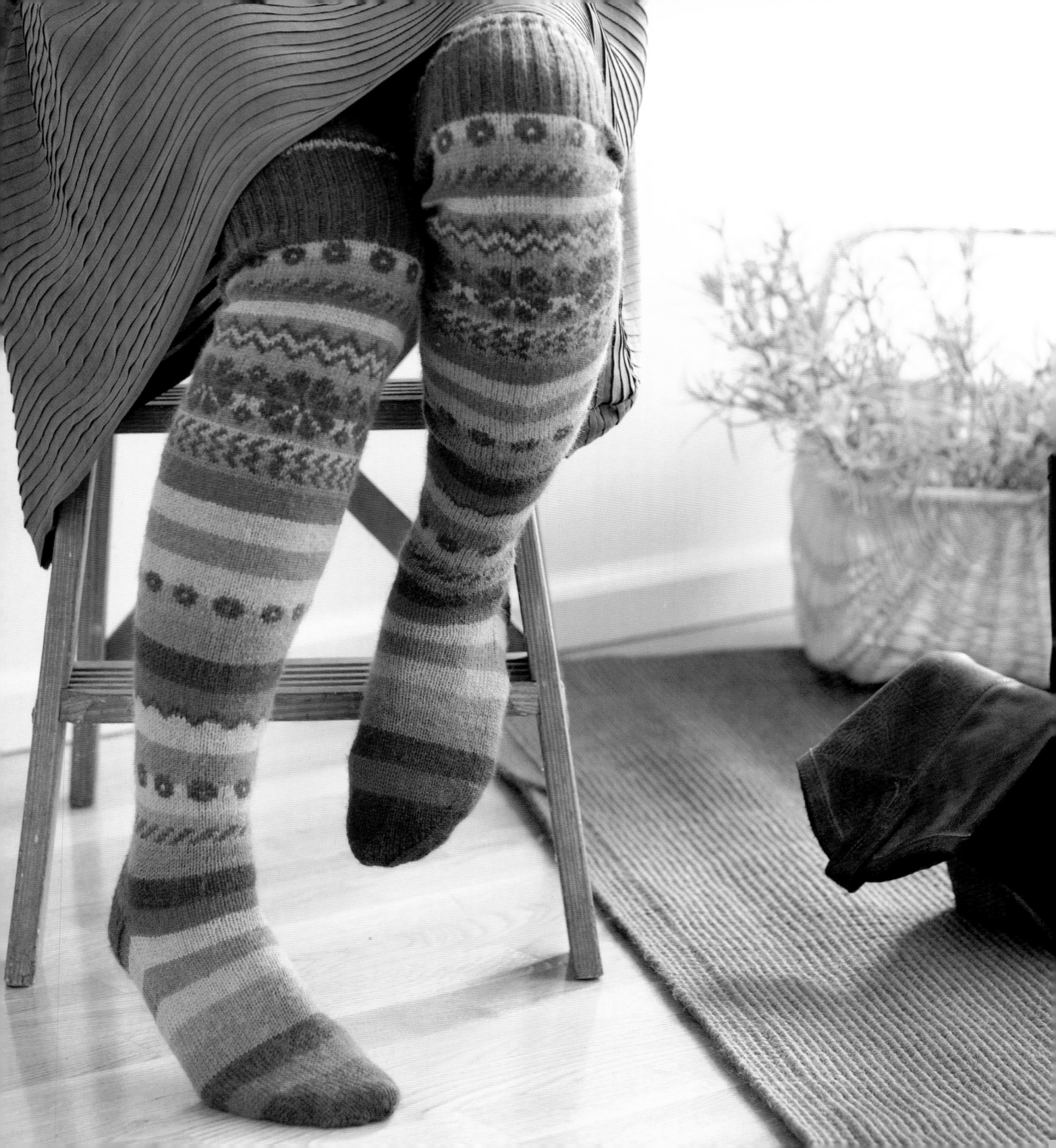

Thigh-High Stripes

DESIGNED BY *Deborah Newton*

finished size

About 7" (18 cm) foot circumference, 9¾" (25 cm) foot length from back of heel to tip of toe (with option for adjusting foot length), 7" (18 cm) ankle circumference immediately above start of heel flap, 9¾" (25 cm) calf circumference midway between end of ribbing and start of heel flap, 11½" (29 cm) circumference at upper leg just below ribbing, and 23½" (59.5 cm) leg length from top of ribbed cuff to base of heel.

yarn

Fingering weight (#1 Super Fine).

Shown here: Classic Elite Alpaca Sox Solids (60% alpaca, 20% merino, 20% nylon; 450 yd [411 m]/100 g): #1831 turquoise, #1876 coffee (brown), #1855 russet (orange), #1843 cornsilk (gold), #1881 granny smith (green), #1854 amethyst (purple), and #1825 rose, 1 skein each.

needles

Size U.S. 2 (2.75 mm): set of 5 double-pointed (dpn).

Adjust needle size if necessary to obtain the correct gauge.

notions

Marker (m); tapestry needle.

gauge

18 sts and 20 rnds = 2" (5 cm) in both solid-color St st and stranded St st colorwork patt, worked in rnds.

> In addition to the lively stripes and stranded colorwork, these long stockings are shaped to fit the contours of the leg."

When I design socks, I want them to be either as dramatic as possible or the simplest kind of mindless knitting. This pair obviously fits the first category! In addition to the lively stripes and stranded colorwork, these long stockings are shaped to fit the contours of the leg. For the best fit, measure your leg snugly because you want the sock to stretch slightly to stay on, and then adapt the stitch count to accommodate your own leg measurements. Change the spacing of the decreases if necessary so they follow the contour of the leg for a close fit. For a thin leg, you might start with fewer stitches than called for in the pattern and space the decreases farther apart; for a wide leg, you might begin with more stitches and work fewer, more widely spaced decreases in the upper leg, and more decreases closer together as you approach the ankle. If your socks slouch, make an elastic garter to tie around the upper leg and fold the ribbed cuff over it. Or make a row of eyelets at the base of ribbing and thread a length of knitted cord through them to be tied in a bow. Or wear a pair of textured tights underneath. Or enjoy the slouch!

notes

+ Take care to maintain the same gauge for in both the solid-color stockinette and stranded colorwork sections. If necessary, use a different needle size for the colorwork to keep the gauge consistent throughout.

+ Use the Fair Isle method of stranding the unused color behind the work as described in Designing with Stranded Colorwork on page 28.

+ Although it was not used for the socks shown here, consider the Jogless Jog technique (page 177) to minimize the "jogs" that can form when changing stripe colors. Be aware that this technique shifts the point where the round begins, so you will need to keep track of where the round originally started (centered on the back of the leg) for shaping purposes.

⊕ **DESIGN TIP:** *While outrageously complicated patterns can be fun and impressive in a sock, they can be more difficult to knit. Ease of execution is arguably an important component of sock design. Patterns that repeat for a relative small number of stitches or rows or ones that flow systematically from one row to the next are much easier to follow.*

Leg

With rose, CO 116 sts. Divide sts evenly among 4 dpn (29 sts on each needle), place marker (pm), and join for working in rnds, being careful not to twist sts. Rnd begins at back of leg. Working in k2, p2 rib, work 2 rnds rose, 3 rnds brown, 3 rnds gold. Change to brown and cont in established rib until piece measures 4" (10 cm) from CO, dec 3 sts evenly spaced on each needle on last rnd—104 sts rem; 26 sts on each needle. Work in St st as foll:

RND 1: Knit with gold.

RNDS 2–6: Work Rnds 1–5 of Chart A, using gold for background color in chart Rnds 1–3 and purple in chart Rnds 4 and 5.

RNDS 7–10: Knit 2 rnds purple, then 2 rnds turquoise.

RNDS 11–14: Work Rnds 1–4 of Chart B, using turquoise for background color in chart Rnds 1 and 2 and rust in chart Rnds 3 and 4.

RNDS 15–20: Knit 2 rnds rust, then 4 rnds green, dec 1 st on each of 2 needles in Rnd 20—102 sts rem.

RNDS 21–32: Work Rnds 1–12 of Chart C and in the last rnd (Rnd 12 of chart), dec 1 st on each on the 2 needles that did not have a dec in Rnd 20—100 sts rem; 25 sts on each needle.

RNDS 33–60: Work Rnds 1–28 of Chart D.

RND 61: (dec rnd) With rust, k1, ssk, knit to last 3 sts, k2tog, k1—1 st dec'd at each end of rnd.

RNDS 62–84: Knit 7 rnds rust, 8 rnds green, then 8 rnds rose and *at the same time* dec 1 st at each end of rnd (as in Rnd 61) in Rnds 67, 73, and 79—92 sts rem after Rnd 84.

RNDS 85–91: Knit 7 rnds gold, dec 1 st at each end of rnd in Rnds 85 and 91—88 sts rem after Rnd 91.

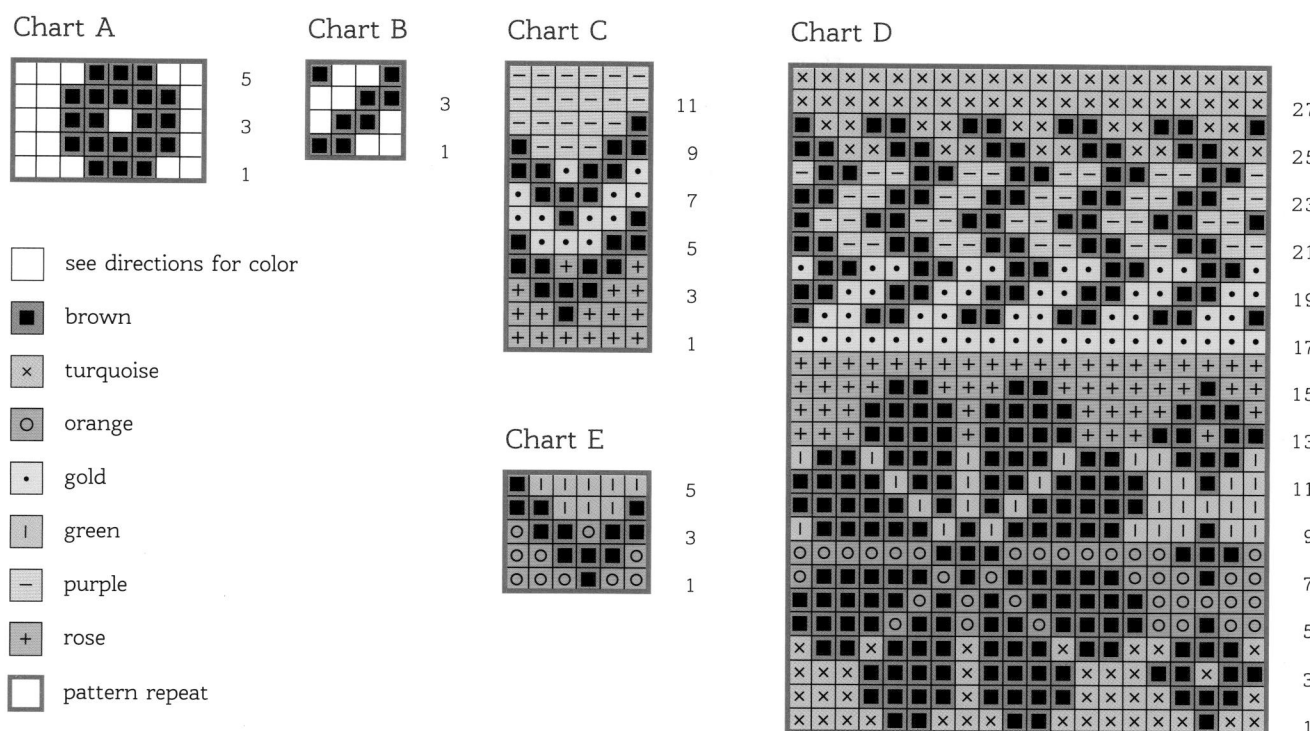

Chart A

Chart B

Chart C

Chart D

Chart E

see directions for color

■ brown

× turquoise

○ orange

• gold

| green

− purple

+ rose

pattern repeat

RNDS 92–96: Work Rnds 1–5 of Chart A, using gold for background color in chart Rnd 1 and purple in chart Rnds 2–5.

RNDS 97–100: Knit 4 rnds purple, dec 1 st at each end of rnd in Rnd 97—86 sts rem.

RNDS 101–121: Knit 8 rnds turquoise, 8 rnds brown, then 5 rnds rust, dec 1 st at each end of rnd in Rnds 103, 109, 115, and 121—78 sts rem after Rnd 121.

RNDS 122–126: Work Rnds 1–5 of Chart E.

RNDS 127–139: Knit 6 rnds green, then 7 rnds rose, dec 1 st at each end of rnd in Rnds 127, 133, and 139—72 sts rem after Rnd 139.

RNDS 140–144: Work Rnds 1–5 of Chart A, using rose for background color in chart Rnd 1 and gold in chart Rnds 2–5.

RNDS 145–151: Knit 4 rnds gold, then 3 rnds purple, dec 1 st at each end of rnd in Rnds 145 and 151—68 sts rem after Rnd 151.

RNDS 152–155: Work Rnds 1–4 of Chart B, using purple for background color every rnd.

RNDS 156–176: Knit 1 rnd purple, 8 rnds turquoise, 8 rnds brown, and 4 rnds rust, dec 1 st at each end of rnd in Rnds 157 and 163—64 sts rem after Rnd 163; piece measures about 21½" (54.5 cm) from CO.

Break yarn.

Heel

NOTE: Work with 3 dpn from here forward.

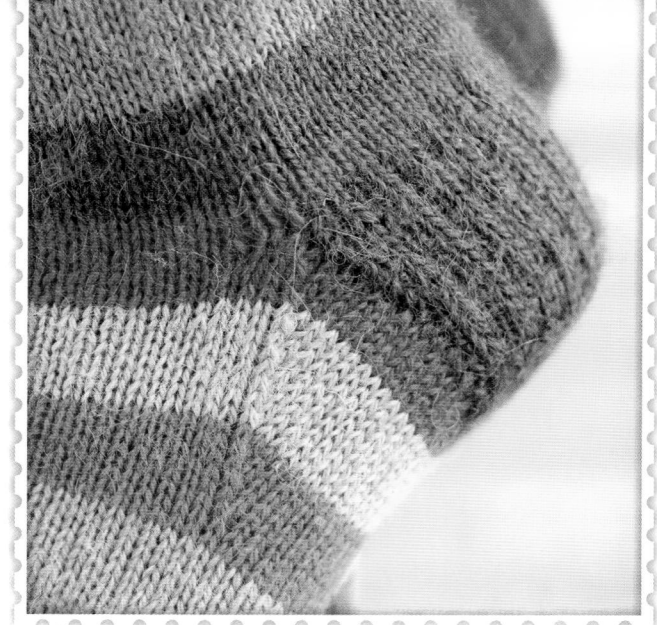

Place the first and last 16 sts of rnd on a single needle for heel—32 heel sts total; former end-of-rnd is in center of heel sts. Divide rem 32 sts evenly on 2 other needles to work later for instep.

HEEL FLAP

Join brown to beg of sts on heel needle with RS facing and work 32 heel sts back and forth in rows as foll:

ROW 1: (RS) *Sl 1 pwise with yarn in back (wyb), k1; rep from *.

ROW 2: (WS) Sl 1 pwise with yarn in front (wyf), p31.

Rep these 2 rows 15 more times, then work RS Row 1 once more—33 heel flap rows total; heel flap measures about 2" (5 cm).

TURN HEEL

With brown, work short-rows to shape heel as foll:

ROW 1: (WS) P18, p2tog, p1, turn work.

ROW 2: (RS) Sl 1 pwise wyb, k5, k2tog, k1, turn.

ROW 3: Sl 1 pwise wyf, purl to 1 st before gap formed on previous row, p2tog (1 st each side of gap), p1 turn.

ROW 4: Sl 1 pwise wyb, knit to 1 st before gap formed on previous row, k2tog (1 st each side of gap), k1, turn.

Rep Rows 3 and 4 until all sts have been worked, omitting the k1 or p1 after the dec on the last rep, and ending with a RS row—18 heel sts rem. Break yarn.

Yarn Note

These socks were knitted in a relaxed two-ply yarn that has a high percentage of alpaca (60%), a reasonable dusting of merino for loft and body (20%), and then a safe amount of nylon (20%) to compensate for the more vulnerable two-ply construction. Because of the yarn's more relaxed ply angle and gentle halo, you don't tend to see the flickering ply shadows that normally would appear in a tighter two-ply yarn. Instead, you get a lovely span of solid, smooth color with a gentle surface halo concealing all the behind-the-scenes techniques. Despite the generous 4" (10 cm) of k2, p2 ribbing at the top of the sock, even Deborah acknowledges that elasticity may be an issue. This sock has a lot of real estate that needs to be held up, and part of staying upright involves a snug fit, so heed her advice on measuring your leg and altering the pattern for the closest fit. Bottom line: Keep elasticity and surface texture in mind when choosing yarns for this sock. The less elastic the yarn, the more careful you'll need to be with the fit; the more elastic the yarn, the more leeway you have. Likewise, color patterning will be brighter and clearer in a smoother yarn than in a yarn with a softer surface. —*Clara Parkes*

GUSSET

Divide 18 heel sts evenly on 2 needles—9 sts on each needle. With RS facing, join rust to last 9 heel sts in center of heel. Pick up and knit sts along edges of heel flap (see Glossary) and rejoin for working in rnds as foll:

JOINING RND: With RS facing and Needle 1, k9 heel sts, then pick up and knit 16 sts along edge of heel flap; with Needle 2, knit 32 instep sts; with Needle 3, pick up and knit 16 sts on other side of heel flap, then k9 heel sts—82 sts total; 25 sts each on Needles 1 and 3, 32 instep sts on Needle 2.

RND 1: Knit.

RND 2: On Needle 1, knit to last 3 sts, k2tog, k1; on Needle 2, knit all instep sts; on Needle 3, k1, ssk, knit to end—2 sts dec'd.

RND 3: Knit—4-rnd rust stripe completed on sole of foot; 8-rnd rust stripe completed on instep.

Rep Rnds 2 and 3 for gusset 8 more times, working 8 rnds green, then 8 rnds rose—64 sts rem; 16 sts each on Needles 1 and 3, and 32 instep sts on Needle 2.

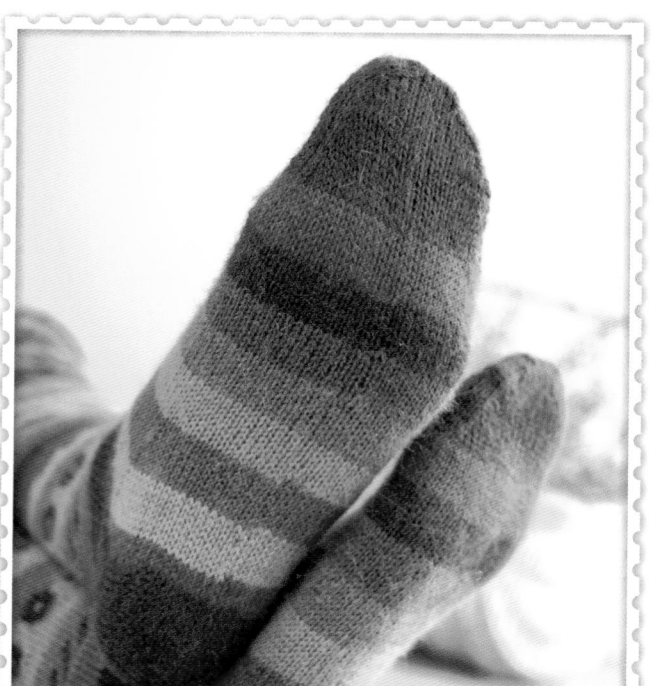

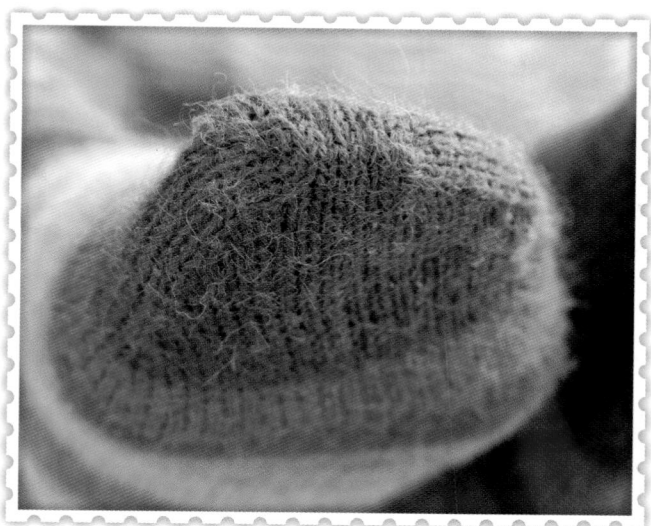

Foot

Work 8 rnds each of gold, purple, turquoise, brown, and rust—foot measures about 7½" (19 cm) from back of heel. If necessary, work even in St st with brown until foot measures 2¼" (5.5 cm) less than desired total length.

Toe

Change to brown if you have not already done so and dec at each side of foot as foll:

RND 1: On Needle 1, knit to last 3 sts, k2tog, k1; on Needle 2, k1, ssk, knit to last 3 sts, k2tog, k1; on Needle 3, k1, ssk, knit to end—4 sts dec'd.

RND 2: Knit.

Rep Rnds 1 and 2 for toe 11 more times—16 sts rem; 4 sts each on Needles 1 and 3, and 8 sts on Needle 2. Knit the sts from Needle 1 onto the end of Needle 3—8 sts each on 2 needles.

Finishing

Cut yarn, leaving a 12" (30.5 cm) tail. Thread tail on a tapestry needle and use the Kitchener st (see page 44) to graft the sts tog. Weave in loose ends. Block lightly.

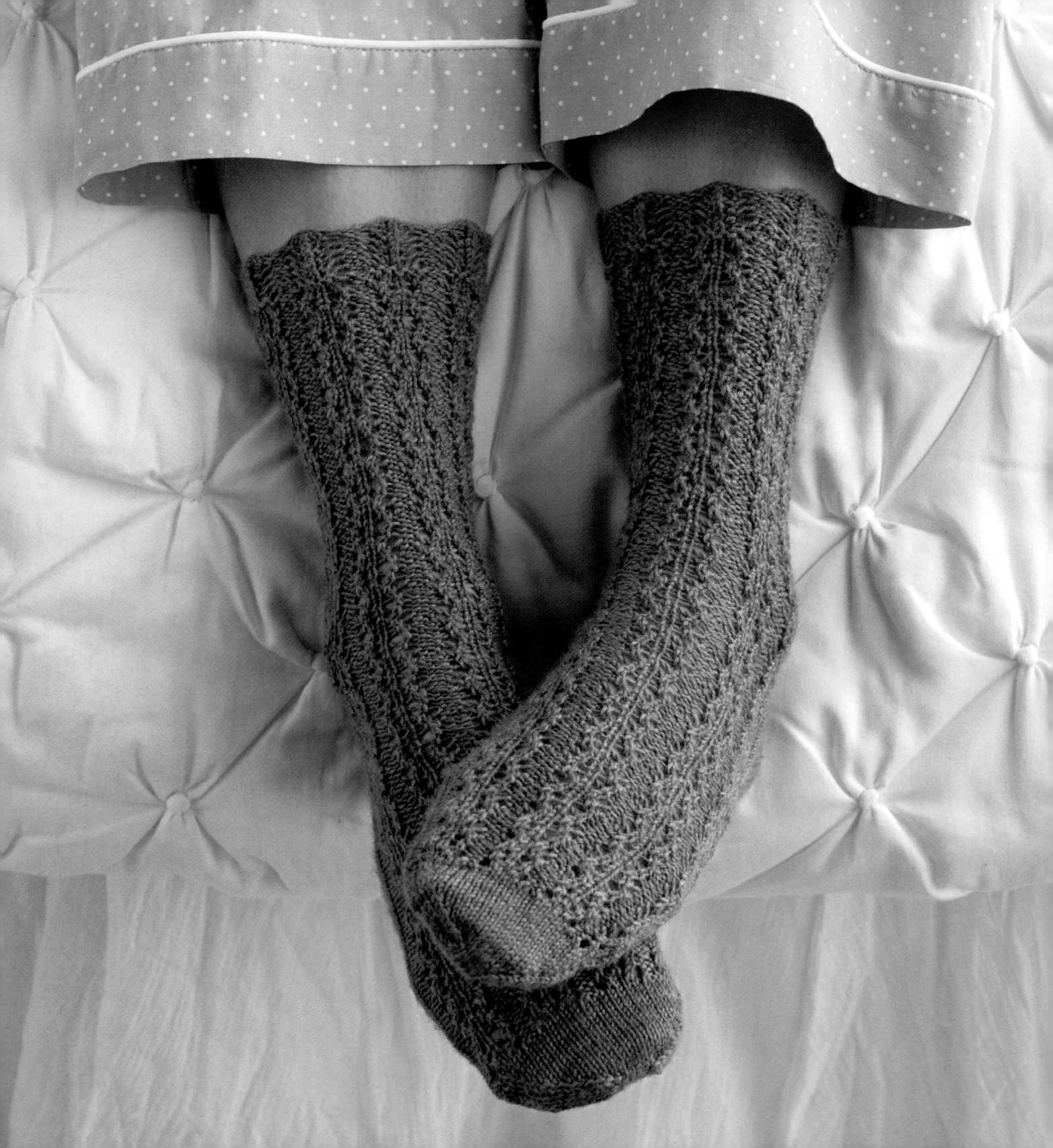

Rose Ribs

DESIGNED BY *Evelyn A. Clark*

finished size

About 7 (8¾)" (18 [22] cm) foot circumference, 9½ (10)" (24 [25.5] cm) foot length from back of heel to tip of toe (with option for adjusting foot length), and 9" (23 cm) leg length from top of leg to base of heel. To fit up to 8 (10)" (20.5 [25.5] cm) foot circumference. Socks shown measure 7" (18 cm) in circumference.

yarn

Fingering weight (#1 Super Fine).

Shown here: Lorna's Laces Shepherd Sock (80% superwash wool, 20% nylon; 215 yd [197 m]/2 oz [56.7 g]): blackberry, 2 skeins.

needles

Size U.S. 1 (2.25 mm): set of 5 double-pointed (dpn).

Adjust needle size if necessary to obtain the correct gauge.

notions

Marker (m); tapestry needle.

gauge

17½ sts and 26 rnds = 2" (5 cm) in St st, worked in rnds.

30 (37) sts of rose rib instep pattern measure 4 (5)" (10 [12.5] cm) wide, slightly stretched (see Notes).

For me, the joy in sock knitting comes from the minimalist aspect of designing a narrow, cylindrical piece of which only part is usually seen and even then mostly from a distance. Because socks often are my meditative knitting, I prefer small repeating motifs that are easily memorized and fun to work. I like to alternate lace with columns of purl stitches for a close fit, and I prefer a tight gauge for a snug feel. For me, sock knitting is all about comfort—comfort with the knitting and comfort with the wearing.

> For me, sock knitting is all about comfort—comfort with the knitting and comfort with the wearing."

The lace pattern in these socks was inspired by a collection of narrow embroidered flower ribbons. I always start by charting several motifs, and it was a happy surprise to see how the decreases curved the little lace flowers into ribbons of roses that could alternate with purl columns along the length of the socks. The simple rose rib pattern repeats over 7 stitches and 8 rounds, so it is easy to memorize. Once I decide on the lace pattern, I have fun planning a top border for the cuff that will flow seamlessly into the lace. However, the border in this project is optional if you would prefer to have uninterrupted lace panels running all the way to the top of the sock.

DESIGN TECHNIQUES

top-down construction, page 36

designing with lace, page 29

working with five double-pointed needles, page 12

any elastic cast-on, page 38

round heel, page 14

wedge toe, page 21

Kitchener stitch, page 44

notes

+ If you prefer to omit the scalloped border, work only Rounds 1 and 2 of the scalloped border pattern, then begin working in the rose rib lace pattern.

+ To check lengths, try the sock on or stretch it widthwise to the indicated circumference before measuring.

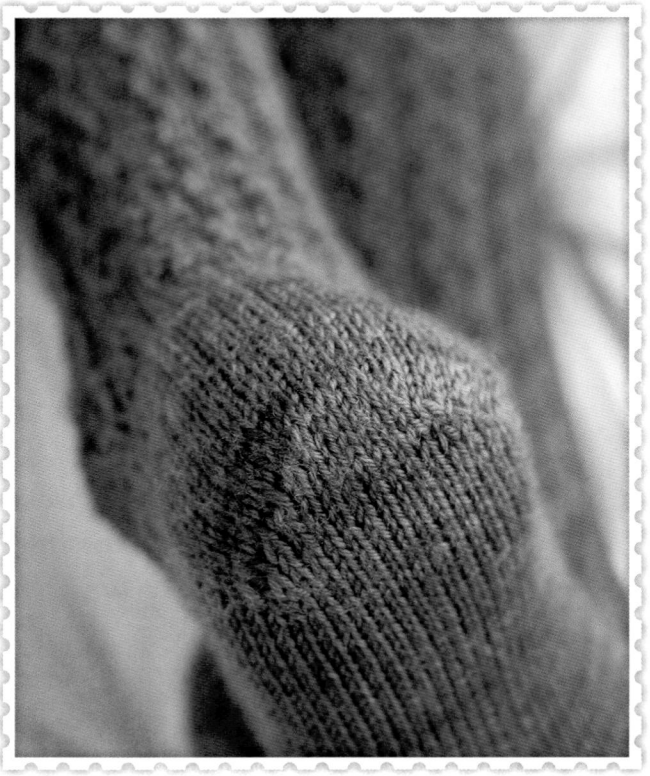

Stitch Guide

SCALLOPED BORDER (MULTIPLE OF 7 STS)

Rnd 1: Purl.

Rnd 2: *P2, k5; rep from *.

Rnd 3: *P2, yo, k1, sl 2 sts as if to k2tog, k1, p2sso, k1, yo; rep from *.

Rnds 4–12: Rep Rnds 2 and 3 four times, then work Rnd 2 once more.

Rnds 13 and 14: Rep Rnds 1 and 2.

ROSE RIB LACE (MULTIPLE OF 7 STS)

Rnd 1: *P2, yo, k2tog, k1, ssk, yo; rep from *.

Rnds 2, 4, and 6: *P2, k5; rep from *.

Rnd 3: *P2, k2tog, yo, k1, yo, ssk; rep from *.

Rnd 5: *P2, ssk, yo, k1, yo, k2tog; rep from *.

Rnd 7: *P2, yo, ssk, k1, k2tog, yo; rep from *.

Rnd 8: Rep Rnd 2.

Rep Rnds 1–8 for patt.

ROSE RIB INSTEP (WORKED OVER 30 [37] STS)

Rnd 1: [P2, yo, k2tog, k1, ssk, yo] 4 (5) times, p2.

Rnds 2, 4, and 6: [P2, k5] 4 (5) times, p2.

Rnd 3: [P2, k2tog, yo, k1, yo, ssk] 4 (5) times, p2.

Rnd 5: [P2, ssk, yo, k1, yo, k2tog] 4 (5) times, p2.

Rnd 7: [P2, yo, ssk, k1, k2tog, yo] 4 (5) times, p2.

Rnd 8: Rep Rnd 2.

Rep Rnds 1–8 for patt.

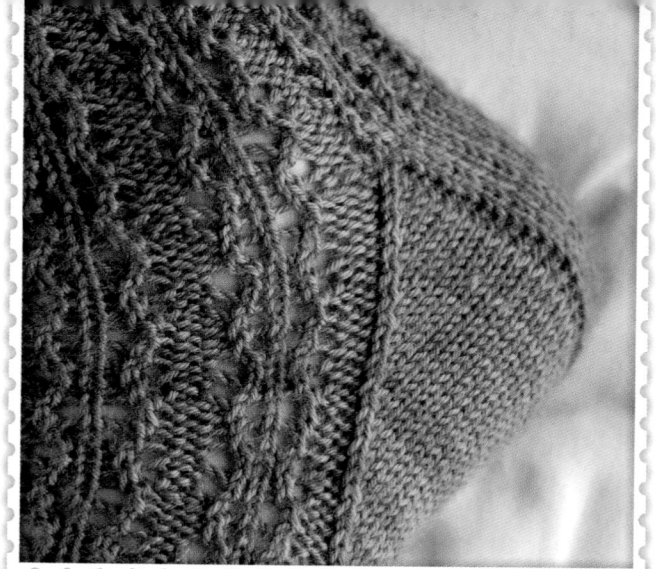

Leg

Loosely CO 56 (70) sts. Divide sts as evenly as possible on 4 dpn. Place marker (pm) and join for working in rnds, being careful not to twist sts.

Work Rnds 1–13 of scalloped border patt (see Notes)—piece measures about 1" (2.5 cm). Rep Rnds 1–8 of rose rib lace patt 9 times or to desired length, ending with Rnd 8 of patt—piece measures about 6½" (16.5 cm) from CO when stretched (see Notes).

Heel

DIVIDING ROW: (WS) With WS facing, sl 1 pwise with yarn in front (wyf), p25 (32) onto a single needle for heel, then divide 30 (37) rem instep sts on 2 needles to work later—26 (33) heel sts; with RS facing, instep sts should beg and end with p2.

HEEL FLAP

Work 26 (33) heel sts back and forth in rows as foll:

ROW 1: (RS) Sl 1, *k1, sl 1 pwise with yarn in back (wyb); rep from * to last 1 (2) st(s), k1 (2).

ROW 2: (WS) Sl 1 pwise wyf, purl to end.

Rep these 2 rows 16 more times for both sizes, then work RS Row 1 once more—36 rows total, including dividing row; 18 chain sts at each selvedge; heel flap measures about 2½" (6.5 cm).

TURN HEEL

Work short-rows as foll:

ROW 1: (WS) Sl 1 pwise wyf, p14 (17), p2tog, p1, turn work.

ROW 2: (RS) Sl 1 pwise wyb, k5 (4), ssk, k1, turn.

ROW 3: Sl 1 pwise wyf, purl to gap formed on previous row, p2tog (1 st each side of gap), p1, turn.

ROW 4: Sl 1 pwise wyb, knit to gap formed on previous row, ssk (1 st each side of gap), k1, turn.

Rep Rows 3 and 4 until all heel sts have been worked, ending with WS Row 4—16 (19) sts rem.

GUSSET

Pick up and knit sts along selvedges of heel flap (see Glossary) and rejoin for working in rnds as foll:

JOINING RND: With Needle 1, pick up and knit 19 sts along selvedge of heel flap; with Needle 2 work Rnd 1 of rose rib instep patt over 30 (37) instep sts; with Needle 3, pick up and knit 19 sts along other selvedge of heel flap, then knit the first 8 (10) heel sts; slip rem 8 (10) heel sts onto beg of Needle 1—84 (94) sts total; 27 (28) sts on Needle 1, 30 (37) instep sts on Needle 2, and 27 (29) sts on Needle 3.

RND 1: On Needle 1, k8 (9), k19 picked-up sts through back loops (tbl); on Needle 2, work Rnd 2 of instep patt; on Needle 3, k19 picked-up sts tbl, k8 (10).

RND 2: On Needle 1, knit to last 2 sts, k2tog; on Needle 2, work instep sts in established patt; on Needle 3, ssk, knit to end—2 sts dec'd.

RND 3: On Needle 1, knit; on Needle 2, work instep sts in established patt; on Needle 3, knit.

Rep Rnds 2 and 3 for gusset 13 (11) more times—56 (70) sts rem; 13 (16) sts on Needle 1, 30 (37) instep sts on Needle 2, and 13 (17) sts on Needle 3.

Foot

Working sts on Needles 1 and 3 in St st, cont instep sts on Needle 2 in established patt until piece measures 8¼" (22 cm) from back of heel for both sizes, or 1¼ (1¾)" (3.2 [4.5] cm) less than desired total foot length (see Notes), ending with Rnd 8 of instep patt.

NOTE: For a deeper St st toe, discontinue instep lace patt sooner and work all sts in St st to the desired length before starting the toe.

Toe

Redistribute sts on next rnd as foll: on Needle 1, k13 (16), then k1 from beg of Needle 2; on Needle 2, k28 (35), then transfer last instep st to Needle 3; on Needle 3: k14 (18)—14 (17) sts on Needle 1, 28 (35) sts on Needle 2, and 14 (18) sts on Needle 3.

Dec each side of toe as foll:

RND 1: On Needle 1, knit to last 3 sts, k2tog, k1; on Needle 2, k1, ssk, knit to last 3 sts, k2tog, k1; on Needle 3, k1, ssk, knit to end—4 sts dec'd.

RND 2: Knit.

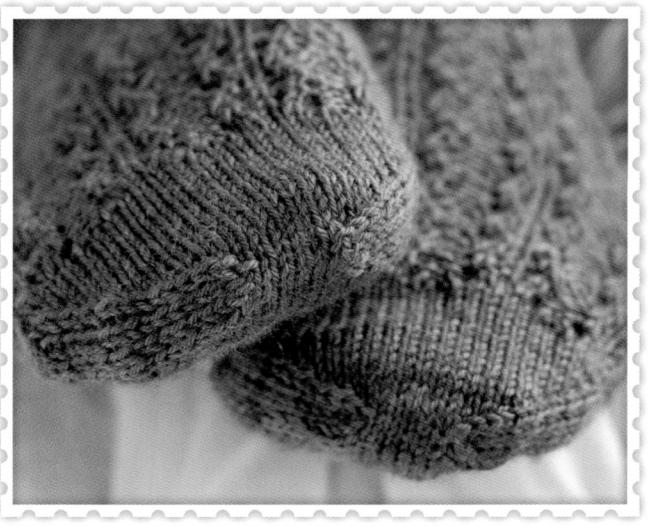

Rep Rnds 1 and 2 for toe 5 (8) more times—32 (34) sts rem. Then rep Rnd 2 only (i.e., dec every rnd) 4 (5) times—16 (14) sts rem; 4 (3) sts on Needle 1, 8 (7) sts on Needle 2, 4 sts on Needle 3 for both sizes.

Finishing

Knit sts from Needle 1 onto the end of Needle 3—8 (7) sts each on 2 needles. Cut yarn, leaving a 12" (30.5 cm) tail. Thread tail on a tapestry needle and use the Kitchener st (see page 44) to graft rem sts tog. Weave in loose ends. Block lightly.

Yarn Note

A smooth, well-rounded traditional four-ply sock yarn gives bright, clean stitch definition to the narrow stocking-stitch lace motif that Evelyn chose to run between vertical ribs of two purl stitches. The ribbing and yarnovers add spring and openness to the sock fabric while also encouraging the lace motif to pop from the purl background. The 20% nylon content in this particular yarn gives welcome reinforcement to the open lace pattern and fine, smooth stockinette along the bottom of the foot and toe. A springy two-ply yarn would likely produce equally attractive results. Just be aware that such a yarn would render the stockinette with a slightly pebbled surface texture and add more openness to the lace pattern. Keep the ply angle in mind, too: The more perpendicular the ply, the bouncier the yarn and the deeper the ply shadows will be; the more parallel the yarn's ply, the more fluid and smooth the fabric will be—although lower twist may also make it more vulnerable to abrasion. The pattern is simple enough that you could get away with a bit more color variation, although a solid or semisolid would display the stitch motif most clearly.

—Clara Parkes

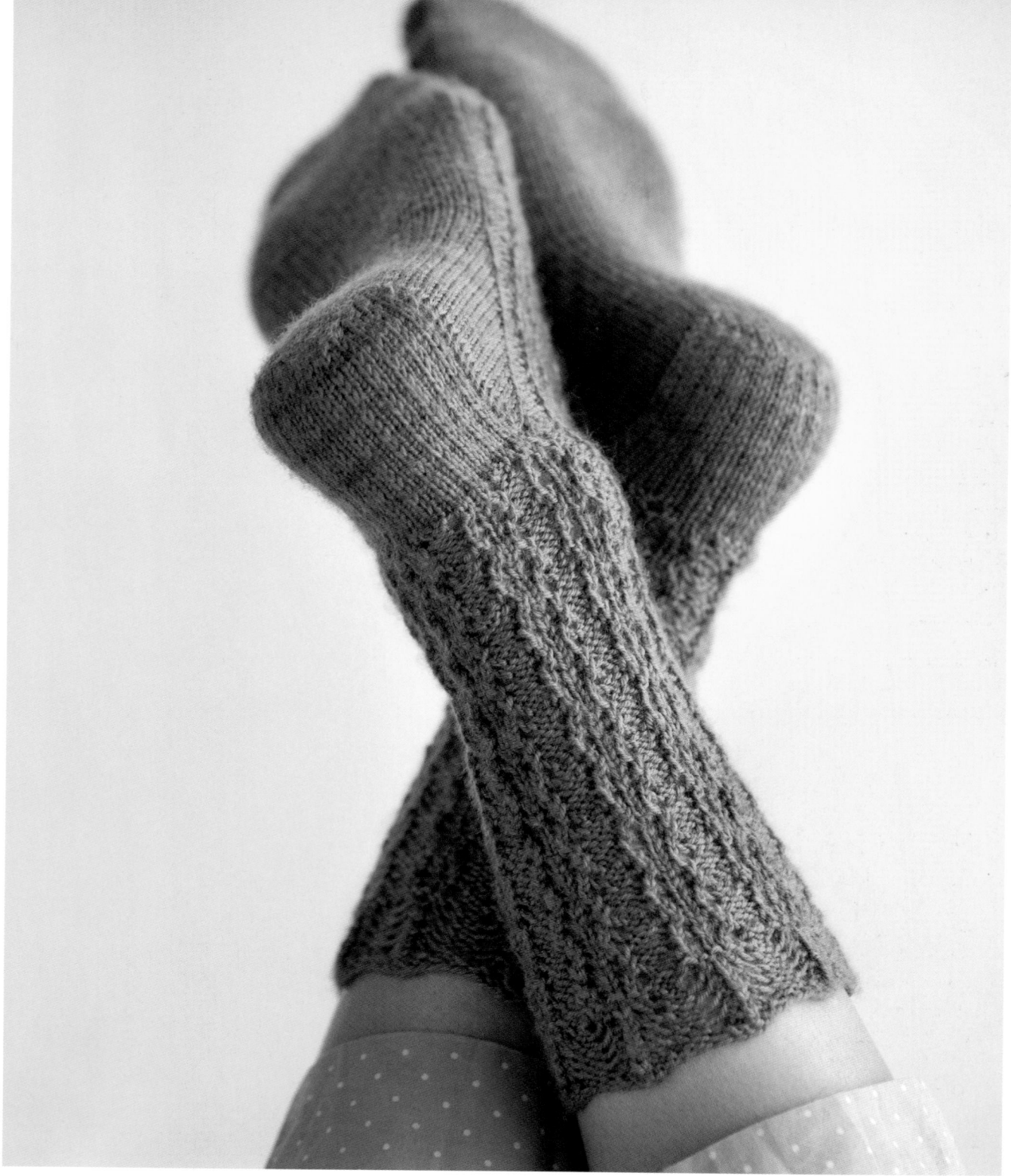

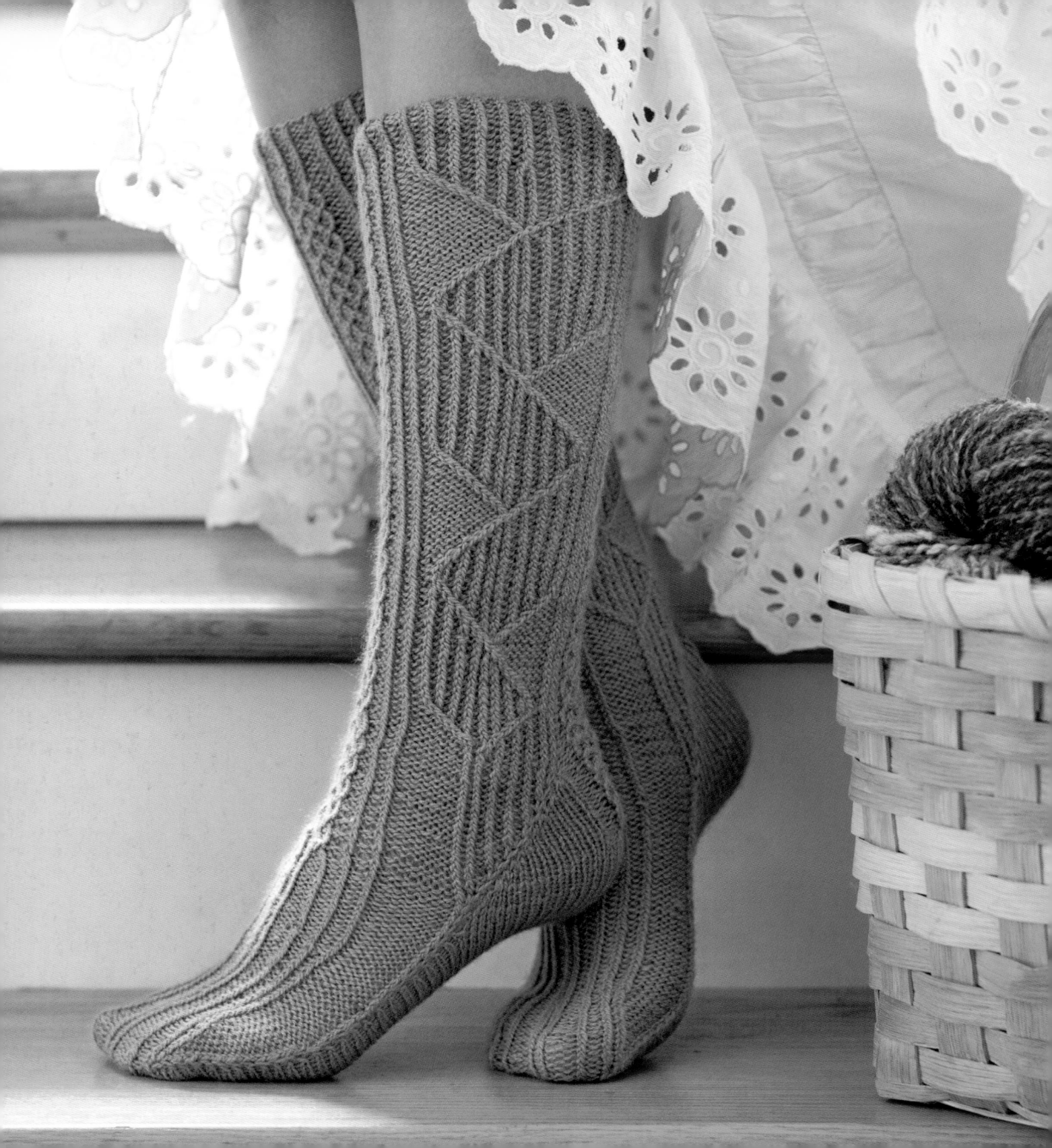

Twisted-Stitch Stockings

DESIGNED BY *Meg Swansen*

finished size

About 7¼" (18.5 cm) foot circumference, 8" (20.5 cm) foot length from back of heel to tip of toe (will stretch to about 9¼" [23.5 cm] and can be adjusted), and 15" (38 cm) leg length from top of cuff to base of heel.

yarn

Sportweight (#2 Fine).

Shown here: Finnish Satakieli (100% wool; 360 [329 m]/100 g): #631 gray-blue, 2 skeins.

needles

Size U.S. 4 (3.5 mm): two 24" (60 cm) circular (cir).

Adjust needle size if necessary to obtain the correct gauge.

notions

Markers (m); waste yarn holder for stitches; coordinating nylon thread for reinforcing toe, foot, and sole (optional); sharp-point sewing needle; tapestry needle.

gauge

19 sts and 16 rnds = 2" (5 cm) in traveling stitch patterns from charts, unstretched and worked in rnds.

14 sts and 20 rnds = 2" (5 cm) in St st, worked in rnds.

The foot shaping on this stocking is Elizabeth Zimmermann's Moccasin Sock design from the early 1970s. In this construction, half a stitch can be snipped along the initial pick-up around the instep, the round unpicked, and the bottom of the foot will fall off, leaving the instep intact. We liken it to retreading a tire.

> *Half a stitch can be snipped along the initial pick-up around the instep, the round unpicked, and the bottom of the foot will fall off, leaving the instep intact."*

For motifs, I turned to my mother's sheepfold pattern and added a classic twisted-stitch honeycomb motif fore and aft that continues along the instep and down the back of the heel. I had to juggle the initial ribbing a bit to sneak in a few increases at the start of the main patterns so the ribbing would flow sensibly from cuff to leg. Worked from the top down, these stockings are shaped with decreases to the ankle. The patterned instep is worked back and forth to the shaped toe, then the center heel stitches are worked back and forth in ever-widening rows for the gusset as a picked-up selvedge stitch is incorporated at the end of each row. Stitches are knitted up around the foot and the moccasin sole is worked in rounds from the "footprint outline" in toward the center of the sole, with heel and toe shaped along the way. Finally, the live stitches are grafted along the center bottom of the foot.

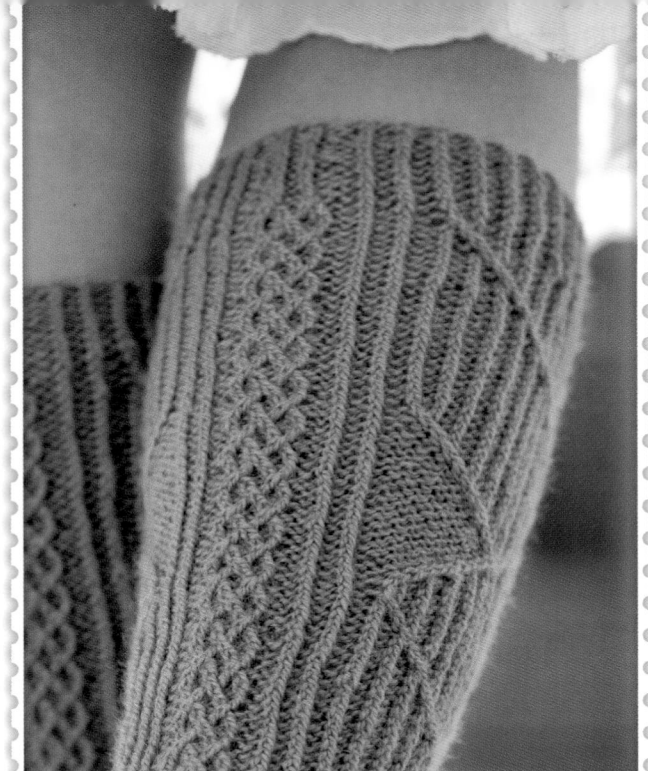

➕ **DESIGN TIP:** *To ensure that the legs and feet are the same length on each sock of a pair, count the number of rows between the cuff and the top of the heel for the leg and count the number of rows between the gusset pick-up round and the first toe decrease for the foot.*

Stitch Guide

RIGHT TWIST (KNIT OVER KNIT)

On RS rows and all rnds: Without removing sts from needle, insert right needle between next 2 sts on left needle from front to back, knit into the back of the second st, then knit into the back of the first st. Sl both sts from left needle tog.

On WS rows: Insert right needle from right to left into the second st on right needle and sl both sts from right needle, allowing the first st to fall free to the back of the work for a moment. Insert the left needle into the loose st from left to right, then sl the st on the right needle back to the left needle. Work the two sts in their new order as [p1tbl] 2 times.

LEFT TWIST (KNIT OVER KNIT)

On RS rows and all rnds: Sl 2 sts to right needle pwise, then insert left needle from left to right into the second st on right needle and sl both sts from right needle, allowing the first st to fall free to the back of the work for a moment. Insert the right needle into the loose st from right to left and replace the st on the left needle. Work the two sts in their new order as [k1tbl] 2 times.

On WS rows: Rearrange sts on left needle as for a RS row or rnd, but work the two sts in their new order as [p1tbl] 2 times.

RIGHT TRAVELER (KNIT OVER PURL)

On RS rows and all rnds: Without removing sts from needle, insert right needle between next 2 sts on left needle from front to back, knit into the back of the second st, then bring the yarn under the tip of the left needle to the front and purl the first st. Sl both sts from left needle tog.

On WS rows: Insert right needle from right to left into the second st on right needle and sl both sts from right needle, allowing the first st to fall free to the back of the work for a moment. Insert the left needle into the loose st from left to right, then sl the st on the right needle back to the left needle. Work the 2 sts in their new order as k1, p1tbl.

LEFT TRAVELER (KNIT OVER PURL)

On RS rows and all rnds: Sl 2 sts to right needle pwise, then insert left needle from left to right into the second st on right needle and sl both sts from right needle, allowing the first st to fall free to the back of the work for a moment. Insert the right needle into the loose st from right to left and replace the st on the left needle. Work the two sts in their new order.

On WS rows: Rearrange sts on left needle as for a RS row or rnd, but work the 2 sts in their new order as p1tbl, k1.

Leg

Using an elastic method (page 38), CO 72 sts. Divide sts evenly on 2 cir needles—36 sts on each needle. Place marker (pm) and join for working in rnds, being careful not to twist sts.

NEXT RND: Working Rib Rnd of all charts (pages 90 and 91), work 15 sts according to Chart A, pm, 21 sts according to Chart B, pm, 15 sts according to Chart A, pm, 21 sts according to Chart C.

Rep the last rnd 9 more times—10 rib rnds total; piece measures about 1¼" (3.2 cm).

NEXT RND: Working Inc Rnd of all charts, work 15 sts of Chart A while inc them to 18 sts, work 21 sts of Chart B while inc them to 22 sts, work 15 sts of Chart A while inc them to 18 sts, and work 21 sts of Chart C while inc them to 22 sts—80 sts.

Work in established chart patts for 83 rnds as foll: For Chart A, work Rnds 1–4 of patt 20 times, then work Rnds 1–3 once more; for Charts B and C, work Rnds 1–83, dec as shown on chart—64 sts rem; 18 sts in each Chart A section; 14 sts each for Charts B and C; piece measures about 11½" (29 cm) from CO.

Moccasin Foot

NOTE: From here, cont working Chart A on instep and at center of heel as established, but rep the Foot Row every row for Charts B and C.

INSTEP

SET-UP RND: (Rnd 4 of Chart A) Ssk, work 11 sts in patt, place last 8 sts just worked (center sts of Chart A) on waste yarn holder to work later for back of heel, work in patt to last 2 sts, k2tog—54 sts rem. Place all sts on one cir needle.

Work instep back and forth in rows, using the knitting (and purling) back-backward technique (page 94) if desired, as foll:

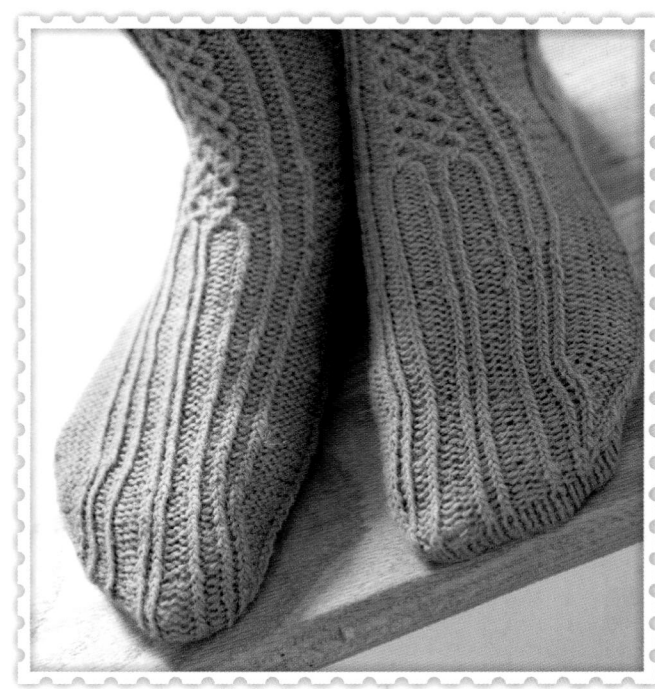

ROW 1: (WS) Work even in patt.

ROW 2: (dec row; RS) Ssk, work in patt to last 2 sts, k2tog—2 sts dec'd.

Rep Rows 1 and 2 ten more times, then work WS Row 1 once more, ending with Row 3 of Chart A—32 sts rem; 18 center sts in patt from Chart A; 7 sts from Chart B or C at each side. Mark each end of last row completed to indicate end of instep shaping.

NEXT ROW: (RS) K1tbl, p7, [k1tbl, p1] 3 times, p1, [k1tbl] 2 times, p1, [p1, k1tbl] 3 times, p7, k1tbl.

NEXT ROW: (WS) P1tbl, k7, [p1tbl, k1] 3 times, k1, [p1tbl, k1] 2 times, k1, [k1, p1tbl] 3 times, k7, p1tbl.

Rep the last 2 rows until piece measures 2" (5 cm) from marked row, or about 6" (15 cm) less than desired total foot length, ending with a WS row.

ᛚ	k1tbl on RS rows and all rnds; p1tbl on WS rows
·	p on RS rows and all rnds; k on WS rows
∕	k2tog on RS rows and all rnds; p2tog on WS rows
∖	ssk on RS rows and all rnds; ssp on WS rows
▨	no stitch

2	k1f&b (see Glossary)
2	p1f&b (see Glossary)
⊠	right twist (see Stitch Guide)
⊠	left twist (see Stitch Guide)
◤⊠	right traveler (see Stitch Guide)
◥⊠	left traveler (see Stitch Guide)

Chart B

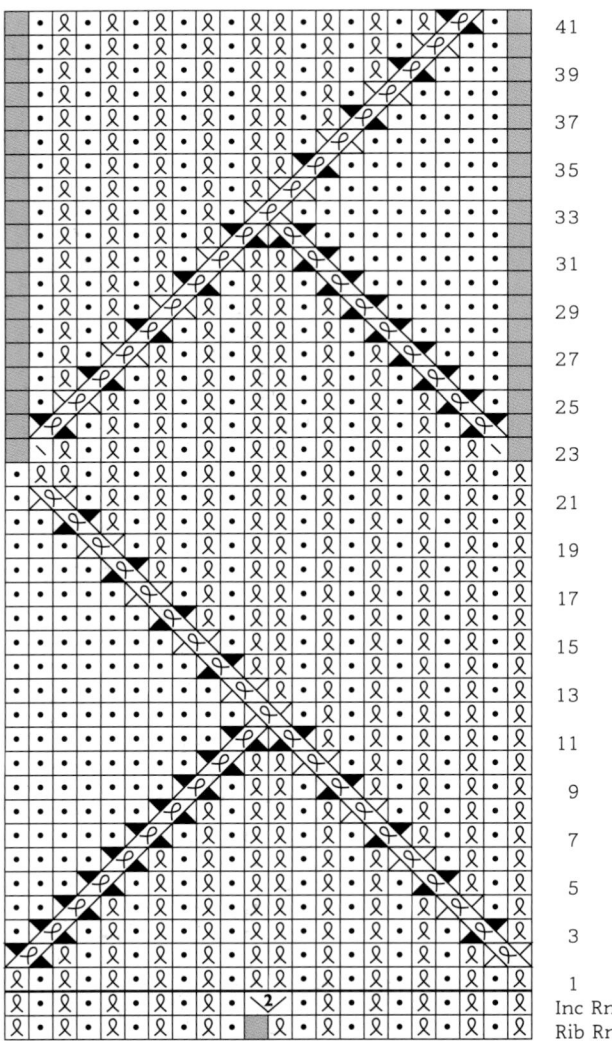

41
39
37
35
33
31
29
27
25
23
21
19
17
15
13
11
9
7
5
3
1
Inc Rnd
Rib Rnd

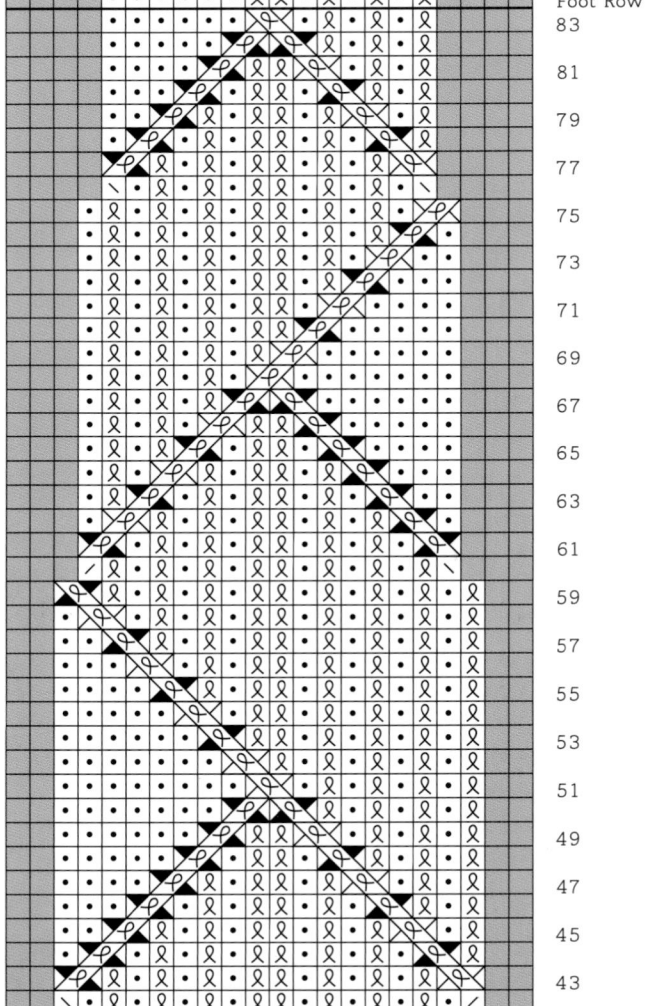

Foot Row
83
81
79
77
75
73
71
69
67
65
63
61
59
57
55
53
51
49
47
45
43

Chart A

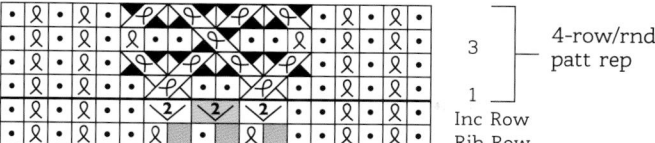

3
1

4-row/rnd
patt rep

Inc Row
Rib Row

Chart C

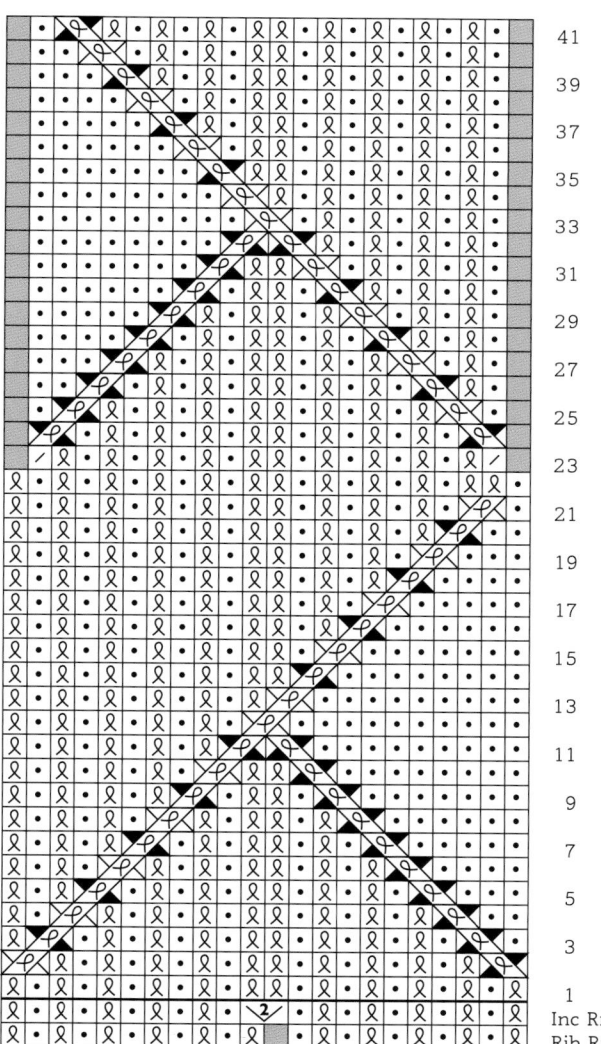

41
39
37
35
33
31
29
27
25
23
21
19
17
15
13
11
9
7
5
3
1

Inc Rnd
Rib Rnd

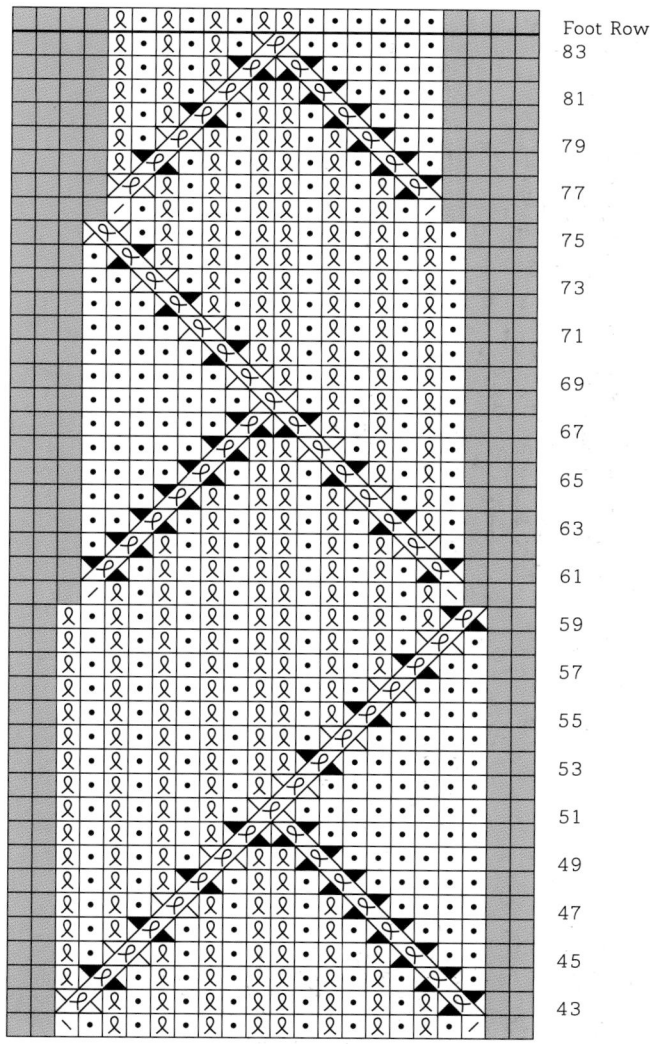

Foot Row
83
81
79
77
75
73
71
69
67
65
63
61
59
57
55
53
51
49
47
45
43

NEXT ROW: (RS) K1tbl, p7, k1tbl, k2tog, p1, k1tbl, p2, [k1tbl] 2 times, p2, k1tbl, p1, ssk, k1tbl, p7, k1tbl—30 sts rem.

NEXT ROW: (WS) P1tbl, k7, [p1tbl] 2 times, k1, p1tbl, k2, [p1tbl] 2 times, k2, p1tbl, k1, [p1tbl] 2 times, k7, p1tbl.

NEXT ROW: (RS) K1tbl, p7, [k1tbl] 2 times, p1, k1tbl, p2, [k1tbl] 2 times, p2, k1tbl, p1, [k1tbl] 2 times, p7, k1tbl.

Rep the last 2 rows until instep measures 3¾" (9.5 cm) from marked row, or about 4¼" (11 cm) less than desired total foot length, ending with a WS row.

Shape Toe

Join reinforcing nylon if desired.

NEXT ROW: (RS) K1tbl, p6, k2tog, pm, k1tbl, p1, k1tbl, p2, [k1tbl] 2 times, p2, k1tbl, p1, k1tbl, pm, ssk, p6, k1tbl—28 sts rem.

NEXT ROW: (WS) Work sts as they appear, working decs of previous row tbl.

DEC ROW: (RS) Work in patt to 2 sts before first m, k2tog, slip marker (sl m), work in patt to next m, sl m, ssk, work in patt to end—2 sts dec'd.

Rep the last 2 rows 7 more times, removing m and working 2 sts tog at each end in final dec row and ending with a WS row—12 sts rem; toe measures about 2¼" (5.5 cm) from start of toe shaping; instep measures about 6" (15 cm) from marked row. Leave sts on needle.

BACK OF HEEL

Place 8 held heel sts on empty needle and rejoin yarn (and reinforcing nylon if desired) with RS facing. The back of the heel is worked back and forth in short-rows while picking up sts along the shaped instep selvedges between the base of the heel sts and the marked row at end of instep shaping (about 1 st picked up for every 2 rows at each side).

ROW 1: (RS) Pick up and purl (see Glossary) 1 st in corner between held sts and instep, work Row 1 of Chart A across 8 sts, pick up and purl 1 st in corner—10 sts.

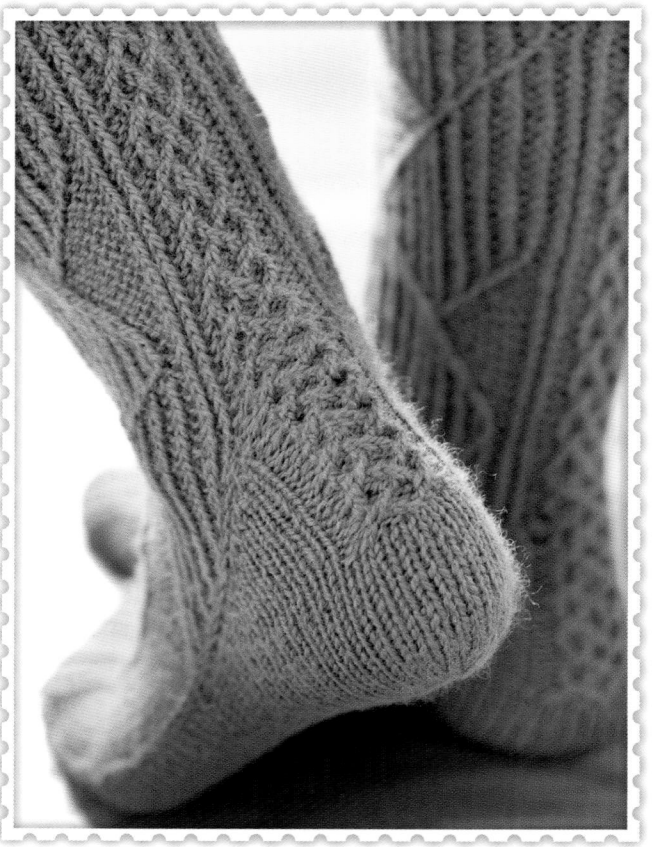

ROW 2: (WS) K1, work 8 sts in patt, k1.

ROW 3: Pick up and purl 1 st from instep selvedge, p1, work 8 sts in patt, p1, pick up and purl 1 st from instep selvedge—12 sts.

ROW 4: K2, work 8 sts in patt, k2.

ROW 5: Pick up and knit 1 st from instep selvedge, pm, p2, work 8 sts in patt, p2, pm, pick up and knit 1 st from instep selvedge—14 sts.

ROW 6: Purl to m, sl m, k2, work 8 sts in patt, k2, sl m, purl to end.

ROW 7: Pick up and knit 1 st from instep selvedge, knit to m, sl m, p2, work 8 sts in patt, p2, sl m, knit to end, pick up and knit 1 st from instep selvedge—2 sts inc'd.

ROWS 8–23: Rep Rows 6 and 7 eight more times, ending with a RS row and removing m in last row—32 heel sts.

BOTTOM OF FOOT

Join reinforcing nylon if desired.

PICK-UP RND: With RS facing and needle holding 32 heel sts (using reinforcing nylon if desired), pick up and knit 29 sts along instep selvedge to held toe sts (about 2 sts for every 3 rows); with second needle, knit 12 toe sts, pick up and knit 29 sts along instep selvedge to heel sts (about 2 sts for every 3 rows)—102 sts total; 61 sts on first needle, 41 sts on second needle.

NEXT RND: On first needle, k23, pm, k32, transfer last 6 sts to beg of next needle; on second needle, k6 transferred sts, k12 toe sts, k6, pm, k23, transfer the first 9 sts of rnd to end of second needle, k9 transferred sts—46 sts on first needle, 56 sts on second needle; marked 14 sts at beg of first needle are center 14 heel sts; marked 24 sts at beg of second needle are 12 toe sts with 6 sts on each side.

Knit 11 rnds—piece measures about 1¼" (3.2 cm) from pick-up rnd.

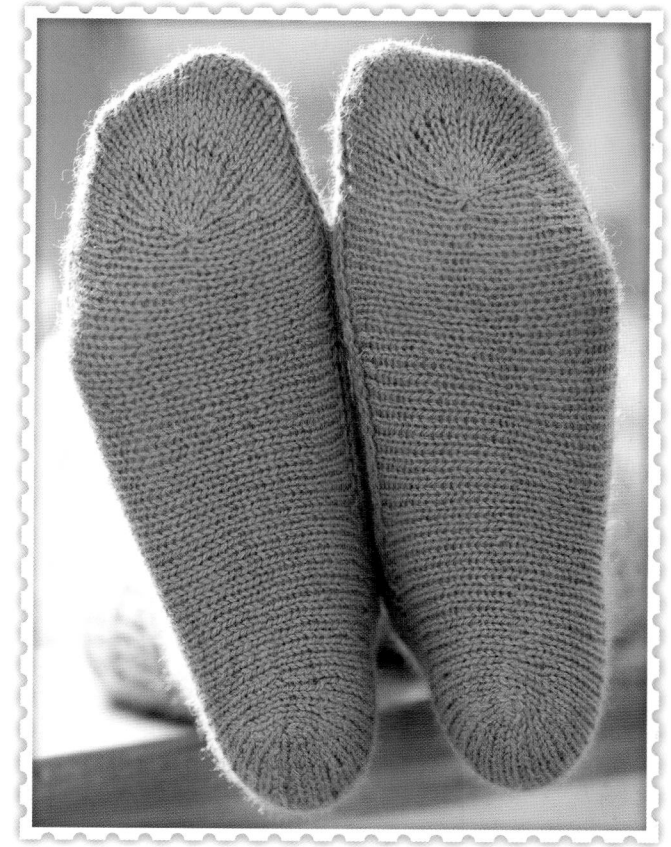

Yarn Note

This sock was designed for Satakieli, a two-ply yarn from Finland that begs for colorwork but also makes a hearty, lovely sock. While lacking the delicacy and bounce of merino wool, Satakieli makes up for these shortcomings with a glossy halo and longer, stronger fibers—both of which translate into a longer-wearing heirloom sock. But just to be sure, Meg suggests you add a strand of nylon to the heel, footbed, and toe. If you're working with a wool/nylon sock yarn blend, you won't have to add the reinforcing nylon unless you're particularly brutal on your socks, and even then the foot can be easily reknitted if it wears out. Keep the yarn's twist and ply in mind as you consider other yarns. By virtue of its two plies,

Satakieli tends to produce slightly nuanced stitches with a hint more shadow than a well-rounded and tightly twisted three- or four-ply yarn. The interplay of shadow and halo add greater depth to the sculptural stitchwork that runs along the top of the foot and up the leg. Elasticity isn't as much of a concern here because the stitch motifs make ample use of twisted-stitch ribbing. Just remember that the tighter the twist and smoother the yarn, the sharper the stitch pattern will be and the less blur you'll have between stitches. You'll want to choose either solid or semisolid color to let the stitch pattern do all the talking.

—*Clara Parkes*

NOTE: For a wider foot, work more rnds here; every extra rnd will add about ¼" (6 mm) to the foot circumference because each rnd counts as 2 rows across the bottom of the foot.

Shape Toe and Heel

DEC RND 1: On first needle, knit to end; on second needle, [k2tog] 12 times, sl m, knit to end—90 sts rem; 46 sts on first needle, 44 sts on second needle; 12 marked toe sts at beg of second needle.

Knit 4 rnds.

DEC RND 2: On first needle, [k2tog] 7 times, sl m, knit to end; on second needle, k1, [k2tog] 5 times, k1, sl m, knit to

end—78 sts rem; 39 sts each needle; 7 marked sts at beg of each needle.

Knit 1 rnd—piece measures about 2" (5 cm) from pick-up rnd. Cut yarn.

Finishing

Thread 24" (61 cm) of yarn on a tapestry needle, draw through 7 marked toe sts and pull tight to gather. Rep for 7 marked heel sts—32 sts rem on each needle. With tails of gathering yarns threaded on a tapestry needle, use the Kitchener st (see page 44) to graft rem sts tog along the center of the sole. Weave in loose ends. Block lightly.

Knitting (and Purling) Back Backward in Twisted Stitch

When you reach the back-and-forth sections on the instep and heel, you may choose to purl back every other row—which means you'd knit the purl sts and purl into the back of the knit sts. Or, you may choose to knit back backward (abbreviated KBB) so the front of the work always faces you.

TO WORK A TWISTED KNIT IN KBB MODE: Insert the left needle tip from right to left in front of the first stitch on the right needle, wrap the yarn counterclockwise around the needle, and pull through a loop while slipping the stitch off the needle.

TO PURL IN KBB MODE: With the yarn in front of the work, insert the left needle tip from right to left into the back of the first stitch on the right needle, wrap the yarn counterclockwise around the needle, and pull through a loop while slipping the stitch off the needle.

TO WORK A TRAVELING STITCH IN KBB MODE: Rearrange the involved sts as necessary, then work the stitches in KBB mode accordingly.

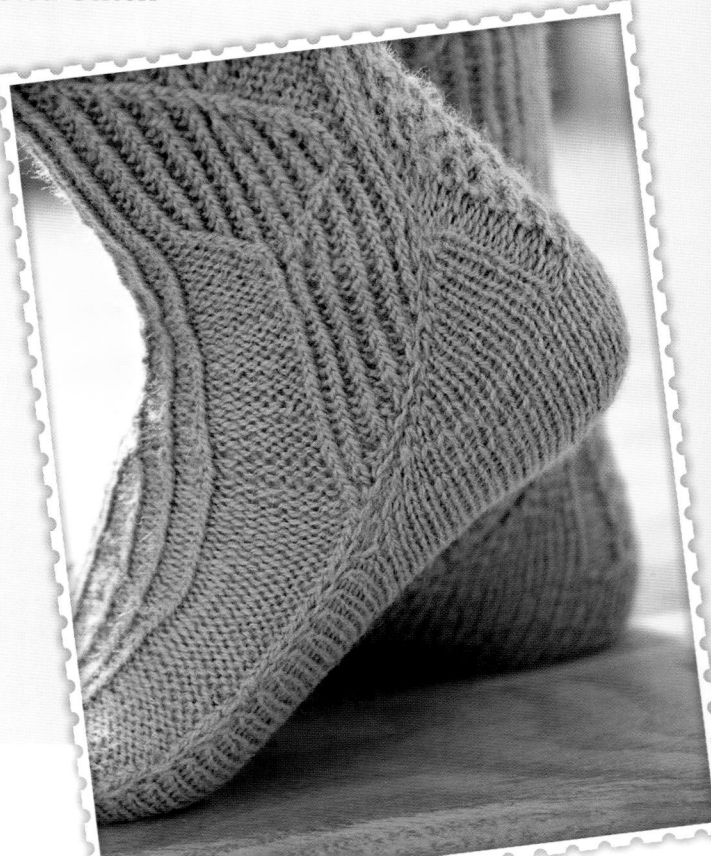

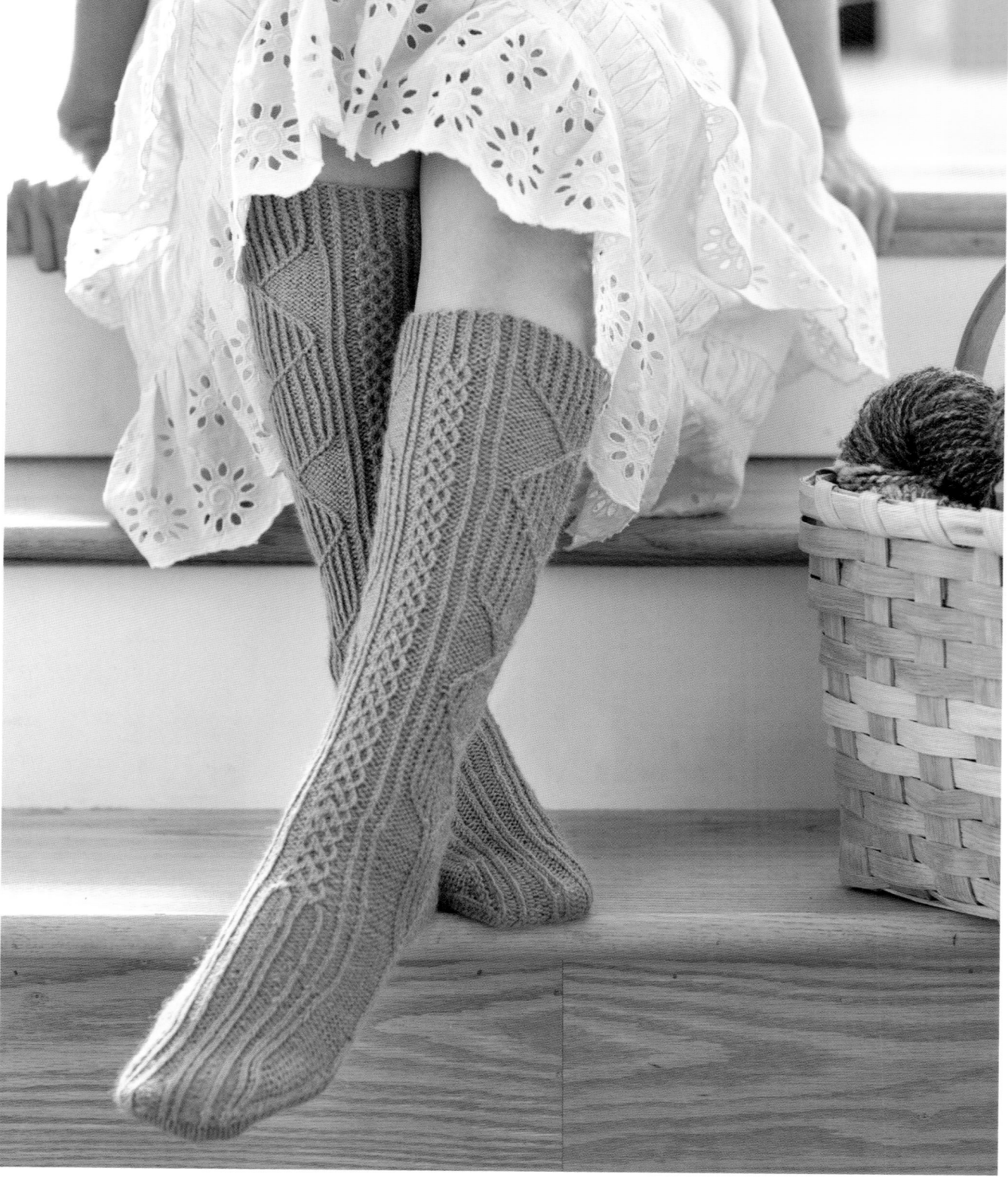

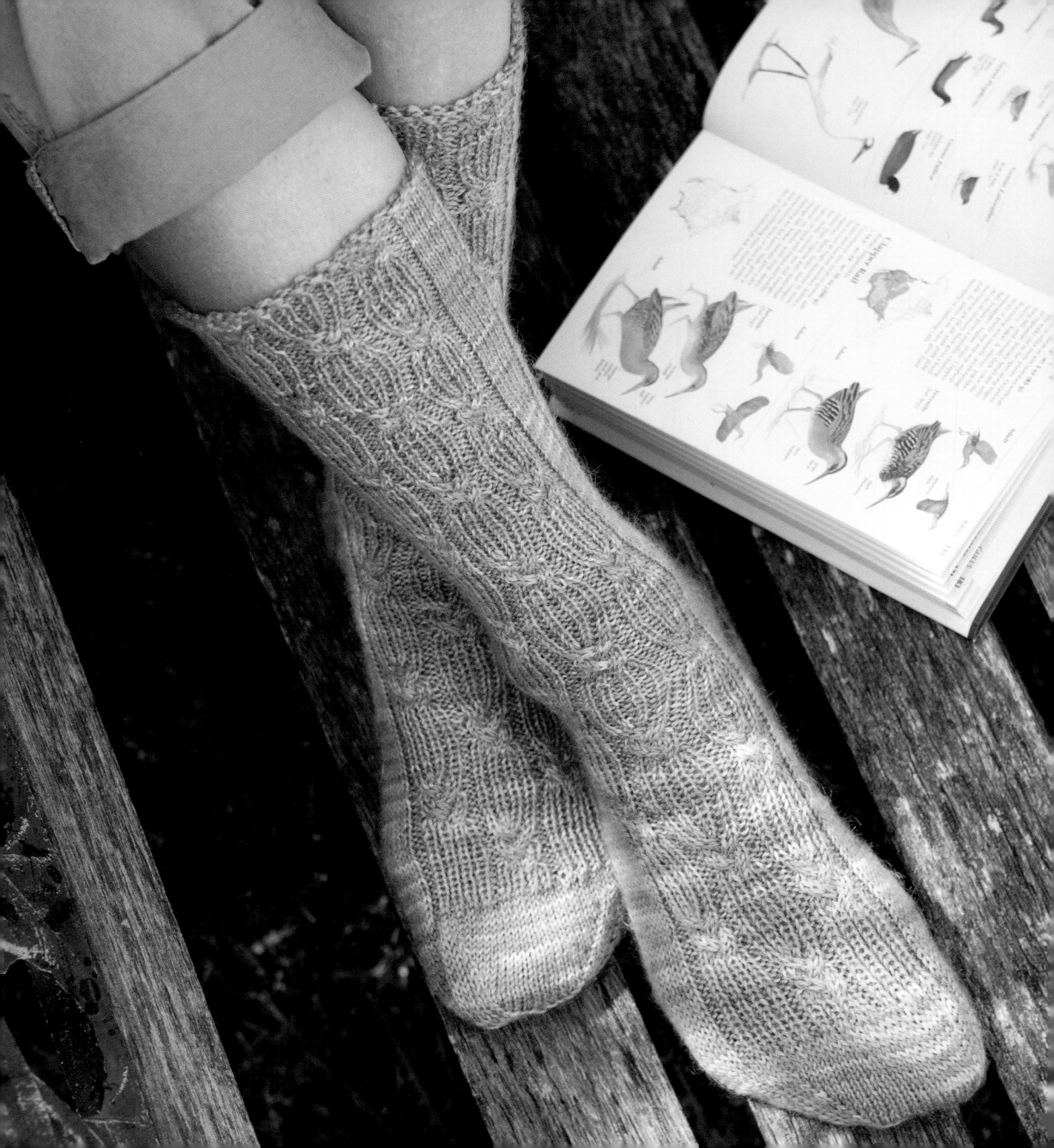

Knot Socks

DESIGNED BY *Nancy Bush*

finished size

About 7½" (19 cm) foot circumference, 9½" (24 cm) foot length from back of heel to tip of toe (with option for adjusting foot length), and 10½" (26.5 cm) leg length from top of cuff to base of heel.

yarn

Fingering weight (#1 Super Fine).

Shown here: Schaefer Yarn Anne (60% superwash merino, 25% mohair, 15% nylon; 560 yd [512 tm]/4 oz [114 g]: almond, 1 skein.

needles

Size U.S. 0 (2 mm): set of 4 double-pointed (dpn).

Adjust needle size if necessary to obtain the correct gauge.

notions

Marker (m); cable needle (cn); tapestry needle.

gauge

18 sts and 23 rnds = 2" (5 cm) in St st, before blocking.

29 sts of Knot pattern from chart measure 2¼" (5.5 cm) wide, before blocking.

My inspiration for this sock design was a pair of socks from Estonia. The original socks were knitted by my friend Maimu Poldoja in a natural white wool yarn. I studied the cables and spent some time making samples to discover how they were worked so that the ribbing melted into the stockinette-stitch cables and then emerged from the other side. I found that by making the cables a bit "unbalanced," each of the 7 rib stitches found a place in the cable. I chose my favorite cast-on—the double-start method—to provide a decorative and very elastic edge. I decided to run ribbing down the back of the leg to add elasticity and give the leg a better fit. I worked a square, or Dutch, heel—the most common for Estonian socks—in the classic heel stitch, which runs to the end of the heel turn. This adds strength and reinforces the heel stitches. The French toe shaping, from the British nineteenth-century *Weldon's* magazines, gives a nice line at the end of the foot that flows from the foot pattern perfectly. I chose to work these socks in Schaefer Anne, a very thin sock yarn that requires small needles for a firm fabric. The nearly solid colorway shows off the textured pattern quite well.

> *I studied the cables and spent some time making samples to discover how they were worked so that the ribbing melted into the stockinette-stitch cables and then emerged from the other side."*

⊕ **DESIGN TIP:** *When working a sock from the top down, the cast-on should be strong and elastic, whether it is purely functional or decorative.*

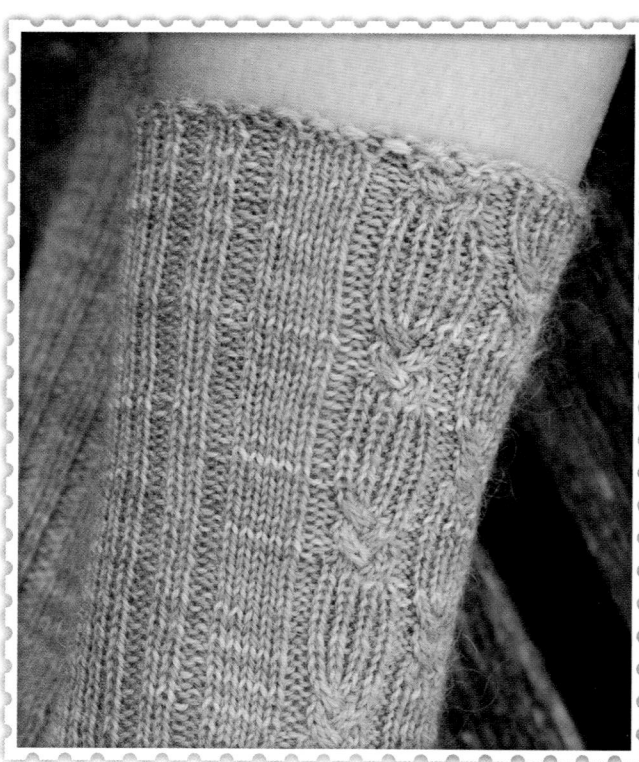

Leg

With yarn doubled and using the Double Start method (page 42), CO 76 sts. Cut off one end of yarn and cont with a single strand. Arrange sts so there are 24 sts on Needle 1, 29 sts on Needle 2, and 23 sts on Needle 3. Place marker (pm) and join for working in rnds, being careful not to twist sts. Rnd begins at back of leg. Purl 1 rnd.

NEXT RND: On Needle 1, [k1, p1] 6 times, k1, p2, k2, p2, k5; on Needle 2, work Rnd 1 of Knot chart over 29 sts; on Needle 3, k5, p2, k2, p2, [k1, p1] 6 times.

Working sts on Needle 1 and Needle 3 as they appear (knit the knits and purl the purls), work sts on Needle 2 according to Rnds 2–20 of chart once, rep Rnds 1–20 three times, then work Rnds 1–17 once more.

NEXT RND: (Rnd 18 of chart) On Needle 1 and Needle 2, work in established patt; on Needle 3, knit the first 5 sts, sl these 5 sts onto the end of Needle 2, and leave the rem 18 sts unworked—98 chart rnds total; piece measures about 8½" (21.5 cm) from CO.

Heel

SET-UP ROW: With RS facing, work heel sts onto one needle, removing end-of-rnd m when you come to it, as foll: Beg with 18 unworked sts at the end of the previous rnd, sl 1 pwise wyb, k2, [sl 1 pwise wyb, k1] 7 times, sl 1 pwise wyb, remove end-of-rnd m, k1, [sl 1 pwise wyb, k1] 7 times, sl 1 pwise wyb, k2, k1 through back loop (k1tbl)—37 heel sts.

Divide rem 39 sts between 2 needles to work later for instep; with RS facing, sts on each side of instep should be k5.

HEEL FLAP

Cont on 37 heel flap sts as foll:

ROW 1: (WS) Sl 1 pwise wyf, k2, p31, k2, p1.

ROW 2: (RS) Sl 1 pwise wyb, k2, [sl 1, k1] 15 times, sl 1, k2, k1tbl.

| | knit | • | purl | 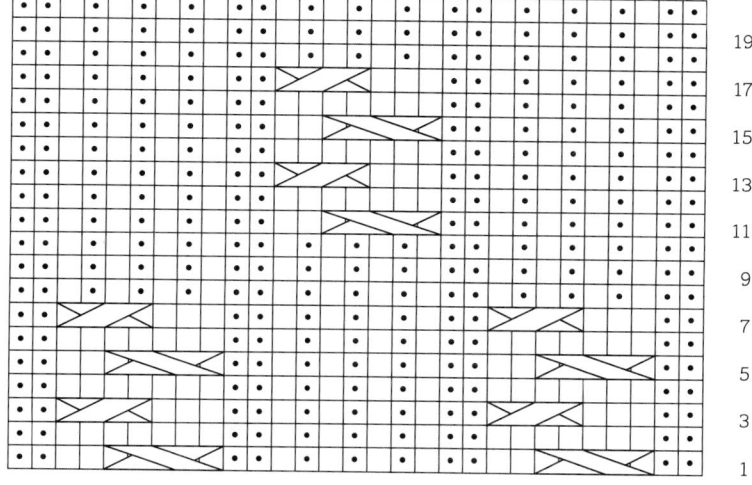 | | sl 2 sts onto cn and hold in back, k2, k2 from cn | | sl 2 sts onto cn and hold in front, k3, k2 from cn |

Knot

19
17
15
13
11
9
7
5
3
1

Rep Rows 1 and 2 for flap 16 more times, then work Row 1 once more—36 rows total including set-up row; 18 chain sts at each selvedge; heel flap measures about 2" (5 cm).

TURN HEEL

Work short-rows as foll:

ROW 1: (RS) Sl 1 pwise wyb, k2, [sl 1 pwise wyb, k1] 10 times, ssk, turn work.

ROW 2: (WS) Sl 1 pwise wyf, p9, p2tog, turn.

ROW 3: Sl 1 pwise wyb, [k1, sl 1] 4 times, k1, ssk, turn.

Rep Rows 2 and 3 for heel turn 11 more times, then work WS Row 2 once more—11 heel sts rem.

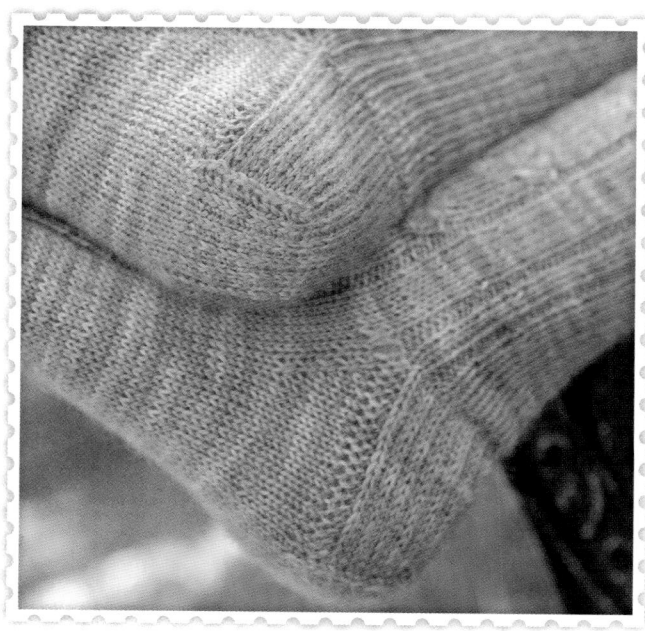

SHAPE GUSSETS

Pick up and knit sts along edges of heel flap (see Glossary) and join for working in rnds as foll:

JOINING RND: With Needle 1, k11 heel sts, then pick up and knit 18 sts (1 st in each chain edge st) along selvedge edge of heel flap; with Needle 2, k5, work Rnd 19 of chart across center 29 sts, k5; with Needle 3, pick up and knit 18 sts (1 st in each chain edge st) along other selvedge edge of heel flap, then knit the first 6 heel sts again—86 sts total; 23 sts on Needle 1, 39 instep sts on Needle 2, 24 sts on Needle 3. Rnd begins at back of heel.

RND 1: On Needle 1, knit to last 3 sts, k2tog, k1; on Needle 2, work instep sts in established patt; on Needle 3, k1, ssk, knit to end—2 sts dec'd.

RND 2: Work even in patt.

Rep Rnds 1 and 2 four more times—76 sts rem; 18 sts on Needle 1, 39 instep sts on Needle 2, 19 sts on Needle 3.

Foot

Cont even in established patt until foot measures 7½" (19 cm) from back of heel, or about 2" (5 cm) less than desired total length, ending with Rnd 10 or 20 of chart.

NOTE: If ending with Rnd 10 or 20 will make the foot too short, discontinue the chart patt and work the instep sts as they appear (without any cables) until foot reaches the desired length.

Toe

Work even in St st for 4 rnds.

NEXT RND: Knit to last 3 sts of Needle 3, k2tog, k1—75 sts rem.

Arrange sts so there are 25 sts on each of 3 needles, keeping the beg of rnd in the same place on sole of foot.

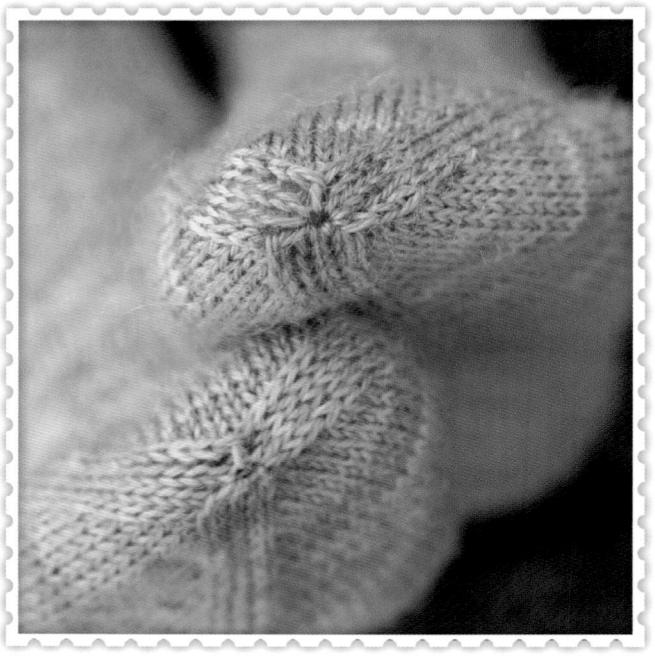

RND 1: *K1, ssk, knit to last 3 sts of needle, k2tog, k1; rep from * for next 2 needles—6 sts total dec'd; 2 sts dec'd on each needle.

RND 2: Knit.

Rep these 2 rnds 5 more times—39 sts rem; 13 sts on each needle. Rep Rnd 1 (i.e., dec every rnd) 4 times—15 sts rem; 5 sts on each needle.

NEXT RND: *K1, sl 1, k2tog, psso, k1; rep from * for next 2 needles—9 sts rem; 3 sts on each needle.

Finishing

Cut yarn, leaving an 8" (20.5 cm) tail. Thread tail on a tapestry needle, draw through rem sts, pull tight to close hole, and fasten off on WS. Weave in loose ends and block under a damp towel or on sock blockers.

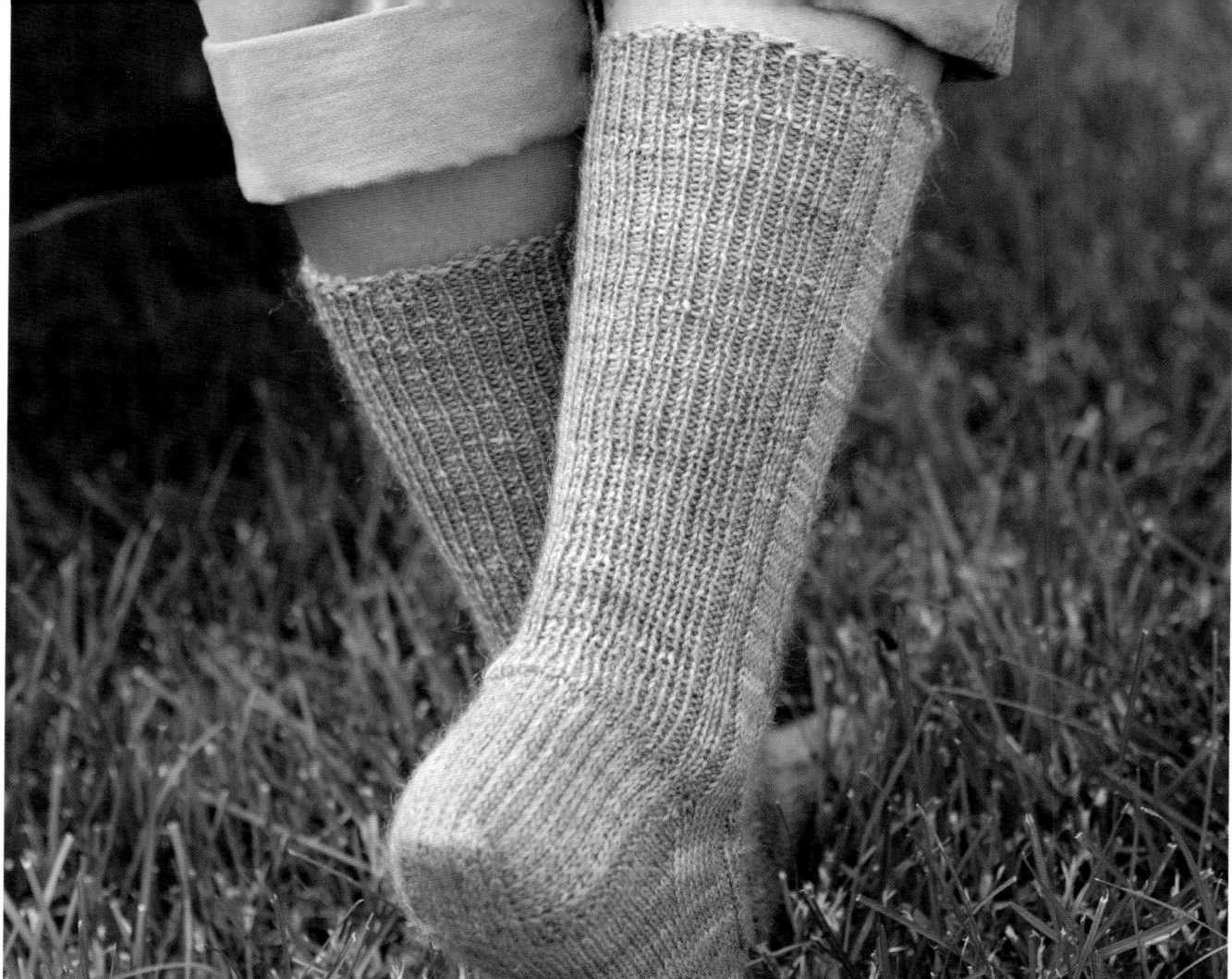

Yarn Note

Despite the presence of 60% superwash merino wool, this particular yarn is one of the more relaxed and fluid ones used in this book. Part of the fluidity comes from the three relaxed plies, and part comes from the addition of 25% mohair. Not only does mohair add luxurious drape to a fabric, but it also lends a distinct halo as its longer, more lustrous fiber ends protrude from the surface. Mohair adds sheen to the otherwise matte merino and also adds strength with its generous staple length and higher tensile strength. Leaving nothing to chance, however, 15% nylon has also been added. The combined loose ply and high mohair content does lessen elasticity, and Nancy cleverly integrated ribbing into the cable pattern and introduced a k1, p1 rib along the back of the leg. Together, these techniques help the sock to hold your leg snugly. Don't be afraid to experiment. The plumper the yarn, the more squishy and sculptural the pattern motif will be. The attractive cabled stitch pattern is best worked in a solid or semisolid colorway. Too much contrast will overpower and eventually conceal all your careful work.

—*Clara Parkes*

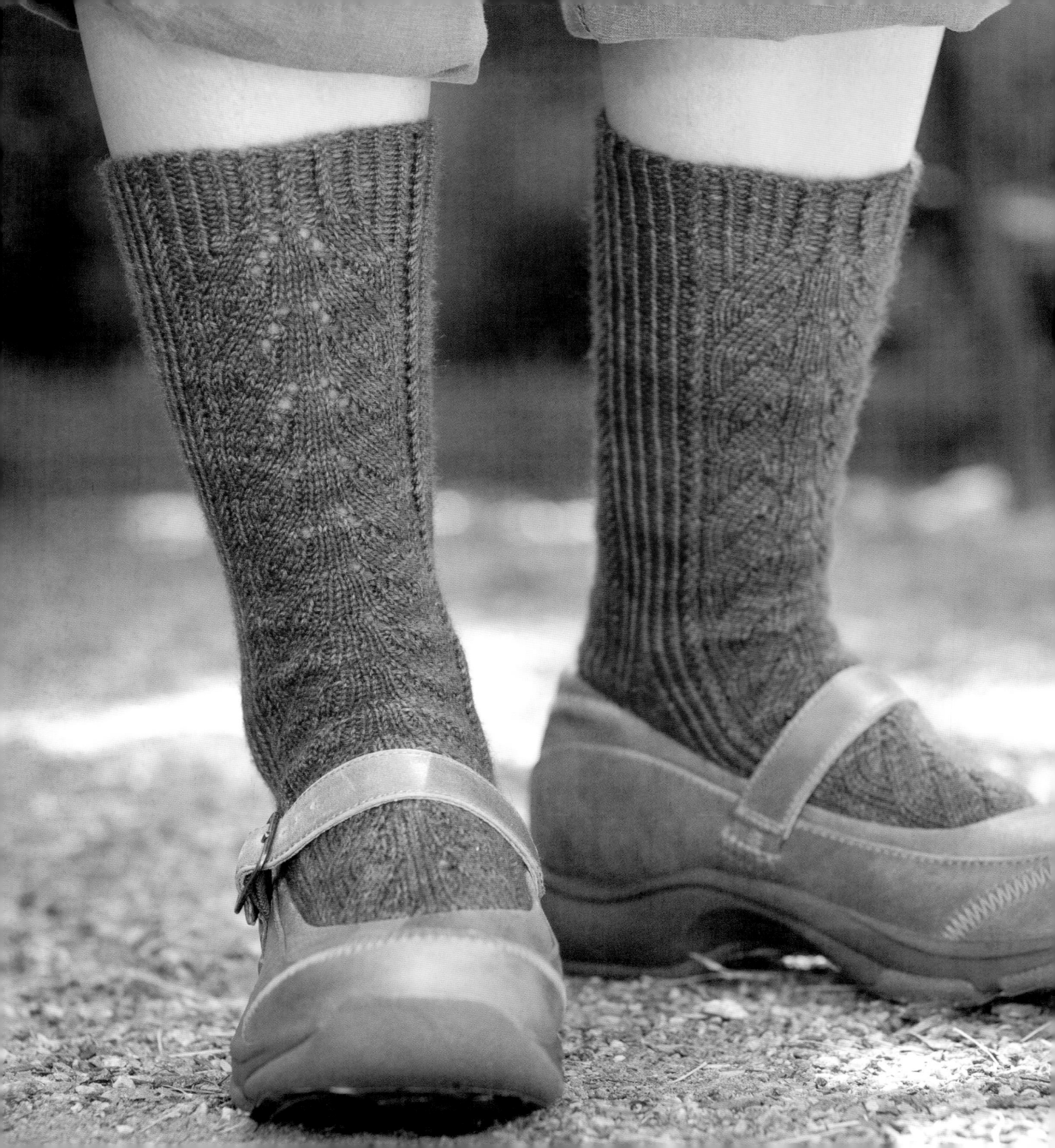

Mock Cables and Lace

DESIGNED BY *Ann Budd*

finished size

About 7½" (19 cm) foot circumference, 10" (25.5 cm) foot length from back of heel to tip of toe (with option for adjusting foot length), and 10½" (26.5 cm) leg length from top of cuff to base of heel.

yarn

Fingering weight (#1 Super Fine).

Shown here: String Theory Bluestocking (80% Blueface Leicester, 20% nylon; 420 yd [384 m]/100 g): canyon, 1 skein.

needles

Upper leg: size 3 (3.25 mm): 40" (100 cm) circular (cir).

Lower leg and foot: size 2 (2.75 mm): 40" cir and 1 spare double-point (dpn) for zigzag bind-off.

Adjust needle size if necessary to obtain the correct gauge.

notions

Marker (m); stitch holder (optional); tapestry needle.

gauge

18 sts and 24 rnds = 2" (5 cm) in St st on smaller needle, worked in rnds.

36 sts of Instep chart measure 3¼" (8.5 cm) wide on smaller needle, worked in rnds.

I like textural patterns, and I especially like textural patterns that look more complicated than they are to knit. For this pair of socks, I chose a lace pattern that gives the illusion of a wide cable along the front and back of the leg. Then I filled in the sides with a twisted k1, p1 rib to provide elasticity and incorporated my favorite non-cable-needle cable stitches—right twists—along the sides of the center panels. The center panel extends along the instep for pattern continuity.

> *I chose a lace pattern that gives the illusion of a wide cable along the front and back of the leg."*

The ribbed cast-on is a modification of the cable cast-on that works into any rib pattern. I worked transition rounds between the ribbed cuff and the main pattern so there wouldn't be a sharp distinction between the cuff and the leg. For the heel flap, I worked a twisted rib pattern, extending some of the ribs from the back of the leg along the edges of the flap. I positioned the gusset decreases on each side of the foot to align with twisted knit stitches from the leg. For fun, I decided to use Priscilla Gibson-Roberts' short-row toe, working the bottom of the toe first and connecting the toe to the instep with a zigzag bind-off that forms a decorative (and altogether comfortable!) ridge on the top of the foot.

notes

+ The short-row toe follows the technique outlined by
Priscilla Gibson-Roberts in *Simple Socks* and in Priscilla's
Dream Socks in *Favorite Socks*.

+ The toe shown is worked in short-rows along the bottom
of the foot, over the end of the toes, and then along the
top of the foot to the base of the toes where it is joined
to the waiting instep stitches with a decorative zigzag
bind-off. If you would prefer an invisible join, work the
toe instructions using the instep stitches instead, working
along the top of the foot, over the end of the toes, and
along the sole of the foot to the base of the toes. Graft
the toe sts to the waiting stitches on the bottom of the
foot using the Kitchener st (see page 44).

Stitch Guide

SSP

Slip 2 sts individually kwise, return these 2 sts to left needle tip,
then purl them tog through their back loops—1 st dec'd.

SSSP

Slip 3 sts individually kwise, return these 3 sts to left needle tip,
then purl them tog through their back loops—2 sts dec'd.

⊕ **DESIGN TIP:** *Use a ribbed cast-on to integrate
the cast-on edge with the first round of ribbing.*

Leg

With larger cir needle, use the k1, p1 cable method (page 40)
to CO 74 sts, following CO Row of the Leg and Heel chart
from left to right for sequence of knit and purl sts 2 times
around. Divide sts into 2 groups of 37 sts each for working the
magic loop technique (page 13), place marker (pm), and join for
working in rnds, being careful not to twist sts. Rnd begins at
side of leg. Work Rnd 2 of chart once, then rep Rnds 1 and 2
five more times—12 cuff rnds total, including CO row; piece
measures about 1¼" (3.2 cm) from CO. Work Rnds 3–12 of chart
once to transition from cuff to leg, then work Rnds 13–22 two
times—piece measures about 4" (10 cm) from CO. Change to
smaller cir needle and work Rnds 13–22 four more times—piece
measures about 7½" (19 cm) from CO.

HEEL FLAP

SET-UP ROW: (RS) Work the first 36 sts of rnd onto a smaller
cir needle for heel according to Row 23 of Leg and Heel chart,
then place rem 38 sts on holder or empty needle to work later
for instep—36 heel sts.

Working back and forth in rows, work WS Row 24 once, then
rep Rows 23 and 24 of chart 17 more times, ending with a WS
row—36 heel flap rows, including set-up row; 18 chain edge sts
at each selvedge.

SHAPE HEEL

Work short-rows as foll:

ROW 1: (RS) K20, ssk, k1, turn work.

ROW 2: Sl 1 pwise with yarn in front (wyf), p5, p2tog, p1, turn.

ROW 3: Sl 1 pwise with yarn in back (wyb), knit to 1 st before
gap formed on previous row, ssk (1 st each side of gap), k1,
turn.

ROW 4: Sl 1 pwise wyf, purl to 1 st before gap formed on
previous row, p2tog (1 st each side of gap), p1, turn.

	knit on RS rows and all rnds; purl on WS rows		k2tog
⅃	k1tbl on RS rows and all rnds; p1tbl on WS rows	\	ssk
•	purl on RS rows and all rnds; knit on WS rows	V	sl 1 pwise wyb on RS; sl 1 pwise wyf on WS
o	yo	⋈	k2tog but do not sl sts from needle, knit the first st again, then sl both sts from needle

Leg and Heel

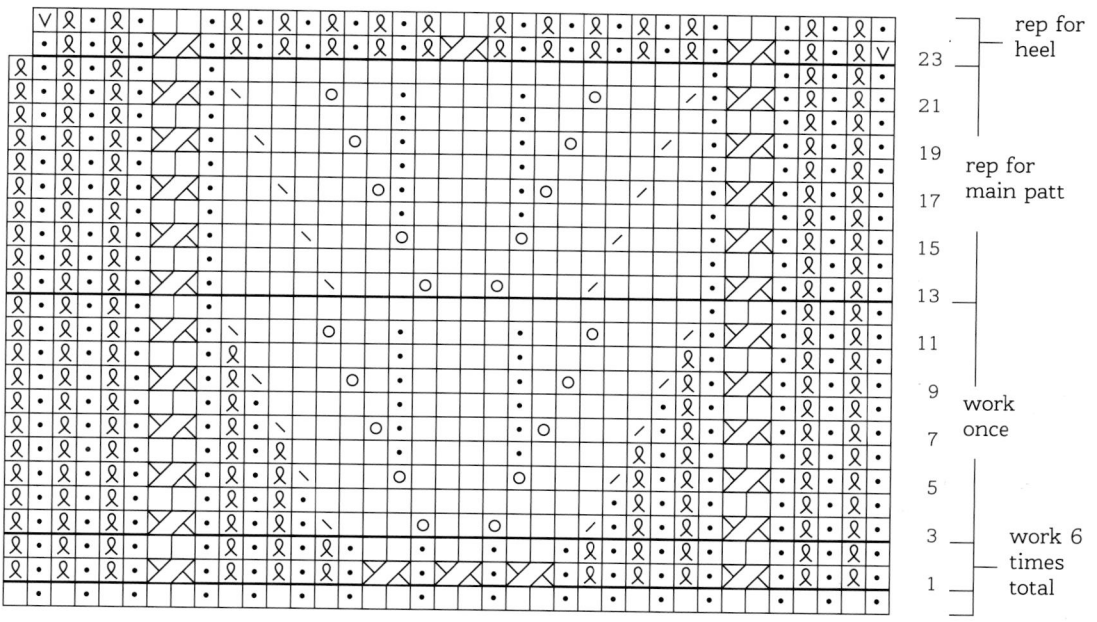

rep for heel — 23

rep for main patt — 17

— 13

work once

work 6 times total

Instep

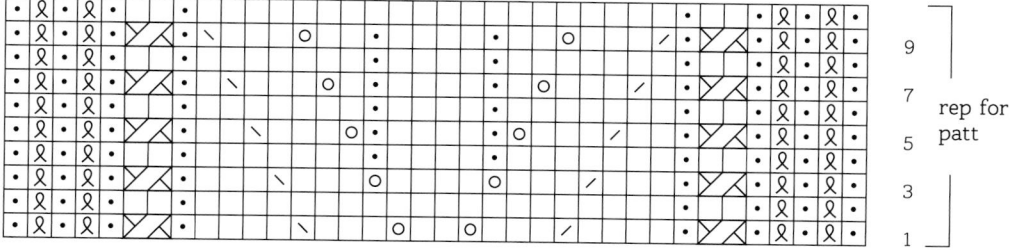

rep for patt

Mock Cables and Lace

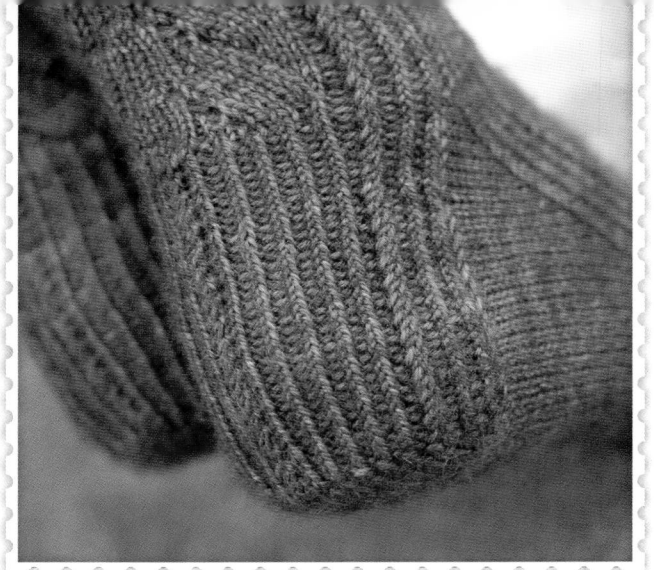

Rep Rows 3 and 4 until all heel sts have been worked, omitting the last k1 on the final rep of Row 3, and omitting the last p1 on the final rep of Row 4—20 heel sts rem. With RS facing, knit the first 10 heel sts and place them on an empty needle or holder, leaving last 10 heel sts on smaller cir needle.

GUSSETS

Pick up and knit sts along edges of heel flap (see Glossary), divide sts into 2 groups, and rejoin for working in rnds as foll:

JOINING RND: For first group of sts, knit last 10 heel sts, then pick up and knit through the back loops (see Glossary) 18 sts along selvedge of heel flap (1 st in each chain-edge st), pick up and knit 1 st in corner at the base of the heel flap, work first 19 instep sts as k1tbl, pm, then first 18 sts from Rnd 1 of Instep chart; for second group of sts, pull out a loop of needle to divide the groups, work last 19 instep sts as last 18 sts from Rnd 1 of Instep chart, pm, k1tbl, then pick up and knit 1 st in corner at the base of the heel flap, then 18 sts along selvedge edge as for the first side, then knit the first 10 heel sts—96 sts total; 48 sts in each group; 36 instep sts between new m. Rnd begs at center of heel; division between groups is in center of marked instep sts.

RND 1: Knit to 2 sts before first instep m, k2tog, slip marker (sl m), work in patt to next instep m, sl m, ssk, knit to end—2 sts dec'd, 1 st from each group.

RND 2: Knit to first instep m, sl m, work instep sts in established patt, sl m, knit to end.

Rep Rnds 2 and 3 ten more times—74 sts rem; 37 sts in each group.

Working sts outside instep patt in St st, work even in established patt until piece measures about 8" (20.5 cm) from back of heel, ending with Rnd 10 of chart. For a longer foot, cont in St st on all sts until foot measures 2" (5 cm) less than desired length before starting toe. For a shorter foot, discontinue instep patt sooner, ending with Rnd 10, then work all sts in St st until foot measures 2" (5 cm) less than desired before starting toe.

Toe

Redistribute sts so the first 18 sts and last 19 sts of the rnd are on smaller cir needle for sole—37 sole sts on one needle. Place rem 37 instep sts on holder or empty needle and remove instep m. Work the sole sts back and forth in short-rows as foll.

FIRST HALF

Work 1 less st in each short-row as foll:

ROW 1: (RS) K36, turn work—1 regular st unworked at end of row.

ROW 2: (WS) Bring yarn from back to front over right needle to create a backward yo, p35, leaving last st unworked, turn—1 st regular st unworked at end of row; 1 regular st and one "paired st" consisting of a yo and the st after it at beg of row.

ROW 3: Bring yarn from front to back over right needle to create a normal yo, knit to paired st at end of row, turn—1 "paired" st and 1 regular st unworked at each end of row.

● **DESIGN TIP:** *Flank a dominant motif with small "filler" patterns to achieve the desired circumference.*

ROW 4: Bring yarn from back to front over right needle to create a backward yo, purl to paired st at end of row, turn.

ROW 5: Bring yarn from front to back over right needle to create a normal yo, knit to paired st at end of row, turn.

Rep Rows 4 and 5 ten more times, adding another paired st at the end of each row, and ending with a RS row—12 paired sts and 1 regular st unworked at each end of row. Last row completed was worked as yo, k1 (to form the 12th pair), k11.

SECOND HALF

Work 1 more st each short-row as foll:

ROW 1: (RS) Cont with the same RS row, k1 (the knit st of the first paired st), correct the mount of the yo so that its leading leg is in front of the needle, k2tog (the yo tog with the knit st of the foll pair), turn work, leaving rem yo of pair unworked.

ROW 2: (WS) Bring yarn from back to front over right needle to create a backward yo, purl to first paired st, p1 (the purl st of paired st), ssp (the yo of pair tog with the purl st of the foll pair; see Stitch Guide), turn, leaving rem yo of pair unworked.

ROW 3: Bring yarn from front to back over right needle to create a normal yo, knit to the first paired st, k1 (the knit st of paired st), correct the mount of the next 2 yo's, k3tog (the 2 yo's with the knit st of the foll pair), turn, leaving rem yo of pair unworked.

ROW 4: Bring yarn from back to front over right needle to create a backward yo, purl to the first paired st, p1 (the purl st of paired st), sssp (the 2 yo's tog with the purl st of the foll pair; see Stitch Guide), turn, leaving rem yo of pair unworked.

Rep Rows 3 and 4 ten more times, ending with a WS row—all sole sts have been worked; 38 sts on sole needle; 37 regular sts and 1 yo paired with the last st on the needle (when viewed from the RS).

Return 37 instep sts to other half of smaller cir needle—38 sole sts in one group; 37 instep sts in other group. Hold sole and instep tog with WS touching and RS facing outward. Using spare dpn in same size as working needle, use the zigzag method (see page 46) to BO all sts, working last regular st on sole needle tog with its paired yo when you come to it. Fasten off last st. Weave in loose ends. Block lightly.

Yarn Note

An ingenious use of stitch trickery gives the effect of broad rippling cables without any of the awkward bulk you'd have if these were actually real four-over-four cables—crucial since the faux cable motif runs along the top of the foot and needs to lie flat inside a shoe. Panels of twisted-stitch ribbing enhance the sock's elasticity, while the use of yarnover increases in the main pattern helps keep the fabric open and stretchy. These design touches combine to give you freedom of yarn choice, whether bouncy or firm, with relative assurance that the sock will still be snug. Visually speaking, remember that the rounder and firmer your yarn, the brighter and better-defined all the ornate stitchwork will be; the "bumpier" the ply structure (especially with two-ply yarns), the more muted and nuanced the stitch pattern will appear. This sample was knitted with a lovely three-ply blend of bluefaced Leicester wool and nylon. Even though the bluefaced Leicester has less crimp than its finewool merino cousin, the sock still hugs the foot tight. A subtle halo adds a hint of coziness, while discreet semisolid coloring enhances the sock's sense of rippling, upward movement.

—*Clara Parkes*

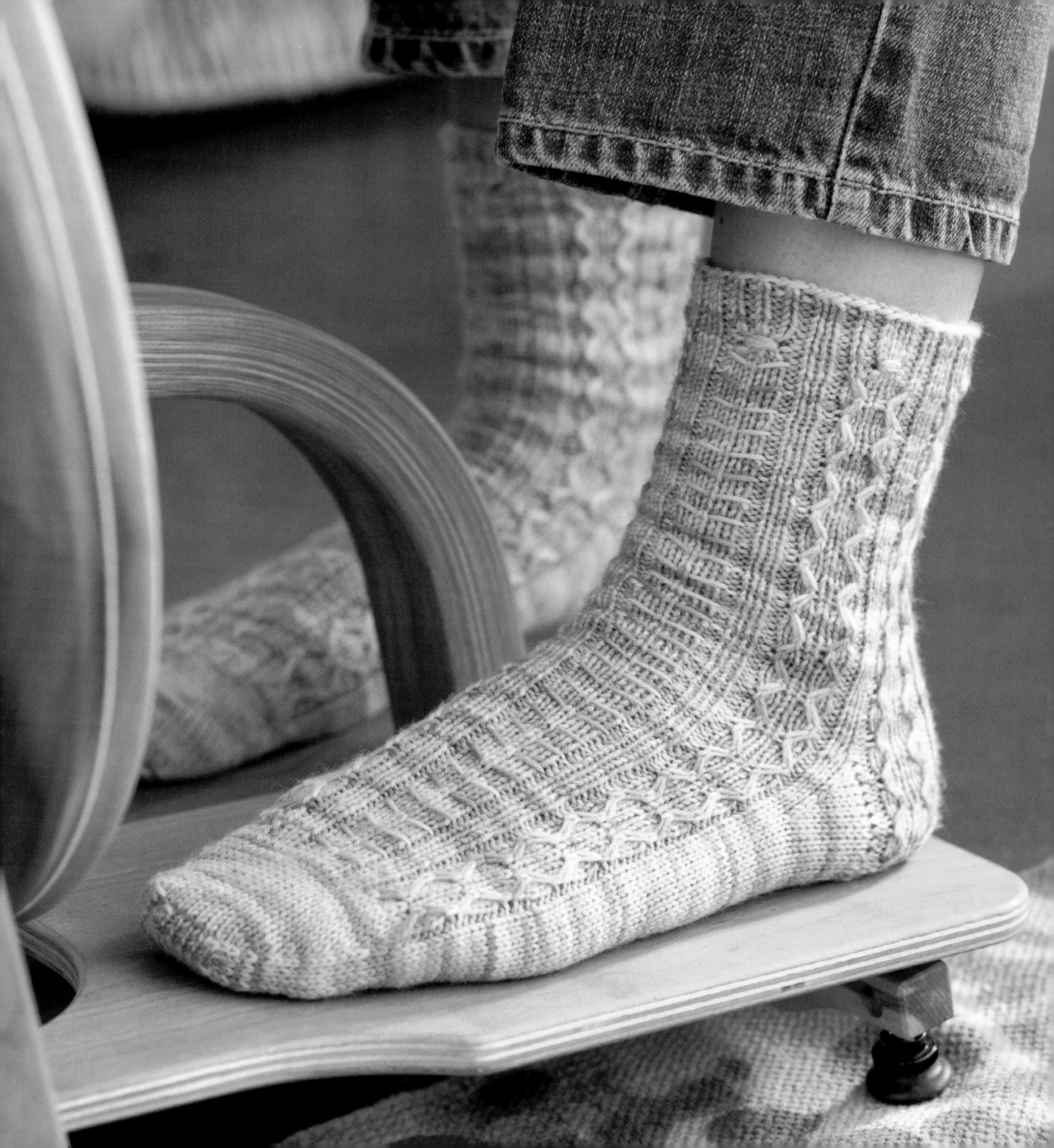

Slip-n-Slide

DESIGNED BY *Chrissy Gardiner*

finished size

About 7" (18 cm) foot circumference (will stretch to fit up to 8" [20.5 cm]), 9¼" (23.5 cm) foot length from back of heel to tip of toe (with option for adjusting foot length), and 7½" (19 cm) leg length from top of cuff to base of heel.

yarn

Fingering Weight (#1 Super Fine).

Shown here: Shalimar Yarns Zoe Sock (100% superwash Merino; 450 yd [411 m]/100 g): saffron, 1 skein.

needles

U.S. size 1 (2.25 mm): set of 4 double-pointed (dpn).

Adjust needle size if necessary to obtain the correct gauge.

notions

Marker (m); tapestry needle.

gauge

16 sts and 24 rnds = 2" (5 cm) in St st, worked in rnds.

31 sts of instep pattern measures 3" (7.5 cm) wide.

When designing socks, I like to use unusual stitch patterns that showcase the yarn in unique ways. These socks began with my idea to use a slip-stitch pattern in which a horizontal strand of yarn is lifted a few rows later to make a little "tent" design. I placed this motif at the center of the pattern, then added a mock cable slip-stitch motif on each side. The mock cables complement the center motif and are worked over the same number of rounds for ease of knitting. I added columns of [p1, k2, p1] between the slipped motifs to make them stand out more, add elasticity to the fabric, and bring the circumference to the right size. To give the cuff a bit of visual interest and maintain the theme of horizontal strands of yarn, I placed a round of smocked stitches between the ribbed cuff and the main leg pattern. To emphasize the vertical lines of the design, I extended the pattern on the back of the leg down into the heel flap. Not only does this make the ankle appear slimmer (always a benefit!), it also eliminates what I find to be a jarring horizontal line at the top of the heel flap.

> *These socks began with my idea to use a slip-stitch pattern in which a horizontal strand of yarn is lifted a few rows later to make a little 'tent' design."*

DESIGN TECHNIQUES

top-down construction, page 36

designing with slip stitches, page 30

working with four double-pointed needles, page 12

any elastic cast-on, page 38

round heel, page 14

wedge toe, page 21

Kitchener stitch, page 44

Stitch Guide

BRIDGE (WORKED OVER 1 ST)

Use right needle tip to lift elongated strand (formed by sl 5 sts two rnds below) onto left needle to the left of the first st, k1 (the first st), then drop elongated strand off left needle so that falls behind and around the knitted st.

SMALL SMOCK (WORKED OVER 3 STS)

*Bring yarn to back, sl 3 sts pwise onto right needle, bring yarn to front, sl the same 3 sts pwise onto left needle; rep from * 2 more times, bring yarn to back and k3 (the wrapped sts).

LARGE SMOCK (3 STS INCREASED TO 5 STS)

*Bring yarn to back, sl 3 sts pwise onto right needle, bring yarn to front, sl the same 3 sts pwise back to left needle; rep from * 2 more times, bring yarn to back and work the 3 wrapped sts as [k1f&b (see Glossary)] 2 times, k1—3 wrapped sts inc'd to 5 sts.

SL 5 WYF (WORKED OVER 5 STS)

Sl 5 sts pwise with yarn in front (wyf), taking care to carry the working yarn loosely but evenly across the front of the slipped sts.

T3L (WORKED OVER 3 STS)

Drop next st (the elongated st that was slipped on previous 2 rnds), k2, insert left needle tip into dropped st from back to front and knit the dropped st.

T3R (WORKED OVER 3 STS)

Sl 2 sts pwise with yarn in back (wyb), drop next st (the elongated st that was slipped on previous 2 rnds), return the 2 slipped sts to left needle, insert left needle tip into dropped st from back to front and knit the dropped st, k2.

⊕ **DESIGN TIP:** *Include some type of ribbed component in the leg pattern to increase elasticity.*

Leg

CO 62 sts. Divide sts so that there are 31 sts on Needle 1, 19 sts on Needle 2, and 12 sts on Needle 3—front-of-leg and instep sts are on Needle 1; back-of-leg and sole sts are on Needles 2 and 3. Place marker (pm) and join for working in rnds, being careful not to twist sts. Rnd begins at side of leg.

RNDS 1–7: *[K1, p1] 2 times, k3, p1, k1, p1, k2, [p1, k1] 3 times, p1, k2, p1, k1, p1, k3, [p1, k1] 2 times; rep from *.

RND 8: (dec rnd) *[K1, p1] 2 times, work small smock (see Stitch Guide) over 3 sts, p1, k1, p1, k2, p1, ssk, k1, k2tog, p1, k2, p1, k1, p1, work small smock over 3 sts, [p1, k1] 2 times; rep from *—58 sts rem.

RND 9: (inc rnd) *[K1, p1] 2 times, k3, p1, k1, p1, k2, p1, work large smock (see Stitch Guide) over 3 sts (inc them to 5 sts), p1, k2, p1, k1, p1, k3, [p1, k1] 2 times; rep from *—62 sts.

RND 10: *K1, p1, k7, p1, k2, p1, k5, p1, k2, p1, k7, p1, k1; rep from *.

NOTE: Sl sts pwise on Rows 11, 12, 15, and 16.

RND 11: *K1, p1, sl 1 with yarn in back (wyb), k5, sl 1 wyb, p1, k2, p1, sl 5 with yarn in front (wyf; see Stitch Guide), p1, k2, p1, sl 1 wyb, k5, sl 1 wyb, p1, k1; rep from *.

RND 12: *K1, p1, sl 1 wyb, k5, sl 1 wyb, p1, k2, p1, k5, p1, k2, p1, sl 1 wyb, k5, sl 1 wyb, p1, k1; rep from *.

RND 13: *K1, p1, T3L (see Stitch Guide), k1, T3R (see Stitch Guide), [p1, k2] 2 times, work bridge (see Stitch Guide) over 1 st, [k2, p1] 2 times, T3L, k1, T3R, p1, k1; rep from *.

RND 14: Rep Rnd 10.

RND 15: *K1, p1, k2, sl 1 wyb, k1, sl 1 wyb, [k2, p1] 2 times, sl 5 wyf, [p1, k2] 2 times, sl 1 wyb, k1, sl 1 wyb, k2, p1, k1; rep from *.

RND 16: *K1, p1, k2, sl 1 wyb, k1, sl 1 wyb, [k2, p1] 2 times, k5, [p1, k2] 2 times, sl 1 wyb, k1, sl 1 wyb, k2, p1, k1; rep from *.

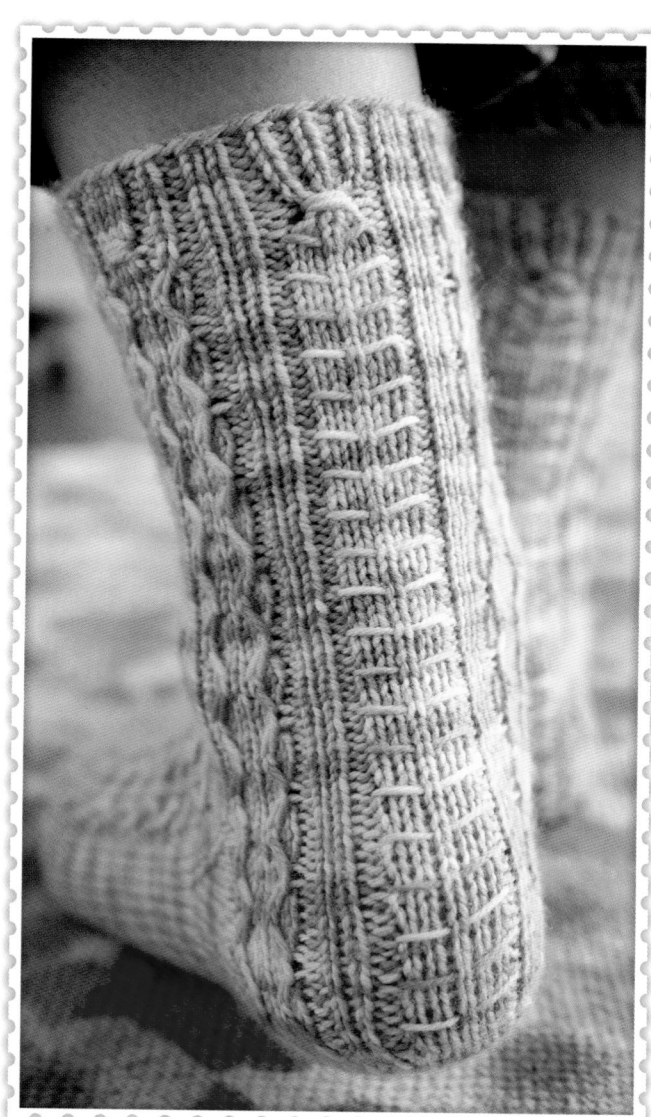

⊕ **DESIGN TIP:** *Extend the leg pattern along the back of the heel for a slimming effect.*

Heel

Work Rnd 11 of patt over first 31 instep sts, divide instep sts on 2 dpn to work later, then place rem 31 sts on a single needle for heel.

HEEL FLAP

Work 31 heel sts back and forth in rows as foll:

ROW 1: (RS) Sl 1 wyb, p1, sl 1 wyb, k5, sl 1 wyb, p1, k2, p1, sl 5 wyf, p1, k2, p1, sl 1 wyb, k5, sl 1 wyb, p1, k1.

ROW 2: Sl 1 wyb, k1, sl 1 wyf, p5, sl 1 wyf, k1, p2, k1, p5, k1, p2, k1, sl 1 wyf, p5, sl 1 wyf, k1, p1.

ROW 3: Sl 1 wyb, p1, T3L, k1, T3R, [p1, k2] 2 times, work bridge over next st, [k2, p1] 2 times, T3L, k1, T3R, p1, k1.

ROW 4: Sl 1 wyb, k1, p7, k1, p2, k1, p5, k1, p2, k1, p7, k1, p1.

ROW 5: Sl 1 wyb, p1, k2, sl 1 wyb, k1, sl 1 wyb, [k2, p1] 2 times, sl 5 wyf, [p1, k2] 2 times, sl 1 wyb, k1, sl 1 wyb, k2, p1, k1.

ROW 6: Sl 1 wyb, k1, p2, sl 1 wyf, p1, sl 1 wyf, [p2, k1] 2 times, p5, [k1, p2] 2 times, sl 1 wyf, p1, sl 1 wyf, p2, k1, p1.

ROW 7: Sl 1 wyb, p1, T3R, k1, T3L, [p1, k2] 2 times, work bridge over next st, [k2, p1] 2 times, T3R, k1, T3L, p1, k1.

ROW 8: Rep Row 4.

Rep Rows 1–8 two more times—heel flap measures about 2" (5 cm).

TURN HEEL

Work short-rows as foll:

ROW 1: (RS) Sl 1 pwise wyb, k16, ssk, k1, turn work.

ROW 2: (WS) Sl 1 pwise wyf, p4, p2tog, p1, turn.

ROW 3: Sl 1 pwise wyb, knit to 1 st before gap formed on previous row, ssk (1 st each side of gap), k1, turn.

RND 17: *K1, p1, T3R, k1, T3L, [p1, k2] 2 times, work bridge over next st, [k2, p1] 2 times, T3R, k1, T3L, p1, k1; rep from *.

RNDS 18–66: Rep Rnds 10–17 six more times, then work Rnd 10 once more—piece measures about 5½" (14 cm) from CO.

NOTE: For a longer leg, rep Rnds 10–17 more times as desired, then work Rnd 10 once.

ROW 4: Sl 1 pwise wyf, purl to 1 st before gap formed on previous row, p2tog (1 st each side of gap), p1, turn.

Rep Rows 3 and 4 until all sts have been worked, omitting the k1 after the dec on the last rep of Row 3 and omitting the p1 after the dec on the last rep of Row 4—17 heel sts rem. Turn work and knit 1 RS row across 17 heel sts.

GUSSET

Pick up and knit sts along edges of heel flap (see Glossary) and rejoin for working in rnds as foll:

JOINING RND: With empty needle, pick up and knit 13 sts along the selvedge of heel flap; with Needle 1, work 31 instep sts according to Rnd 12 of patt; with Needle 2, pick up and knit 13 sts along other selvedge of heel flap, then knit first 8 heel flap sts again; with Needle 3, knit last 9 heel flap sts again, knit to last 3 picked-up sts, k2tog, k1—73 sts; 31 instep sts on Needle 1, and 21 sts each on Needles 2 and 3. Rnd begins at side of foot at start of instep sts.

RND 1: On Needle 1, work instep sts in established patt; on Needle 2, k1, ssk, knit to end; on Needle 3, knit—1 st dec'd on Needle 2 only.

RND 2: On Needle 1, work instep sts in established patt; on Needle 2, knit; on Needle 3, knit to last 3 sts, k2tog, k1—1 st dec'd on Needle 3 only.

Rep the last 2 rnds 4 more times, then work Rnd 1 once more—62 sts total; 31 instep sts on Needle 1, 15 sts on Needle 2, 16 sts on Needle 3.

Foot

Working sts on Needles 2 and 3 in St st, cont instep sts on Needle 2 as established until piece measures 7" (18 cm) from back of heel, or about 2¼" (5.5 cm) less than desired total foot length, ending with Rnd 10 or 14 of patt.

Toe

Cont in St st, dec at each side of toe as foll:

RND 1: Knit.

RND 2: On Needle 1, k1, ssk, knit to last 3 sts, k2tog, k1; on Needle 2, k1, ssk, knit to end; on Needle 3, knit to last 3 sts, k2tog, k1—4 sts dec'd.

Rep Rnds 1 and 2 for toe 8 more times—26 sts rem. Then rep Rnd 2 only (i.e., dec every rnd) 3 times—14 sts rem; 7 instep sts on Needle 1, 3 sts on Needle 2, 4 sts on Needle 3.

Finishing

Arrange the sts so that there are 7 instep sts on one needle and 7 sole sts on another needle. Cut yarn, leaving a 14" (35.5 cm) tail. Thread tail on tapestry needle and use the Kitchener st (page 44) to graft sts of instep and sole tog. Weave in loose ends. To block, dampen socks and lay flat to dry or place on sock blockers.

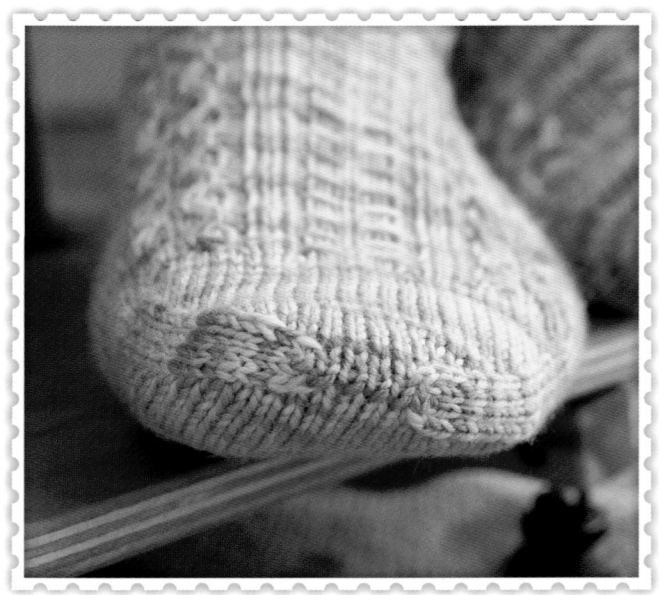

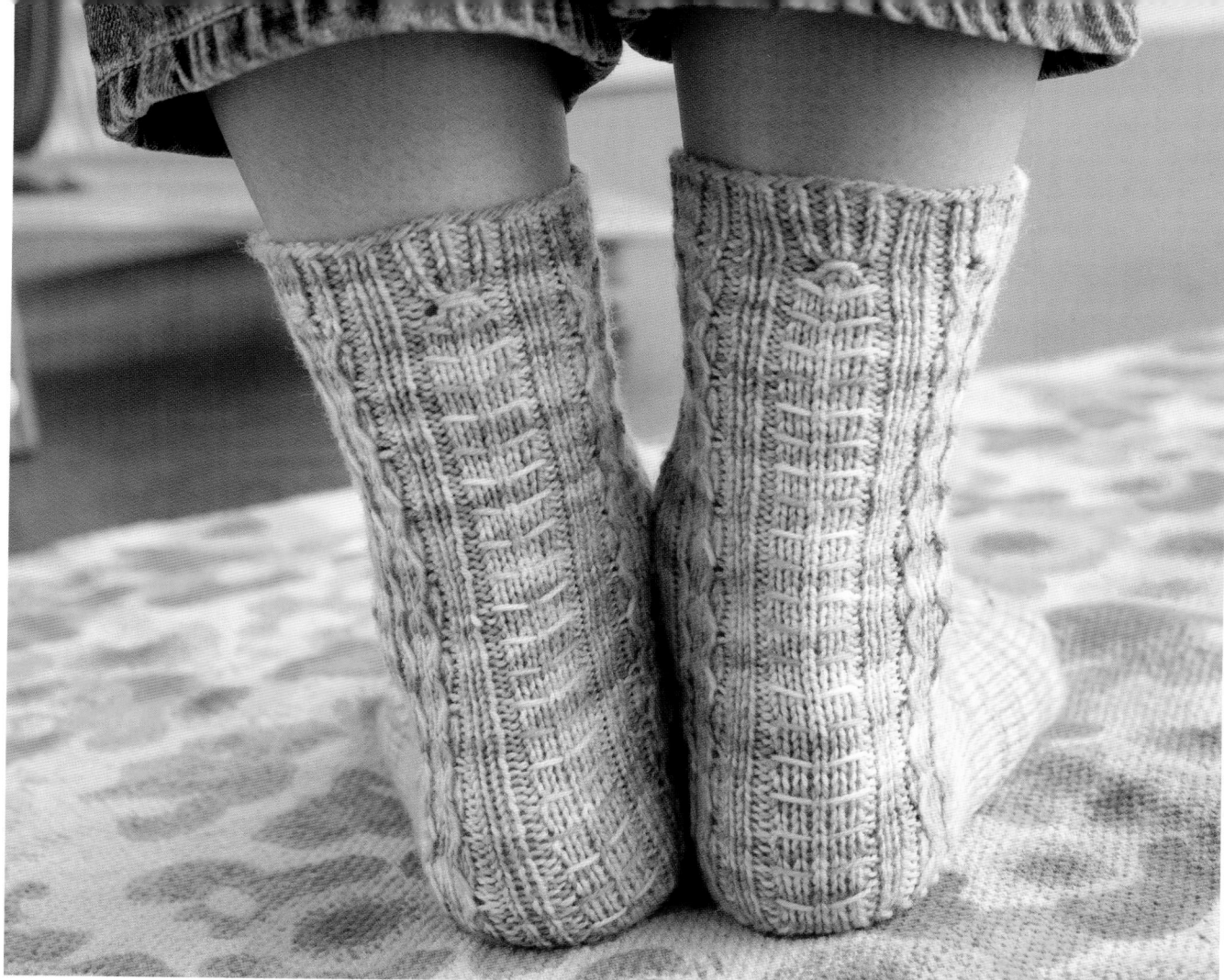

Yarn Note

These socks are worked in a soft three-ply superwash merino whose slight halo helps fill gaps between stitches and create a more cohesive fabric. The yarn's rounded structure renders the movement of slipped stitches beautifully while retaining a soft wooly quality. Semisolid coloring further softens the stitch pattern and enhances the flickering nature of the motif. But you could just as easily use a smoother four-ply solid if you long for more crisp, sculptural precision. If you choose a more loosely twisted two-ply, consider a yarn with nylon to help compensate for the decreased durability, especially along the heel and instep where slipped stitches run several rows at a time above the fabric surface. While the slipped stitches do help thicken the fabric in those areas, the slipped stitches are innately more vulnerable to abrasion. Alternating columns of ribbing give this sock sufficient elasticity for you to experiment with lower-elastic yarns or cotton blends if you desire.

—*Clara Parkes*

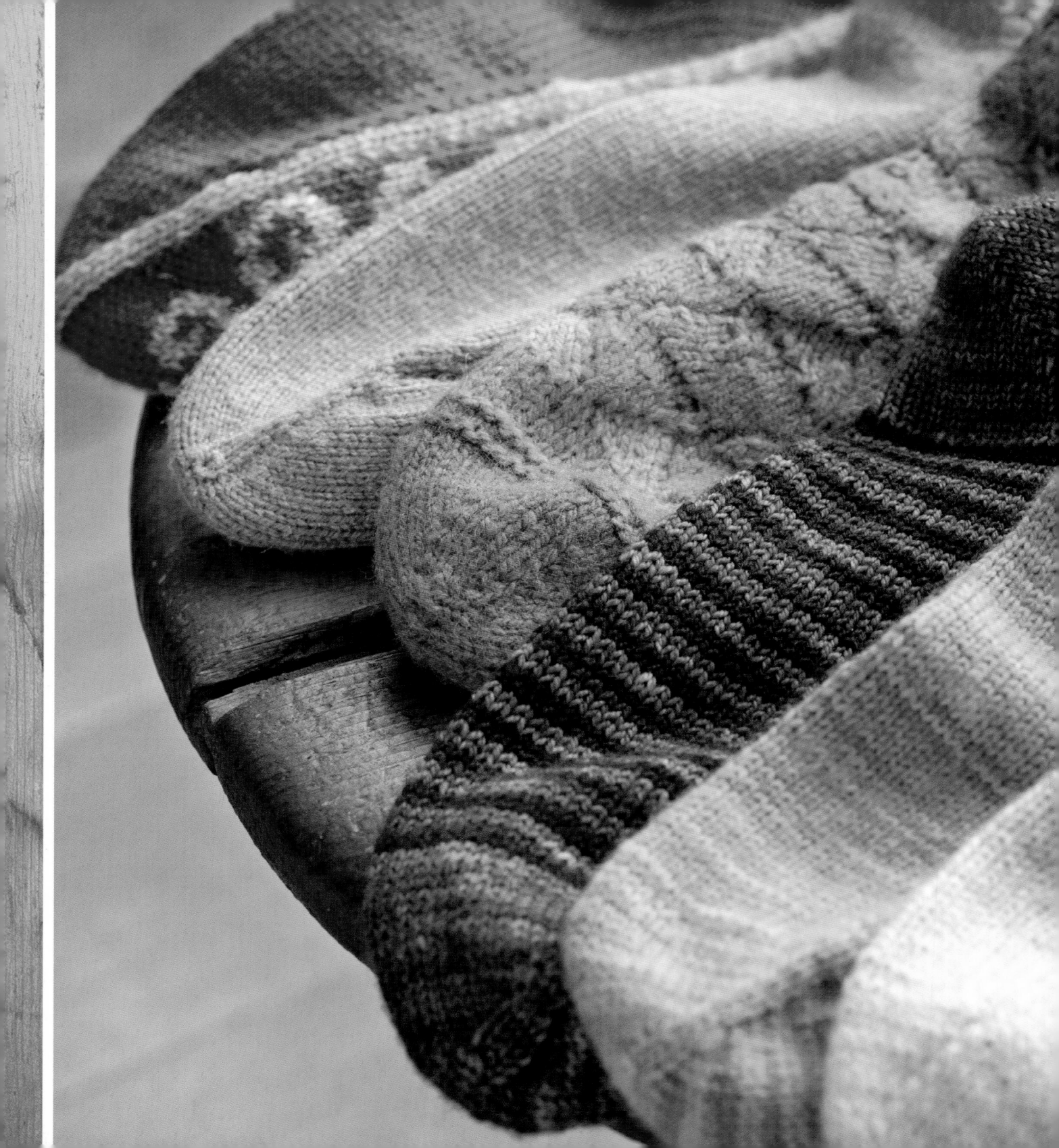

Toe-Up
Construction

Socks worked from the toe up are gaining popularity worldwide. To begin, stitches are cast on for the tip of the toe. Stitches are then increased at regular intervals to shape the toe and bring the foot circumference to the desired size, then the foot is worked to the desired length.

If a round heel is worked (see page 16), stitches are increased to shape the gussets along the way, then the stitches are divided with half on a holder to work later for the instep and the rest worked back and forth in rows to shape the heel and gussets. The gusset shaping is eliminated if a short-row heel (see page 20) is worked. The stitches are then rejoined for working in the round, and the leg is worked upward to where stitches are bound off at the top of the cuff.

The advantage to working socks from the toe up is that you can try on the foot along the way to ensure the correct circumference and length. If you have a limited amount of yarn, you can work the foot to the proper size, then end the leg when the yarn runs out. There are a variety of ways the heel can be shaped, none of which involves picking up stitches, and there is no need for the Kitchener stitch.

The main disadvantage to this direction of construction is that the entire texture or color pattern needs to be worked out before the foot is begun. Depending on the number of rows in the pattern repeat and the length of the foot, a pattern that begins nicely at the toe might end at an awkward place at the heel or cuff.

The seven patterns in this section are all worked from the toe up. In them, you'll find a variety of cast-ons designed specifically for working in rounds, a number of ways to shape the heels and toes, and an assortment of elastic bind-offs. Of course, you'll also find exciting integration of texture, color, and design.

Toe-Up Cast-Ons 〰〰〰〰〰〰〰〰〰〰〰〰〰〰〰

When knitting a sock from the toe up, the cast-on row forms the tip of the toe. Most methods mimic the look of a single row of knitting, with the instep stitches extending from one side of the cast-on stitches and the sole stitches extending from the other side.

Turkish/Eastern Cast-On

This method is worked by first wrapping the yarn around two parallel needles, then using a third needle to knit the loops on each of the two needles. The loops on one needle are the foundation for the instep and the loops on the other needle are the foundation for the sole. This method is used for the toe of Up-Down Entrelac (page 122), Stealth Argyles (page 138), and Toe-Up Travelers (page 166) and is demonstrated on the accompanying DVD.

Hold two double-pointed needles parallel to each other. Leaving a 4" (10 cm) tail hanging to the front between the two needles, wrap the yarn around both needles from back to front half the number of times as desired stitches (four wraps shown here for 8 stitches total), then bring the yarn forward between the needles (figure 1).

Use a third needle to knit across the loops on the top needle, keeping the third needle on top of both the other needles when knitting the first stitch (figure 2).

With the right side facing, rotate the two cast-on needles like the hands of a clock so that the bottom needle is on the top (figure 3).

Knit across the loops on the new top needle (figure 4).

Rotate the needles again and use a third needle to knit the first 2 stitches of the new top needle. There will now be 2 stitches each on two needles and 4 stitches on another needle (figure 5).

The two needles with 2 stitches each will form the bottom of the foot; the needle with 4 stitches will form the top of the foot. Using a fourth needle, begin working in rounds.

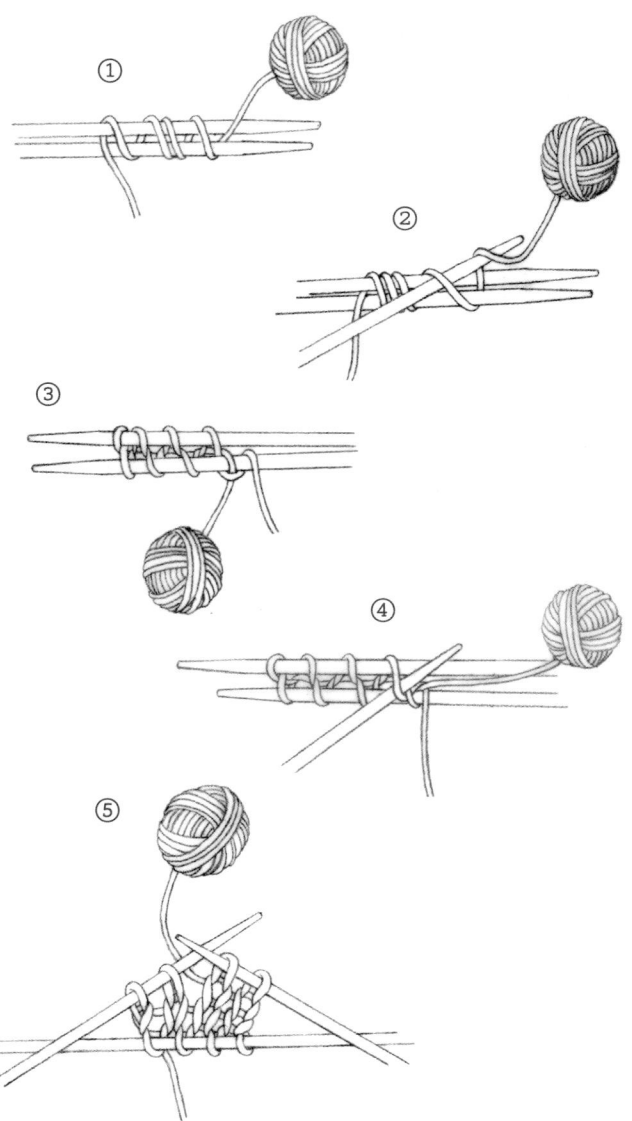

Judy's Magic Cast-On

This amazingly simple cast-on is named for its founder, Judy Becker. It wraps the yarn around two parallel needles in such a way as to mimic a row of stockinette stitch between the two needles. This technique is used for Terpander (page 144) and Pussy Willow Stockings (page 160) and is demonstrated on the accompanying DVD.

Leaving a 10" (25.5 cm) tail, drape the yarn over one needle, then hold a second needle parallel to and below the first and on top of the yarn tail (figure 1).

Bring the tail to the back and the ball yarn to the front, then place the thumb and index finger of your left hand between the two strands so that the tail is over your index finger and the ball yarn is over your thumb (figure 2). This forms the first stitch on the top needle.

*Continue to hold the two needles parallel and loop the finger yarn over the lower needle by bringing the lower needle over the top of the finger yarn (figure 3), then bringing the finger yarn up from below the lower needle, over the top of this needle, then to the back between the two needles.

Point the needles downward, bring the bottom needle past the thumb yarn, then bring the thumb yarn to the front between the two needles and over the top needle (figure 4).

Repeat from * until you have the desired number of stitches on each needle (figure 5).

Remove both yarn ends from your left hand, rotate the needles like the hands of a clock so that the bottom needle is now on top and both strands of yarn are at the needle tip (figure 6).

Using a third needle, knit the half of the stitches from the top needle (figure 7). There will now be the same number of stitches on two needles and twice that number of stitches on the bottom needle.

The two needles with the smaller number of stitches will form the bottom of the foot; the needle with the most stitches will form the top of the foot.

Using a fourth needle, begin working in rounds.

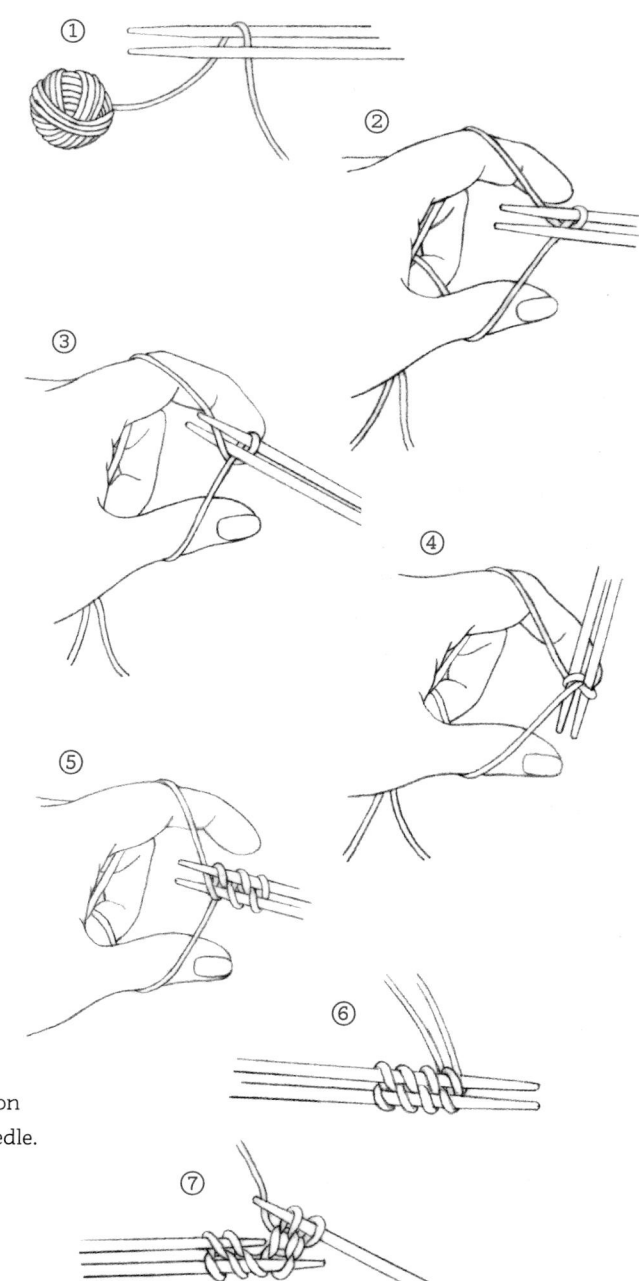

Toe-Up Bind-Offs

One of the drawbacks of knitting socks from the toe up is that the bind-off edge is at the top of the leg. If the bind-off is at all tight or inelastic, the sock will be difficult to stretch over the heel, will bind at the top of the leg, and possibly will not stay up. Fortunately, there are a number of bind-off techniques that ensure an elastic edge and comfortable fit.

Sewn Bind-Off

This method is worked using a tapestry needle and forms an elastic edge that has a ropy appearance much like a purl row. It is ideal for finishing off garter stitch. This method is used for the Toe-Up Travelers on page 166 and is demonstrated on the accompanying DVD.

Cut the yarn, leaving a tail about 4 times the circumference of the knitting to be bound off, and thread the tail onto a tapestry needle.

Working from right to left, *insert tapestry needle purlwise (from right to left) through the first 2 stitches (figure 1) and pull the yarn through.

Bring tapestry needle knitwise (from left to right) through the first stitch (figure 2), pull the yarn through, then slip this stitch off the knitting needle.

Repeat from * for the desired number of stitches.

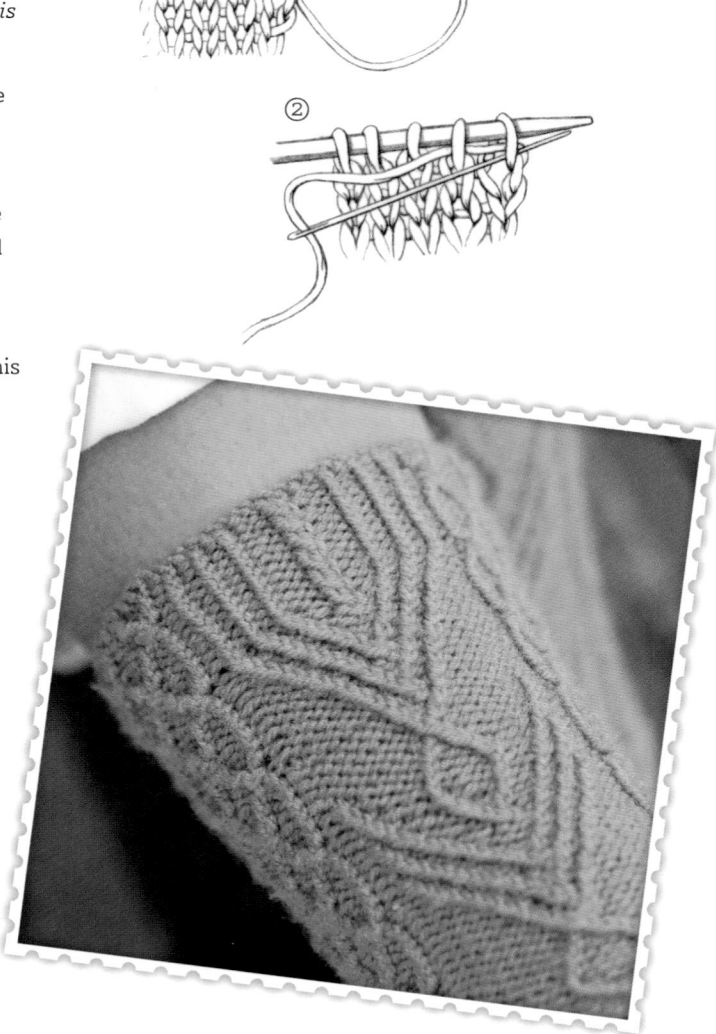

TOE-UP TRAVELERS, PAGE 166

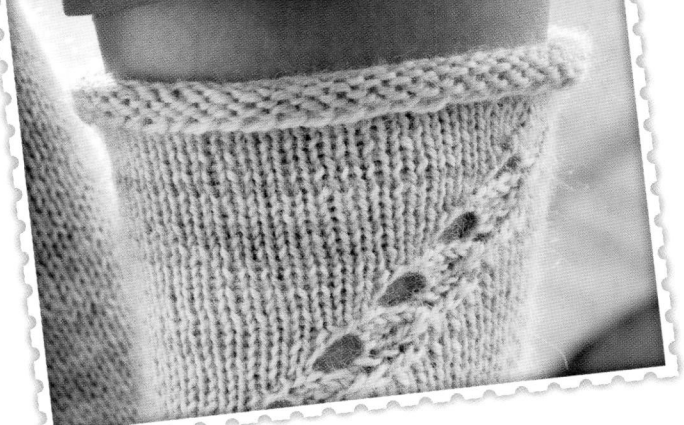

PUSSY WILLOW STOCKINGS, PAGE 160

Jeny's Surprisingly Stretchy Bind-Off

This aptly named bind-off is the brain child of Jeny Staiman. The elasticity comes from a yarnover "collar" that is worked in conjunction with each stitch. When viewed straight down from above, the bind-off edge of the ribbing will have a hinged appearance at each transition between knit and purl stitches. This bind-off is used in Pussy Willow Stockings on page 160 and is demonstrated on the accompanying DVD.

TO COLLAR A KNIT STITCH: Bring working yarn from back to front over needle in the opposite direction of a normal yarnover (figure 1), knit the next stitch, then lift the yarnover over the top of the knitted stitch and off the needle (figure 2).

TO COLLAR A PURL STITCH: Bring working yarn from front to back over needle as for a normal yarnover (figure 3), purl the next stitch, then lift the yarnover over the top of the purled stitch and off the needle (figure 4).

To begin, collar each of the first 2 stitches to match their knit or purl nature. Then pass the first collared stitch over the second and off the right needle—1 stitch is bound off.

*Collar the next stitch according to its nature (figure 5), then pass the previous stitch over the collared stitch and off the needle (figure 6).

Repeat from * until 1 stitch remains on the right needle. Cut the yarn, leaving a 6" (15 cm) tail, then pull on the loop of the last stitch until the tail comes free.

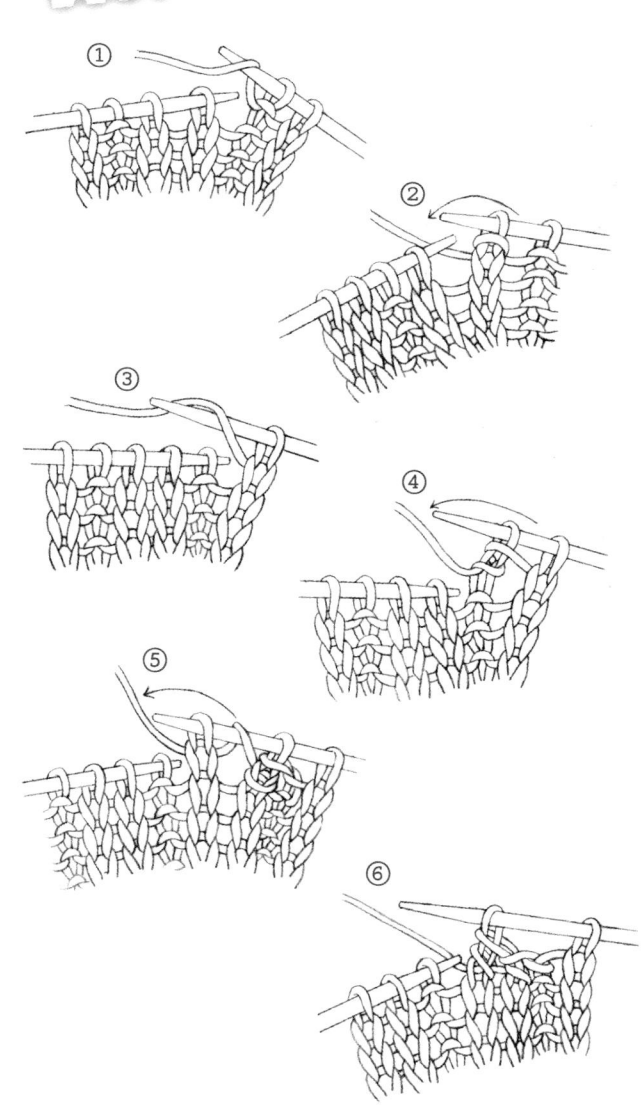

Decrease Bind-Off

This method forms a flexible bind-off that is commonly used on lace shawls. For socks, it ensures sufficient elasticity to stretch over the heel. Instead of lifting 1 stitch over another and off the needle, 2 stitches are worked together similar to working a ssk decrease, then the remaining stitch is returned to the left needle to be worked together with the next stitch. This method is used for Stealth Argyles on page 138 and is demonstrated on the accompanying DVD.

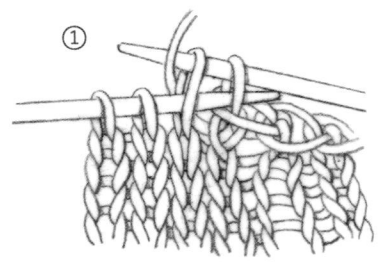

Slip the first stitch, knit the second stitch, then *knit these 2 stitches together by inserting the left-hand needle into the front both from left to right and knitting them together through their back loops with the right needle (figure 1).

Knit the next stitch (figure 2).

Repeat from * for the desired number of stitches.

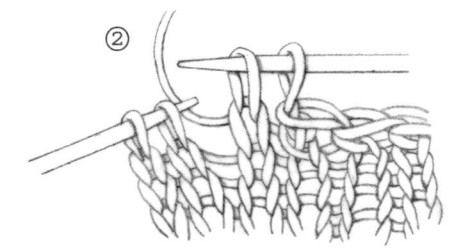

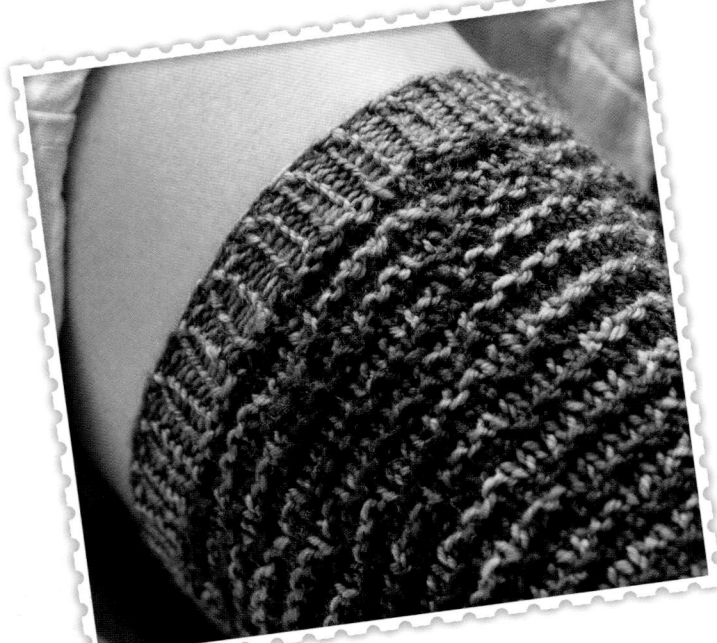

STEALTH ARGYLES, PAGE 138

Tubular Bind-Off

Also called the invisible ribbed bind-off, this method produces an extremely elastic edge that follows a k1, p1 rib. The edge had a rounded appearance that when viewed straight down from above looks as though the stitches are continuous from the right side to the wrong side of the piece. This method is used to finish the Half-Stranded Socks on page 152.

Cut the yarn, leaving a tail about 3 times the circumference of the knitting to be bound off, and thread the tail onto a tapestry needle.

STEP 1: Working from right to left, insert the tapestry needle purlwise (from right to left) through the first (knit) stitch (figure 1) and pull the yarn through.

STEP 2: Bring the tapestry needle behind the knit stitch, then insert it knitwise (from left to right) into the second stitch (this will be a purl stitch; figure 2), and pull the yarn through.

STEP 3: *Insert the tapestry needle into the first knit stitch knitwise and slip this stitch off the knitting needle.

STEP 4: Skip the first purl stitch, insert the tapestry needle purlwise into the next knit stitch (figure 3), and pull the yarn through.

STEP 5: Insert the tapestry needle into the first purl stitch purlwise and slip this stitch off the knitting needle.

STEP 6: Bring the tapestry needle behind the knit stitch, then insert it knitwise into the second stitch (this will be a purl stitch; figure 4), and pull the yarn through.

Repeat from * until 1 stitch remains on the knitting needle. Insert the tapestry needle purlwise through this last stitch, draw the yarn through, and pull tight to secure.

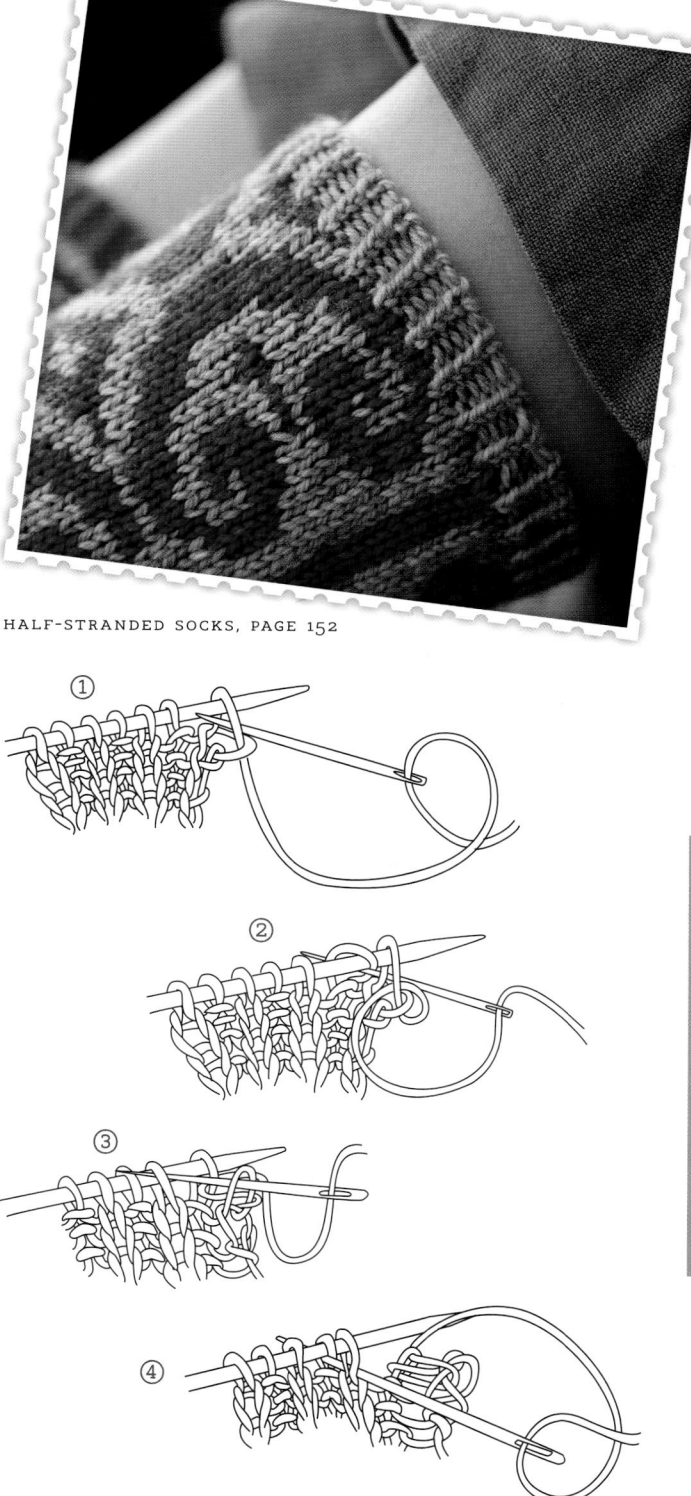

HALF-STRANDED SOCKS, PAGE 152

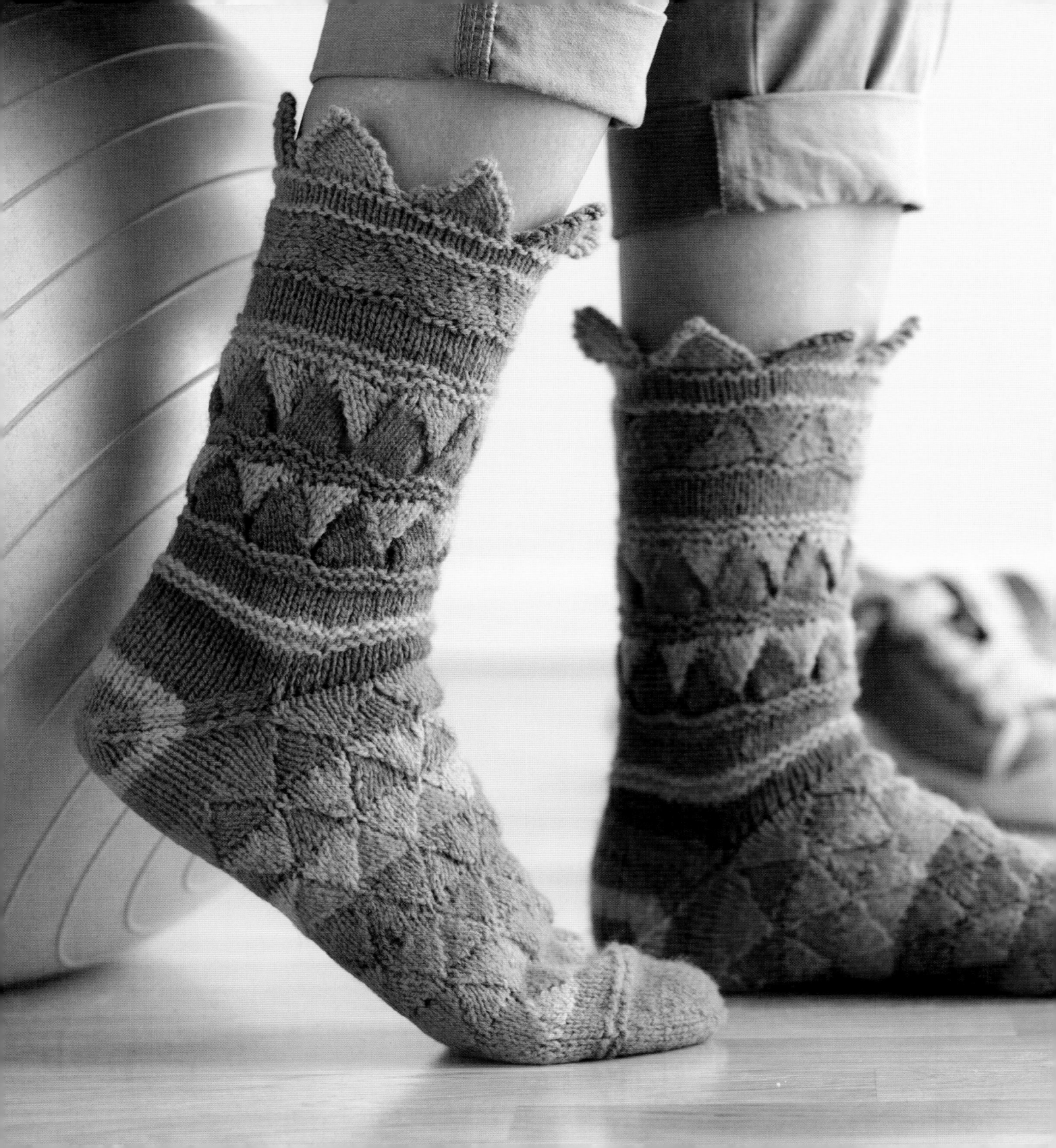

finished size

About 8½" (21.5 cm) foot circumference, 10" (25.5 cm) foot length from back of heel to tip of toe (with option for adjusting foot length), and 10" (25.5 cm) leg length from tip of tallest cuff point to base of heel flap.

yarn

Sportweight (#2 Fine).

Shown here: Kathryn Alexander Designs Hand-Dyed Wool (100% wool; 22 yd [20 m]/5 g): 30 hand-dyed colors: mulberry, turquoise, orange-gold, pinky violet, yellow-green, gray-blue, grass green, pink, mustard yellow, rust, bright blue, violet, teal, rusty orange, gray-violet, olive, gold, coral-orange, bright teal, coral, green, copper, blue, lavender, rosy magenta, dark teal green, orange, light sage green, dusty purple, and cantaloupe.

Visit www.kathrynalexander.net to order a kit of all the yarns used in this pattern.

needles

Sizes U.S. 1, 2, and 3 (2.25, 2.75, and 3.25 mm): set of 5 double-pointed (dpn) each.

Adjust needle size if necessary to obtain the correct gauge.

notions

Waste yarn for provisional cast-on; marker (m); tapestry needle.

gauge

12 sts and 18 rnds = 2" in St st on size U.S. 2 (2.75 mm) needles, worked in rnds.

Up-Down Entrelac

DESIGNED BY *Kathryn Alexander*

My love for color is evident in all of my designs—most incorporate as many colors as possible. These socks are no different. But, because I don't like to carry the multiple yarns required to get such wild patterns through color stranding, I tend to work many of my patterns in a variety of entrelac shapes—squares, rectangles, base triangles, and fill-in triangles. By changing colors for each shape, I can introduce more colors for a riotous effect—these socks incorporate a total of thirty muted

By changing colors for each shape, I can introduce more colors for a riotous effect—these socks incorporate a total of thirty muted colors of my hand-dyed yarn."

colors of my hand-dyed yarn. I arranged the shapes to produce a variety of textural surfaces and separated them with colorful garter ridges. So that I could work an afterthought or peasant heel that wouldn't interfere with the entrelac patterning, I worked the legs top down from the cuff to the heel, then I worked the foot toe up from the tip of the toe to the heel. For the heel, I first connected the instep stitches with a three-needle bind-off, then worked the remaining heel stitches in the round, working a series of stripes to echo the lively color pattern on the leg and foot.

DESIGN TECHNIQUES

top-down leg construction, page 36
toe-up foot construction, page 114
designing with entrelac, page 32
working with five double-pointed needles,
page 12
invisible provisional cast-on (for leg), page 43
Turkish/Eastern cast-on (for toe), page 116
peasant heel, page 19
Kitchener stitch, page 44

Stitch Guide

LEFT-LEANING 6-STITCH TRIANGLE (WORKED OVER 6 STS)

Row 1: (RS) K2, turn work.

Row 2: Sl 1 pwise with yarn in front (wyf), p1, turn.

Row 3: K3, turn.

Row 4: Sl 1 pwise wyf, p2, turn.

Row 5: K4, turn.

Row 6: Sl 1 pwise wyf, p3, turn.

Row 7: K5, turn.

Row 8: Sl 1 pwise wyf, p4, turn.

Row 9: (RS) K6, do not turn—1 triangle completed.

RIGHT-LEANING 6-STITCH TRIANGLE (WORKED OVER 6 STS)

Row 1: (WS) P2, turn work.

Row 2: Sl 1 pwise with yarn in back (wyb), k1, turn.

Row 3: P3, turn.

Row 4: Sl 1 pwise wyb, k2, turn.

Row 5: P4, turn.

Row 6: Sl 1 pwise wyb, k3, turn.

Row 7: P5, turn.

Row 8: Sl 1 pwise wyb, k4, turn.

Row 9: (WS) P6, do not turn—1 triangle completed.

RIGHT-LEANING 6-STITCH RECTANGLE

Rows 1, 3, 5, and 7: (RS) K6, turn work.

Rows 2, 4, and 6: P5, p2tog (last rectangle st tog with triangle st after it), turn—1 triangle st joined in each row.

Row 8: (WS) P5, p3tog (last rectangle st tog with next 2 triangle sts)—1 rectangle completed; 6 rectangle sts; no sts rem from triangle being joined.

LEFT-LEANING 6-STITCH RECTANGLE

Rows 1, 3, 5, and 7: (WS) P6, turn work.

Rows 2, 4, and 6: K5, ssk (last rectangle st tog with triangle st after it), turn—1 triangle st joined in each row.

Row 8: (RS) K5, sl 1 kwise wyb, k2tog, (2 triangle sts tog), pass slipped rectangle st over—1 rectangle completed; 6 rectangle sts; no sts rem from triangle being joined.

WS FILL-IN TRIANGLE

Row 1: (RS) Sl 1 pwise wyb, k1, turn work.

Row 2: Sl 1 pwise wyf, p2, turn—1 st worked from triangle below.

Row 3: Sl 1 pwise wyb, k3, turn.

Row 4: Sl 1 pwise wyf, p4, turn—1 st worked from triangle below.

Row 5: Sl 1 pwise wyb, k5, turn.

Row 6: Sl 1 pwise wyf, p6, turn—1 st worked from triangle below.

Row 7: Sl 1 pwise wyb, k5, sl 1 kwise wyb, k2tog, psso.

Row 8: Sl 1 pwise wyf, p1, p2tog, p2, p3tog (last fill-in triangle st tog with 2 sts from triangle below)—6 fill-in triangle sts rem.

RS FILL-IN TRIANGLE

Row 1: (WS) Sl 1 pwise wyf, p1, turn work.

Row 2: Sl 1 pwise wyb, k2, turn—1 st worked from triangle below.

Row 3: Sl 1 pwise wyf, p3, turn.

Row 4: Sl 1 pwise wyb, k4, turn—1 st worked from triangle below.

Row 5: Sl 1 pwise wyf, p5, turn.

Row 6: Sl 1 pwise wyb, k6, turn—1 st worked from triangle below.

Row 7: Sl 1 pwise wyf, p5, p3tog, turn.

Row 8: Sl 1 pwise wyb, k1, k2tog, k2, sl 1 kwise wyb, k2tog (2 sts from triangle below), psso—6 fill-in triangle sts rem.

notes

+ The leg is worked from the top down and the foot is worked from the toe up. The leg and foot are joined across the top of the instep using the three-needle bind-off, then the remaining stitches of the sole and back of the leg are joined in the round for working a peasant heel.

+ The small gaps between the rectangles in the triangle/rectangle bands of the leg are a deliberate design element.

+ For the socks shown, the toe measures 2½" (6.5 cm) long, the heel measures 2" (5 cm) long, and the entrelac section of the foot measures about 5½" (14 cm) long. For a longer or shorter foot, work more or fewer rounds with turquoise at the end of the toe before beginning the foot triangles. For a longer or shorter leg, work more or fewer rounds with bright teal at the end of the ankle before placing the leg stitches on hold. Every 2 rounds added or removed will lengthen or shorten the pieces by about ¼" (6 mm).

+ Instead of turning the work and purling the small number of stitches for each entrelac triangle or rectangle, you can substitute knitting in reverse for the purl rows (see Glossary). This allows you to work entirely with right side of the piece facing you and speeds up the process.

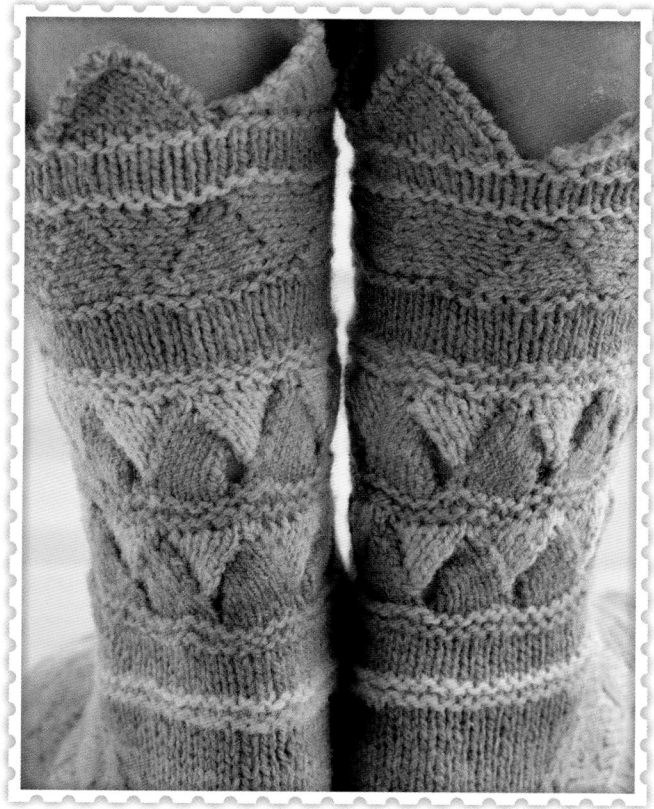

Cuff

TRIANGLE BAND

With mulberry and size U.S. 2 (2.75 mm) needles, use a provisional method (see page 43) to CO 6 sts. Knit 1 RS row. *With mulberry, purl 1 WS row, then work Rows 1–9 of Left-Leaning 6-st Triangle (see Stitch Guide), ending with a RS row. Slide sts to beg of needle in position to work another RS row. With turquoise, knit 1 RS row, then work Rows 1–9 of Right-Leaning 6-st Triangle (see Stitch Guide), ending with a WS row. Slide sts to beg of needle in position to work another WS row. Rep from * 7 more times—16 triangles, 8 of each color; piece measures about 9" (23 cm) from CO.

Carefully remove waste yarn from provisional CO and place live sts on spare needle. Hold ends of band tog with RS touching and WS facing out, being careful not to twist band. With turquoise, use the three-needle method (see Glossary) to BO live sts tog with provisional CO sts to form a ring.

TOP EDGING

Hold top triangle band horizontally with the predominantly turquoise selvedge running along the top. With orange-gold, size U.S. 2 (2.75 mm) needles, and RS facing, pick up and knit 5 sts along the selvedge of each turquoise triangle and 2 sts along the top of selvedge of each mulberry triangle—56 sts total. Purl 1 rnd. With pinky violet, knit 3 rnds. With yellow-green, knit 2 rnds, then purl 1 rnd, then knit 2 rnds.

TOP TRIANGLES

Make 7 short-row top triangles, each worked over an 8-st section using a different color. With WS facing, join mustard yellow and work triangle as foll:

ROW 1: (WS) P8.

ROW 2: P1, k1, turn work.

ROW 3: Sl 1 pwise wyf, p1, turn.

ROW 4: P1, k2, turn.

ROW 5: Sl 1 pwise wyf, p2, turn.

ROW 6: P1, k3, turn.

ROW 7: Sl 1, p3, turn.

ROW 8: P1, k4, turn.

ROW 9: Sl 1, p4, turn.

ROW 10: P1, k5, turn.

ROW 11: Sl 1, p5, turn.

ROW 12: P1, k6, turn.

ROW 13: Sl 1, p6, turn.

ROW 14: [P1, k1] 4 times, turn.

Break yarn, thread tail on a tapestry needle, and draw through 8 live triangle sts. Pull the tail just tight enough to make a nice equal-sided triangle, then weave in tail on WS. With WS facing, join pink to beg of sts to the left of the triangle just completed and work a second triangle in the same manner. Working each triangle on the 8 sts to the left of the previous triangle when WS is facing, work 5 more triangles in gray-blue, light sage green, rusty orange, pinky violet, and turquoise—no live sts rem at top of cuff.

Leg

Hold cuff with RS facing and top triangles pointing down.

PICK-UP RND: With grass green and size U.S. 2 (2.75 mm) needles, pick up and knit 5 sts along the selvedge of each mulberry triangle and 2 sts along the top of selvedge of each turquoise triangle—56 sts total.

Purl 1 rnd. Change to gray-blue and knit 5 rnds. Change to size 1 (2.25 mm) needles. With pink, knit 1 rnd, then purl 1 rnd while dec 2 sts evenly spaced—54 sts rem. With mustard yellow, knit 1 rnd, then purl 1 rnd. With grass green, knit 1 rnd.

Yarn Note

This is a perfect pairing of yarn and design upon which there really is no improvement. The lofty two-ply yarn is made from the fibers of Columbia sheep raised by Kathryn's brother. Spun to her exact specifications, the yarn is then hand-dyed by Kathryn in a palette specifically intended for each design. The Columbia wool is both soft and sturdy, with a generous staple length for strength, plus a forgiving elasticity that makes entrelac easy. After washing, the yarn relaxes and gains cohesion, forgiving any slightly irregular tension and possible gaps between the entrelac triangles on the foot. The design benefits from the natural bloom of Kathryn's yarn, so if substituting, be sure to choose a yarn that also has a slightly fuzzy surface. If you're particularly hard on your heels, consider wearing these socks with open-heeled shoes or clogs—both for maximum longevity and greater visibility.

—*Clara Parkes*

FIRST TRIANGLE/RECTANGLE BAND
Left-Leaning Triangles

With grass green, work Rows 1–9 of Left-Leaning 6-st Triangle (see Stitch Guide). *With RS still facing, work Rows 1–9 of triangle over the next 6 sts to complete another triangle; rep from * 7 more times—9 triangles completed; 54 sts in 9 groups of 6 sts each.

Right-Leaning Rectangles

Turn work so WS is facing and join rust to the top of the long side of any triangle, close to the needle. With WS facing, pick up and purl (see Glossary) 5 sts along triangle selvedge from tip of triangle to bottom of "valley" between triangles, then purl 1 st from triangle on left-hand needle—6 rectangle sts; 1 triangle st has been joined. Work Rows 1–8 of Right-Leaning 6-st Rectangle (see Stitch Guide)—all sts of triangle have been joined. *With WS still facing, pick up and purl 5 sts along selvedge of next triangle, then purl 1 triangle st—6 sts. Work Rows 1–8 of rectangle once more to complete another rectangle. Rep from * 7 more times—9 rectangles completed; 54 sts in 9 groups of 6 sts each.

SECOND TRIANGLE/RECTANGLE BAND

With bright blue, knit 1 rnd, then purl 1 rnd. With violet, knit 1 rnd, then purl 1 rnd. With yellow-green, knit 1 rnd.

Right-Leaning Triangles

Turn work so WS is facing. With yellow-green, work Rows 1–9 of Right-Leaning 6-st Triangle. *With WS still facing, work Rows 1–9 over the next 6 sts to complete another triangle; rep from * 7 more times—9 triangles completed; 54 sts in 9 groups of 6 sts each.

Left-Leaning Rectangles

Turn work so RS is facing and join teal to the top of the long side of any triangle, close to the needle. With RS facing, pick up and knit 5 sts along triangle selvedge from tip of triangle to bottom of "valley" between triangles, then knit 1 st from

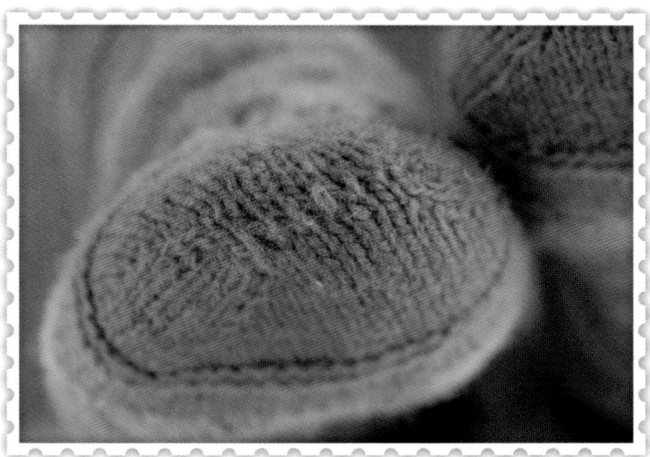

triangle on left-hand needle—6 rectangle sts; 1 triangle st has been joined. Work Rows 1–8 of Left-Leaning 6-st Rectangle (see Stitch Guide)—all sts of triangle have been joined. *With RS still facing, pick up and knit 5 sts along selvedge of next triangle, then knit 1 triangle st—6 sts. Work Rows 1–8 once more to complete another rectangle. Rep from * 7 more times—9 rectangles completed; 54 sts in 9 groups of 6 sts each.

ANKLE

With rusty orange, knit 1 rnd, then purl 1 rnd. With gray-violet, knit 1 rnd, then purl 1 rnd. With olive, knit 4 rnds. With gold, knit 1 rnd, then purl 1 rnd. With coral-orange, knit 1 rnd, then purl 1 rnd. With bright teal, knit 1 rnd while inc 2 sts evenly spaced—56 sts total. With bright teal, knit 3 more rnds—leg measures about 8" (20.5 cm) from tip of top points (see Notes for adjusting leg length). Place foot sts on holder or empty set of needles.

Foot
TOE

With lavender, size U.S. 2 (2.75 mm) needles and using the Turkish/Eastern method (page 116), CO 16 sts, 8 sts each on 2 needles. Knit 1 rnd on all sts. Working back and forth in rows on sts of one needle, work 5 rows in St st, beg and ending with a RS row—8 sts each on 2 needles; 6-row St st rectangle between needles.

JOINING RND: With RS still facing and empty needle, pick up and knit 3 sts along selvedge of rectangle; with another needle, k8 from needle at bottom of rectangle; with another needle, pick up and knit 3 more sts along other selvedge of rectangle—22 sts total; 8 sts each on top and bottom needle, 3 sts each on 2 side needles. Place marker (pm) and join for working in rnds. Rnd begins at top of rectangle at start of 8-st top needle.

INC RND: *K1, use the lifted method (see Glossary) to inc 1 st, knit to last st of needle, use the lifted method to inc 1 st, k1, knit 3 sts from side needle; rep from * once more—4 sts inc'd, 2 sts inc'd on top and bottom needles.

Knit 1 rnd even. Rep the last 2 rnds 5 more times—46 sts; 20 sts each on the top and bottom needles; 3 sts each side needle.

NEXT RND: *K1, use the lifted method to inc 1 st, knit to end needle, k3 sts from side needle; rep from * once more—48 sts; 21 sts each on top and bottom needles, 3 sts each side needle.

Redistribute sts evenly on 3 or 4 needles. With olive, knit 1 rnd, then purl 1 rnd. With rusty orange, knit 1 rnd, then purl 1 rnd. With turquoise, knit 4 rnds—toe measures about 2½" (6.5 cm). See Notes for adjusting foot length.

FOOT TRIANGLES

Change to size U.S. 1 (2.25 mm) needles.

Left-Leaning Triangles

With gold and RS facing, knit 1 rnd. Work Rows 1–9 of Left-Leaning 6-st Triangle. *With RS still facing, work Rows 1–9 of triangle over the next 6 sts to complete another triangle; rep from * 6 more times—8 triangles completed; 48 sts in 8 groups of 6 sts each.

WS Fill-in Triangles

Turn work so WS is facing and join coral to the top of the long side of any left-leaning triangle, close to the needle. With WS facing, pick up and purl 5 sts along triangle selvedge from tip of triangle to bottom of "valley" between triangles, then purl 1 st from triangle on left-hand needle—6 fill-in triangle sts; 1 st worked from left-leaning triangle. Work Rows 1–8 of WS Fill-in Triangle (see Stitch Guide)—all sts of left-leaning triangle have been worked. *With WS still facing, pick up and purl 5 sts along selvedge of next left-leaning triangle, then purl 1 triangle st from left-hand needle—6 fill-in triangle sts. Work Rows 1–8 of fill-in triangle once more to complete another triangle. Rep from * 6 more times—8 fill-in triangles completed; 48 sts in 8 groups of 6 sts each.

Right-Leaning Triangles

With green and WS facing, purl 1 rnd. Work Rows 1–9 of Right-Leaning 6-st Triangle. *With WS still facing, work Rows 1–9 over the next 6 sts to complete another triangle; rep from * 6 more times—8 triangles completed; 48 sts in 8 groups of 6 sts each.

RS Fill-in Triangles

Turn work so RS is facing and join copper to the top long side of any right-leaning triangle, close to the needle. With RS facing, pick up and knit 5 sts along triangle selvedge from tip of triangle to bottom of "valley" between triangles, then knit 1 st from triangle on left-hand needle—6 fill-in triangle sts; 1 st worked from right-leaning triangle. Work Rows 1–8 of RS Fill-in Triangle (see Stitch Guide)—all sts of right-leaning triangle have been worked. *With RS still facing, pick up and knit 5 sts along selvedge of next right-leaning triangle, then knit 1 triangle st from left-hand needle—6 fill-in triangle sts. Work Rows 1–8 of fill-in triangle once more to complete another triangle. Rep from * 6 more times—8 fill-in triangles completed; 48 sts in 8 groups of 6 sts each.

This completes a 4-tier set of foot triangles comprised of 1 tier each of left-leaning triangles, WS fill-in triangles, right-leaning triangles, and RS fill-in triangles as given above. Work 2 more 4-tier sets using the foll colors:

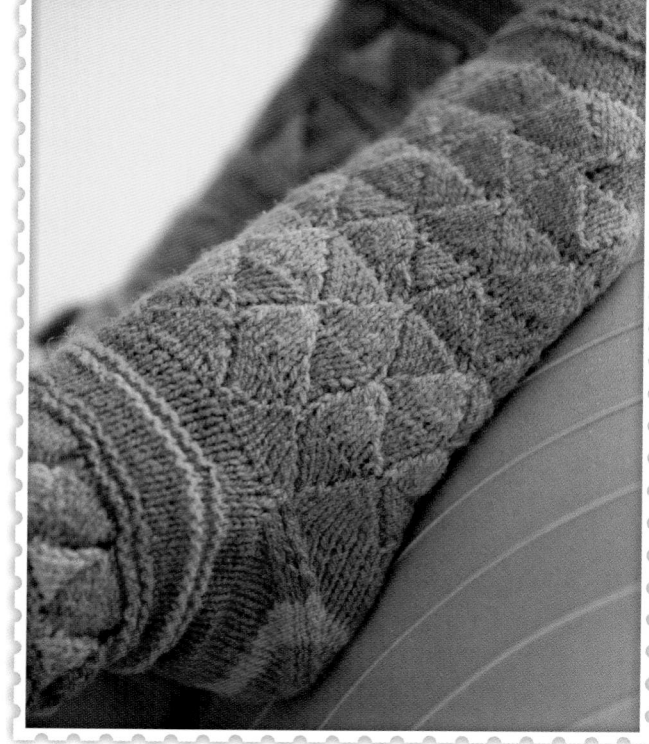

SET 1: Left-leaning triangles, blue; WS fill-in triangles, rosy magenta; right-leaning triangles, dark teal green; RS fill-in triangles, violet.

SET 2: Left-leaning triangles, orange; WS fill-in triangles, yellow-green; right-leaning triangles, turquoise; RS fill-in triangles, light sage green.

With dusty purple, work a tier of left-leaning triangles. With rusty orange, work a tier of WS fill-in triangles and *at the same time* work WS Row 8 of each fill-in triangle as foll to inc each triangle from 6 to 7 sts: Sl 1 pwise wyf, p5, p3tog (last fill-in triangle st tog with 2 sts from triangle below)—56 sts in 8 groups of 7 sts each.

With rusty orange, knit 1 rnd—foot measures about 8" (20.5 cm) from tip of toe.

Join Leg to Foot

Flatten the foot so the toe incs are positioned evenly on side of the toe to identify the instep half and sole half of the foot sts. Arrange foot sts on 3 needles with 28 sts on one needle for instep, and 28 sole sts divided evenly on 2 needles with 14 sts on each needle. Flatten the leg so the top point in light sage green is in the center of one side, in the middle of the front of the leg. Arrange foot sts on 3 needles with 28 sts on one needle for front of the leg and 28 back-of-leg sts divided evenly on 2 needles with 14 sts on each needle. Hold needles with 28 sts each for top of foot and front of leg tog with RS touching and WS facing out. With size 3 (3.25 mm) needles and bright teal, join sts tog using the three-needle bind-off method (see Glossary)—56 sts rem; 28 back of leg sts, and 28 sole sts.

Heel

Transfer all sts to size U.S. 2 (2.75 mm) needles, 14 sts each on 4 needles. Join lavender in corner between back of leg sts and sole sts, at start of sole sts.

JOINING RND: *Pick up and knit 1 st in corner, k28 sts, pick up and knit 1 st in corner; rep from * once more—60 sts; 15 sts each on 4 needles.

NEXT RND: Knit.

DEC RND: *On Needle 1, k1, ssk, knit to end; on Needle 2, knit to last 3 sts, k2tog, k1; rep from * for Needles 3 and 4—4 sts dec'd.

Rep the shaping of the last 2 rnds 8 more times and *at the same time* change colors for stripes as foll: 1 rnd lavender, 4 rnds olive, 4 rnds cantaloupe, 7 rnds turquoise—24 sts rem; heel measures about 2" (5 cm) from joining rnd.

Finishing

Place 12 heel sts from sole of foot on one needle, and 12 heel sts from back of leg on another needle—12 sts each on 2 needles. With teal threaded on a tapestry needle, use the Kitchener st (page 44) to graft the sts tog. Weave in loose ends. Block lightly.

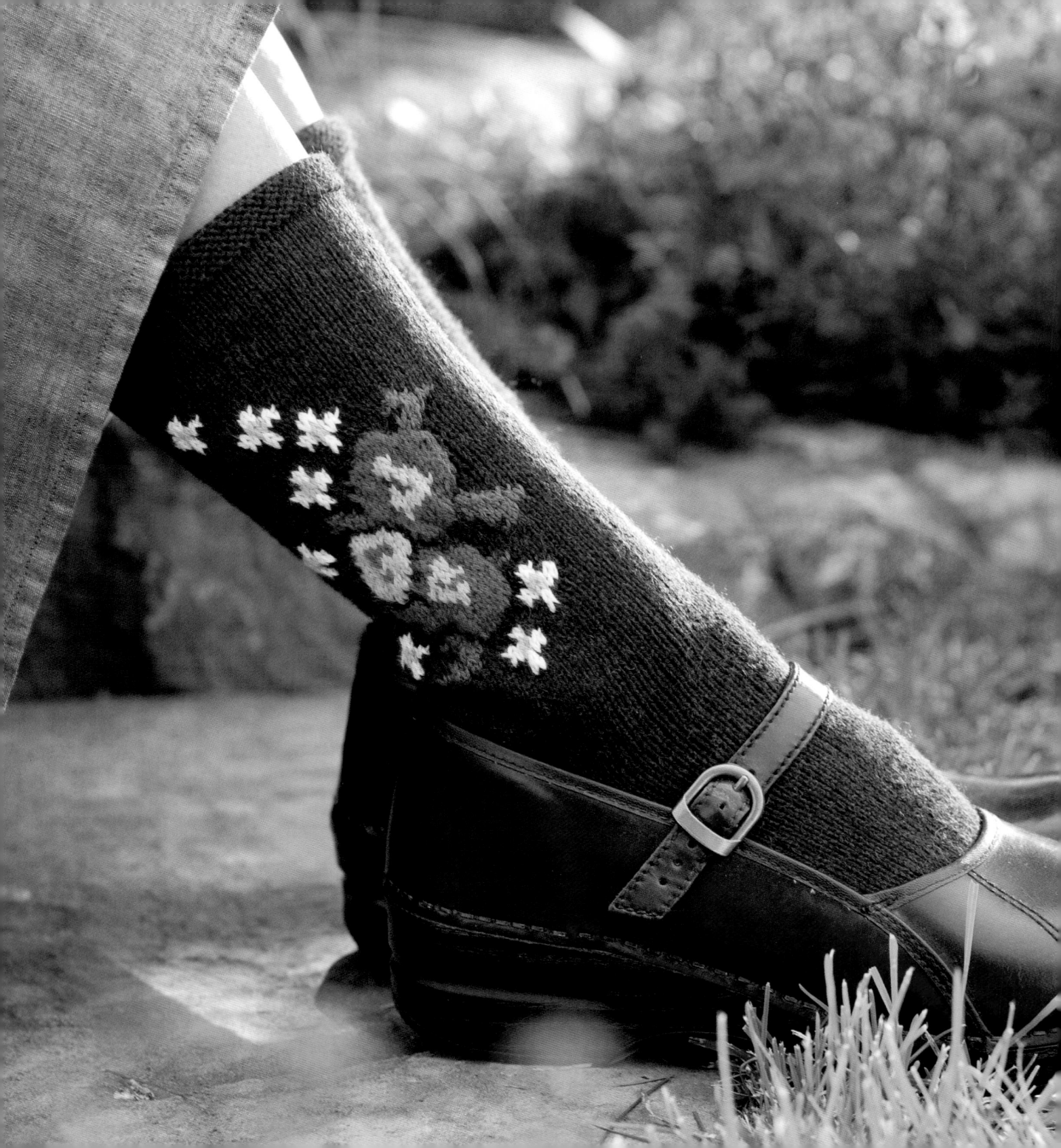

Bulgarian Blooms

DESIGNED BY *Priscilla Gibson-Roberts*

finished size

About 7½ (8, 8½, 8¾, 9¼)" (19 [20.5, 21.5, 22, 23.5] cm) foot circumference, 9½ (9½, 9¾, 9¾, 9¾)" (24 [24, 25, 25, 25] cm) foot length from back of heel to tip of toe (with option for adjusting foot length), and 10" (25.5 cm) leg length from top of cuff to base of heel. Socks shown measure 8" (20.5 cm) in circumference.

yarn

Fingering weight (#1 Super Fine).

Shown here: Brown Sheep Cotton Fine (80% cotton, 20% merino; 222 yd [203 m]/50 g): #CW045 cavern (black; MC), 2 skeins; #CW930 candy apple (dark red), #CW210 tea rose (pink), #CW100 cotton ball (white), #CW460 jungle green, and #CW345 gold dust,1 skein each.

needles

Foot and lower leg: size 0 (2 mm): set of 5 double-pointed (dpn).

Upper leg and cuff: size 1 (2.5 mm): set of 5 dpn.

Adjust needle size if necessary to obtain the correct gauge.

notions

Markers (m); waste-yarn for provisional cast-on; tapestry needle.

gauge

18 sts and 25 rnds = 2" (5 cm) in St st on smaller needles, worked in rnds.

> *For these socks, I chose to center the design on the outside half of each leg.*

During my studies of historical knitting, I have become enamored with intarsia patterns worked in the round and short-row heels, both of which are included in these socks. In true Bulgarian patterns, the design extends from the instep up the front of the leg. This places part of the design inside the shoe, especially with the clogs that I like to wear. The design could be placed higher on the foot where it wouldn't be covered by a shoe, but that always seems a little off-balance to me. For these socks, I chose to center the design on the outside half of each leg.

To work intarsia in the round "in the old way," both the background and pattern stitches are worked as for normal color stranding in the first round, then the design yarns are dropped at the end of the pattern section while the background yarn continues to the end of the round. For the following round, the background and design stitches are worked separately in two steps. Upon reaching the design, the background stitches are knitted, and the pattern stitches are slipped with the background yarn held in back to create floats across the wrong side. The work is turned and the pattern stitches are purled back to the start of the design (when viewed from the right side). The work is turned once more and the background color is worked to the end of the round.

131

DESIGN TECHNIQUES

toe-up construction, page 114

intarsia in the round, page 136

working with five double-pointed needles,
page 12

invisible provisional cast-on, page 43

short-row heel (and toe), page 25

notes

+ These socks begin with a provisional cast-on across the top of the foot at the base of the toes. The short-row toe shaping is worked along the top of the foot to the tip of the toes, then along the sole of the foot to the base of the toes. The stitches from the sole of the foot and the provisional cast-on are joined for working in the round and the foot is worked from the toe to the heel.

+ The short-row heel is worked the same as the short-row toe, except that it is worked using the stitches from the sole half of the foot.

+ In the charts, the main color is shaded a slightly darker gray on the two-step intarsia rounds (see sidebar on page 136) to make it easier to keep your place in the patterns.

Stitch Guide

SSP

Slip 2 sts individually kwise, return these 2 sts to left needle tip, then purl them tog through their back loops—1 st dec'd.

SSSP

Slip 3 sts individually kwise, return these 3 sts to left needle tip, then purl them tog through their back loops—2 sts dec'd.

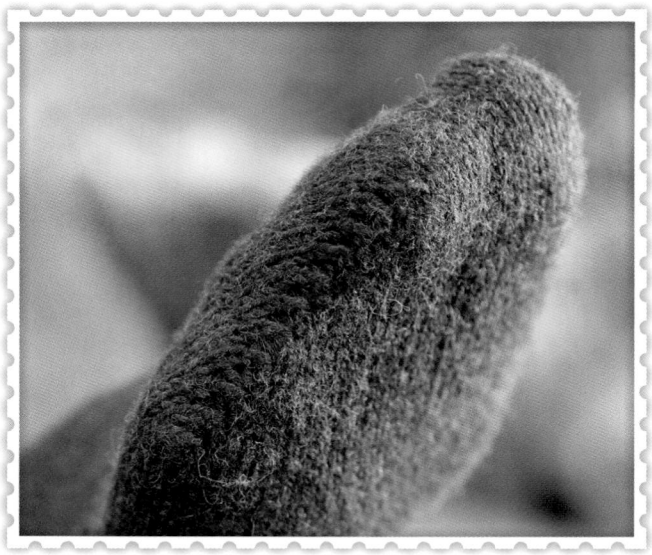

Toe

With waste yarn, MC, smaller dpn, and using the invisible provisional method (page 43), provisionally CO 34 (36, 38, 40, 42) sts.

FIRST HALF

Work short-rows as foll:

ROW 1: (RS) Knit to last st (leave last st unworked), turn work.

ROW 2: (WS) Yo backward (from back to front; see Glossary), purl to last st (leave last st unworked), turn.

ROW 3: Yo as usual (from front to back), knit to 1 st before yo formed on previous row, turn.

ROW 4: Yo backward, purl to 1 st before yo formed on previous row, turn.

Rep Rows 3 and 4 for first half 8 (8, 9, 10, 10) more times, ending with a WS row—14 (16, 16, 16, 18) center sts between last pair of yarnovers.

SECOND HALF

ROW 1: (RS) Yo as usual, k14 (16, 16, 16, 18) to first yo, correct the mount of the yo (so that leading side of loop is on the front of the needle), k2tog (yo tog with next st), turn work.

ROW 2: (WS) Yo backward, p15 (17, 17, 17, 19) to first yo, ssp (yo tog with next st; see Stitch Guide), turn.

ROW 3: Yo as usual, knit to first yo of 2 yos, correct mount of yo loops as before, k3tog, (2 yos tog with next st), turn.

ROW 4: Yo backward, purl to first yo of 2 yos, sssp (2 yos tog with next st; see Stitch Guide), turn.

Rep Rows 3 and 4 for second half 8 (8, 9, 10, 10) more times, ending with a WS row—35 (37, 39, 41, 43) sts on needle; 34 (36, 38, 40, 42) original sts plus 1 yo at start of last WS row.

NEXT ROW: (RS) Yo as usual, k17 (18, 19, 20, 21) to middle of needle—18 (19, 20, 21, 22) sts each on 2 dpn, including yos; working yarn is between these 2 needles.

Carefully remove waste yarn from provisional CO and place 34 (36, 38, 40, 42) live sts on 2 dpn for instep so that there are 17 (18, 19, 20, 21) sts on each needle.

JOINING RND: Resuming where you left off, knit to yo, sl yo to next needle, ssk (yo tog with first st of next needle), knit to end of needle; on the foll needle, work to last st, sl yo from beg of next needle to end of working needle and k2tog (last st tog with transferred yo)—68 (72, 76, 80, 84) sts; 17 (18, 19, 20, 21) sts each on 4 dpn; toe measures about 1½ (1½, 1¾, 2, 2)" (3.8 [3.8, 4.5, 5, 5] cm) from needles to tip of flattened toe; working yarn is at side of toe.

Foot

Place marker (pm) for beg of rnd. Work even in St st (knit every rnd) until piece measures 8 (8, 8, 7¾, 7¾)" (20.5 [20.5, 20.5, 19.5, 19.5] cm) from beg, or about 1½ (1½, 1¾, 2, 2)" (38 [3.8, 4.5, 5, 5] cm) less than desired total foot length.

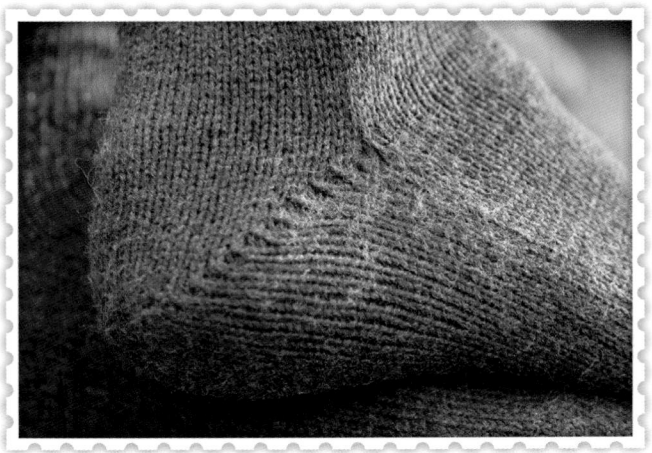

Heel

The heel is worked with short-rows just as the toe, beg with the bottom of the heel (sole) sts. Place 34 (36, 38, 40, 42) sole sts onto 1 dpn for ease in working, leaving 34 (36, 38, 40, 42) instep sts on 2 needles to work later.

FIRST HALF

Work short-rows on sole sts as foll:

ROW 1: (RS) Knit to last st (leave last st unworked), turn work.

ROW 2: (WS) Yo backward, purl to last st (leave last st unworked), turn.

ROW 3: Yo as usual, knit to 1 st before yo formed on previous row, turn.

ROW 4: Yo backward, purl to 1 st before yo formed on previous row, turn.

Rep Rows 3 and 4 for first half 8 (8, 9, 10, 10) more times, ending with a WS row—14 (16, 16, 16, 18) sts between last pair of yarnovers.

SECOND HALF

ROW 1: (RS) Yo as usual, k14 (16, 16, 16, 18) to first yo, correct the mount of the yo, k2tog (yo tog with next st), turn work.

ROW 2: (WS) Yo backward, p15 (17, 17, 17, 19) to first yo, ssp (yo tog with next st), turn.

ROW 3: Yo as usual, knit to first yo of 2 yos, correct mount of yo loops as before, k3tog (2 yos tog with next st), turn.

ROW 4: Yo backward, purl to first yo of 2 yos, sssp (2 yos tog with next st), turn.

Rep Rows 3 and 4 for second half 8 (8, 9, 10, 10) more times, ending with a WS row—35 (37, 39, 41, 43) sts on needle; 34 (36, 38, 40, 42) original sts plus 1 yo at beg of last WS row.

NEXT ROW: (RS) Yo as usual, k17 (18 19, 20, 21) to middle of heel needle—70 (74, 78, 82, 86) sts; 17 (18, 19, 20, 21) sts each on 2 instep dpns; 18 (19, 20, 21, 22) sts each on 2 heel dpns, including yos; working yarn is between the 2 heel needles.

JOINING RND: Knit to yo, sl yo to next needle, k2tog (yo tog with first instep st), knit to last st on second instep needle, sl yo at beg of foll needle to instep needle and ssk (last instep st tog with transferred yo)—68 (72, 76, 80, 84) sts; working yarn is at side of sock, at end of instep sts.

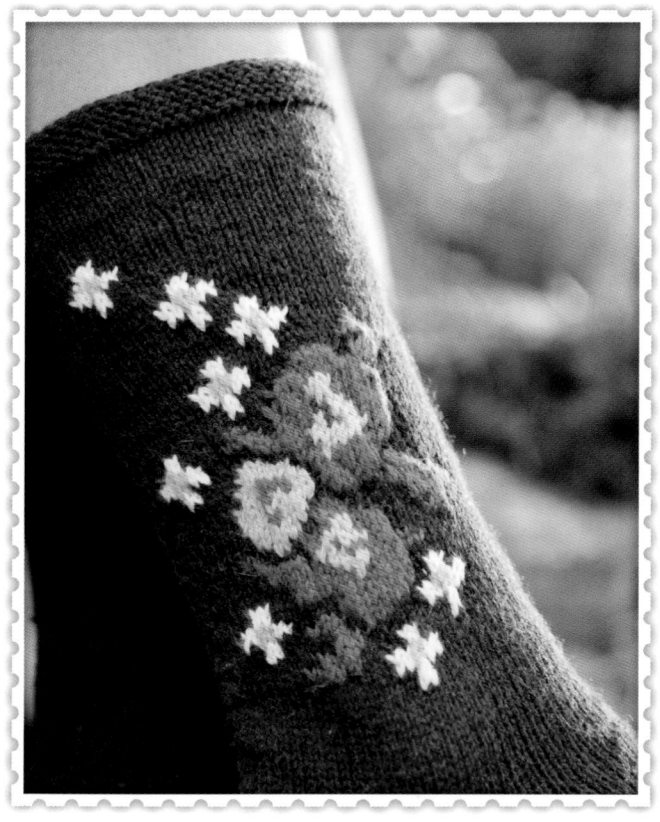

Yarn Note

Brown Sheep Cotton Fine is 80% cotton and 20% merino, which is a perfect blend for warm-weather climates. Its multiple-ply cabled construction makes it extremely durable. It is, however, rather limited in elasticity. Those with generous calves will want to check the finished measurements and adjust stitches as necessary for a comfortable fit. Fortunately, the intarsia pattern is centered on the side of the leg in such a way that you can add or subtract from overall stitches (to a degree) without having to touch the chart. Your other option is to choose a yarn with higher elasticity, either from the addition of spandex or from a higher percentage of wool—not just any wool but springy wool from breeds such as Merino or Cormo. Also keep in mind how the fibers and yarn will affect the colorwork. A smooth worsted-spun yarn will make the flowers pop with great clarity—but any irregularities in tension or colorwork will be quite visible. Mercerized cotton would brighten up the sock but reduce the elasticity even more. A yarn with a slightly softer surface will help conceal those irregularities while still rendering the flowers clearly.

—Clara Parkes

MC ● dark red Ⅰ pink · white × green + gold

NOTE: The main color is shaded a slightly darker gray every other row to make it easier to keep your place in the pattern.

Left Leg

Right Leg

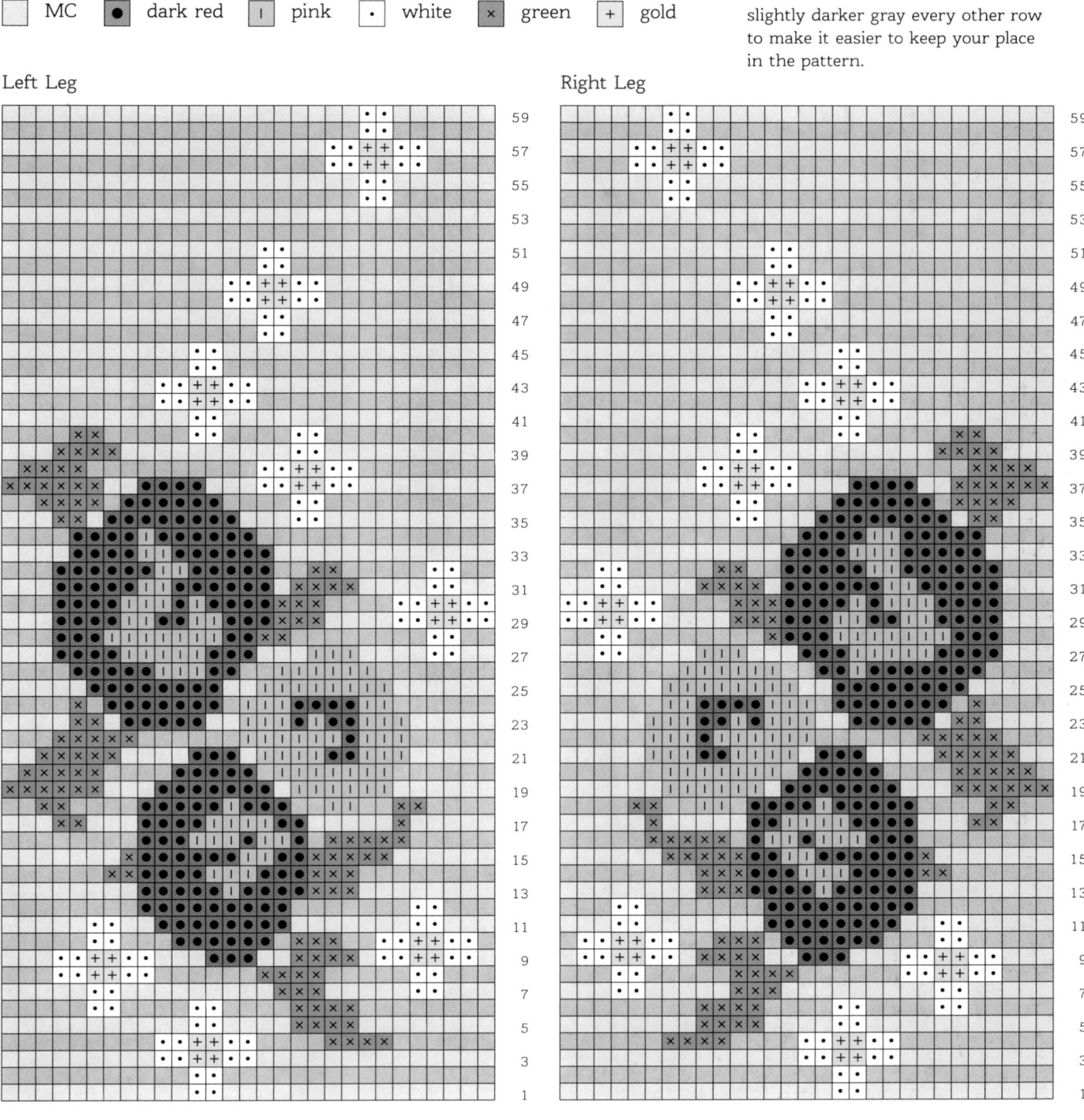

Leg

Work even in St st for 20 rnds.

NEXT RND: Remove end-of-rnd m, work 17 (18, 19, 20, 21) sts of first needle, and pm for new beg of rnd at center back leg.

Using the intarsia in the round method shown at right, work chart patt on side of each leg as foll.

LEFT LEG

NEXT RND: K3 (4, 5, 6, 7), pm, work Rnd 1 of Left Leg chart over next 29 sts, pm, knit to end.

Working sts between new m according to chart patt, work Rnds 2–14 of chart. Change to larger needles and work Rnds 15–59 of chart. With MC, knit 1 rnd while inc 4 sts evenly spaced—72 (76, 80, 84, 88) sts. With MC, work even in St st until piece measures about 9½" (24 cm) from base of heel.

RIGHT LEG

NEXT RND: K36 (39, 42, 45, 48), pm, work Rnd 1 of Right Leg chart over next 29 sts, pm, k3 (4, 5, 6, 7).

Working sts between new m according to chart patt, work Rnds 2–14 of chart. Change to larger needles and work Rnds 15–59 of chart. With MC, knit 1 rnd while inc 4 sts evenly spaced—72 (76, 80, 84, 88) sts. With MC, work even in St st until piece measures about 9½" (24 cm) from base of heel.

BOTH LEGS

Work in garter st (purl 1 rnd; knit 1 rnd) for 8 rnds—4 garter ridges; piece measures about 10" (25.5 cm) from base of heel. Loosely BO all sts.

Finishing

Weave in loose ends. Block lightly.

Intarsia in the Round

This method of working intarsia patterns in the round prevents excessively long floats in designs that have stitches worked in the main color interspersed with the pattern stitches. The designs can range from simple, single-color motifs to complex designs involving several colors.

Work this technique in a series of 2 rounds as follows:

ROUND 1: Working from right to left, work the motif as for normal color standing of main and pattern colors, with the unused yarn stranded across the back of the work. At the left edge of the motif, drop the pattern color(s), and use the main color to finish the round.

ROUND 2: This round is worked in two steps, the first in the main color and the second in the design color(s).

- **STEP 1:** Work with the main color (shown as light) to the right edge of the motif, then continue across the motif, knitting all the main-color stitches in the motif while slipping all the pattern-color stitches (shown as dark) purlwise with yarn in back. Drop the main color at the left edge of the motif. Both the main color and the pattern color are now at the left edge of the motif (figure 1).

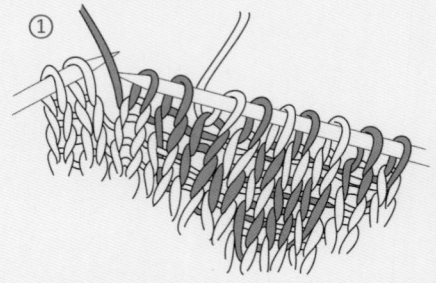

- **STEP 2:** Turn the work so that the wrong side is facing, pick up the pattern color, which is now at the right edge of the motif when viewed from the wrong side, cross it over the main color (figure 2), and work to the end of the motif, purling the pattern-color stitches and slipping the main-color stitches (the ones that were worked in Step 1 purlwise with yarn in front. Drop the pattern color at the end of the motif, in position to work Step 1 on the next round (figure 3). Turn the work so that the right side is facing. If you are working on a circular needle, slip all of the motif stitches purlwise to where the main color is waiting. If you are working on double-pointed needles, you can reposition the stitches so all motif stitches are on one needle, eliminating the need to slip stitches to get to where the main color is waiting—simply move to the next needle. Pick up the main color (figure 4) and work to the end of the round.

Repeat Rounds 1 and 2 to complete the motif. If you prefer not to turn the work and purl the motif stitches, you can knit them in reverse (see Glossary) so that the right side of the work is always facing you.

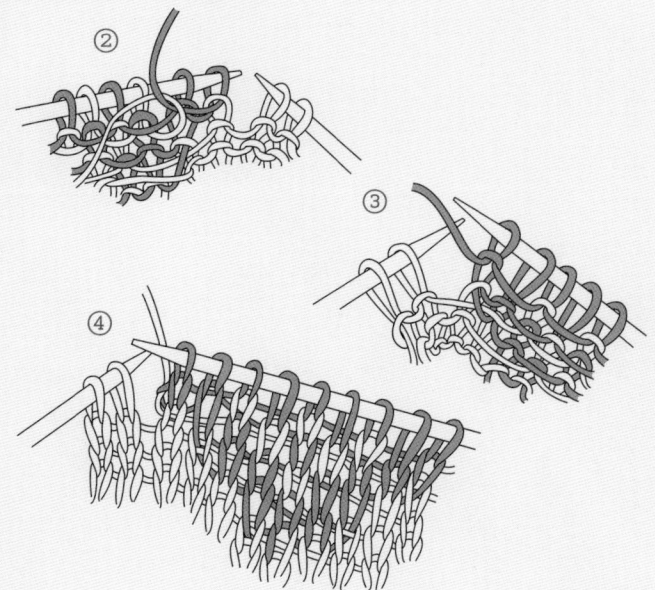

NOTE: I used the method above for one of the sample socks shown. For the other sock, I discovered an easier way to work Round 2. I knit with the main color to the start of the first motif, slipped the motif colors purlwise with yarn in back, knit the first main color stitch after the first motif, and stopped. Then, without turning the work, I twisted the motif color with the main color, and knit the motif stitches (the stitches just slipped) in reverse. Before continuing with the main color, I adjusted the tension of its float behind the motif. Then I knit to the next motif, slipped its stitches, knit only the first main color stitch after the motif, and repeated the process. Working in small sections and adjusting the tension of the main color strand after each motif made it easier to maintain an even tension and increased the speed of the knitting.

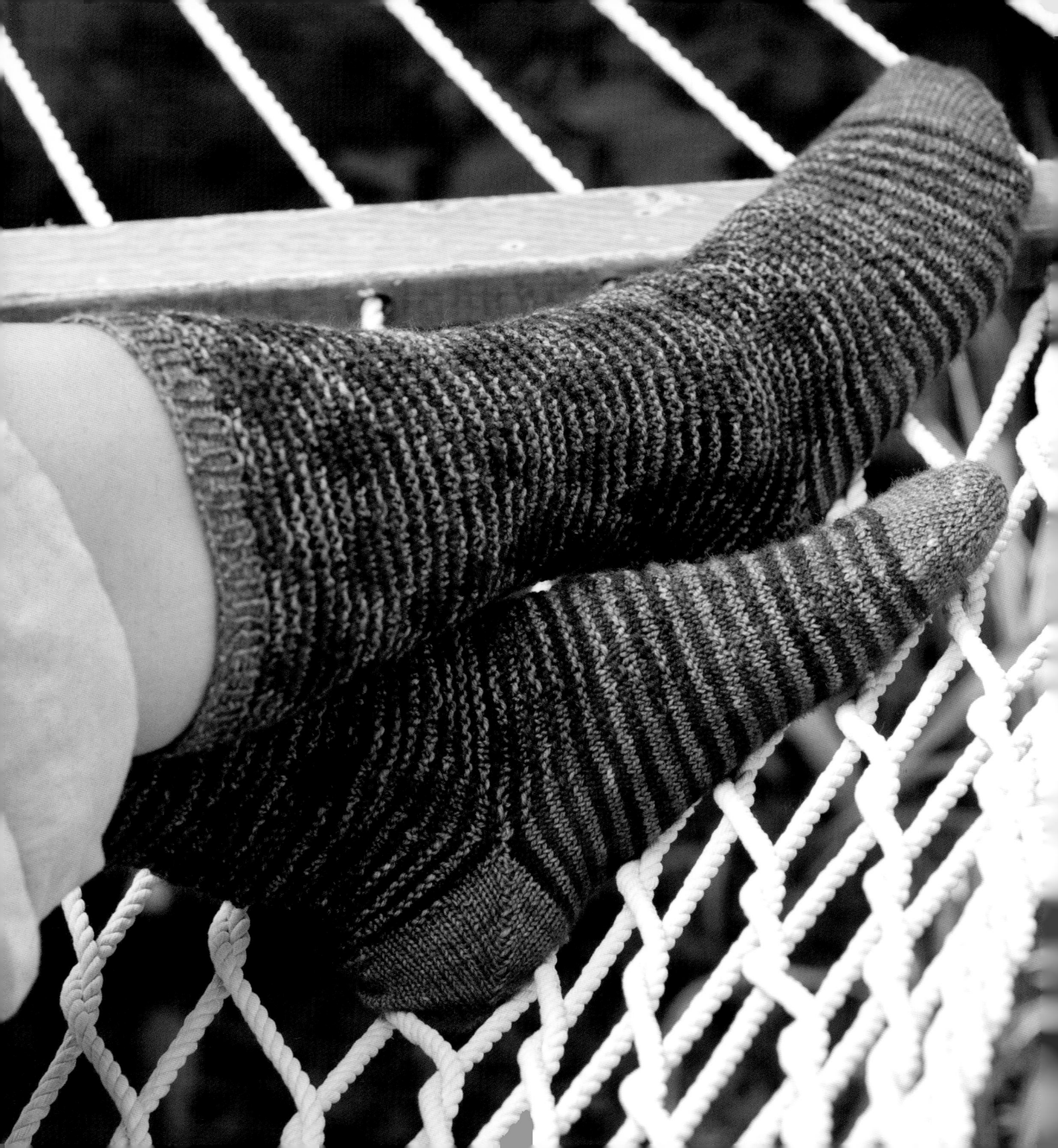

Stealth Argyles

DESIGNED BY *Eunny Jang*

finished size

About 8" (20.5 cm) foot circumference, 9½" (24 cm) foot length from back of heel to tip of toe, and 14½" (37 cm) leg length from top of cuff to base of heel.

yarn

Fingering weight (#1 Super Fine).

Shown here: Malabrigo Sock (100% merino; 440 yd [420 m]/100 g): #855 aguas (A) and #810 cordovan (B), 1 skein each.

needles

Foot and lower leg and foot: size U.S. 2 (2.75 mm): set of 4 double-pointed (dpn).

Upper leg: size U.S. 3 (3.25 mm): set of 4 dpn.

Adjust needle size if necessary to obtain the correct gauge.

notions

Removable marker (m); tapestry needle.

gauge

16 sts and 23 rnds = 2" (5 cm) in St st on smaller needles, worked in rnds.

These stockings are an exploration of shadow knitting (a combination of knit and purl stitches worked in two-color stripes) and movement. Because patterns produced by shadow knitting only reveal themselves when viewed at certain angles, the patterns magically appear and disappear as the piece moves. My initial plan was to knit the socks from side to side so that the shadow-knitted argyle pattern would run vertically up the leg where the motifs would be visible to viewers as the wearer walked. But I quickly discovered that even the broadest calf doesn't provide enough flat area to make a motif readable. Instead, I ended up working the socks from the toe up in traditional rounds. In this orientation, the classic argyle pattern is always visible to the most important onlooker—that is, the wearer.

> *Because patterns produced by shadow knitting only reveal themselves when viewed at certain angles, the patterns magically appear and disappear as the piece moves."*

Except for the solid-color toe, heel, and cuff ribbing, these socks are worked entirely in shadow knitting. Beginning with a Turkish/Eastern cast-on, the socks are worked from the toe to the short-row heel, then the calf is shaped by changing needle size. A special bind-off that involves decreased stitches ensures that the cuff doesn't bind the top of the leg.

notes

+ The calf shaping is created by changing needle size, not by increasing stitch count.

+ For a tighter or looser fit, use smaller or larger needles.

+ The fabric should be only slightly stretched to achieve the correct fit; too much stretch will distort the shadow knitting pattern.

+ To hide the jog produced by knitting circular stripes, carry the unused color up along the inside of the sock, always trapping the yarns when changing colors. To trap the old color before knitting the first stitch of the new color, cross the two colors as for intarsia, bringing the new color behind the old. Before changing colors again, tug gently on the old color to align the stripes.

⊕ DESIGN TIP: *If you find it easier to make knit stitches than purl stitches, arrange the stitches so that the first stitch of every needle is a knit stitch, even if that isn't how the needle arrangement is specified in the pattern. This will make the transition from one needle to the next easier to execute.*

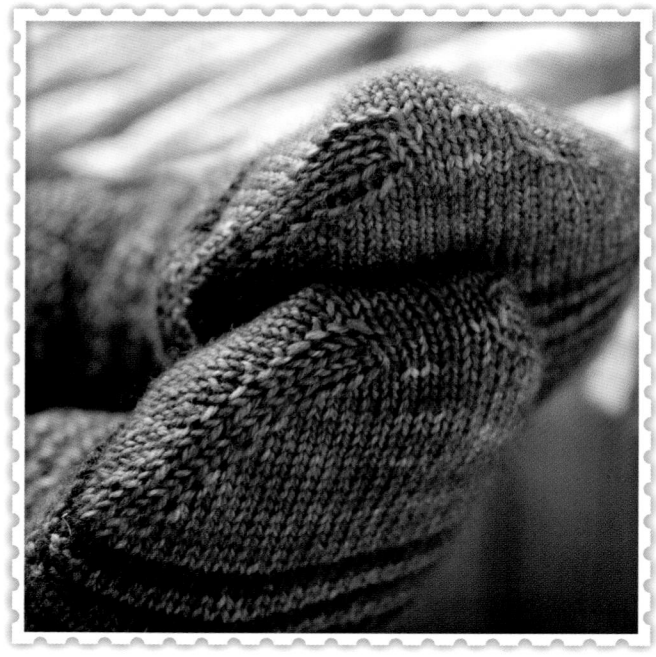

Toe

With A, smaller needles, and using the Turkish/Eastern method (see page 116), CO 8 sts each on 2 needles. Knit 1 rnd, dividing sts so that there are 8 sts on Needle 1 and 4 sts each on Needle 2 and Needle 3—16 sts total.

INC RND: On Needle 1, k1, M1R (see Glossary), knit to last st, M1L (see Glossary), k1; on Needle 2, k1, M1R, knit to end; on Needle 3, knit to last st, M1L, k1—4 sts inc'd.

Inc 4 sts in this manner every rnd for the next 5 rnds—40 sts total; 20 sts on Needle 1, 10 sts each on Needle 2 and Needle 3.

NEXT RND: Knit.

Rep the last 2 rnds (i.e., inc 4 sts every other rnd) 6 times— 64 sts; 32 sts on Needle 1, 16 sts each on Needle 2 and Needle 3.

NEXT RND: Knit, inc 1 st in the center of Needle 1—65 sts; 33 sts on Needle 1, 16 sts each on Needle 2 and Needle 3; toe measures about 1¾" (4.5 cm) long.

Foot

Join B and work set-up patt from Rnd 1 of Argyle Shadow chart (page 143) as foll: On Needle 1, work 16-st patt rep 2 times, then work 1 st at end of chart once; on Needle 2, knit; on Needle 3, knit—instep sts in patt are on Needle 1, sole sts in St st are divided evenly between Needle 2 and Needle 3. Rnd begins at side of foot at start of Needle 1.

Changing colors every 2 rnds using the almost jogless join technique (see Notes), cont instep sts in established patt and work sole sts in St st until piece measures 8" (20.5 cm) from tip of toe, or about 1½" (3.8 cm) less than desired total foot length, ending after completing a 2-rnd stripe with B.

Heel

The heel is worked back and forth in short-rows (see Glossary) with A.

FIRST HALF

SET-UP ROW: Work next chart rnd on 33 sts of Needle 1, place sts just worked on 2 dpn to work later for instep, place all 32 sole sts from Needle 2 and Needle 3 onto a single needle for heel, knit to last heel st, wrap next st (formerly the last st of rnd), turn work.

Make a note of the instep chart rnd just completed so that you can resume the patt on the leg with the correct rnd later. Cont on 32 heel sts with A as foll:

ROW 1: (WS) Purl to last st, wrap next st, turn work— 1 wrapped st at each end of needle.

ROW 2: (RS) Knit to 1 st before previously wrapped st, wrap next st, turn.

ROW 3: Purl 1 st before previously wrapped st, wrap next st, turn.

Rep Rows 2 and 3 ten more times, ending with a WS row— 8 sts rem unwrapped in the center of heel; 12 wrapped sts at each side.

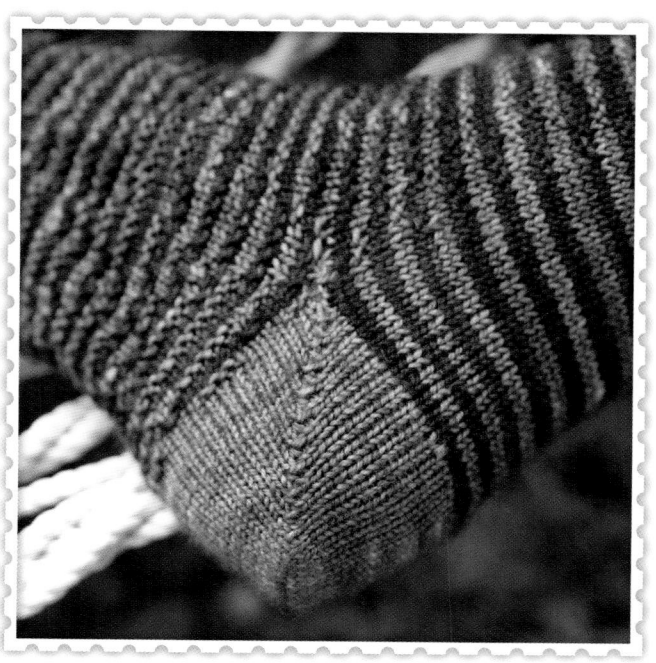

SECOND HALF

ROW 1: (RS) Knit to first wrapped st, knit this st tog with its wrap, wrap next st, turn work—st just wrapped is now double-wrapped.

ROW 2: (WS) Purl to first wrapped st, purl this st tog with its wrap, wrap next st, turn—st just wrapped is now double-wrapped.

ROW 3: Knit to first wrapped st, knit this st tog with both its wraps, wrap next st, turn work.

ROW 4: Purl to first wrapped st, purl this st tog with both its wraps, wrap next st, turn work.

Rep Rows 3 and 4 nine more times, ending with WS Row 4—1 wrapped st rem at each end of needle.

NEXT ROW: (RS) Knit to last st, knit last st tog with both its wraps, turn.

NEXT ROW: (WS) Sl 1 pwise with yarn in front (wyf), purl to last st, purl last st tog with both its wraps, turn.

NEXT ROW: Sl 1 pwise with yarn in back (wyb), knit to last 2 sts, k2tog; do not turn work—31 heel sts rem.

⊕ **DESIGN TIP:** *Make sure that the bind-off edge in socks worked from the toe up is elastic enough to allow the socks to stretch over the heel and not bind at the top of the leg.*

Leg

With A, rejoin for working in the rnd as foll: On Needle 1, work established chart patt across first 32 instep sts (this should be the second rnd of a 2-rnd A stripe), sl last instep st to beg of next needle; on Needle 2, knit the st transferred from end of Needle 1, k15; on Needle 3, k16—64 sts total; 32 sts on Needle 1; 16 sts each on Needle 2 and Needle 3. Rnd begins at side of leg at start of Needle 1.

Cont established chart patt on all sts, working the 16-st patt rep 4 times around for each rnd (do not work the single st outside patt rep at end of chart).

Cont in patt until piece measures about 6" (15 cm) from base of heel. Change to larger needles and cont in patt until piece measures about 13½" (34.5 cm) from base of heel or 1" (2.5 cm) less than desired total leg length, ending with Rnd 4 or Rnd 32 of chart.

RIBBING

Change to smaller needles. With A only, work in k1, p1 rib for 1" (2.5 cm). Loosely BO all sts as foll: K1, *p1, return both sts to left needle, p2tog (1 st dec'd), k1, return both sts to left needle, ssk (1 st dec'd); rep from * until 1 st rem. Cut yarn and fasten off last st.

Weave in loose ends. Block lightly.

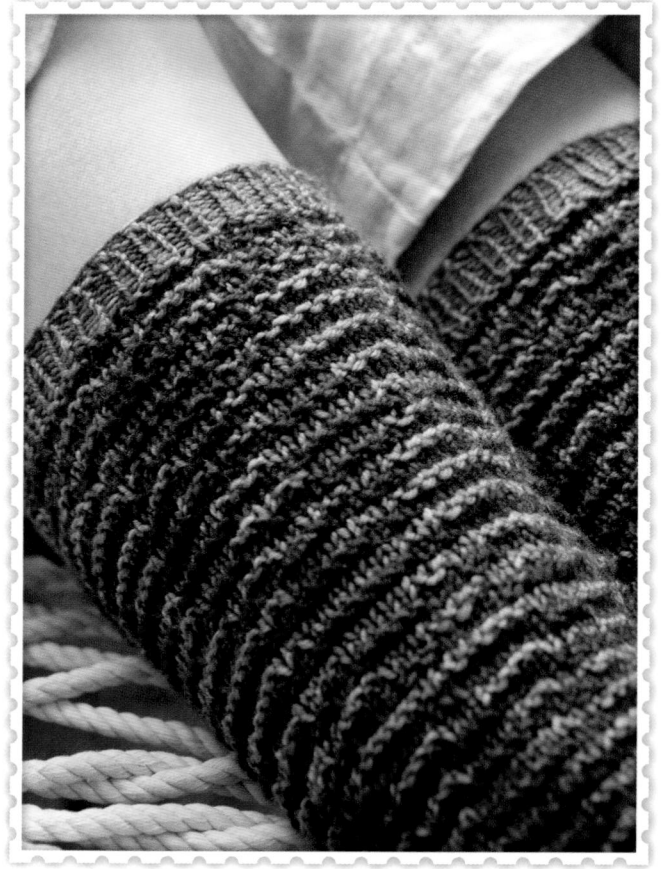

Yarn Note

Here's a fun pattern that offers a lot of yarn flexibility. Shadow knitting produces a somewhat hybrid garter-stitch fabric with extraordinary horizontal stretch to it, meaning that this sock's cuff will fit all but the most generous calves—even if you use a yarn with less elasticity to it. The fabric's ability to stretch means that it is relatively reluctant to snap back and hold snug, and that's where the inch of ribbing along the top becomes essential. The rounded surface of this Malabrigo three-ply yarn gives the purl ridges a soft fullness that would become bumpier and far more dramatic in a springy two-ply yarn. Keep this yarn's overall tensile strength in mind, especially around high-wear areas such as the heel. Here it's worked in a smooth and potentially vulnerable stockinette short-row heel. In terms of color, the flickering semisolid Malabrigo adds a lovely depth and nuance to the pattern. Be cautious of colorways that involve more than one color, however, as the contrasting variegation may weaken the clarity of the shadow pattern.

—*Clara Parkes*

Argyle Shadow

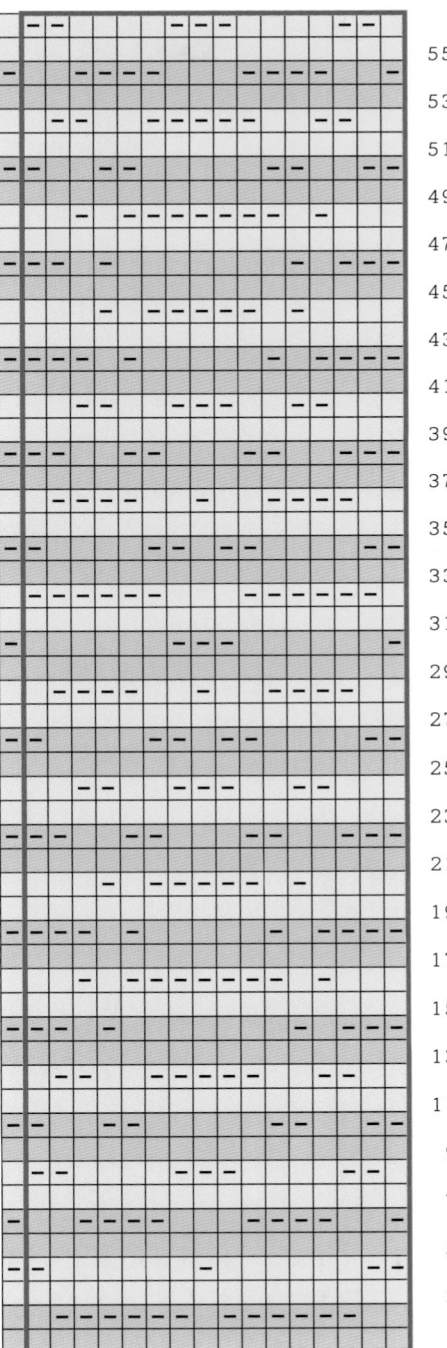

knit with A

- purl with A

knit with B

- purl with B

pattern repeat

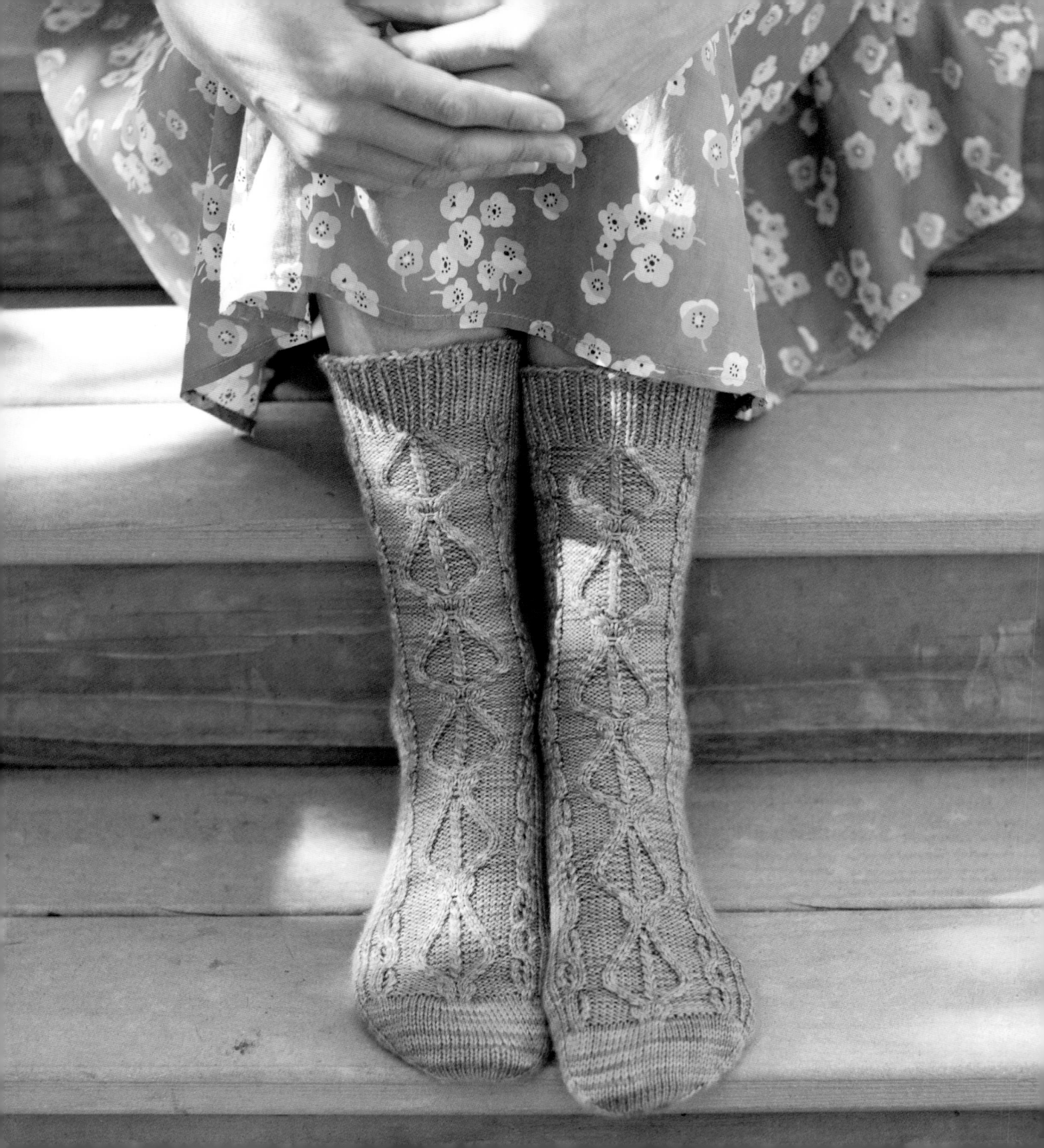

Terpander

DESIGNED BY *Melissa Morgan-Oakes*

finished size

About 7" (18 cm) foot circumference; 9½" (24 cm) foot length from back of heel to tip of toe, and 9¾" (25 cm) leg length from top of cuff to base of heel.

yarn

Fingering weight (#1 Super Fine).

Shown here: Dye Dreams Classy Sox (80% superwash merino, 10% cashmere, 10% nylon; 490 yd [448 m]/100 g): #1211 moss, 1 skein.

Note: This yarn has been discontinued; substitute the fingering-weight yarn of your choice.

needles

Size U.S. 1 (2.25 mm): 40" (100 cm) circular (cir).

Adjust needle size if necessary to obtain the correct gauge

notions

Removable marker; markers (m); cable needle (cn); tapestry needle.

gauge

19 sts and 24 rnds = 2" (5 cm) in St st, worked in rnds.

36 sts of Terpander chart measures about 3¼" (8.5 cm) wide.

Yarn talks to me. Sometimes a skein calls out that it wants to be a specific object. Sometimes it just says "Buy me! I am going to be wonderful." Most projects generate a lot of arguments in my head about yarn or design or execution, but things happen along the way and the result is often far from my initial plan—but better for the diversion. Getting out of my own way and allowing a thing to be what it wants to be is vital to my design process (and a good plan for life as well). I had initially intended to use this yarn for a lace project. As I swatched, though, the yarn insisted on the more rugged look of cables.

> *Getting out of my own way and allowing a thing to be what it wants to be is vital to my design process (and a good plan for life as well)."*

I named these socks for Terpander, an ancient Greek poet and musician who used a lyre in composition and performance. None of his work exists in print form; his music was passed on by oral tradition and he was most famed for his drinking songs. The shape of the cables in this pattern brings to mind his favored musical instrument; the decadence of the cashmere in this yarn creates a bit of revelry for the feet—a taste of bacchanal for tired toes.

notes

+ Dye Dreams yarn company closed their doors during the production of this book so Classy Sox is no longer available. You may substitute the fingering weight yarn of your choice (see the note by Clara Parkes on page 148).

+ These instructions are for working two socks at the same time using the magic loop method on a single long circular needle (page 13).

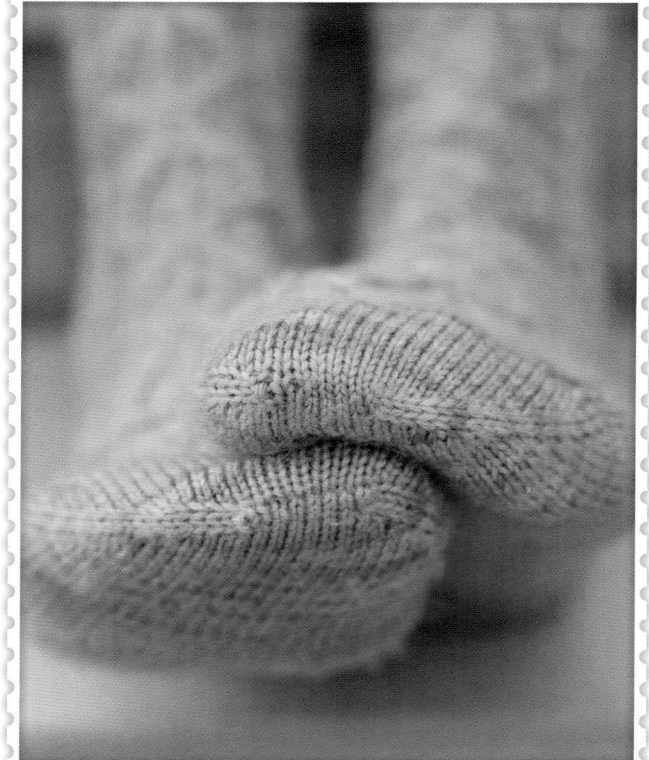

Toes

Using Judy's Magic method (page 117), CO 16 sts for Sock B, then, with a separate ball of yarn, CO 16 more sts for Sock A.

NEXT RND: Knit around all 16 stitches of each sock. Place a removable marker on the first stitch of sock A to denote the beg of rnds; move this marker up as you work.

INC RND: Side 1: On Sock A, *k1, M1 (see Glossary), knit to last st, M1, k1; rep from * for Sock B. Side 2: Rotate the work and rep from * of Side 1 across Sock B, then across Sock A—4 sts inc'd each sock.

Rep the inc rnd 6 more times—44 sts each sock (22 sts each side of each sock).

NEXT RND: Knit all sts of each sock.

NEXT RND: Rep the inc rnd—4 sts inc'd each sock.

Rep the last 2 rnds (i.e., inc every other rnd) 6 more times—72 sts each sock (36 sts each side of each sock); toe measures about 1¾" (4.5 cm) from CO.

Feet

RND 1: Side 1 (instep): Work Rnd 1 of Terpander chart across each sock. Side 2 (sole): Knit across each sock.

Cont in this manner, working chart on instep sts and knitting all sole sts until pieces measure about 4¾" (12 cm) from tip of toe, or 4¾" (12 cm) less than desired total foot length.

GUSSETS

RND 1: Side 1: Work chart patt as established on instep sts for each sock. Side 2: For each sock, k1, M1, knit to last st M1, k1—2 sts inc'd on sole of each sock.

RND 2: Side 1: Work chart patt as established. Side 2: Knit.

Rep these 2 rnds 17 more times—36 gusset rnds total; 108 sts each sock; 36 instep sts on Side 1 of each sock, and 72 sole sts on Side 2 of each sock.

Heels

Work chart patt across instep Side 1 of both socks. Make a note of the chart rnd just completed so that you can resume the patt on the leg with the correct rnd later. Rotate work to beg heel with Side 2 of Sock B and work each heel individually (i.e., work the heel turn and heel flap on Sock B first, then work the heel turn and heel flap on Sock A) as foll.

TURN HEEL

Work the 72 sole sts back and forth in short-rows as foll:

ROW 1: (RS) K18, place marker (pm), k35, sl 1 pwise with yarn in back (wyb), pm, bring yarn to front, return slipped st to left needle, turn work—36 center sts between m; 18 sts outside m at each side.

NOTE: Work "wrap next st" on foll rows as sl 1 pwise with wyb, bring yarn to front, return slipped st to left needle.

ROW 2: (WS) Purl to 1 st before m, wrap next st, turn.

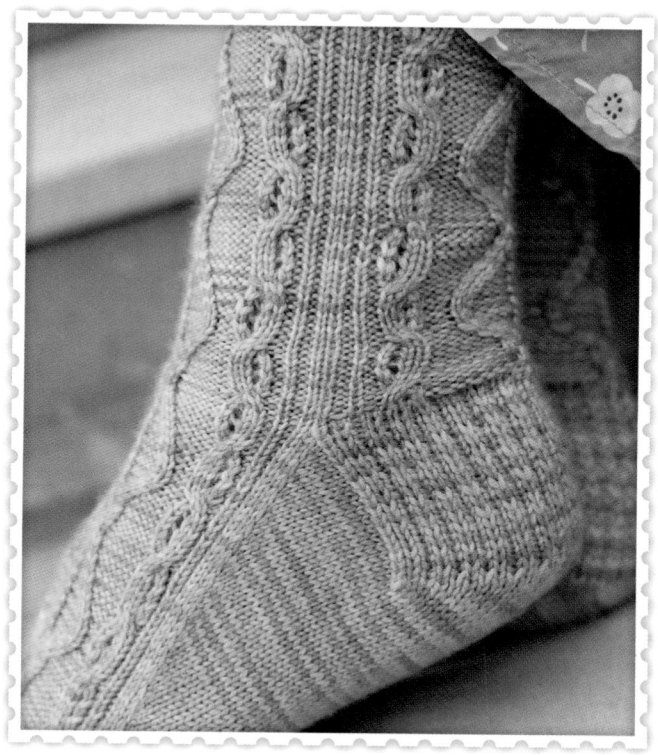

ROW 3: Knit to 2 sts before previously wrapped st, wrap next st, turn.

ROW 4: Purl to 2 sts before previously wrapped st, wrap next st, turn.

Rep Rows 3 and 4 for heel turn 6 more times, then work RS Row 3 once more—last row completed is worked as k4, wrap next st.

HEEL FLAP

NOTE: Work "wrap tog with wrapped st" on WS rows by lifting the wrap onto the left needle and purling it tog with wrapped st; on RS rows by lifting the wrap onto the left needle and knitting it tog with wrapped st. This hides the wrap.

Work back and forth in rows, working the wraps tog with their wrapped sts (i.e., hiding the wraps) when you come to them, as foll:

ROW 1: (WS) Purl to 1 st before m (hiding wraps as you come to them), lift the wrap of next st onto left needle, sl both the st and its wrap pwise to right needle, remove m, return both st and wrap to left needle, p3tog (the wrapped st, its wrap, plus the next st), turn work—1 st dec'd.

ROW 2: (RS) Sl 1 pwise wyb, knit to 1 st before m (hiding wraps as you come to them), lift the wrap of next st onto left needle, sl both the st and its wrap kwise to right needle, remove m, sl the foll st kwise, k3tog tbl (the wrapped st, its wrap, plus the next st), turn—1 st dec'd.

ROW 3: Sl 1 pwise wyf, purl to 1 st before gap formed on previous row, p2tog (1 st each side of gap), turn—1 st dec'd.

ROW 4: *Sl 1 pwise wyb, k1; rep from * to 1 st before gap formed on previous row, ssk (1 st each side of gap), turn—1 st dec'd.

Rep Rows 3 and 4 for heel flap 16 more times, ending with RS Row 4—36 heel sts rem; heel flap measures about 2¼" (5.5 cm).

Work the heel turn and heel flap on the sts of Side 2 for Sock A.

Legs

Rejoin for working both socks simultaneously in rnds as foll:

JOINING RND: Side 1: Cont charted patt as established across both insteps. Side 2: Work the same chart rnd across both sets of heel sts—72 sts for each sock (36 sts each side of both socks).

NOTE: If desired, pick up an extra stitch where the heel and instep meet to prevent a hole from forming as you resume working in the round, then dec the extra st on the foll rnd.

Cont in chart patt as established until leg measures about 6" (15 cm) from top of heel flap, ending with Rnd 24 or 48 of chart—piece measures about 8¼" (21 cm) from base of heel flap.

CUFF

Work in k1, p1 rib across all sts until each piece measures 1½" (3.8 cm) from last chart rnd and 9¾" (25 cm) from base of heel flap.

Finishing

Loosely BO all sts. Weave in loose ends. Block lightly.

Yarn Note

Here Melissa uses a simple, straightforward three-ply merino with a dusting of cashmere and nylon (10% each) for luxury and strength, respectively. The results are smooth and cohesive, rendering the cable motif in a soft and approachable high relief. At times the stitches are so well-rounded that they almost appear to hover over their reverse stockinette background. If you want more precision and drama to the cables, consider swapping out the cashmere in favor of bright, lustrous silk. Cottons aren't out of the question, but you'll absolutely need some percentage of elasticity—either from wool or, simpler yet, Lycra (which is a brand name for spandex). In these socks, a ribbed panel running along each side of the leg provides the much-needed elasticity. Also be aware that cables use more yarn per square inch of fabric, so any relatively dense yarn will feel even heavier when knitted in this cable pattern. Keep the coloring simple, either a solid or semisolid. Colorways with any dramatic multi-hue contrasts will overpower the beautiful cables.

—*Clara Parkes*

Terpander

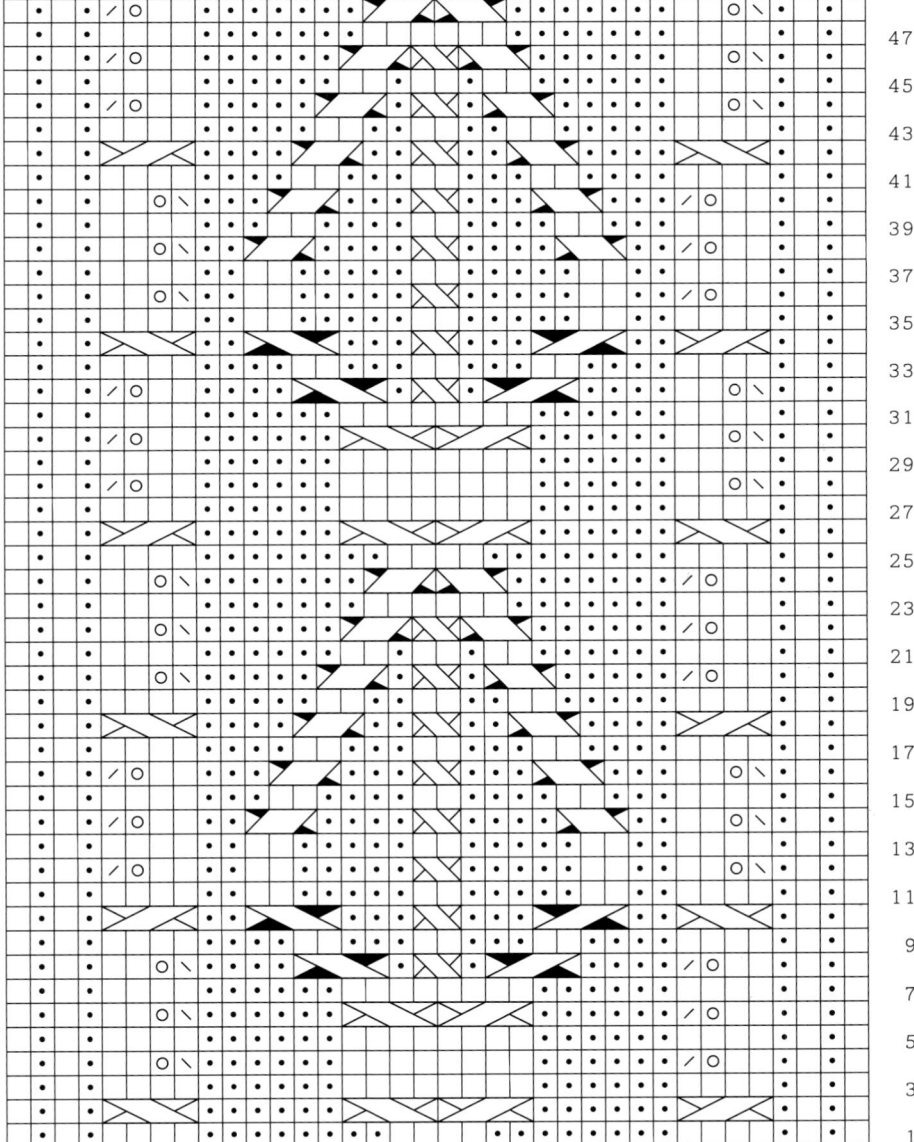

Legend

☐	knit
•	purl
○	yo
╱	k2tog
╲	ssk
⋈	sl 1 st onto cn and hold in front, k1, k1 from cn
⟋	sl 1 st onto cn and hold in back, k2, p1 from cn
⟍	sl 2 sts onto cn and hold in front, p1, k2 from cn
⋈	sl 2 sts onto cn and hold in back, k2, k2 from cn
⋈	sl 2 sts onto cn and hold in front, k2, k2 from cn
◤	sl 2 sts onto cn and hold in back, k2, p2 from cn
◣	sl 2 sts onto cn and hold in front, p2, k2 from cn

Row numbers (right side): 1, 3, 5, 7, 9, 11, 13, 15, 17, 19, 21, 23, 25, 27, 29, 31, 33, 35, 37, 39, 41, 43, 45, 47

Terpander

Working Two Socks at a Time

Many knitters suffer from Single Sock Syndrome—they happily knit the first sock, then never seem to cast on stitches for the mate. This isn't a problem if you work two socks simultaneously on the same needles.

To work two socks at a time, you'll need either two short circular needles or one long circular needle as described on page 13 (unless you knit one sock inside the other, which is a nice parlor trick but one that doesn't guarantee two socks of the same size). You will also need two separate balls of yarn (one for each sock). If working from the toe up, cast on the toe stitches for each sock using a separate ball of yarn so that the stitches that correspond to the top of each foot (instep stitches) are on one needle and the stitches that correspond to the bottom of each foot (sole stitches) are on another needle (figure 1). If working top down, cast on the leg stitches for each sock with a separate ball of yarn so that the stitches that correspond to the front of each leg are on one needle and the stitches that correspond to the back of each leg are on another needle (figure 2).

The trick is to remember to work each sock with its own ball of yarn. If you mistakenly use the same ball for both socks, even for just half a round, the two will be forever joined. For each round of toe-up knitting, knit the instep stitches of the first sock with ball A, then work the instep stitches of the second sock with ball B, then work the sole stitches of the second sock with ball B, then work the sole stitches of the first stock with ball A. If the pattern calls for working the sole stitches before the instep, simply reverse the words sole and instep in the descriptions above. When it's time to work the heel, work the entire heel of the first sock, then the entire heel of the second sock.

To prevent the two balls of yarn from hopelessly tangling on one another, take a moment as you switch from one sock to the other to make sure the strands from the two balls are not twisted around each other. This will also help you remember to switch balls between the two socks. If you need to join new yarn, do it at least 1" (2.5 cm) away from the end of the needle to prevent confusion later.

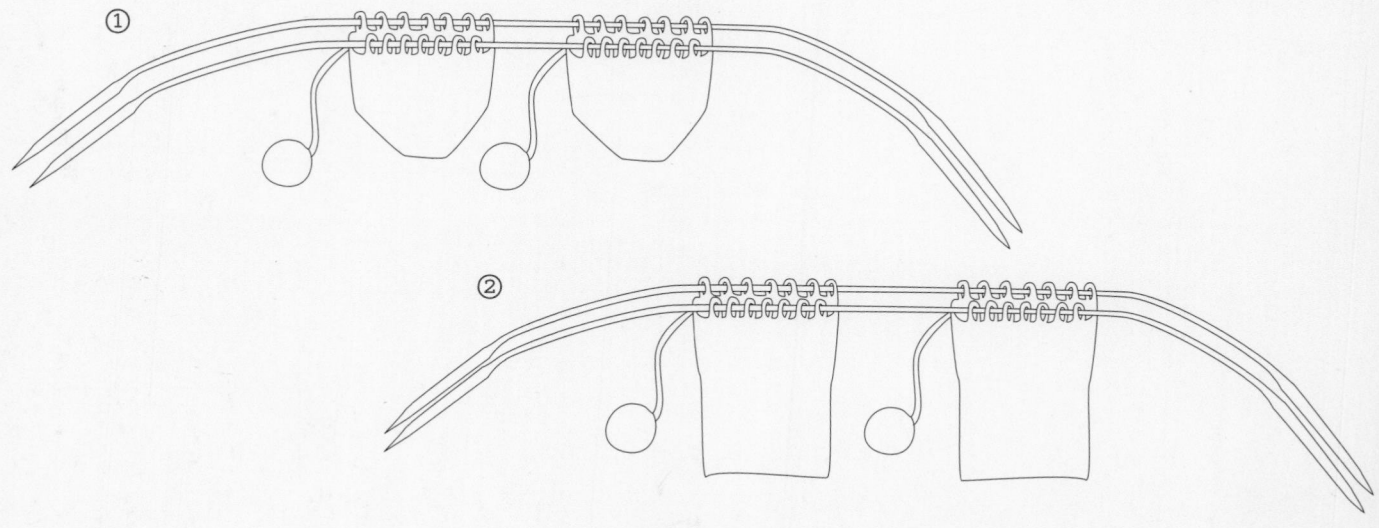

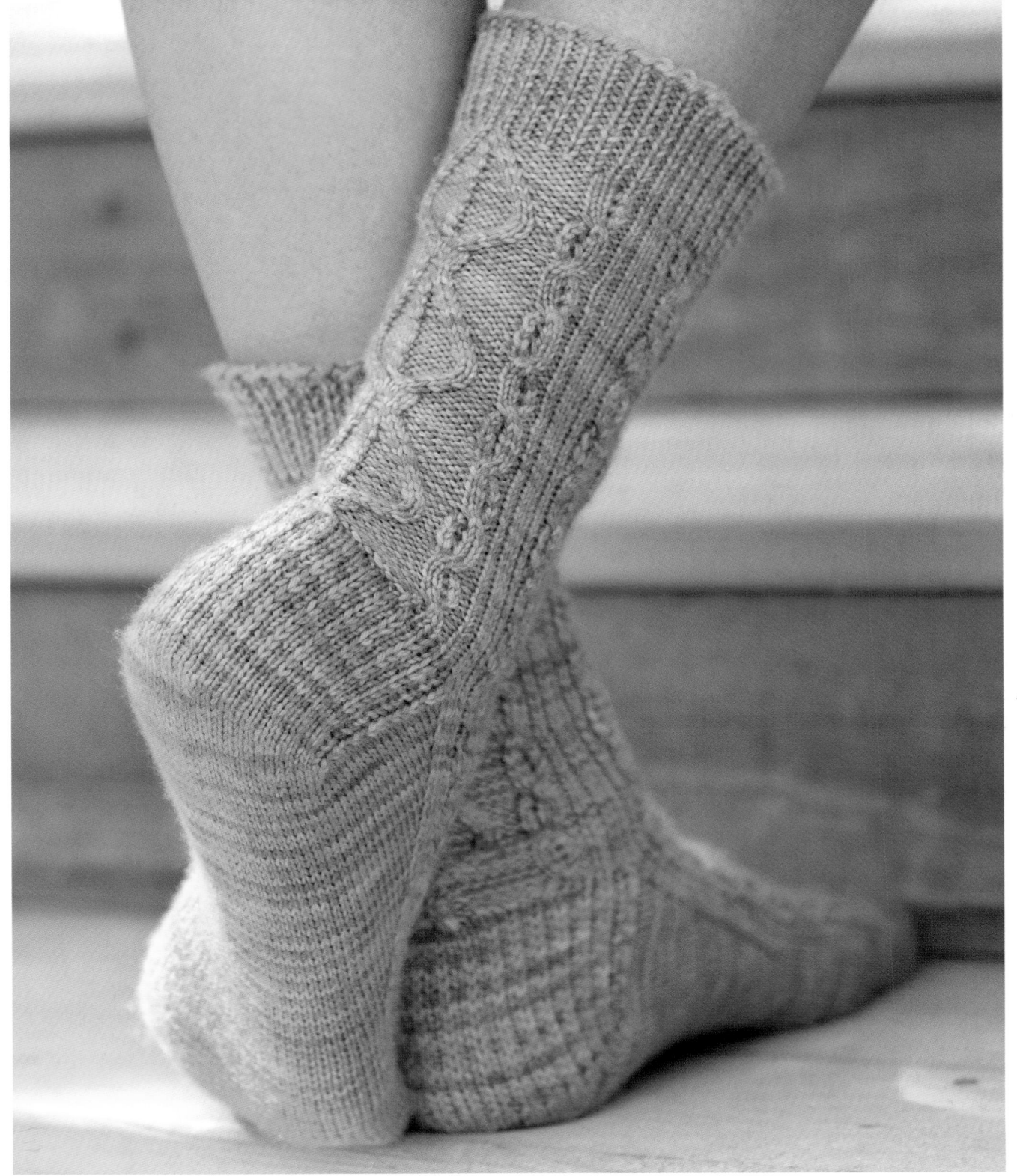

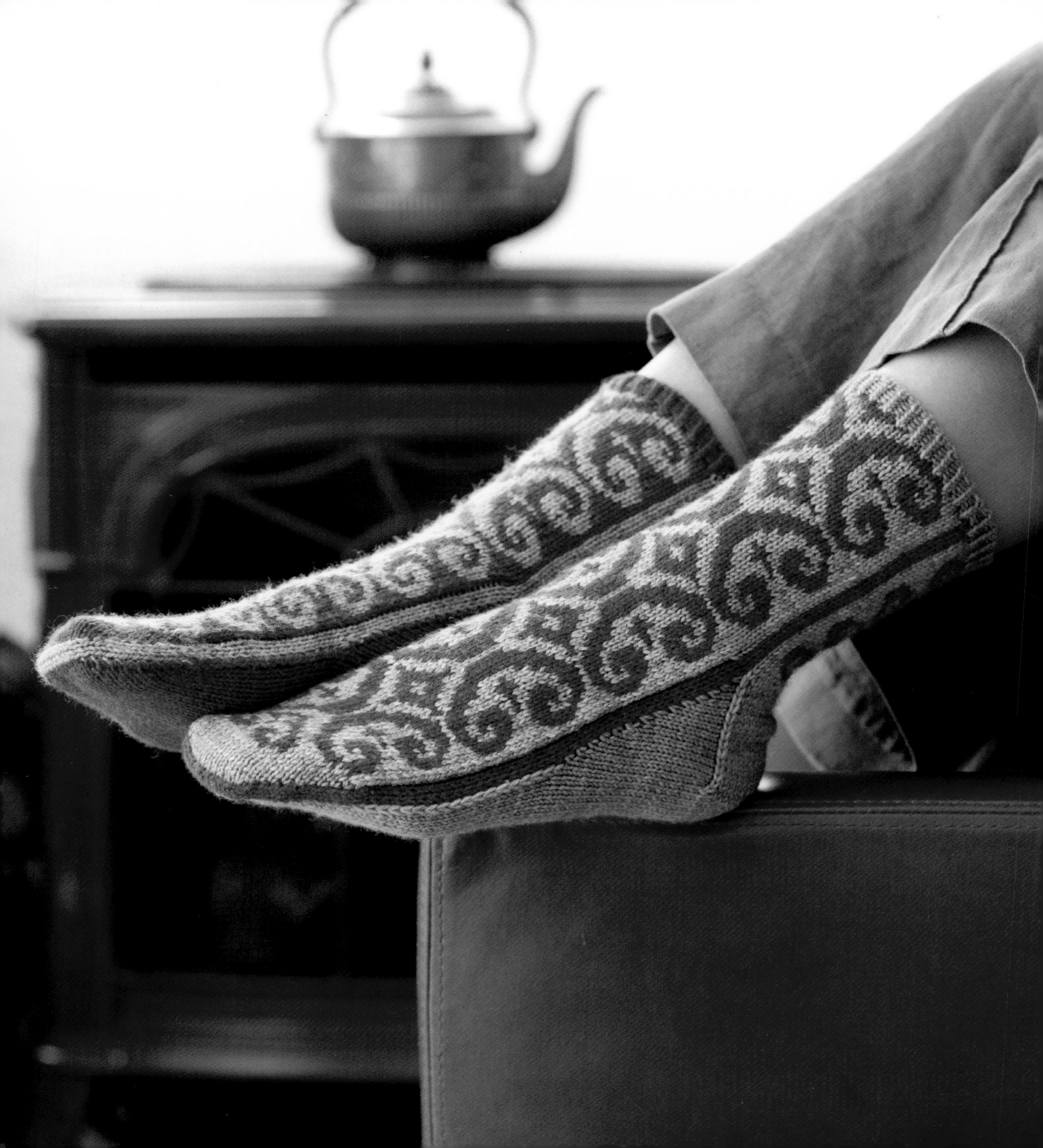

Half-Stranded Socks

DESIGNED BY *Anna Zilboorg*

finished size

About 7½" (19 cm) foot circumference, 10" (25.5 cm) foot length from back of heel to tip of toe (with option for adjusting foot length), and 8¼" (21 cm) leg length from top of cuff to base of heel.

yarn

Fingering weight (#1 Super Fine).

Shown here: Simply Socks Yarn Company Simply Sock Yarn Solids (80% wool, 20% nylon; 175 yd [160 m]/50 g): cranberry and camo, 1 skein each.

needles

Foot and heel: size U.S. 2 (2.75 mm): set of 5 double-pointed (dpn).

Leg: size U.S. 3 (3.25 mm): set of 5 dpn.

Adjust needle size if necessary to obtain the correct gauge.

notions

Removable markers; stitch holder; tapestry needle.

gauge

18 sts and 20 rows/rnds = 2" (5 cm) in both solid-color St st and stranded St st colorwork on smaller needles.

This peculiar sock construction enables a stranded color pattern to be worked on the instep alone, which makes the sock fit your normal shoe size. Furthermore, it allows any portion of the sole to be removed and reknitted. If a hole develops, snip a row of yarn on the sole anywhere between the heel turn and the end of toe, then ravel the sole as far as necessary. Replace the sole by picking up stitches and joining them to the instep in the same manner as originally worked, then graft the live stitches at the snipped row.

> *The colorwork pattern marches up the front and back of the leg to the cuff. For fun, I reversed the colors on the second sock."*

To create the color pattern, I drew the outline of the instep on graph paper, then doodled patterns until I came up with a design I liked. In order to extend the instep pattern into the toe, I elongated the traditional Eastern toe band to extend around the toes so I could work the top and the bottom separately on each side of the band. When the instep was finished, I knitted the sole while attaching it and increasing for gussets by simply omitting decreases when joining the sole and instep. Cat Bordhi's well-fitting short-row turn and heel flap completed the foot. The colorwork pattern marches up the front and back of the leg to the cuff; then the sock ends with an elastic tubular bind-off. For fun, I reversed the colors on the second sock.

notes

+ For the first sock, use cranberry for color A and camo for color B. To work the second sock with the colors reversed, use camo for color A and cranberry for color B.

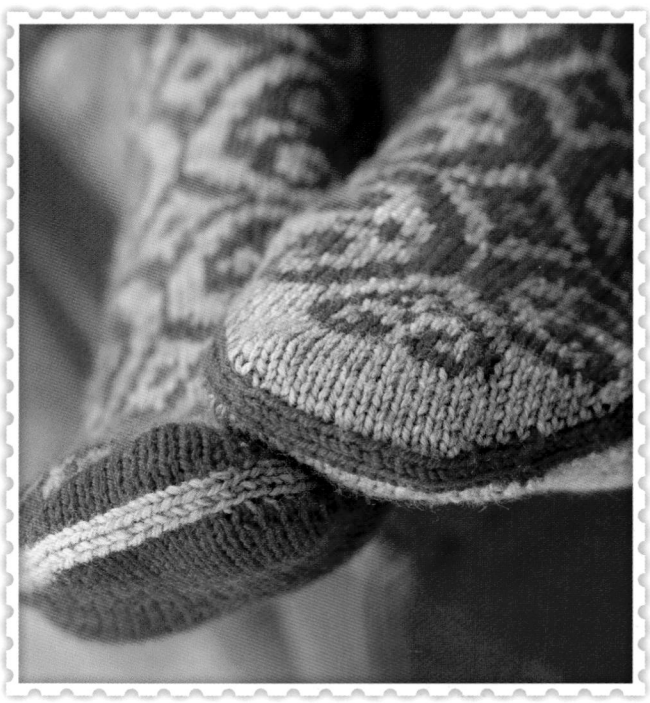

Toe Band

With B and smaller needles, use the backward-loop method (see Glossary) to CO 5 sts onto 1 dpn. Band begins at side of toes and is worked around the tip of the toes to the other side. Turn the needle upside down so that the CO loops are on top. With B and a second dpn, pick up and knit 4 sts from base of CO.

NOTE: The CO sts can be left on the dpn to work later or placed on a holder.

Work toe band using B on 4 picked-up sts as foll:

ROW 1: (WS) Sl 1 pwise with yarn in front (wyf), p3.

ROW 2: (RS) Sl 1 pwise with yarn in back (wyb), k3.

Rep these 2 rows 30 more times—62 rows completed; 31 chain edge sts along each selvedge. Cut yarn and place sts on holder. Mark the center chain edge st along each selvedge to indicate the center of the toe on both instep and sole of foot—15 chain edge sts on each side of marked st on each selvedge.

Top Half of Foot

TOE

Hold toe band horizontally with CO sts on the right and held sts at end of band on the left.

PICK-UP ROW: With A, RS facing, and beg 5 chain edge sts before marked st, pick up and knit 1 st from each of 5 chain edge sts to marked st, pick up and knit 1 st in marked st (remove marker), then pick up and knit 1 st in each of next 5 chain edge sts—11 sts total.

ROW 1: (WS) Sl 1 pwise wyf, p10, turn work.

ROW 2: (RS) Pick up and knit 1 st from the next chain edge st at beg of needle and place picked-up st on right needle, knit to end, then pick up and knit 1 st from the chain edge st at end of needle—2 sts inc'd.

ROW 3: Sl 1 pwise wyf, purl to end.

ROWS 4–7: Rep the last 2 rows 2 more times—17 toe sts.

⊕ DESIGN TIP: *For a graceful look, extend the leg pattern along the top of the instep, being careful to avoid bulky patterns that could be uncomfortable in a shoe.*

NEXT ROW: (RS) Establish patt from Row 1 of Front chart (page 159) as foll: Pick up and knit 1 st with A from next chain edge st at beg of row, work chart patt in stranded St st to end (joining B when necessary), pick up and knit 1 st with A from next chain edge st at end of row—19 toe sts.

Cont in patt from chart, picking up 1 st at each end of every RS row as shown, until Row 13 has been completed—31 toe sts; all chain edge sts on instep side of toe band have been used.

NEXT ROW: (WS) Work Row 14 of chart to end, return 4 CO sts to left needle, then use B to work across CO sts as p2tog through back loops (tbl; see Glossary), p2—34 sts total; 31 sts in chart patt, 3 band sts.

NEXT ROW: (RS) With B, sl 1 pwise wyb, k2; with A and B work Row 1 of main patt rep of chart to end; return rem 4 held band sts to left needle, then use B to work across held sts as k2tog, k2—37 sts total; 31 center sts in chart patt, and 3 band sts at each side.

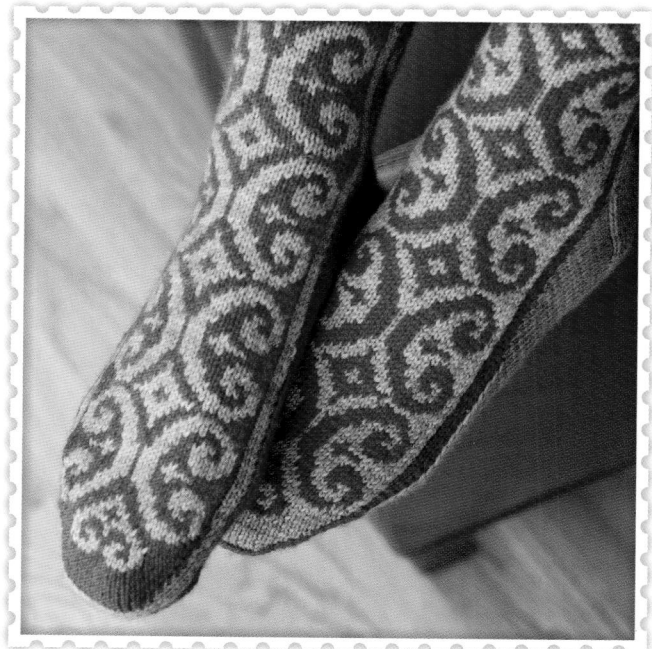

INSTEP

Working 3 band sts at each side with B and slipping the first st of every row as established, cont in patt from chart until Row 22 has been completed, then work Rows 1–22 of main patt rep once more, then work Rows 1–14 of the main patt rep again—piece measures about 8" (20.5 cm) from center of band at tip of toe.

NOTE: To adjust foot length, work more or fewer rows in chart patt; every row added or removed will lengthen or shorten the foot by about 1/10" (2.5 mm). Make a note of the last chart row completed so you can determine where to start the pattern on the back of the heel later (see box on page 157).

Not counting any sts actually on the needle, mark the 14th chain edge down from the needle at each side to indicate where gusset shaping will begin later. Place sts on holder.

Bottom Half of Foot

TOE

Hold toe band horizontally with rem chain edge uppermost. Working entirely with A and omitting chart patt, work toe as for top half of foot until there are 31 toe sts on needle.

SOLE

With A, purl 1 WS row. Work sole back and forth in rows, joining to a chain edge st color B band on each side of instep at the end of every row as foll:

ROW 1: (RS) Sl 1 pwise wyb, knit to last st, sl 1 kwise (last sole st), pick up and knit 1 st from chain edge of instep, insert left needle tip into front of 2 sts on right needle, and k2tog (last sole st tog with picked-up st).

ROW 2: (WS) Sl 1 pwise wyf, purl to last st, sl 1 pwise wyf (last sole st), pick up and purl (see Glossary) 1 st from chain edge of instep, insert left needle tip into back of 2 sts on right needle, p2tog (last sole st tog with picked-up st).

Rep Rows 1 and 2 until you have joined a chain edge st at each side just below the st marked for start of gusset shaping, ending with a WS row.

SHAPE GUSSETS

Inc for gussets by picking up at each side without working any decs as foll:

NEXT ROW: (RS) Sl 1 pwise wyb, knit to end, pick up and knit 1 st from chain edge of instep—1 st inc'd.

NEXT ROW: (WS) Sl 1 pwise wyf, purl to end, pick up and purl 1 st from chain edge of instep—1 st inc'd.

Rep the last 2 rows 13 more times, dividing sole sts onto 2 needles if there are too many to fit comfortably on 1 needle, ending with a WS row—59 sts. Knit 1 RS row.

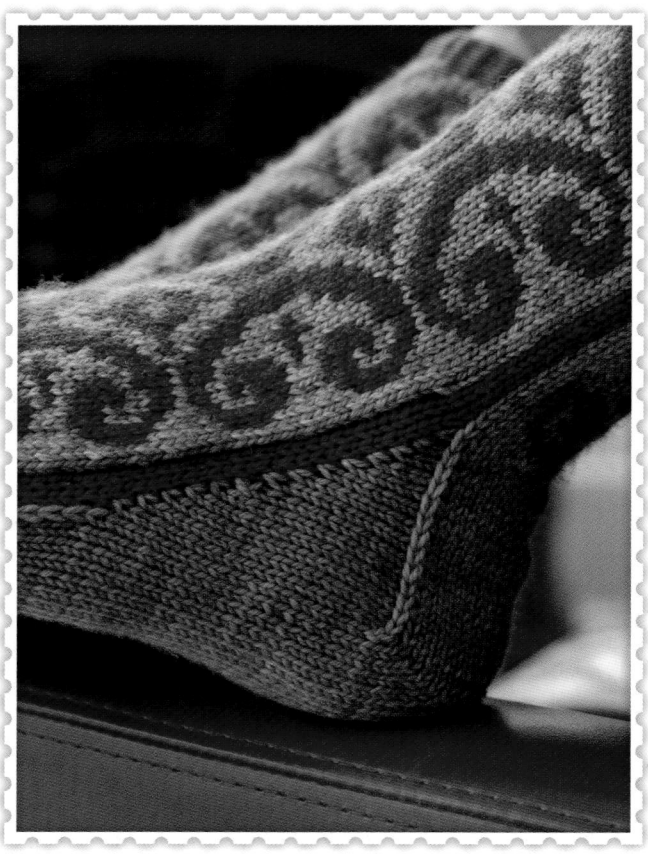

Heel

Place markers (m) on each side of center 31 sole sts—14 sts outside m at each side.

TURN HEEL

Work short-rows (see Glossary) as foll:

ROW 1: (WS) Sl 1 pwise wyf, purl to first m, sl m, p30 to 1 st before next m, wrap next st, turn work.

ROW 2: (RS) K29 to 1 st before m, wrap next st, turn.

ROW 3: Purl to 1 st before previously wrapped st, wrap next st, turn.

ROW 4: Knit to 1 st before previously wrapped st, wrap next st, turn.

Rep the last 2 rows 8 more times—last row completed is worked as k11, wrap next st, turn.

NEXT ROW: (WS) Purl to 1 st before m, working wraps tog with wrapped sts, sl next st temporarily to right needle, remove m, return slipped st to left needle, and purl the last wrap and wrapped st tog with the first st after m—58 sts rem.

NEXT ROW: (RS) Sl 1 pwise wyb, knit to 1 st before m, working wraps tog with wrapped sts, sl next st to right needle, remove m, return slipped st to left needle, knit the last wrap and wrapped st tog with the first st after m—57 sts rem.

HEEL FLAP

NEXT ROW: (WS) Sl 1 pwise wyf, purl to 1 st before gap formed on previous row, p2tog (1 st each side of gap), turn work—1 st dec'd.

NEXT ROW: (RS) Sl 1 pwise wyb, knit to 1 st before gap formed on previous row, ssk (1 st each side of gap), turn—1 st dec'd.

Heel Flap Pattern Placement

The heel flap instructions assume that the top half of the foot ended with Row 14 of the Front chart. The heel flap contains 26 rows. The center flap stitches are worked in solid-color stockinette for the first 20 rows and according to Rows 1–6 of the Back chart for the last 6 rows. In order for the Front and Back patterns to be aligned for the leg, Row 7 of the Back chart and Row 15 of the Front chart should be worked on the same round, just as they are in the joining round at the start of the leg instructions.

If you worked more or fewer rows on the top half of the foot to adjust the foot length, you will need to start the Back chart earlier or later on the heel flap to keep the patterns aligned. For example, if you worked 4 rows fewer on the top half of the foot and ended with Row 10 of the Front chart, begin the Back chart 4 rows later on the heel flap—after completing 24 rows instead of 20 rows. Work Rows 1 and 2 of the Back chart on the last 2 heel flap rows, work the joining round according to Row 3 of the Back chart and Row 11 of the Front chart, then work 4 more rounds, ending with Round 7 of the Back chart and Round 15 of the Front chart to align the patterns.

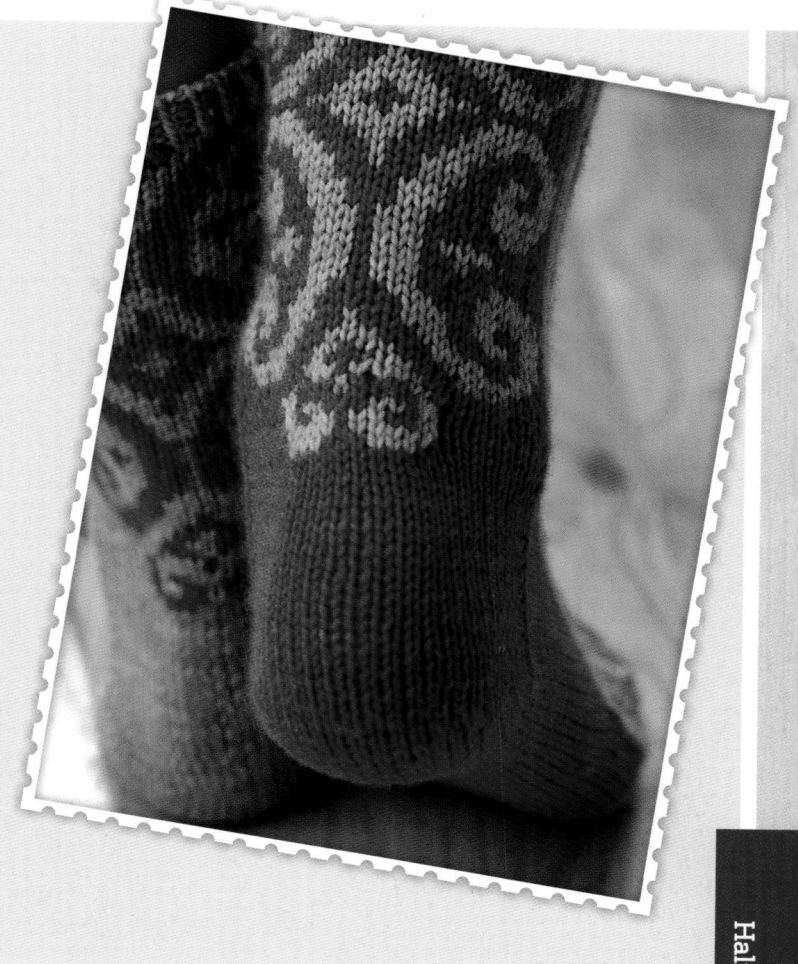

Rep the last 2 rows 9 more times—37 sts rem; 20 heel flap rows completed. Mark the center 31 sts—3 sts outside m at each side. Beg with Row 1 of chart as a WS row, work Back chart (page 159) over center 31 sts while cont to dec for flap as foll:

NEXT ROW: (WS) Sl 1 pwise wyf, purl to m, sl m, work chart patt over center 31 sts, sl m, purl to 1 st before gap formed on previous row, p2tog (1 st each side of gap), turn—1 st dec'd.

NEXT ROW: (RS) Sl 1 pwise wyb, knit to m, sl m, work chart patt over center 31 sts, sl m, knit to 1 st before gap formed on previous row, ssk (1 st each side of gap), turn—1 st dec'd.

Cont in patt from chart, rep the shaping of the last 2 rows 2 more times, ending with RS Row 6 of chart—31 heel sts rem; heel flap measures about 2¾" (7 cm).

Leg

Change to larger needles and place 37 held instep sts on needles.

JOINING RND: With B, work 3 sts at beg of instep as k2tog, k1; with A and B, work Row 15 of Front chart over 31 sts; with B, work 3 sts at end of instep as k1, ssk; with A and B, work Row 7 of Back chart as a RS row over 31 sts, pm for beg of rnd at side of leg—66 sts; 3-st sections at each side of instep have been dec'd to 2 sts each.

Working 2-st sections separating front and back patts with B and working all chart rows as RS rnds, work even in patt until Rnd 14 of Back chart has been completed, ending with Rnd 22 of Front chart. Working patt from Front chart across 31 patt sts on both front and back of leg, work Rnds 1–22 of main patt rep once more, then work Rnds 23–26 once—piece measures about 7¾" (19.5 cm) from start of heel flap. Cut off B.

CUFF
With A, knit 1 rnd across all sts.

NEXT RND: *K1 tbl, p1; rep from *.

Rep the last rnd 4 more times—5 rib rnds total; piece measures about 8¼" (21 cm) from start of heel flap.

Finishing
Cut yarn, leaving a 30" (76 cm) tail. Thread tail on tapestry needle and use the tubular method (page 121), BO all sts. Weave in loose ends. Block lightly.

Make a second sock, reversing the colors (see Notes).

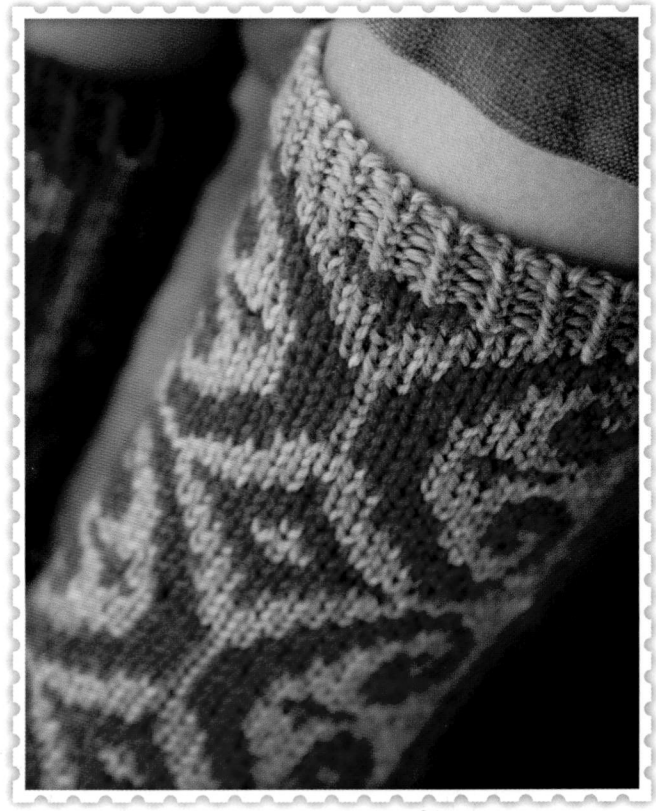

Yarn Note

Yarn choices can have consequences, and here's a sock that was designed expressly with those consequences in mind: Its sole can be raveled and reknitted whenever it grows too thin. Three strands of 80% merino reinforced with 20% nylon are plied together at a near-perpendicular angle, producing a very round, bouncy yarn with a high degree of abrasion resistance—exactly what you want in a sock yarn and especially welcome in patterns that have a smooth stockinette heel such as this one. The elasticity is important here because the top of the foot and the entire cuff are knitted in stranded colorwork. A decorative skiff of twisted k1, p1 ribbing runs along the top to add finality and keep the edge from curling. Because of the relative inelasticity of stranded colorwork and the cuff's need to expand at least one-third its circumference to accommodate your heel every time you put on the sock, you'll want to stick with a yarn that has a good amount of elasticity to it. Don't be shy about using semisolids for the main and contrasting colors or, at a minimum, the main color. The variation in hue adds movement and depth without distracting from the beautiful color patterning. —*Clara Parkes*

Back

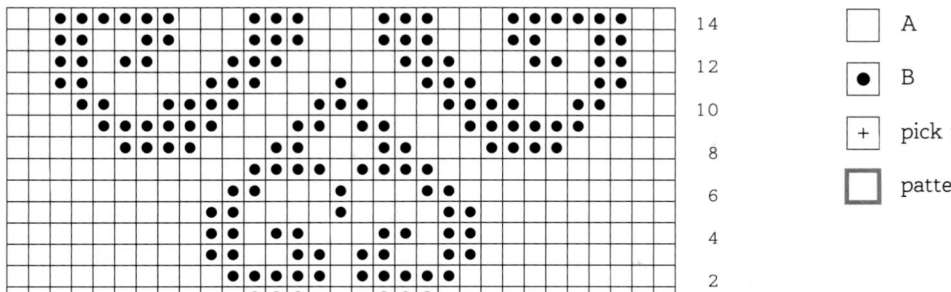

14
12
10
8
6
4
2

	A
•	B
+	pick up 1 st with A
	pattern repeat

Front

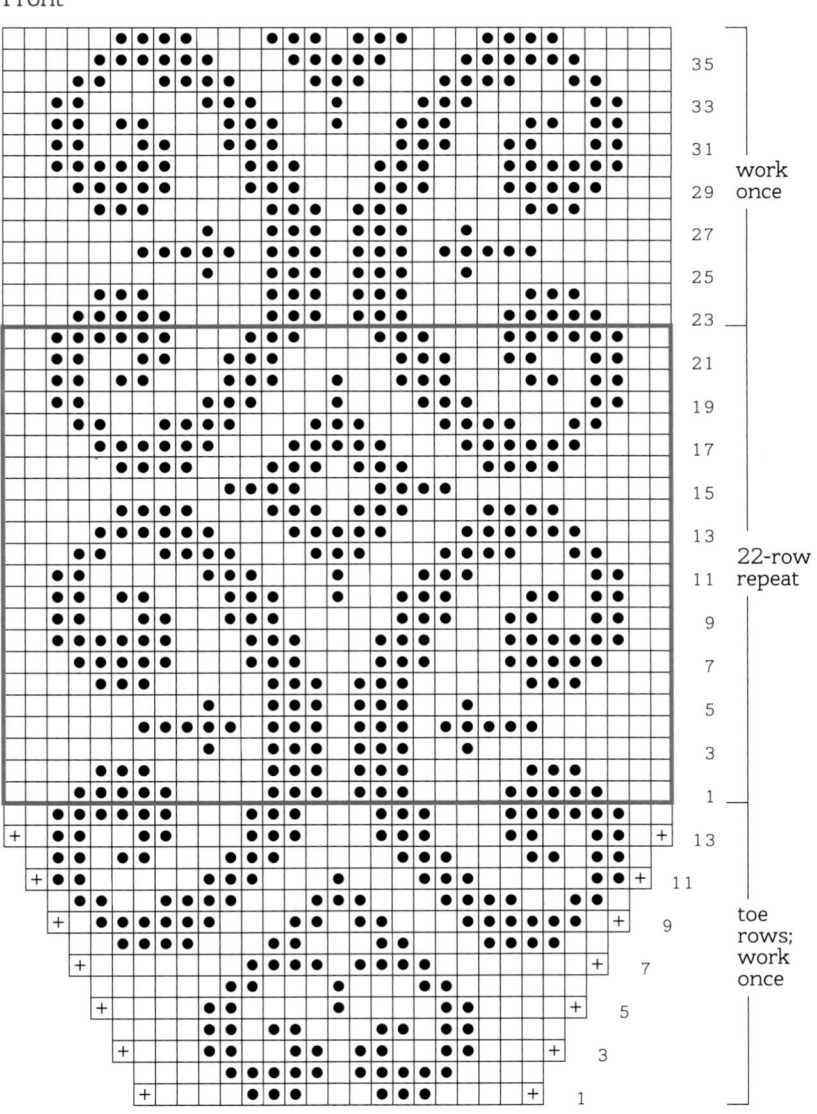

35
33
31
29

work once

27
25
23
21
19
17
15
13
11
9
7
5
3
1

22-row repeat

13
11
9
7
5
3
1

toe rows; work once

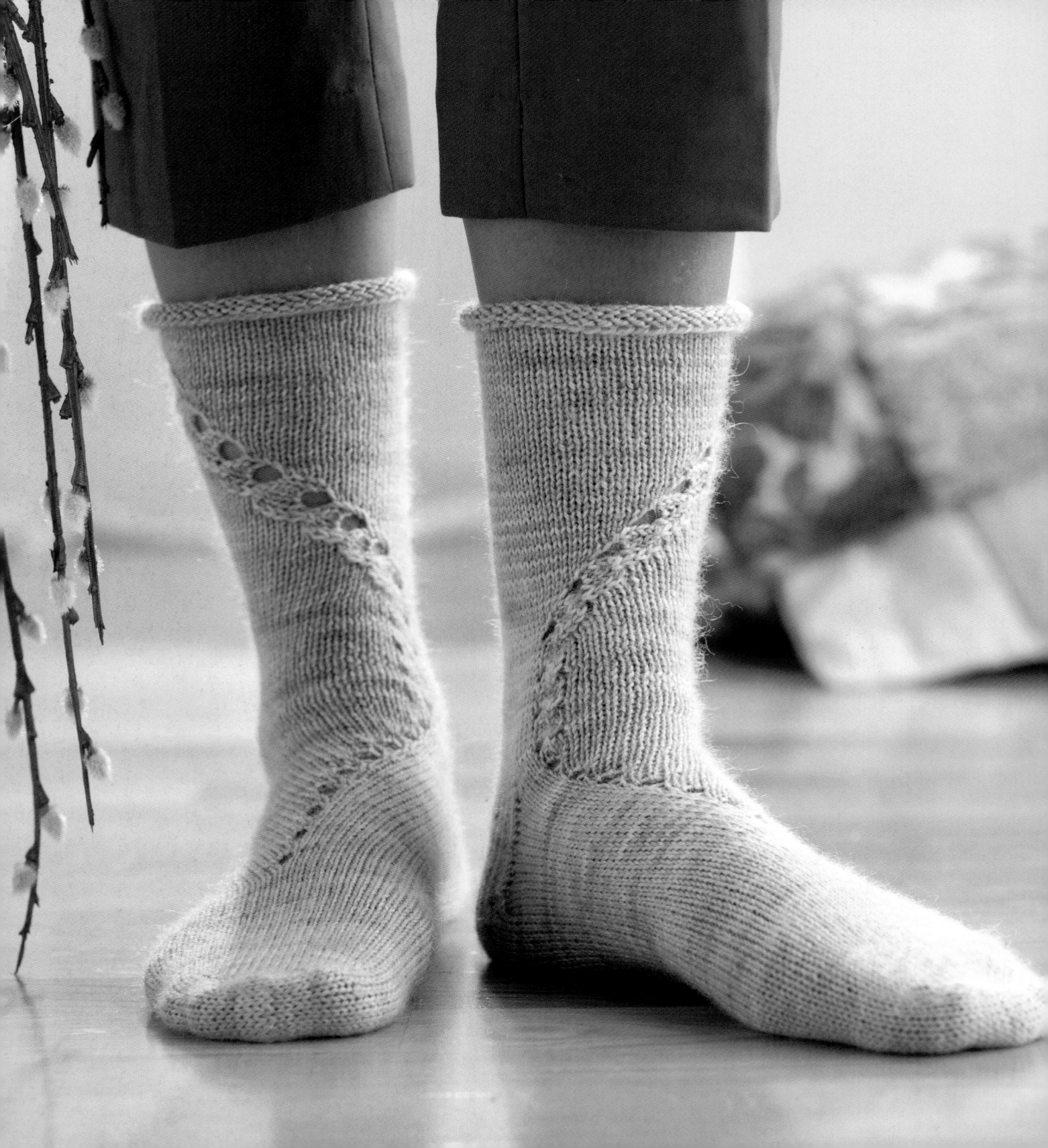

Pussy Willow Stockings

DESIGNED BY *Cat Bordhi*

finished size

About 7 (8)" (18 [20.5] cm) foot circumference (will stretch to accommodate a foot about 1" [2.5 cm] larger), 9½" (24 cm) foot length from back of heel to tip of toe (with option for adjusting foot length), and 9½" (24 cm) leg length from top of leg to base of heel flap, with upper edge allowed to roll. Socks shown measure 7" (18 cm) in circumference (to fit a foot about 8" [20.5 cm] in circumference).

yarn

Fingering weight (#1 Super Fine).

Shown here: Fleece Artist Somoko (65% merino, 20% kid mohair, 10% nylon, 5% silk; 383 yd [350 m]/4 oz): salt spray, 1 skein.

needles

Size U.S. 1 (2.5 mm): two 24" (60 cm) circular (cir).

Adjust needle size if necessary to obtain the correct gauge.

notions

4 unique markers (m; designated A, B, C, and D, or in 4 different colors or styles); tapestry needle.

gauge

16 sts and 22 rnds = 2" (5 cm) in St st worked in rnds.

My inspiration usually comes from nature and, like nature, a design arises organically, revealing its unique expression moment by moment. Where I live, spring is announced by the emergence of pussy willows on formerly bare branches. For this design, I wanted to transform the charming catkins— sleek little furry shapes marching up smooth branches—into a pair of delicate socks. I began with a toe capped by a horizontal band to form a smooth and comfortable covering, similar to the shape of a catkin. Once the lower foot was complete, I began to expand the instep by working a diagonal branch with yarnovers (increasing 3 stitches every 5 rounds) to represent young catkins. Based on the basic formula in *New Pathways for Sock Knitters,* I knew these increases could be placed anywhere on the instep. I worked the heel in a fortified heel stitch, twisting the elongated, vulnerable slipped stitches to shorten them and tighten the yarn's plies. At the ankle, the pussy willow stem continues vertically for a while, then begins to lean outward as the catkins reach maturity, with each yarnover hole crowned with a bouffant catkin. I finished the cuff with a simple rolled edge, preserving the serene stockinette background and letting the pussy willow branch hold center stage.

> *My inspiration usually comes from nature and, like nature, a design arises organically, revealing its unique expression moment by moment."*

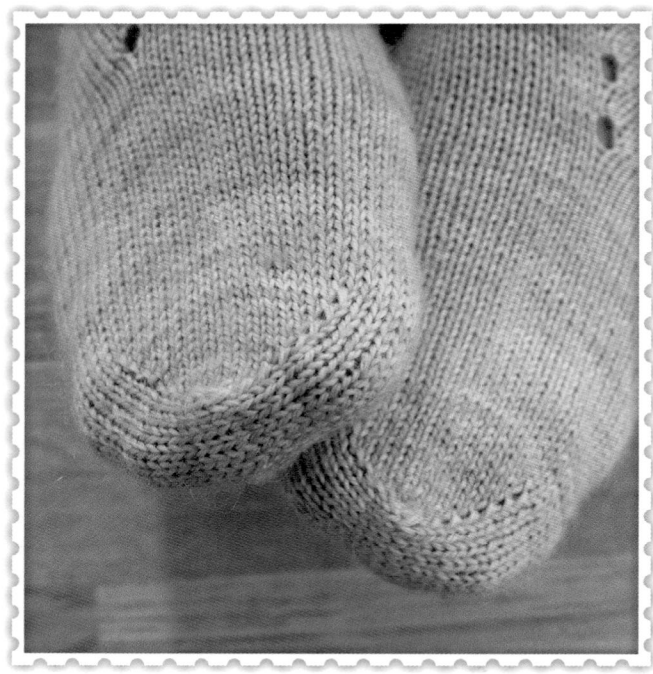

notes

+ If you do not have markers labeled A, B, C, and D, use markers in four different colors or four different styles and assign one of the letters to each marker.

Moccasin Toe

Using Judy's Magic method (see page 117), CO 24 sts total (12 sts each on 2 cir needles). Knit across 12 sts on first needle to set up for working toe.

RND 1: (inc rnd) On first needle, *k1, M1 (see Glossary), k10, M1, k1; on second needle, rep from *—28 sts; 14 sts each needle.

RND 2: Knit.

RND 3: (inc rnd) On first needle, k2, M1, place marker (pm) A (see Note), k10, pm B, M1, k2; on second needle, k2, M1, pm C, k10, pm D, M1, k2—32 sts; 16 sts each needle.

RND 4: Knit.

RND 5: Knit to m A, M1, slip marker (sl m) A, k10, sl m B, M1, knit to m C, M1, sl m C, k10, sl m D, M1, knit to end—4 sts inc'd.

Rep Rnds 4 and 5 for shaping 5 (7) more times—56 (64 sts); 28 (32) sts each needle. Knit 3 rnds even, removing markers—toe measures about 1½ (1¾) (3.8 [4.5] cm) from CO.

Foot

Rearrange sts as foll: K14 (16) and transfer sts just worked to adjacent end of second needle, knit the next 28 (32) sts with first needle for instep, knit next 28 (32) sole sts with second needle. Round begins at start of first needle that holds instep sts. Work even in St st (knit every rnd) until foot measures 4 (3½)" (10 [9] cm) from tip of toe, or about 5½ (6)" (14 [15] cm) less than desired total foot length.

Instep Expansion

Work each sock as foll.

RIGHT SOCK

SET-UP RND: On instep needle, k17 (19) to 3 sts after center of needle, pm A, knit to end.

RND 1: Knit to m A, sl m A, yo, knit to end—1 st inc'd on instep needle.

RND 2: Knit to m A, sl m A, work (k1, yo, k1) in yo of previous rnd, knit to end—2 sts inc'd on instep needle.

RNDS 3–5: Knit.

Rep these 5 rnds 7 (8) more times, then work Rnds 1–3 once more—83 (94) sts total; 55 (62) sts on instep needle; 28 (32) sts on sole needle; m A is still positioned after the first 17 (19) sts of instep needle.

LEFT SOCK

SET-UP RND: On instep needle, k11 (13) to 3 sts before center of needle, pm A, knit to end.

RND 1: Knit to m A, yo, sl m A, knit to end—1 st inc'd on instep needle.

RND 2: Knit to 1 st before m A, work (k1, yo, k1) in yo of previous rnd, sl m A, knit to end—2 sts inc'd on instep needle.

RNDS 3–5: Knit.

Rep these 5 rnds 7 (8) more times, then work Rnds 1–3 once more—83 (94) sts total; 55 (62) sts on instep needle; 28 (32) sts on sole needle; m A is still positioned after first 11 (13) sts of instep needle.

Heel

NOTE: The heel is worked back and forth in rows. If you purl more loosely than you knit, use a smaller needle for the purl rows to keep the gauge sufficiently tight.

SET-UP RND: (counts as Rnd 4 of instep patt) On the first needle, k1 and slip the st just worked to end of second needle, knit the next 13 (15) sts while inc 5 (6) sts evenly spaced, knit the center 28 (31) instep sts leaving m A in place, knit the last 13 (15) sts while inc 5 (6) sts evenly spaced; do not work sts on second needle—93 (106) sts total; 64 (73) sts on instep needle; 29 (33) sts on heel needle.

TURN HEEL

Work the heel back and forth in short-rows (see Glossary) on 29 (33) heel sts as foll:

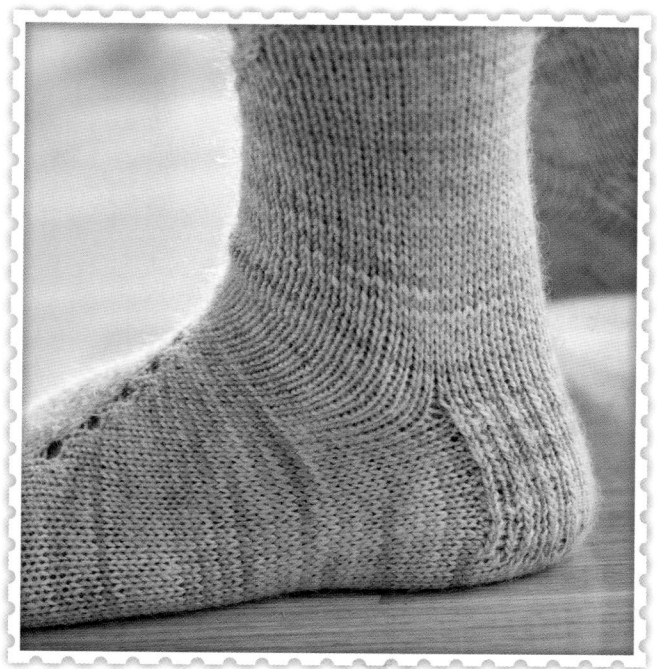

ROW 1: (RS) Knit to last 2 sts, wrap next st, turn work.

ROW 2: (WS) Purl to last 2 sts, wrap next st, turn.

ROW 3: Knit to 1 st before previously wrapped st, wrap next st, turn.

ROW 4: Purl to 1 st before previously wrapped st, wrap next st, turn.

Rep Rows 3 and 4 for heel turn 5 (6) more times—7 (8) wrapped sts at each end of needle; 13 (15) center sts between last pair of wrapped sts.

NEXT ROW: (RS) Knit to wrapped st, work next 6 (7) sts tog with their wraps, work rem wrapped st tog with its wrap while working it tog with last st as k2tog, turn—1 heel st dec'd; 28 (32) heel sts rem.

NEXT ROW: (WS) Sl 1 pwise with yarn in front (wyf), purl to wrapped sts, work next 6 (7) sts tog with their wraps, work rem wrapped st tog with its wrap while working it tog with last st as p2tog, turn—1 heel st dec'd; 27 (31) heel sts rem.

BACK OF HEEL

Slip the first 18 (21) sts of instep needle to end of heel needle—45 (52) sts on heel needle; 46 (52) sts on instep needle; with RS facing, working yarn is at left needle tip, at start of 27 (31) heel-turn sts.

NOTE: In this variation on the standard slip-stitch heel, the slipped sts are twisted by slipping them pwise through the back loop (sl 1 tbl) to shorten and tighten the elongated slip stitches, thereby increasing durability. The sts just before the ssk and p2tog decs at the ends of the rows are also twisted to tighten these potentially loose columns of sts.

ROW 1: (RS) Sl 1 tbl with yarn in back (wyb), k1tbl, [sl 1 tbl, k1] 11 (13) times, [k1tbl] 2 times, ssk (last heel st tog with st after it), turn work—1 st dec'd from heel needle.

ROW 2: (WS) Sl 1 tbl wyf, [p1tbl] 2 times, p22 (26), p1tbl, p2tog (last heel st tog with next st from instep needle), turn work—1 st dec'd from instep needle.

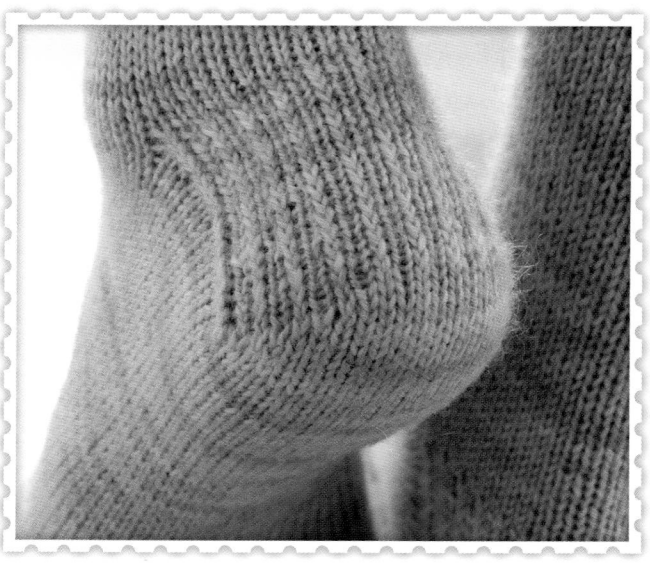

Rep Rows 1 and 2 for heel 15 (18) more times—29 (33) sts on heel needle; 30 (33) sts on instep needle; slip-stitch heel flap measures about 2 (2½)" (5 [6.5] cm) high.

JOINING RND: (counts as Rnd 5 of instep patt) With RS facing and heel needle, sl 1 tbl, k1tbl, [sl 1 tbl, k1] 11 (13) times, [k1tbl] 2 times, ssk, k1; with instep needle, knit to last st, transfer last st to heel needle; with heel needle, work transferred st and first heel st as k2tog, knit to end—57 (64) sts total; 28 (32) sts on heel needle; 29 (32) sts on instep needle. Rnd begins at side of leg at start of instep sts.

Yarn Note

Graceful, fluid stitchwork moves across a sea of stockinette—all of which is enhanced by a yarn whose two relaxed plies contain a blend of 65% merino, 20% kid mohair, 10% nylon, and 5% silk. The merino gives bounce and substance to the mix, while the 20% kid mohair lends much of the exquisite luster and smoothness. The 10% nylon adds welcome strength to the vulnerable stockinette, while 5% silk adds even more luster to the finished result. This sock yearns to be knitted in a semisolid colorway to bring flickering movement to the surface, although it could work in a gently variegated colorway as well. The sock also longs for a yarn with luster, whether that comes from silk or mohair or even bamboo. Elasticity will be an issue, however, as this sock has no ribbing to hold it snugly on your leg; therefore you'll want to make sure the sock has a bit a negative ease. Check the finished measurements and modify the cuff as necessary so that the sock will fit comfortably. If you need even greater elasticity or are creating this for someone whose calf circumference you don't know, consider a 100% merino yarn with as perpendicular a twist as possible—or even a yarn with a small percentage of elastic. Just remember that you'll lose some of the smooth, glossy stockinette effect in the process.

—*Clara Parkes*

Ankle

Work each sock as foll:

RIGHT SOCK

RND 1: Knit to m A, sl m A, yo, ssk, knit to end.

RND 2: Knit to m A, sl m A, work (k1, yo, k1) in yo of previous rnd, sl 2 sts as if to k2tog, k1, p2sso, knit to end.

RNDS 3–5: Knit.

Rep these 5 rnds 3 more times.

LEFT SOCK

RND 1: Knit to 2 sts before m A, k2tog, yo, sl m A, knit to end.

RND 2: Knit to 4 sts before m A, sl 2 sts as if to k2tog, k1, p2sso, work (k1, yo, k1) in yo of previous rnd, sl m A, knit to end.

RNDS 3–5: Knit.

Rep these 5 rnds 3 more times.

Leg

NOTE: The beg of the rnd shifts to accommodate the yo patt as it spirals around toward the outside of the leg. Transfer sts between needles as necessary to work the patt.

Work each sock as foll.

RIGHT SOCK

SET-UP: Knit to m A.

RND 1: Sl m A, yo, ssk, knit to m A.

RND 2: Sl m A, work (k1, yo, k1) in yo of previous rnd, sl 2 sts as if to k2tog, k1, p2sso, knit to m A.

RNDS 3–5: M1, sl m A, k3, ssk, knit to m A.

Rep Rnds 1–5 eight more times—leg measures about 8 (8½)" (20.5 [21.5] cm) from base of heel flap.

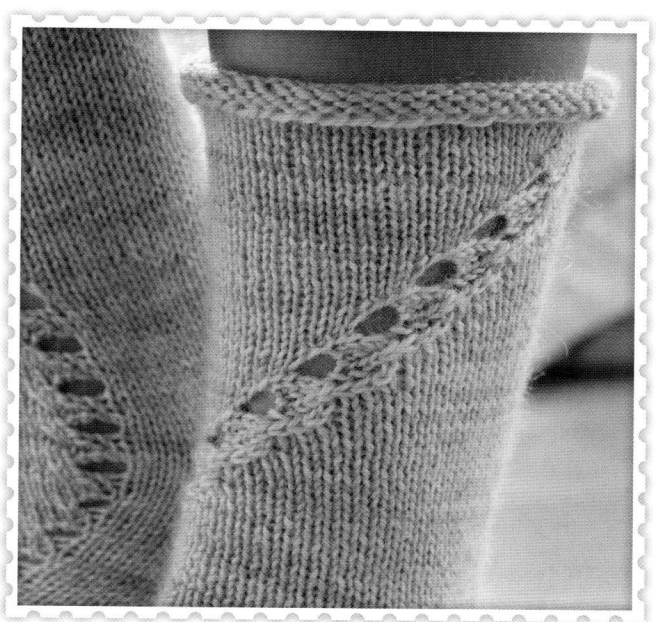

LEFT SOCK

SET-UP: Knit to 2 sts before m A.

RND 1: K2tog, yo, sl m A, knit to 4 sts before m A.

RND 2: Sl 2 sts as if to k2tog, k1, p2sso, work (k1, yo, k1) in yo of previous rnd, sl m A, knit to 5 sts before m A.

RNDS 3 AND 4: K2tog, k3, sl m A, M1, knit to 5 sts before m A.

RND 5: K2tog, k3, sl m A, M1, knit to 2 sts before m A.

Rep Rnds 1–5 eight more times—leg measures about 8 (8½)" (20.5 [21.5] cm) from base of heel flap.

CUFF (FOR BOTH SOCKS)

Knit every rnd until piece measures 9¾" (25 cm) from base of heel flap. Purl 2 rnds.

Finishing

Using Jeny's Surprisingly Stretchy method (page 119), BO all sts; top edge will roll to the RS. Weave in loose ends. Block lightly.

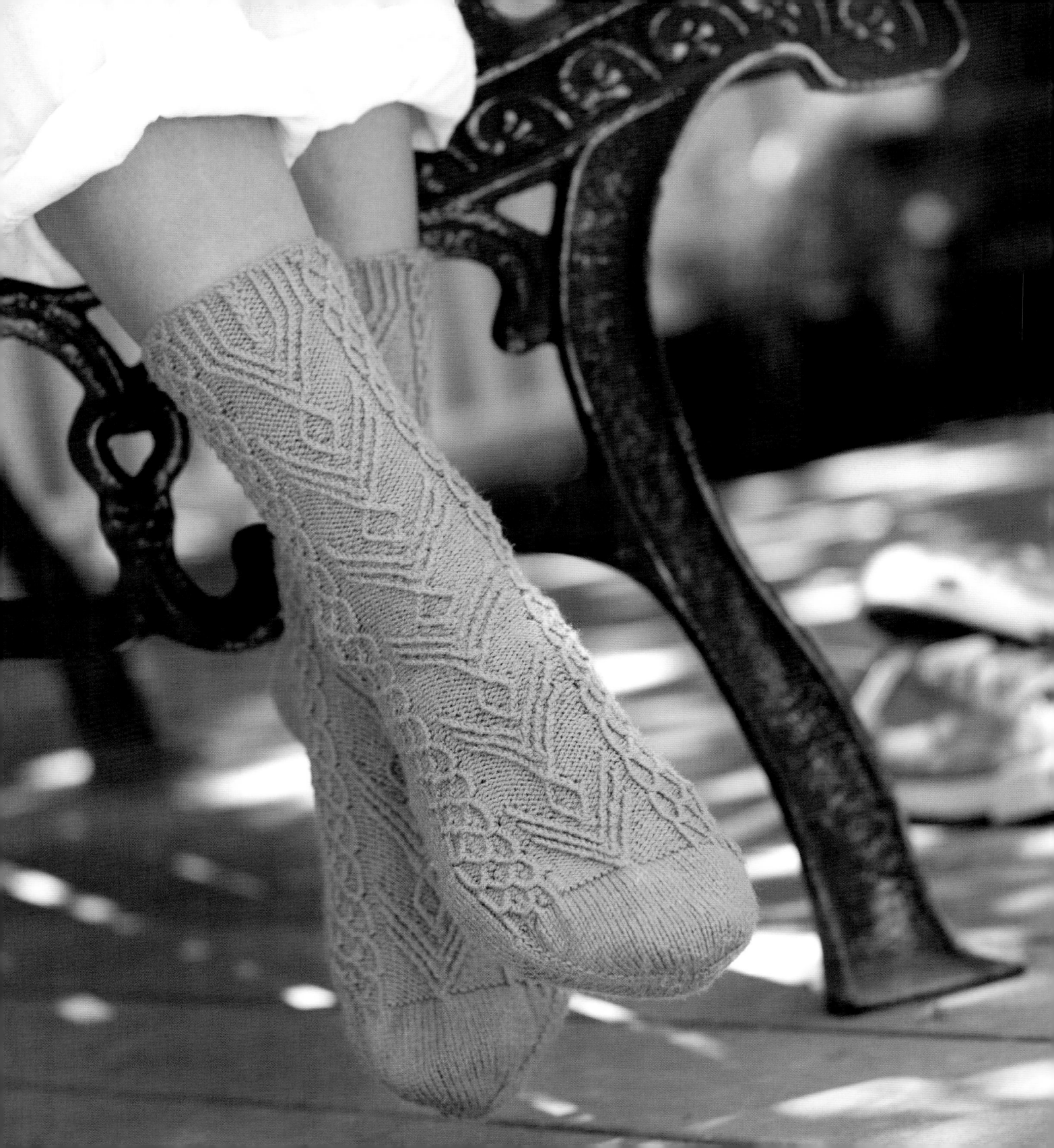

Toe-Up Travelers

DESIGNED BY *Ann Budd*

finished size

About 7½" (19 cm) foot circumference, 10" (25.5 cm) foot length from back of heel to tip of toe, and 8½" (21.5 cm) leg length from top of cuff to base of heel.

yarn

Fingering weight (#1 Super Fine).

Shown here: Quince & Company Tern (75% wool, 25% silk; 226 yd [206 m]/50 g): #750 kelp, 2 skeins.

needles

Foot and lower leg: size U.S. 1 (2.25 mm): set of 5 double-pointed (dpn).

Upper leg: size U.S. 2 (2.75 mm): set of 5 dpn.

Adjust needle size if necessary to obtain the correct gauge.

notions

Markers (m); cable needle (optional); tapestry needle.

gauge

18 sts and 26 rnds = 2" (5 cm) in St st on smaller needles, worked in rnds.

40 sts of Wings Instep chart measures 3" (7.5 cm) wide on smaller needles.

I began these socks with the traveling-stitch "wing" pattern that I found in a Japanese book of stitch patterns called *Knitting Patterns Book 250*. Because I wanted the pattern to flow along the front of the leg and instep in the same orientation as was shown in the pattern book, I had to work the socks from the toe up. Then I added another pattern at the sides of the leg to bring the stitch count to an appropriate number for a leg circumference. The pattern I chose involves twisted stitches to coordinate with the main stitch pattern, but I added 4-stitch groups of wrapped stitches to add to the textural look. For design continuity on the front of the leg, I extended the wrapped-stitch pattern along the instep. I chose to work a short-row heel to minimize design interruption at the heel, but it would have looked equally good if I extended the wrapped-stitch pattern along the flap of a round heel (worked from the toe up). For the cuff, I maintained the wrapped-stitch pattern at the sides of the leg but discontinued the traveling stitches in the wings pattern and added a tiny cable pattern at the center of the motif. A stretchy sewn bind-off forms an elastic edge at the cuff.

> *I wanted the pattern to flow along the front of the leg and instep in the same orientation it was shown in the pattern book."*

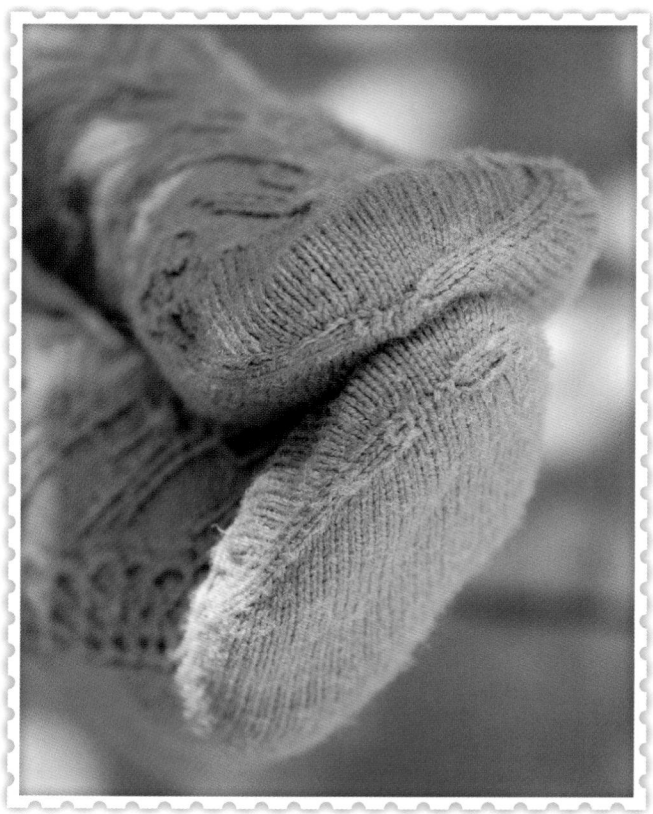

notes

+ The twisted stitches are easiest to work using needles that have long sharp tips.

+ To lengthen the foot, work the desired number of additional rounds of stockinette stitch after reaching the total number of foot stitches but before beginning the charted pattern.

+ To increase the foot circumference, work more toe increases, then distribute the extra stitches evenly between the instep and sole. Work the extra instep stitches in the purl columns on each side of the main motif (between the wings and the wrapped stitches) where they will cause the least disruption. Work the extra sole stitches in stockinette stitch. When working the first half of the heel, repeat the required rows until a right-side row of "paired sts, k14" has been worked, then work the second half as written. Distribute the extra stitches on the back of the leg in the purl columns flanking the wings pattern, just as for the instep (which continues along the front of the leg).

⊕ **DESIGN TIP:** *Traditionally, cuffs are worked in some type of rib pattern. If possible, a ribbed cuff is best integrated with the leg if the knit or purl stitches in the cuff flow uninterrupted into the knit or purl stitches in the leg pattern.*

Stitch Guide

4-ST WRAP

Insert right needle between the 4th and 5th sts on left needle, draw up a loop and place it on left needle, knit the new loop tog with the st after it, then k2, k1tbl.

SSP

Slip 2 sts individually kwise, return these 2 sts to left needle tip, then purl them tog through their back loops—1 st dec'd.

SSSP

Slip 3 sts individually kwise, return these 3 sts to left needle tip, then purl them tog through their back loops—2 sts dec'd.

Toe

With two smaller dpn held tog and using the Turkish/Eastern method (page 116), CO 8 sts. Divide sts on 3 dpn so that there are 2 sole sts on Needle 1, 4 instep sts on Needle 2, and 2 sole sts on Needle 3; rnd begins at center of sole (between Needles 1 and 3).

INC RND: On Needle 1, knit to last st, M1 (see Glossary), k1; on Needle 2, k1, M1, knit to last st, M1, k1; on Needle 3, k1, M1, knit to end—4 sts inc'd.

Rep the inc rnd on the next 7 rnds—40 sts. Rep the inc rnd every other rnd 10 times—80 sts; 20 sole sts on Needle 1, 40 instep sts on Needle 2, and 20 sole sts on Needle 3.

Foot

Working the sole sts in St st as established, work 40 instep sts (Needle 2) in patt from Wings Instep chart (page 170) until Rnds 1–24 of chart have been worked 3 times, ending at the end of instep sts (Needle 2) on Rnd 24 of chart (leave sts of Needle 3 unworked)—72 chart rnds completed; piece measures about 8" (20.5 cm) from tip of toe (see Notes for adding length).

Heel

Arrange sts so that all 40 sole sts (Needle 1 and Needle 3) are on the same needle for the heel and divide the 40 instep sts on 2 needles to work later. Work the 40 sole stitches back and forth in short-rows in two halves as foll.

FIRST HALF

Work 1 less st each short-row as foll:

ROW 1: (RS) K39, turn work—1 regular st unworked at end of needle.

ROW 2: (WS) Bring yarn from back to front over right needle to create a backward yo, p38, leaving last st unworked, turn—1 regular st unworked at end of row; 1 regular st and 1 "paired st" consisting of a stitch plus a yo at beg of row.

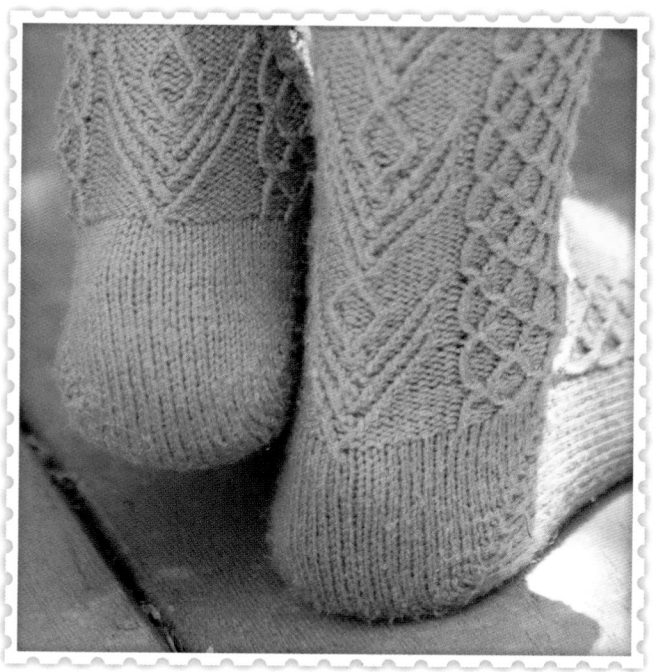

ROW 3: Bring yarn from front to back over right needle to create a normal yo, knit to paired st at end of row, turn—1 paired st and 1 regular st unworked at each end of row.

ROW 4: Bring yarn from back to front over right needle to create a backward yo, purl to paired st at end of row, turn.

ROW 5: Bring yarn from front to back over right needle to create a normal yo, knit to paired st at end of row, turn.

Rep Rows 4 and 5 ten more times, adding another paired st at the end of each row and ending with a RS row—12 paired sts and 1 regular st unworked at each side. Last row completed was worked as "yo, k1 (to form the 12th st/yo pair), k14."

SECOND HALF

Work 1 more st each short-row as foll:

ROW 1: (RS) Cont with the same RS row, k1 (the knit st of the paired st), correct the mount of the yo so that its leading leg is in front of the needle, k2tog (the yo tog with the knit st of the foll paired st), turn work, leaving rem yo of the pair unworked.

	knit
ℓ	k1tbl
·	purl
ℓ▭	4-st wrap (see Stitch Guide)
	sl 1 st onto cn and hold in front, k1tbl, k1tbl from cn
	sl 1 st onto cn and hold in back, k1tbl, p1 from cn
	sl 1 st onto cn and hold in front, p1, k1tbl from cn

Wings Instep

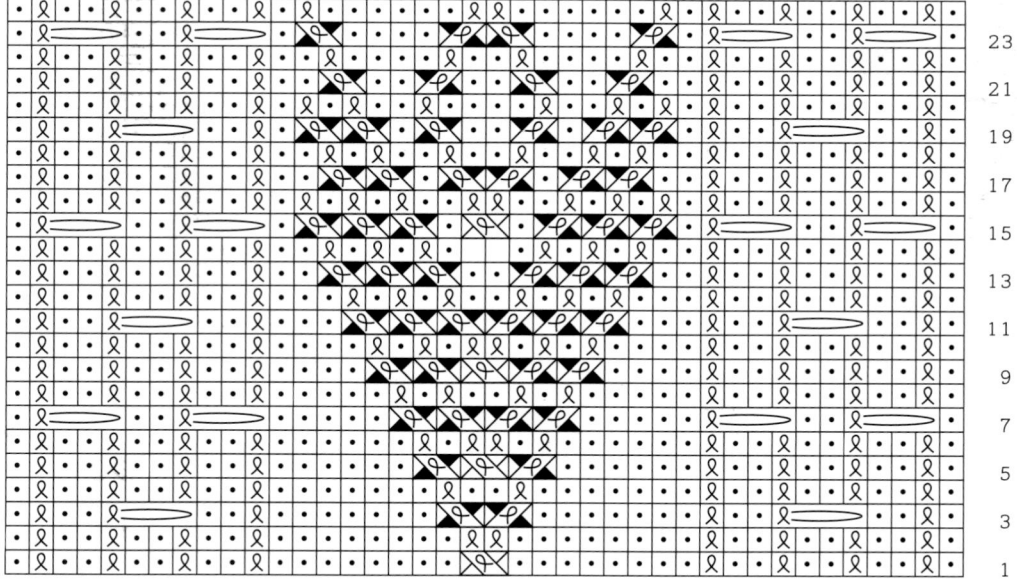

23
21
19
17
15
13
11
9
7
5
3
1

Wings Leg

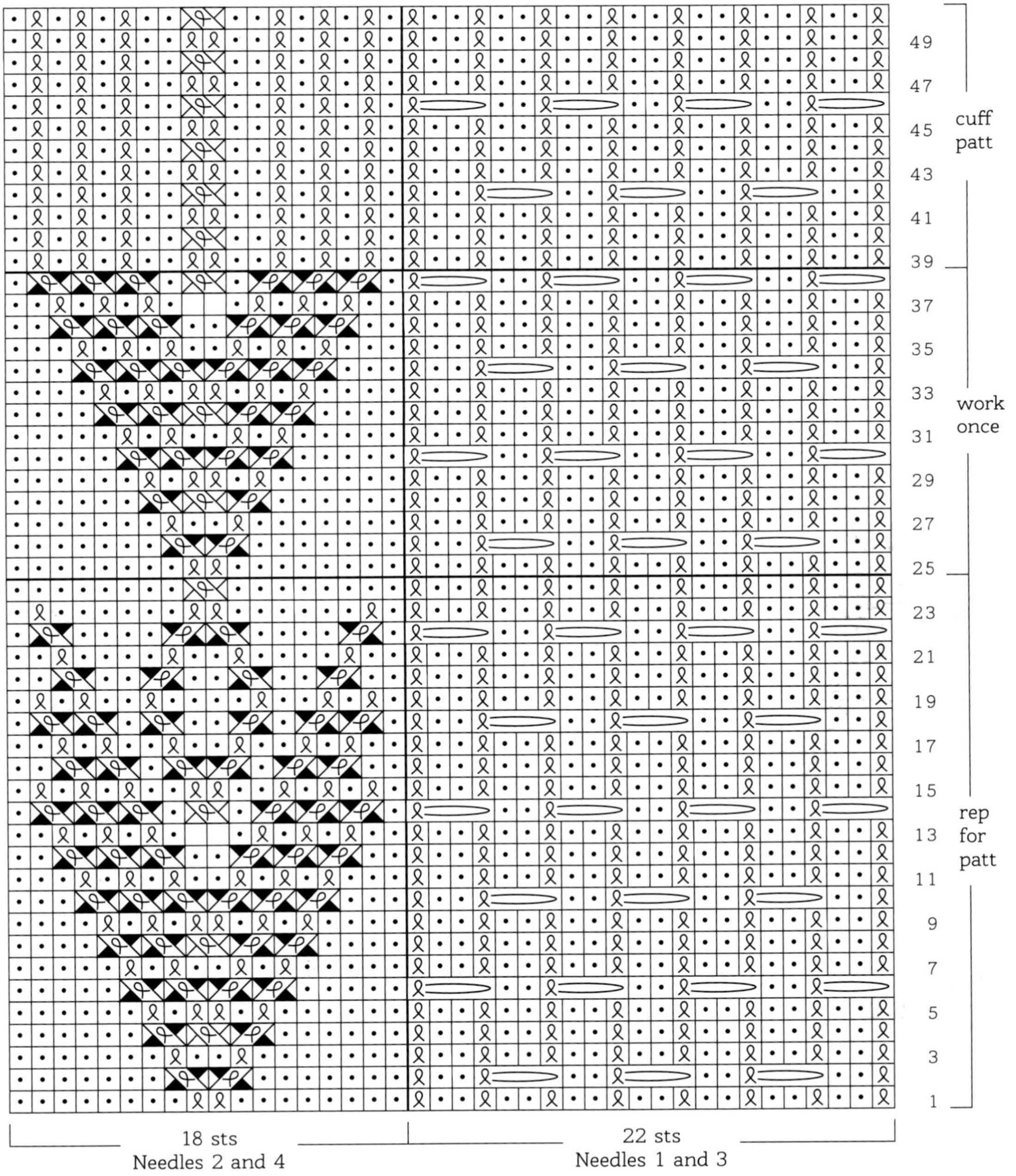

49
47
45   cuff patt
43
41
39
37
35
33   work once
31
29
27
25
23
21
19
17
15
13   rep for patt
11
9
7
5
3
1

18 sts	22 sts
Needles 2 and 4	Needles 1 and 3

ROW 2: (WS) Bring yarn from back to front over right needle to create a backward yo, purl to the first paired st, p1 (the purl st of the pair), ssp (the yo of the pair tog with the purl st of the foll pair; see Stitch Guide), turn, leaving rem yo of pair unworked.

ROW 3: Bring yarn from front to back over right needle to create a normal yo, knit to the first paired st, k1 (the knit st of the pair), correct the mount of the next 2 yo's, k3tog (the 2 yo's tog with the knit st of the foll pair), turn, leaving rem yo of the pair unworked.

ROW 4: Bring yarn from back to front over right needle to create a backward yo, purl to the first paired st, p1 (the purl st of the pair), sssp (the 2 yo's tog with the purl st of the foll pair; see Stitch Guide), turn, leaving rem yo of pair unworked.

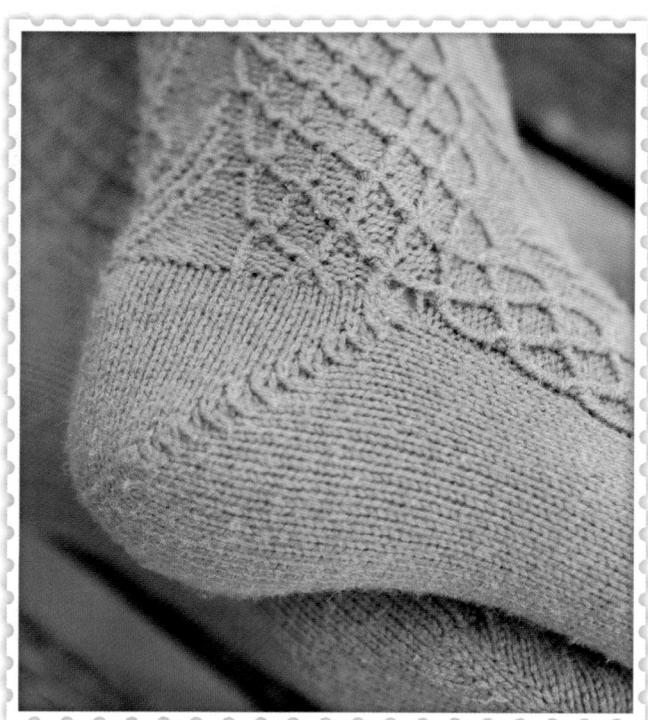

Rep Rows 3 and 4 until all heel sts have been worked, ending with a WS row—there will be 41 sts on the needle; 40 regular sts and 1 yo paired with the last st on the needle (when viewed from the RS).

JOINING ROUND

With RS facing, bring yarn from front to back to create a normal yo, knit to the paired st at the end of the needle, k1 (the knit st of the pair), transfer the yo to the beg of the instep sts and work it tog with the first instep st as p2tog (counts as the first st from Rnd 1 of Wings Instep chart), work the next 38 sts according to the chart, transfer the yo at the beg of the heel sts to the end of the instep needle and work it tog with the last instep st as ssp (counts as last st from Rnd 1 of chart), then work the first 29 sts from Rnd 1 of Wings Instep chart again over the first 29 heel sts, leaving rem 11 heel sts unworked—80 sts total.

Leg

Rearrange sts on 4 dpn as foll: Place 11 rem unworked sts and next 11 sts on Needle 1 for 22 sts in wrapped-st patt at side of leg, place next 18 sts on Needle 2 for main motif at front of leg, place next 22 sts on Needle 3 for wrapped-st patt at other side of leg, and place rem 18 sts on Needle 4 for main motif at back of leg. Rnd begs at start of Needle 1 with 22 sts in wrapped-st patt. Work Rnds 1–24 of Wings Leg chart once, then work Rnds 1–14 once more—piece measures about 5½" (14 cm) from base of heel. Change to larger dpn and work Rnds 15–38 once—piece measures about 7½" (19 cm) from base of heel. Work Rnds 39–50 for cuff—12 cuff rnds total; piece measures about 8½" (21.5 cm) from base of heel.

Finishing

Cut yarn, leaving a 26" (66 cm) tail. Thread tail on a tapestry needle and use the sewn method (see page 118) to BO all sts.

Weave in loose ends. Block to measurements.

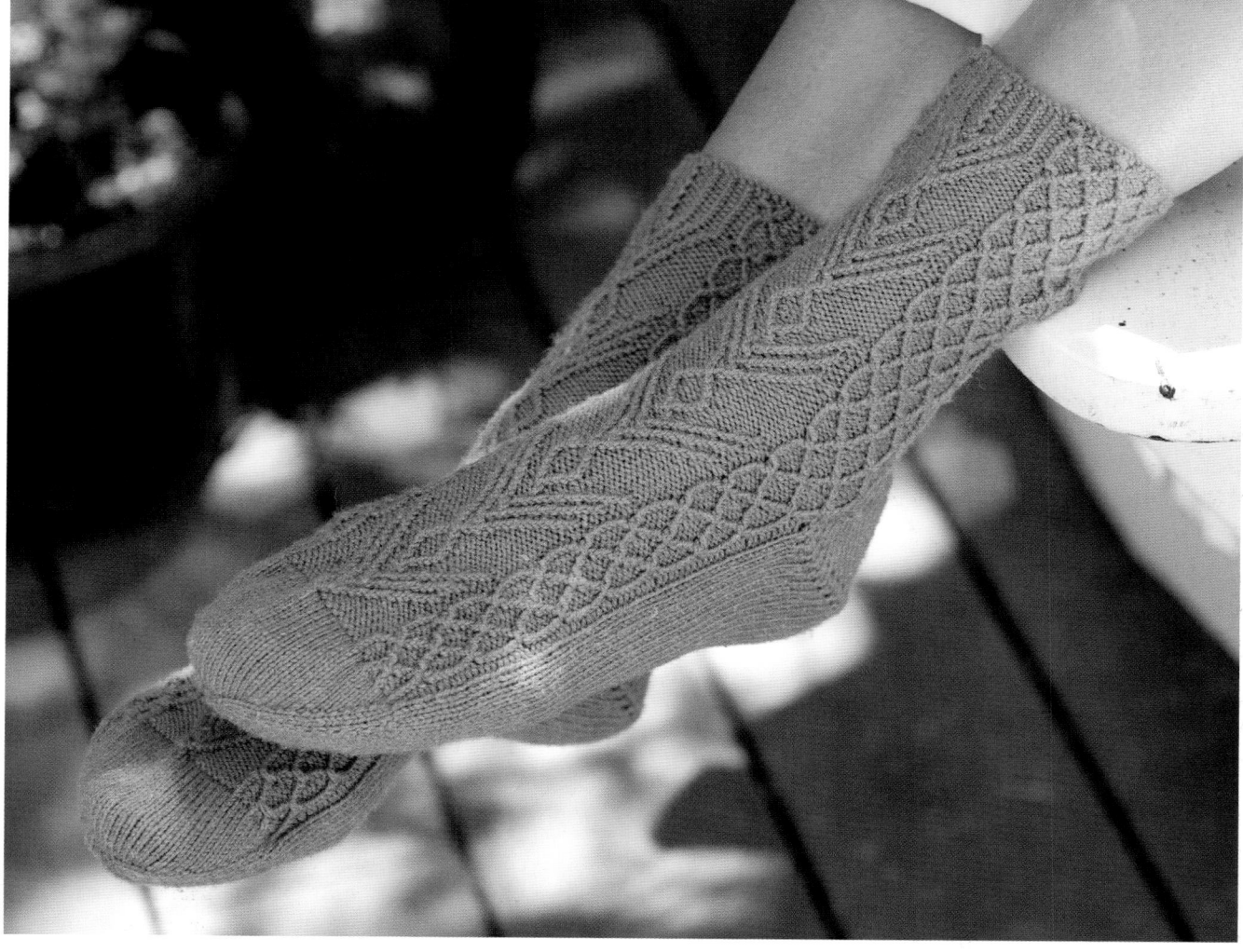

Yarn Note

A well-rounded three-ply wool/silk blend from Quince & Company is a fitting match for this ornate design. The yarn's near perpendicular plies and predominant wool content give loft, bounce, and strength to the fabric while also rendering the intricate pattern of twisted and wrapped stitches with great clarity. A generous dusting of undyed silk (25%) gives a glassy halo to the stitches while helping the raised-stitch motif stand out even more from its reverse stockinette background. The silk also gives this yarn a hint more density and strength, though not as much abrasion resistance as you'd get from nylon. A yarn with dyed silk would have a deeper glow, while you'd get a more matte effect in 100% wool or a wool/nylon blend. For optimal stitch definition, steer toward yarns with three or more plies—or even a multiple-plied cable-style yarn. If you want to add a touch of wobble and nuance to the motif, try a springy two-ply yarn instead. Either way, you'll want to stick with a solid or semisolid colorway to preserve the stitch pattern.

—*Clara Parkes*

Glossary

Abbreviations

beg(s)	begin(s); beginning
BO	bind off
CC	contrasting color
cm	centimeter(s)
cn	cable needle
CO	cast on
cont	continue(s); continuing
dec(s)	decrease(s); decreasing
dpn	double-pointed needles
foll	follow(s); following
g	gram(s)
inc(s)	increase(s); increasing
k	knit
k1f&b	knit into the front and back of same stitch
kwise	knitwise, as if to knit
m	marker(s)
MC	main color
mm	millimeter(s)
M1	make one (increase)
p	purl
p1f&b	purl into front and back of same stitch
patt(s)	pattern(s)
psso	pass slipped stitch over
p2sso	pass 2 slipped stitches over
pwise	purlwise, as if to purl
rem	remain(s); remaining
rep	repeat(s); repeating
rev St st	reverse stockinette stitch
rnd(s)	round(s)
RS	right side
sl	slip
sl st	slip st (slip 1 stitch purlwise unless otherwise indicated)
ssk	slip 2 stitches knitwise, one at a time, from the left needle to right needle, insert left needle tip through both front loops and knit together from this position (1 stitch decrease)
st(s)	stitch(es)
St st	stockinette stitch
tbl	through back loop
tog	together
WS	wrong side
wyb	with yarn in back
wyf	with yarn in front
yd	yard(s)
yo	yarnover
*	repeat starting point
( )	alternate measurements and/or instructions
[ ]	work instructions as a group a specified number of times

Bind-Offs

See pages 44–47 and 118–121.

THREE-NEEDLE BIND-OFF

Place the stitches to be joined onto two separate needles and hold the needles parallel so that the right sides of the knitting face together. Insert a third needle into the first stitch on each of the two needles (figure 1) and knit them together as one stitch (figure 2), *knit the next stitch on each needle the same way, then use one of the left needle tips to lift the first stitch over the second and off the needle (figure 3). Repeat from * until no stitches remain on the first two needles. Cut yarn and pull tail through the last stitch to secure.

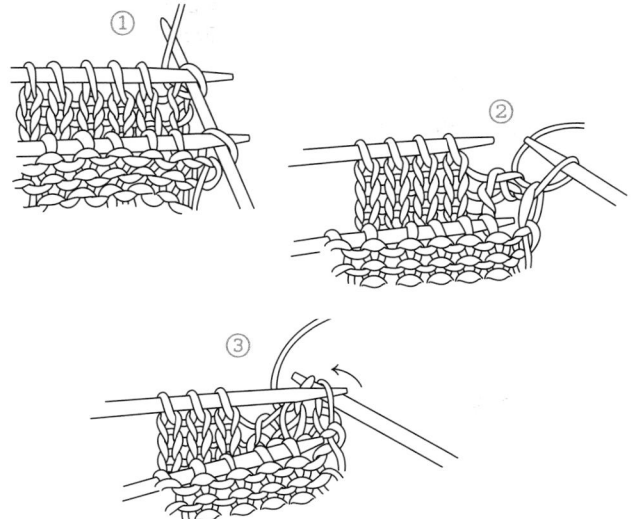

Cast-Ons

See pages 38–43 and 116–117.

BACKWARD-LOOP CAST-ON

*Loop working yarn and place it on needle backward so that it doesn't unwind. Repeat from *.

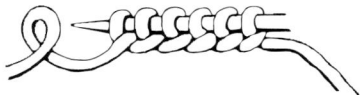

Decreases

PURL 2 TOGETHER THROUGH BACK LOOPS (P2TOGTBL)

Bring right needle tip behind two stitches on left needle, enter through the back loop of the second stitch, then the first stitch, then purl them together.

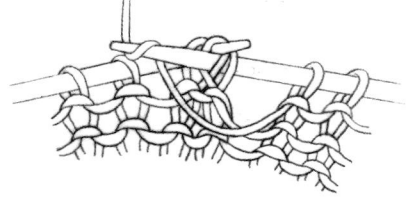

SLIP, SLIP, KNIT (SSK)

Slip two stitches individually knitwise (figure 1), insert left needle tip into the front of these two slipped stitches, and use the right needle to knit them together through their back loops (figure 2).

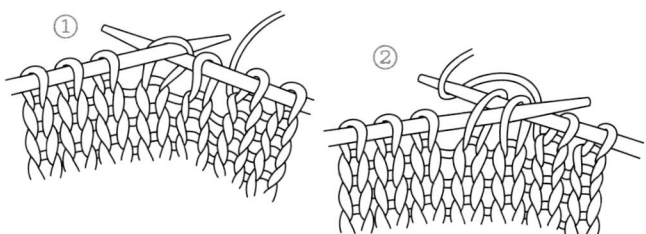

Increases

BACKWARD YARNOVER

Short-row toe and heels are constructed with short-rows that produce an hourglass shape. Each short-row begins with a yarnover that is instrumental in preventing gaps at the short-row turns. When the knit side is facing, work the yarnover in the usual manner, bringing the yarn forward under the needle, then over the top to the back. When the purl side is facing, bring the yarn to the back under the needle, then over the top to the front. This forms a "backward" yarnover—the leading side of the loop is on the back of the needle—with the distance traveled by the yarn equal to that of the standard yarnover on the knit side, an important distinction for truly even stitches. The stitch mount of the backward yarnover is corrected later in the heel.

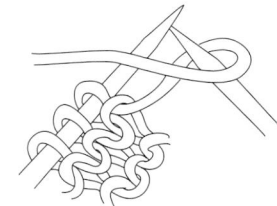

BAR INCREASE (K1F&B)

Knit into a stitch but leave it on the left needle (figure 1), then knit through the back loop of the same stitch (figure 2) and slip the original stitch off the needle (figure 3).

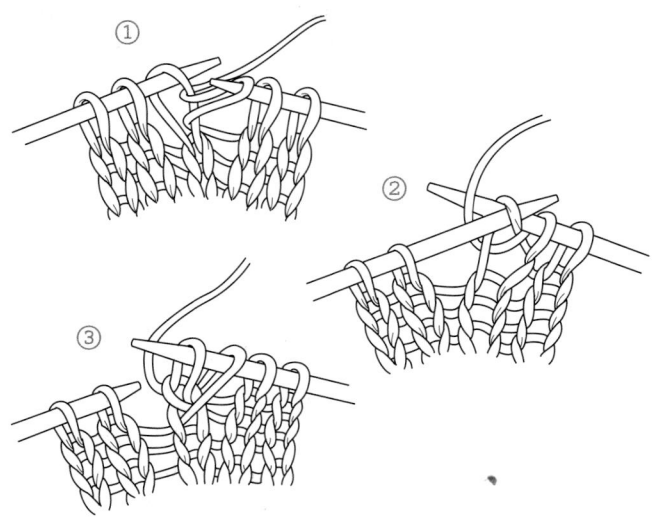

RAISED MAKE-ONE INCREASE (M1)

NOTE: Use the left slant if no direction of slant is specified.

Left Slant (M1L)

With left needle tip, lift the strand between the last knitted stitch and the first stitch on the left needle from front to back (figure 1), then knit the lifted loop through the back (figure 2).

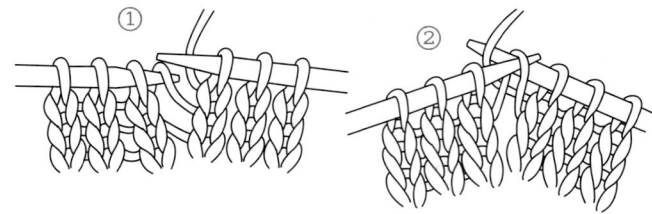

Right Slant (M1R)

With left needle tip, lift the strand between the needles from back to front (figure 1), then knit the lifted loop through the front (figure 2).

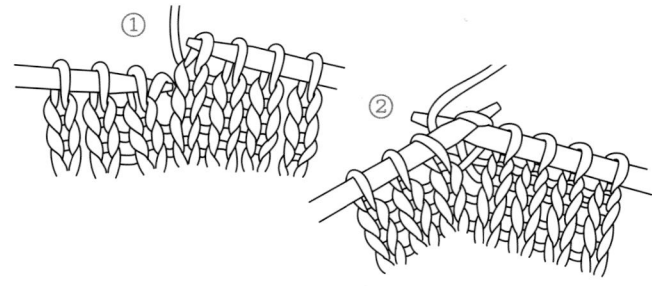

Purlwise (M1P)

With left needle tip, lift the strand between the needles from front to back (figure 1), then purl the lifted loop through the back (figure 2).

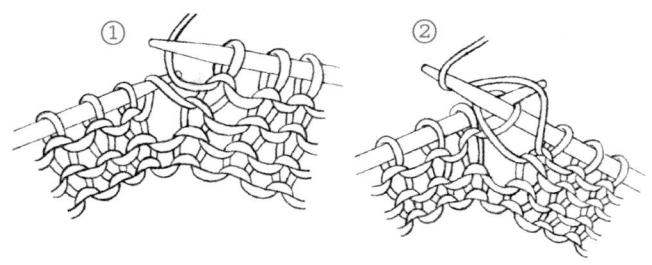

LIFTED INCREASE

NOTE: If no slant direction is specified, use the right slant.

Right Slant (LRI)

Knit into the back of the stitch (in the "purl bump") in the row directly below the stitch on the needle (figure 1), then knit the stitch on the needle (figure 2), and slip the original stitch off the needle.

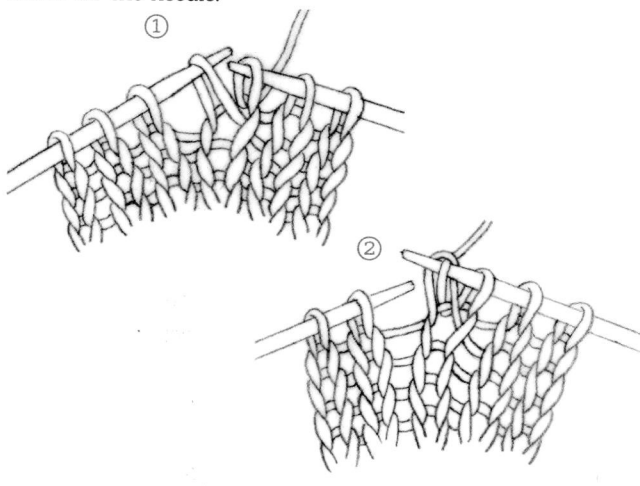

Left Slant (LLI)

Insert left needle tip into the back of the stitch below the stitch just knitted (figure 1), then knit this stitch (figure 2).

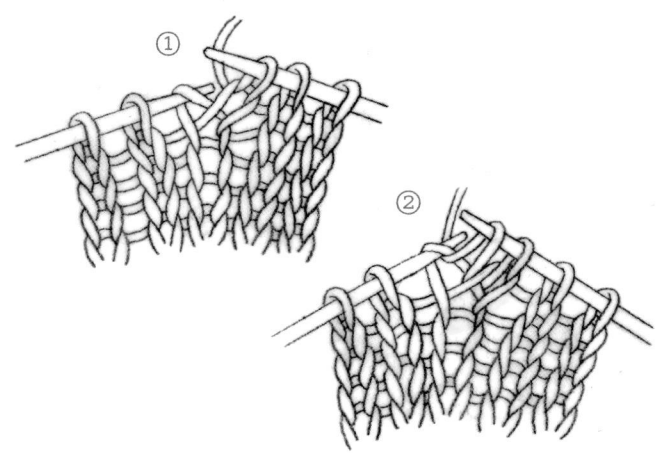

Jogless Jog

When color stripes are knitted in rounds, "jogs" can form between the last stitch of one color on one round and the first stitch of another color on the next round. Meg Swansen has a clever technique for eliminating these jogs and creating invisible "seams" in circular knitting.

Let's say you've knitted a stripe with A and you want to knit a second stripe with B. Drop A and work to the end of the round with B, then work the first stitch of the round again with B by using the right needle tip to lift the stitch in the row below onto the needle (figure 1), then knitting this lifted stitch together with the first stitch of the round (figure 2). Although the first stitch has been knitted twice, it was worked into the row below the second time and therefore shows up for just one round. There is no jog between the two colors, but the beginning of the round shifts one stitch to the left. Each time you change colors, work the first stitch of the round a second time into the row below the stitch on the needle to eliminate subsequent jogs. The beginning of the round will shift one stitch to the left at every color change.

Because each color stripe appears as a complete circle, a round can begin with any stitch. When it's time to shape the heel, shift the stitches on the needles as necessary to put the beginning of the round at the desired place, join new yarn, and continue as usual.

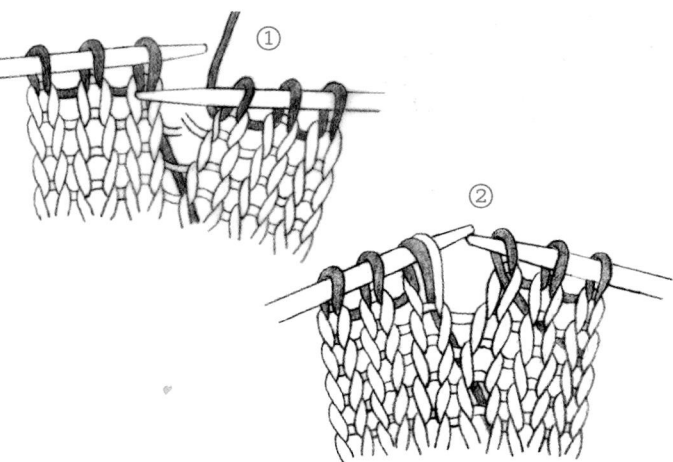

Knitting in Reverse

To create a standard knit stitch in reverse, enter the stitch with the left needle tip from left to right behind the right needle tip, wrap the yarn from back to front, coming up and over the left needle tip, then pull the yarn wrap through the loop to form a new stitch on the left needle, letting the loop drop from the right needle.

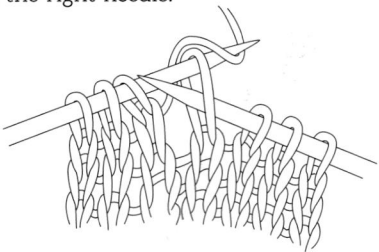

Pick Up and Knit

There are a variety of ways to pick up and knit stitches along the gusset edges. The following methods are demonstrated on the accompanying DVD.

PICK UP A SINGLE LOOP

For very little bulk along the pick-up edge, pick up gusset stitches through the front half of the edge stitches. *Insert the needle under the front half of the selvedge stitch (figure 1), wrap the yarn around needle (figure 2), and pull a loop through. Repeat from * for the desired number of stitches (figure 3).

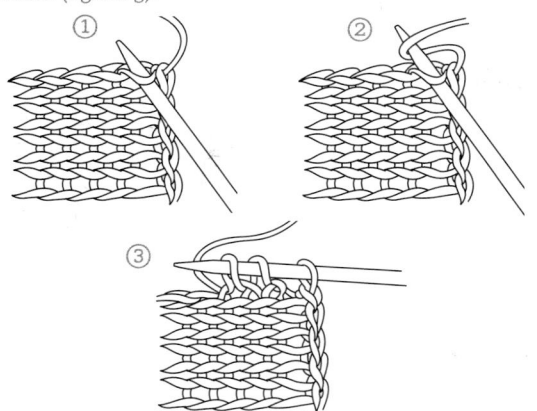

PICK UP BOTH LOOPS

For a sturdier join, pick up the gusset stitches through both halves of the edge stitch. *Insert the needle under both halves of the selvedge stitch (figure 1), wrap the yarn around needle (figure 2), and pull a loop through. Repeat from * for the desired number of stitches (figure 3).

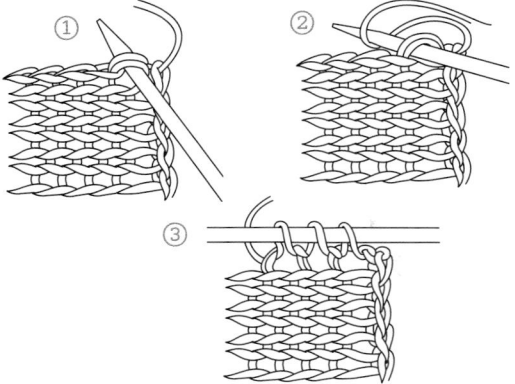

PICK UP THROUGH THE BACK LOOPS

For a very snug join, pick up the gusset stitches by working into the back loop of either the first half or both halves of each edge stitch. *Use the needle in your left hand to lift the selvedge stitch, then insert the right needle into the back of the lifted stitch (figure 1), wrap the yarn around the right needle (figure 2), and pull a loop through. Repeat from * for the desired number of stitches (figure 3).

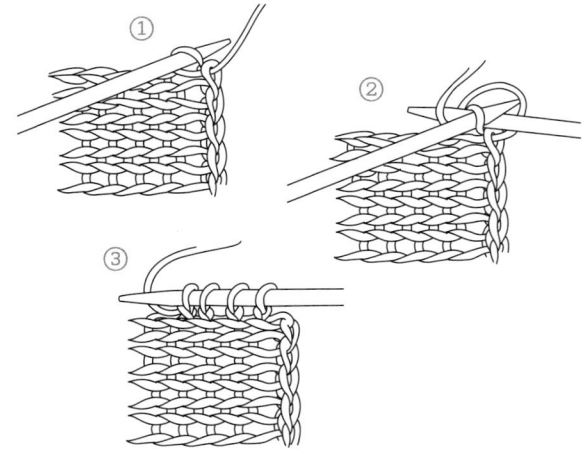

Pick Up and Purl

With wrong side of work facing and working from right to left, *insert needle tip under both legs of the selvedge stitch from the far side to the near side (figure 1), wrap yarn around needle, and pull a loop through (figure 2). Repeat from * for desired number of stitches.

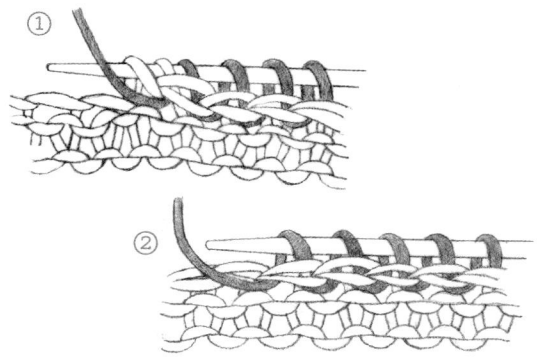

Short-Rows

SHORT-ROWS KNIT SIDE

Work to turning point, slip next stitch purlwise (figure 1, above right), bring the yarn to the front, then slip the same stitch back to the left needle (figure 2, above right), turn the work around and bring the yarn in position for the next stitch—one stitch has been wrapped, and the yarn is correctly positioned to work the next stitch. When you come to a wrapped stitch on a subsequent row, hide the wrap by working it together with the wrapped stitch as follows: Insert right needle tip under the wrap (from the front if wrapped stitch is a knit stitch; from the back if wrapped stitch is a purl stitch; figure 3, above right), then into the stitch on the needle, and work the stitch and its wrap together as a single stitch.

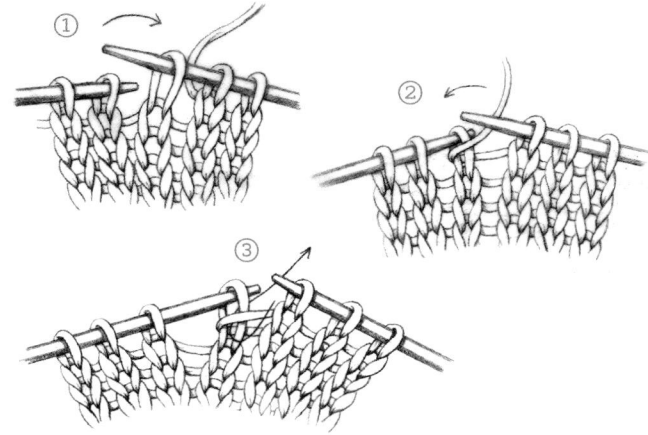

SHORT-ROWS PURL SIDE

Work to the turning point, slip the next stitch purlwise to the right needle, bring the yarn to the back of the work (figure 1), return the slipped stitch to the left needle, bring the yarn to the front between the needles (figure 2), and turn the work so that the knit side is facing—one stitch has been wrapped, and the yarn is correctly positioned to knit the next stitch. To hide the wrap on a subsequent purl row, work to the wrapped stitch, use the tip of the right needle to pick up the wrap from the back, place it on the left needle (figure 3), then purl it together with the wrapped stitch.

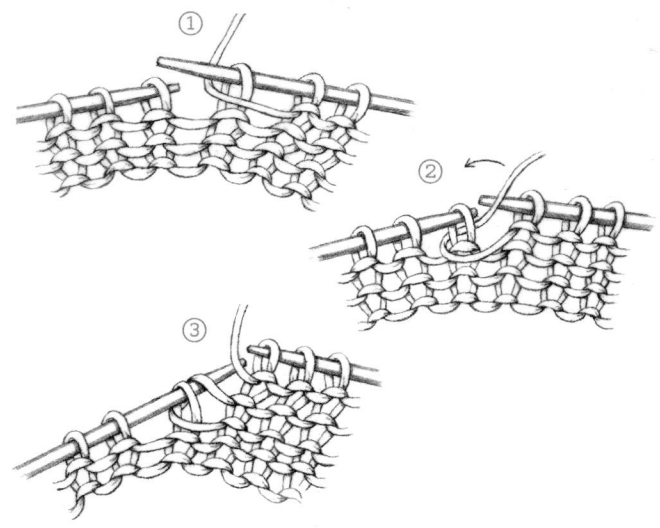

Contributors

COOKIE A debuted her pattern line, Cookie A Knitwear Designs, in 2007 and became an instant hit. In the short time since then, she has written two books about knitting socks—*Sock Innovation* and *Knit.Sock.Love*. Cookie teaches internationally and can be found online at cookiea.com.

KATHRYN ALEXANDER is a passionate spinner, dyer, and knitter who has brought entrelac knitting to the mainstream through her inventive patterns and kits. For a full selection of Kathryn's work, visit kathrynalexander.net.

An expert at bringing a dressmaker's approach to knitwear design, **VÉRONIK AVERY** is the author of *Knitting Classic Style* and *Knitting 24/7* and the founder of St-Denis Yarns, which are sourced, manufactured, and distributed solely in North America.

CAT BORDHI is a creative, free-thinking knitter who delights in experimenting with technique and breaking the rules. She has shared her knowledge in her books, *Socks Soar on Two Circular Needles, A Treasury of Magical Knitting, A Second Treasury of Magical Knitting, New Pathways for Knitters,* and *Personal Footprints* and numerous YouTube knitting tutorials.

NANCY BUSH is passionate about traditional knitting techniques, especially when it comes to socks. She is the author of several books on sock knitting, including *Folk Socks, Folk Knitting in Estonia, Knitting on the Road,* and *Knitting Vintage Socks*. Nancy teaches workshops in the United States and abroad, is a regular contributor to *PieceWork* magazine, and is owner of The Wooly West, a mail-order knitting shop (woolywest.com) in Salt Lake City.

A Pacific Northwest native, **EVELYN A. CLARK** is addicted to lace knitting and delights in sharing her addiction with others. She is the author of *Knitting Lace Triangles* and her designs have been published by knitting magazines and yarn companies. You can find her work at evelynclarkdesigns.com.

CHRISSY GARDINER designs and knits from her home in Portland, Oregon, where she lives with her husband, two kids, three cats, two rabbits, and two chickens. She is author of *Toe-Up!: Patterns and Worksheets to Whip Your Sock Knitting Into Shape*. You can find more of Chrissy's work at gardineryarnworks.com.

PRISCILLA GIBSON-ROBERTS has a life-long passion for textiles. In additional to knitting and spinning "in the old way," she became passionate about socks when she learned they were the first knitted objects. Her books include *Ethnic Socks & Stockings* and *Simple Socks*, both of which provide readers with the basics to design on their own.

As the proprietor of the online studio KnitSpot, **ANNE HANSON** strives to provide patterns that "elevate a knitter's experience, provide engaging opportunities to learn new skills, and result in expert-looking finished projects." Visit Anne at knitspot.com.

EUNNY JANG is editor of *Interweave Knits* magazine and co-host of *Knitting Daily TV*. In the rare times that she isn't knitting or editing, Eunny cooks, runs long distance, wakeboards, and follows the Yankees from her home in Fort Collins, Colorado.

MELISSA MORGAN-OAKES, a self-taught knitter, is author of *Two-at-a-Time Socks* and *Toe-Up 2-at-a-Time Socks* and teaches at venues around the country. She and her family live on a farm in western Massachusetts.

DEBORAH NEWTON of Providence, Rhode Island, designs all kinds of knitwear for magazines and yarn companies, as well as fabrics for Seventh Avenue. She is the author of *Designing Knitwear*.

An expert in knitting yarns, CLARA PARKES is the publisher of KnittersReview.com and author of *The Knitter's Book of Yarn* and *The Knitter's Book of Wool*. Her forthcoming book is called *The Knitter's Book of Socks: The Yarn Lover's Ultimate Guide to Creating Socks that Fit Well, Feel Great, and Last a Lifetime*. She is also a frequent contributor to *Interweave Knits* and *Twist Collective*.

MEG SWANSEN, daughter of the esteemed Elizabeth Zimmermann, is a renowned knitwear designer, author, and teacher. She is the owner of Schoolhouse Press (schoolhousepress.com), which specializes in knitting books, DVDs, and products of interest to knitters.

ANNA ZILBOORG took her love and knitting around the world and into the hills. The result is countless knitting designs published in various magazines and a number of books, two of which feature sock designs: *Socks for Sandals and Clogs* and *Magnificent Mittens and Socks*. Anna is also author of *Knitting for Anarchists*, a must-read for understanding how stitches are formed.

Sources for Supplies

BROWN SHEEP COMPANY
100662 County Rd. 16
Mitchell, NE 69357
brownsheep.com

CASCADE YARNS
PO Box 58168
1224 Andover Park East
Tukwila, WA 98188
cascadeyarns.com

CLASSIC ELITE YARNS/ST. DENIS
122 Western Ave.
Lowell, MA 01851
classiceliteyarns.com

ELEMENTAL AFFECTS
17555 Bubbling Wells Rd.
Desert Hot Springs, CA 92241
elementalaffects.com

FLEECE ARTIST
fleeceartist.com

KATHYRN ALEXANDER KITS
PO Box 202
Johnsonville, NY 12094
kathrynalexander.net

KNITTING FEVER, INC./MALABRIGO
PO Box 336
315 Bayview Ave.
Amityville, NY 11701
knittingfever.com

LORNA'S LACES
4229 N. Honore St.
Chicago, IL 60613
(773) 935-3803
lornaslaces.net

PAGEWOOD FARM
pagewoodfarm.com

QUINCE & COMPANY
quinceandco.com

SATAKIELI
Distributed in the U.S. by
Schoolhouse Press
6899 Cary Bluff
Pittsville, WI 54466
schoolhousepress.com
and
The Wooly West
PO Box 58306
Salt Lake City, UT 84158
woolywest.com

SCHAEFER YARN
3514 Kelly's Corners Rd.
Interlaken, NY 14847
schaeferyarn.com

SHALIMAR YARNS
shalimaryarns.com

SIMPLY SOCKS YARN COMPANY
PO Box 382
Woodburn, IN 46797
simplysockyarn.com

STRING THEORY
132 Beech Hill Rd.
Blue Hill, ME 04614
stringtheoryyarn.com

Bibliography

A, Cookie. *Sock Innovation: Knitting Techniques & Patterns for One-of-a-Kind Socks*. Loveland, Colorado: Interweave, 2009.

An excellent tutorial on how to design socks.

Bordhi, Cat. *New Pathways for Sock Knitters: Book One*. Friday Harbor, Washington: Passing Paws Press, 2007.

Groundbreaking ways to shape the instep of a sock.

———. *Personal Footprints for Insouciant Sock Knitters*. Friday Harbor, Washington: Passing Paws Press, 2009.

Introduction to an innovative technique for working socks entirely in the round.

Budd, Ann, and Anne Merrow, eds. *Favorite Socks: 25 Timeless Designs from Interweave*. Loveland, Colorado: Interweave, 2006.

A collection of the most popular sock patterns from Interweave publications.

Bush, Nancy. *Folk Knitting in Estonia: A Garland of Symbolism, Tradition and Technique*. Loveland, Colorado: Interweave, 1999.

Estonian knitting history, patterns, and techniques for socks, mittens, and gloves.

———. *Folk Socks: The History & Techniques of Handknitted Footwear*. Loveland, Colorado: Interweave, 1994.

The foundations and history of sock knitting.

Gardiner, Chrissy. *Toe-Up!: Patterns and Worksheets to Whip Your Sock Knitting into Shape*. Portland, Oregon: Sydwillow Press, 2009.

A comprehensive course in toe-up socks with custom worksheets.

Galeskas, Bev. *The Magic Loop*. East Wenatchee, Washington: Fiber Trends, 2002.

A description of how to knit socks on one long circular needle.

Gibson-Roberts, Priscilla. *Ethnic Socks & Stockings: A Compendium of Eastern Design & Technique*. Sioux Falls, South Dakota: XRX Books, 1995.

Everything you need to know about the art of sock knitting as practiced in Eastern Europe and the Middle East.

———. *Simple Socks: Plain and Fancy*. Fort Collins, Colorado: Nomad Press, 2001.

An excellent description of short-row heels and toes.

———. *"Traditional Techniques for Creating Ethnic Intarsia Designs,"* in *Interweave Knits*, Fall 2003. Pages 90–93.

A primer on various ways to work intarsia in the round.

Høxbro, Vivian. *Shadow Knitting*. Loveland, Colorado: Interweave, 2004.

An excellent overview of shadow knitting and projects to knit.

Jang, Eunny. *"Entrelac: Knitting Block by Block,"* in *Interweave Knits*, Spring 2007. Pages 22–28.

A comprehensive tutorial on knitting entrelac flat or in the round.

Johnson, Wendy D. *Socks from the Toe Up: Essential Techniques and Patterns from Wendy Knits*. New York: Potter Craft, 2009.

How-tos, tips, and techniques for knitting socks from the toe up.

Morgan-Oakes, Melissa. *2-at-a-Time Socks: The Secret of Knitting Two at Once on One Circular Needle*. North Adams, Massachusetts: Storey Publications, 2007.

Techniques and patterns for working two top-down socks at a time.

———. *Toe-Up 2-at-a-Time Socks*. North Adams, Massachusetts: Storey Publications

Techniques and patterns for working two toe-up socks at a time.

Index

Check out even more beautiful patterns

and expert advice in these sock knitting resources from Interweave

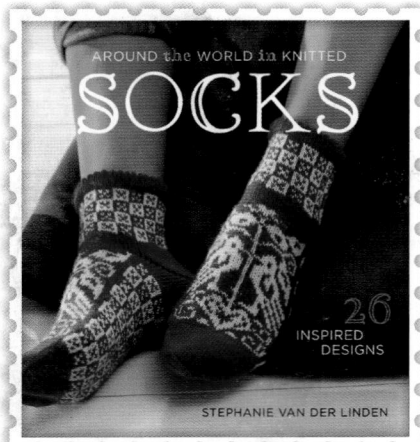

**Around the World
in Knitted Socks**
26 Inspired Designs
Stephanie van der Linden
ISBN 978-1-59668-230-6
$24.95

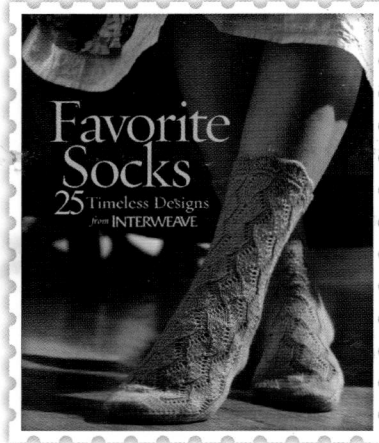

746.432 B927
Budd, Ann,
Sock knitting master class
:innovative techniques + patterns from top
COLLIER
04/12

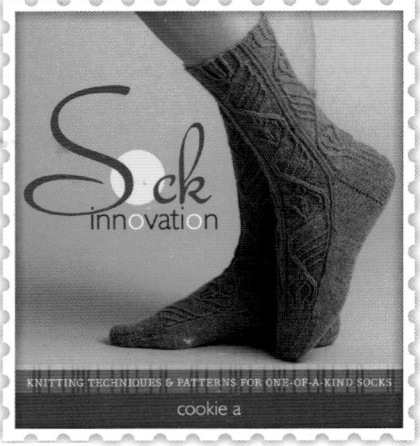

HCOLW

Sock Innovation
...tting Techniques & Patterns
for One-of-a-Kind Socks
Cookie A.
ISBN 978-1-59668-109-5
$22.95

INTERWEAVE KNITS

knitting daily

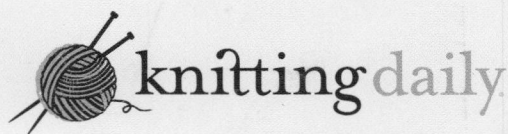

From cover to cover, *Interweave Knits* ma...   ...Daily.com, an online community
presents great projects for the beginner t...   ...ur passion for knitting. You'll get
advanced knitter. Every issue is packed fu...   ...sletter, free patterns, projects store,
captivating smart designs, step-by-step i...   ...even updates, galleries, tips and
easy-to-understand illustrations, plus we...   ...and more. Sign up for *Knitting Daily* at
lively articles sure to inspire. **interweave**...   ...y.com.

TIU interweave.com